Approaches to Semiotics

43

Editorial Committee

Thomas A. Sebeok
Roland Posner
Alain Rey

MOUTON PUBLISHERS · THE HAGUE · PARIS · NEW YORK

Description:
Sign, Self, Desire

Description:
Sign, Self, Desire

Critical Theory
in the wake of Semiotics

Marc Eli Blanchard

Professor of French & Comparative Literature
University of California, Davis

MOUTON PUBLISHERS · THE HAGUE · PARIS · NEW YORK

ISBN: 90-279-7778-X (casebound)
        90-279-3488-6 (paperback)
Jacket design by Jurriaan Schrofer
© 1980, Mouton Publishers, The Hague, The Netherlands
Printed in Great Britain

Acknowledgements

Some of the material in the book has appeared in another form and under a different title in various journals. Permission to recast is most gratefully acknowledged. In Part One, parts of chapters 1 and 4 appeared as: "Sémiostyles: le rituel de la littérature" in *Semiotica* 14(4):297–328 (1975); Chapter 5 appeared as: "Sur les mythe poétique: essai d'une sémiostylistique rimbaldienne' in *Semiotica* 16(1): 67–86 (1976); Chapter 6 appeared as: "Searching for Narrative Structure" in *Diacritics* 7(1): 2–17 (1977). In Part Two, Chapter 8 appeared as: "*Daphnis et Chloe*: histoire de la mimesis" in *Quaderni Urbinati di Cultura Classica* 20: 39–62 (1975); Chapter 9 appeared as: "The Eye of the Beholder: on the Semiotic Status of Paranarratives" in *Semiotica* 22(3–4): 235–268 (1978); Chapter 10 appeared as: "Le je(u) de Montaigne" in *Neophilologus* 61 (3): 347–355 (1977); Chapter 11 appeared as: "Style pastoral, style des Lumières" in *Studies on Voltaire and the Eigtheenth Century* 106: 331–346 (1973). In Part Three, Chapter 14 appeared as: "The Tree and the Garden: Pastoral Poetics and Milton's Rhetoric of Desire" in *Modern Language Notes* 91: 1540–1568 (1976).

A special note of thanks to Bell and Hyman Publishers, Hogarth Press Ltd., Holt, Rinehart and Winston, the Institute of Psychoanalysis, the Loeb Classical Library, the Estate of C.K. Moncrieff and Chatto and Windus, Random House, Sigmund Freud Copyrights, and the Society of Authors, the literary representative of the estate of James Joyce, for their kind permission to reprint material from their publications. To Princeton University Press I am grateful for permission to reproduce the pictures of "Heracles slaying Busiris" (E.H. Gombrich's *Art and Illusion*, Princeton, 1960: plate 94), currently at the Kunsthistorisches Museum in Vienna, and of "Alexander's victory over Darius" (*Art and Illusion*: plates 96 and 97) currently at the Museo Nazionale in Naples.

I also want to thank the following persons for their time and advice: Carol Anderson, Michel Beaujour, Howard Bloch, Peter Brooks, Ruby Cohn, Phillip Lewis, Louis Martin, Marolyn Morford, Mary Jo Muratore, Arline Targum and Marcia Trattner. Finally, to Manfred Kusch and Lars Lerup, who have been with me all along, to Thomas Sebeok, who made the book possible at all, my indebtedness is greater than words can express. Any mistakes, however, remain my own.

Davis, California, 1975–1978

Contents

Introduction

I have written this book in an attempt to clarify what, ten years after the *Structuralist controversy* (Donato and Macksey 1971), can now be termed the *"semiotic controversy"*. What is semiotics? Does it offer an alternative to the traditional historical, psychological, thematic, or stylistic approach to literature? And to what degree does it differ from the structural approach pioneered in the sixties in reaction against all the above? At a time when semiotics aspires to account for all human activity, including art and literature, in terms of communication and sign systems, the recent debate on the status of the sign initiated by Derrida and expanded by the poststructuralist (Deleuze, Kristeva, Lyotard) also makes one wonder whether the whole semiotic enterprise, once so imperial with its goal of charting paths of communication through all the various fields of knowledge, has not failed, due partially to the excesses of an obsessive and repressive categorization. To these questions I have tried to respond in the following pages, from a particular, even a personal commitment, which should become more readily apparent as the book unfolds through its second and third parts. My own evolution from a strict Saussurean constructionism to a position where I have been trying to conform a theory based on the homogeneous classifications of language (*langue*) to the textual idiosyncrasies of personal styles of speech (*parole*), and my exploration of the resources of phenomenology and psychoanalysis could, perhaps, be construed as a reflection of the state of flux of semiotics today. It should also suggest the possibility of expanding the field of semiotics to include disciplines which were first rejected as irrelevant to semiotic studies, because it was feared they might lead back to the pitfalls of psychologism and subjectivism (theory of knowledge and phenomenology), or those disciplines which have now been recast to fit a semiolinguistic mold (a psychiatry and psychoanalysis based on the Lacanian reduction of the unconscious to a language).

Actually, my purpose is to show that the limitations of semiotics lie in the application of a strict Saussurean model to literary texts and in the dismissal of elements of stylistic and semantic analysis through reductive operations where the critic concerns himself with codes, but not with the processes of encoding and decoding which make these codes possible. Already, post-structuralist analyses may have shown the way in the development of meaningful alternatives in semiotics. Taking, for instance, the notions of redundancy of information one could show that the hypothesis of *textual effects* laid out by Derrida to account for the *dissemination*, the endless diffraction of the principle of identity and difference, explains how a stylistic feature can not only constitute pertinent linguistic information based on a series of stable phonological oppositions ([bat]— [cat]), but also suggest a new— translinguistic— context, which destablilizes these oppositions and jolts our system of references. Because signs are used to communicate not only a finished product, the message, but also the processes which make the ongoing production of that message possible, a text functions much like a painting, which communicates a clearly identifiable narrative message, while also displaying the diacritical marks of that message all across the canvas without allowing a clear distinction of what is form and what is substance. Thus, with Derrida, the inability of the critic to distinguish between tenor and vehicle in the metaphor, between two signified or a signified and its referent, is a cornerstone of the whole enterprise of deconstruction and name-playing. Is the *hymen* the ceremonial ritual or the vaginal (virginal) membrane? Is the *margin* that which includes or excludes (Derrida 1972, 1974)? Taking another example, this time from Kristeva, one could assume a dialectic of the text between a *semiological* (Saussurean, symbolic) principle which regulates the text from within according to the rules of its own linguistic universe, and a *semiotic* (non-Saussurean, non-symbolic) principle which regulates it from without according to psychic and social determinants. Thus Mallarmé's struggle with the decomposition and the recomposition of the art object suggests a vision of the poet as both social outcast and murderer of his own textual tradition (Kristeva 1974, 1977; see also chapters 5 and 14).

For my part, however, I believe that new perspectives in semiotics must now come from a reconsideration of the relations between signs and the conscious or unconscious subject producing them. That is to say, the operations of construction and deconstruction, the manifestations of drives, the experience of intensities, whatever their dissemination, their negativity, remain a part of the activity of the subject in general. Moreover, this activity is determined, in the last instance, not so much by sociolinguistic processes well beyond the control of any single writing or speaking subject, but rather by processes of individual stylistic production activated by the subject himself, insofar as he is already *both* a writer and a reader who, by personally interpreting linguistic differences, produces textual displacements beyond the realm of an amalgamated *langue*. This dual determination to abide by the subject and to adopt a median way between the rigid requirements of linguistic semiotics and the vertigo of deconstruction implies that we rid ourselves of what I should like to call the *progress and closure imperative* — by which I mean the accepted notion that texts *do indeed always tell a story,* complete with a beginning and an end, whether it be the story of a clearly referenced subject (the hero or his narrator), or that, more abstruse, of an anonymous semiotic process which constantly stimulates and deflects desire beyond the limits of a specific subject.

In this respect, it is striking that from Propp to Greimas to Barthes, models of interpretation are constructed around short stories (from Russian and Lithuanian folktales to Maupassant's *Tales* to Balzac's *Sarrasine*), and not around more elaborate works (novels or plays), thus propounding the illusion that narratives will always open and close according to fairly predictable patterns. Even a writer as wary of an ideology of beginning and end as Derrida, will, in his account of Mallarmé's construction of *mimesis* in *Mimique* imply that the reading of any text is always predicated on the acknowledgement of some sort of (temporary and replaceable) narrative sequence, due to the manifestation of either a universal *sentiment linguistique* (Chomsky's generative *competence*) or that of an all-purpose plurivalent grammatical code: every text thus ends up constituting a two-part narrative — one literal and the other figurative, repeating it (Derrida 1972: 200-317). This hegemony of the narrative model not only entails a closed system of beginning and end, but also and primarily suggests a general anxiety about sequences, about what is to follow what, simply by virtue of syntagmatic and paradigmatic arrangements, or in the name of *difference* or *delay*. Whether what follows follows logically or unexpectedly as shadow follows light or echo sound, the Hegelian model is there: present in its dialectic of same and other resolved into a new sameness. In the first case (the semioticians of narrative), the contents of any narrative are reducible to a dialectic inversion, as the end of the narrative presents the reader with a situation which is exactly the reverse of the beginning: the Fair Princess has been freed; the hero has overcome, and so on. In the second case (Derrida and the poststructuralists), this dialectic resolution is exposed for what it is, a process allowing the introduction of a rational, ordered difference into an otherwise incomprehensible (dis)order. Both these interpretations of narrative, however, leave aside those segments of a text which are different precisely in that they seek to escape narrative governance and promote *description* as a substitute for *narration*. Finely exposed on the edges of narrative in the secluded and pastoral *loci* of the text, description may not really escape the dialectic at work in the narrative process, but it clearly and unmistakably refuses progress, movement and displacement, even pits itself against it, denying narrativity itself. Contemplation and inaction without the beginning and end or hero of a story, description is an experience which is possible only within a modified semiotic structure designed not to reduce it, but to save it and protect it. This brings us to the next point: because they are obsessed with stating or denying beginnings, narrative models do not allow for a theory of description. Moreover, as a semiotics of narrative operates mostly at the level of *content*, the semiotician spends no time discussing the insertion of his models into a text whose peculiarities of *form* and *style* may invalidate those models. He has little patience and no substantive explanation for these stylistic features, except to say that being part of a linguistic context, they should not require procedures different from those in use in the determination of other units of language. However, because styles effect not only a presentation but also a transformation of reality, every narrative always includes a fictionalization process. It seems to me, therefore, that such concepts as *the image of the narrator, the image of the reader*, indicating the inscription, the representation of the writer's and the reader's consciousness in the text, terms already, albeit lamely, introduced in structuralist terminology, need to be consolidated and taken literally to mean that we must concern ourselves with the substance of appearance and representation in literary texts. Focusing our attention on the style of description and freed from the obligation to make progress from one point (decidable or undecidable) to another, we are now at leisure to examine the textural or surface applications of a theory of description based on the premise that we speak and tell essentially *to describe*: to say personally and in our own manner what we have to say about the world, in terms which not only do not help construe narrative, but may in fact attempt to delay it. In this way, I hope, the term *ritual*, which appears somewhat cryptically at the end of the first chapters, may slowly acquire its full significance, as we delve into the fiction of the narrative and its signs — our growing awareness of a reading that goes nowhere leading to an awareness of ourselves in relation to our own desire.

The book more clearly places itself in and out of the present controversy: in, because it attempts to go beyond semiotics, as developed in the sixties and the seventies; but out, because it chooses to stay within the *eudaimonic* perspective attacked by Derrida, and looks forward to possibilities of reconstructing the self in the dual image of the writer and the reader, thereby attempting to enjoy the *appearance*, the *presence* of fiction through the manipulation of the signs of that fiction. Description, so far a marginal, or to use a term become fashionable, *supplementary*, extension of narrative, thought to lie beyond the purview of structural analysis and to be unfit, as it were, for narrative consumption, may now appear as the new frontier of semiotic studies, the *locus* of the manipulation.

Before we proceed, however, I must make two general remarks. First, this is a collection of essays and strictly speaking, not a book (a work of literature and art, where the aesthete-critic enjoys, albeit at a distance, the fruits of his vacarious creation;[1] whence the apparent discontinuity between essays, collected next to one another not so much by reason of semantic contiguity as by reason of semiotic form. Thus a text on Homer and the Sophists may appear next to one on Milton, which may itself be contiguous to one on Montaigne. This discontinuity, however, is in some way appropriate to my subject, as each text may be considered as yet another descriptive locus, a shelter for sign, self and desire, excerpted from the ongoing metacritical rumor surrounding us. In fact, it is actually no accident if many of the texts display their insularity, not only as a matter of form, but paradoxically as a matter of content as well. In several instances, what the semiotician seeks to isolate as pockets of displaced, though unconsumed meaning, can be reapprehended or reclassified (the French would say *récupéré*) as an instance of cultural or literary history, as *genre*: the genre of pastoral, which, from Homer to Joyce and beyond, haunts Western culture, as the place where the sign is still experienced as the restriction of an interdict, and where there is properly no room for intruders: men, women and their serpent, the first perpetrator of narrative in the history of the Western text.

Second, and last, I must acknowledge the presence in this field of Edward Said (1976), who has already attempted to work through structuralism and semiotics to begin anew. My own enterprise, however, is different, in that it seeks not the understanding of how one begins to communicate, in the first place, but rather wishes, for a moment at least, to immobilize the flow of stories, of their history and their grammar.

NOTES

1. I thought this would be the appropriate place to register, if only in passing, my protest against *the current fetishism of the well-rounded critical book* in American academia — a fetishism

derived, like all fetishisms, from economic necessities and contradictions, which might explain some of the antipathy still extant against intellectual trends (structuralism and poststructuralism, semiotics) appearing to threaten the ideology of the individual, the free, the complete critic. Edmund Wilson (1968), while pursuing different objectives, has already made the point in the *Fruits of the MLA*.

Part One: Sign

1

Semiotics and Linguistics

Studies in semiotics have developed out of three major events: (1) a revival of the theory of signs (Saussure); (2) even more important, a restructuring of the levels of content-expression (Hjelmslev); and (3) the establishing of a semiological level coherent and distinct from the semantic level.[1] In the last few years, particularly in France, a number of works have appeared where an attempt is made to apply the more fundamental laws of semiotics to literary texts and the visual arts. Especially noticeable among such works since that of Barthes (1970), are those of Marin (1971); the bilingual essays (in French and English) edited by Kristeva *et al.* (1971); Greimas (1970); Coquet (1973); Damisch (1973); Rastier and Greimas (1973); and the more recent works by Kristeva (1974, 1977) and Greimas (1976). In Italy, the publications of such scholars as Umberto Eco (1971, 1975), Cesare Segre (1973) and the periodical *VS*, edited by Eco and his group, have contributed to the development of a strictly Saussurean semiotics, in contradistinction with the efforts of French poststructuralists. In Germany, Helmut Bonheim (1975) has turned his attention to a classification of the various *types* of narrative discourses. In Holland, T. A. van Dijk (1972) has been engaged in the elaboration of a generative grammar of literary texts, and finally, in America, Seymour Chatman (1971a, 1971b, 1972, 1978) has long been investigating the relationship of rhetoric to narrative structures, while Fredric Jameson (1971) and Jonathan Culler (1975) have, on their part, provided useful reviews of Continental semiotics. Let us add to these brief notes another one stressing the influence for the dissemination of linguistic and semiotic research of such international journals as *Semiotica, Poétique,* and *Poetics,* and we shall be in a better position to discuss the *semiotic scene.*[2]

However, before launching into a critical examination of the current semiotic conjuncture, it is important to define more clearly some of the semiotician's epistemological bases, and more particularly, to emphasize the relationship between semiology and linguistics.

Saussure had suggested in his *Cours de la linguistique générale* (1971:33) that linguistics was but one part of a vast scientific domain, constituted by the structural encyclopedia of the sign sciences. And, in most instances, semiotics has indeed recognized its major debt to linguistics: were it not for certain recent developments, one could say that the semiotician of today is working on a purely linguistic model with linguistic methods. What are these developments? First, it appears that linguistics, and structural linguistics in particular, is almost exclusively interested in the strictly synchronic aspect of language (*langue*), thereby neglecting the possibilities of a diachronic study of language or individual speech, while semiotics, operating in the anthropological (Lévi-Strauss), sociological (Barthes), and psychoanalytical (Lacan) field, is deeply involved with the examination of *langue* (society) — *parole* (individual) relationships. In tackling the study of corpuses where, through the patient investigation of an as yet unknown (spoken or gestural) idiolect, it hopes to reach a system of *langue*, semiotics paradoxically recognizes a certain primacy of *parole* over *langue* — a primacy that is, moreover, underscored by the essentially diachronic nature of every investigation. When Lévi-Strauss analyzes the main concepts of the Nambikwara culture, before revealing its organizational structure, one could say, in Hjelmslevian terms, that he establishes in the conscious and human process of *parole*, the relationship of a particular *expression-form* with an *expression-substance*, in a process which involves the release of a symbolic or semiotic import from the expression-substance and form (*parole*) to the level of the system (*langue*). In *Tristes Tropiques*, for example, the study of the nominal classes of Nambikwara and other linguistic families of Central and South America eventually leads to the discussion of the basic traits of the couple as *manifested* in the attitudes of the two sexes toward each other (Lévi-Strauss 1973: 305-317). It is on these same principles that Greimas (1966: 42-54) establishes a semiotic relationship (expression-form/content-form) and semantic relationship (expression-substance/content-substance) between a world of representation (process/*parole*-text) and a world of concepts (system/*langue*).

Now, however urgent the demands of semiotic discourse for the elaboration of a metasemiotics distinct from linguistics, insofar as the linguistic model still prevails in any structural study, and insofar as semiotics, like linguistics, uses a model, this distinction is very hard to maintain. Rather than a strict separation between linguistics and semiotics, there is between them a *semiolinguistic collusion* — albeit not overlap — in the methods of the human sciences. To the epistemologist, this collusion can only be justified *a posteriori* by means of the following argument: (1) all signs of the world function on the model of *natural* language signs; and (2) all discourses regarding signs (metasemiotics) must borrow, for the sake of coherence and comprehensibility, the terminology of a discourse on natural language (metalinguistics). In carrying out the first part of the analysis prescribed by Greimas under the title of *normalization*[3], the semiotician must thus define a model of analysis which will enable him to reduce the *process* of a text to a *system*. In so doing, he strives to establish an objective context where relationships between parts of signs and the signs themselves are well defined. This can be done with literature proper, "journalese," or any other form of writing, so long as there can be established and maintained conditions which permit a structural reduction of the text under consideration. In this way, for example, disregarding the personal level (personal pronouns) in a literary text facilitates the elaboration of the first categories of a grammar of narrative: category of *actants*/category of *performance* or *faire* (see chapters 3 and 4). These categories, in turn, represent the first step in an attempt to extend to the area of narrative proper structures of identities and differences which have been a basic tenet of the study of natural languages in the last seventy-five years.

However, a system of identities and differences alone, whereby sentences and propositions are programmed without reference to a pragmatics and the capacity of the subject to make explicit certain choices, while also internalizing (for example fantasizing about) others, will not suffice, as semiotics is not only a search for simple differential meaning but also for the functions of meaning *in discourse*. To this extent, the relationships between expression and content are not only built on the principle of identity and difference, but equally on the principle of identity and equivalence. At the logical and syntactic level of language, the determination of meaning is made as much on the principle of equivalence as on that of difference, and it often happens, for instance, that an irreconcilable lexical difference in a specific context can later be resolved in the overall context revealed by a linguistic and semiotic analysis. Thus Claude Brémond (1973) can envisage equivalences between seemingly distinct or opposite phases of a narrative; thus, in Lévi-Strauss' *The Raw and the Cooked* (1969: 125–126), where the hero of the Bororo myth is transformed from a deer to a jaguar, Greimas can show that the lexical difference (man $\neq$ deer; jaguar $\neq$ deer) is summed up in a paradigmatic equivalence of code, without any basic structural modification to the narrative (Greimas 1970: 49–93).

Before we end this discourse on the relations between semiotics and linguistics, let us note in passing that using or adapting a linguistic model which refers to language as the social creation *par excellence*, semiotics resolutely affirms its human and social vocation. On one side, the bulk of its research is now oriented toward problems of communication in the field of natural as well as nonnatural languages — including a cosmological language without individual reference, which Greimas studies in his "Conditions d'une sémiotique du monde naturel" (1970: 49-93). This research is particularly dynamic, since it introduces into the semiolinguistic perspective an element which had until then been completely banned from theoretical investigation: the referent (be it animate or inanimate, human or nonhuman)— not as absolute or eternal reference, but rather *as a place* for the manifestation of that which is both understood (*sens*) by and perceivable (*sensible*) to man. On the other side, as regards natural languages proper and a semiotics more strictly derived from linguistic principles, the work of a Barthes or a Metz on systems produced by a consumer society (fashion, food, mass media, film) proposes an entirely contemporary vocation for semiology; and the interest expressed by certain Soviet semioticians in processes which had previously been considered irrational (magic, cards, games) coincides perfectly with the aspirations of this new humanism (Barthes 1957, 1964; Metz 1971; Kristeva 1968). Finally, as far as literary semiotics is concerned, let us remark, without going into detail, that the tendency on the part of the semiotician to study collective (folklore) texts— that is, texts whose desubjectivization and normalization make them more readily available to the structuralist activity— can be justified in the context of a shift in intercultural relationships. Indeed, the return to Propp's theories (1958) on the Russian folktale and the attempt to apply those theories to all narrative systems (at the level, for instance, of a *narrative logic*) constitutes nothing less than an attack on the elitist and privileged individualism of a tradition known as *literature* in the proper sense of the word, and of which oral folklore represented until now but a primitive and unwritten stage. Through a typology of narrative levels, based on classes of actions and character functions, semiotics proposes the establishment of a universal model of narrative, which it remains confident it can extend to all genres and subgenres anywhere, as literature is but a sophisticated system of signs which a society only articulates and diversifies in order to communicate to itself and others contextual and behavioral changes. From this it follows that semiotic investigations, replacing a sociology of literature today outmoded, lean toward the reconstruction of traditional relations between the work and its environment in terms of exchanges (of signification), instead of simple cause and effect relations.

NOTES

1. I am introducing here a Hjelmslevian terminology, now traditional in structuralist criticism. Let us remember that, in order to do away with the classic determination of form through content, Hjelmslev recognized in the linguistic *content*, in its *process* and its *system*, a specific *form*, the *content-form*, which is independent of, and stands in arbitrary relation to, the *purport*, and forms it into a *content-substance* (1961: 47–60); likewise at the level of expression. In this way, the sign is a sign for both a signifying system of expression and one of content. The whole design must be seen in the context of a new description of language, giving up the traditional view of pure sign systems in favor of two analyses eventually yielding (on either level) a restricted number of entities hopefully matchable in what is known as *isomorphic process*.

    As regards *semiotics vs. semiology*, Riffaterre rather curiously distinguishes between "*semiotics*, the study of signs, of which linguistics is a part," and "*semiology*, conceived as being a part of linguistics" (1971: 269; my translation), while Jakobson (1973: 280) links Saussure's "semiology" to Peirce's "semiotics." In the next pages, I shall be using the two interchangeably. In some of the texts which follow, however, placing myself in a poststructuralist perspective, I shall be using *semiotics* in contradistinction with *semiology* (see in particular chapter 14). As for the opposition semiotics *vs.* linguistics, Benveniste had already written in 1963: "Far from language being the one to be subordinated to society, it is society which must be recognized as *langue* in order to begin. . . " (1966: 32–45; my translation). One year later, in his *Eléments de sémiologie* (1964), Barthes, returning to Hjelmslev, then to Saussure, demonstrated the importance of the dichotomies, *langue/parole* and *process/system* in semiology.

2. *The Semiotic Scene* now happens to be the name of the bulletin issued by the recently constituted *Semiotic Society of America*.

3. *Normalization* refers to "the first elements of a syntax and a lexematics of semantic language, that is to say, the metalinguistic framework in which to place the explicit [*manifestés*] contents of the corpus under description" (Greimas 1966: 158 ff; my translation).

2

From Language Signs to Narrative Signs

While it is clear that the study of signs has opened new perspectives in the field of knowledge by offering the hope that all branches of human activity, including literature, can be known according to models derived from the linguistic model, the application of semiotics to specific literary texts raises several important questions. It should, first, be decided whether semiotics can really abide by a (linguistic) model, where the unit of reference (at least for all types of structural linguistics) is still the sentence, and be applied to areas where the unit of reference can no longer be the sentence, because what is at stake there is not the theory of the sign, but the practical ways in which signs become parts of larger systems. For a long time now, the unit of reference in literary semiotics has been the narrative unit (*unité de récit*)— on the premise that *literature* only exists with reference to what it has to say, to tell someone, and that how it tells is what enables us to distinguish between various forms of narrative. Here I do not wish to enter the controversy of what is literary and what is not, nor of how this literariness should be defined (a good model could be provided by Jakobson's definition of the poetic function) — because semioticians, and specifically semi-oticians of literature, are still divided as to whether specific privileges should be granted the semiotics of literature. They are still debating whether these specific privileges derive from peculiarities in the way in which semiotic models of literature function, or whether this attempt to define a literary specificity is not the saving remnant of an ideology which, as such (semioticians are concerned with structures of languages, not with the relation between a particular structure and its referent) has nothing to do with semiotics: the ideology of the good, the beautiful and a literary *je ne sais quoi* always beyond the reach of the linguist.

Now there are several ways to define a narrative unit. One can simply admit that the narrative unit is determined by a linguistic structure beyond the sentence but not very different from the one activating single sentences: and in this sense, a narrative only differs from a linguistic unit to the degree to which it represents an accumulation of linguistic units. This tendency has been well-exemplified by critics like Genette (1966, 1969, 1972) who simply consider narrative texts as resulting from the concatenation of various linguistic phenomena: thus accounting for the process of the Proustian narrative, its acquisition and production, by studying the development of the metonymy and its relation to the production of metaphor (1972: 42–63). However, there is an ambiguity in definitions of this kind as the critic who insists that the mechanisms of narrative are dependent on rules regulating specific linguistic phenomena, be it metonymy or any other, also reserves the right to introduce subjective, nonlinguistic considerations between code and message (Genette's *voice*): which is one of the reasons we shall leave Genette aside in our search for a *semiostylistic theory*.

The other way to define a narrative unit is to start from generative grammar and to attempt to generalize to *narrative units* structures originally conceived at the level of the string sentence. Hypothesizing that a narrative order increases the probability of paradigms through the concatenation of linguistic features, one could follow Levin and others and scan the text for structures of *couplings* working at various intervals (see e.g. Levin 1962: 30–41); or, having first posited that a text functions as a result of multiple relations between a deep-structure or a surface structure, one could also entertain the principle that one single surface sentence may contain several interpretations, and vice versa: that a sentence can operate in several ways in the text.[1] But, as one discovers that there is no syntax without a semantics, whereas the reverse could still be possible, this system of *text grammars* finally ends up relying on semantic concepts of what is the semantic notion underlying the syntax of a particular text. Thus we might have to return to a simpler system where narrative structures would, as van Dijk himself admits (1972: 187), *both* syntactically *and* semantically *represent* (and perhaps mime?), the text: that is, a system where the complexity of narrative (character/plot/thought) is reduced to evolving typologies of meaning which account for the staging, the fictionalization of syntactic phenomena in relation with the patterns of a specific text. This explains why narrative models combining syntax and semantics (Brémond 1973; Greimas 1966, 1970, 1976) always have a tendency to mix the abstract and the anthropomorphic (agent/patient; addressor/addressee). The real question, however, is, as we shall see in a moment, whether these typologies are valid in all cases; that is, not only for the fairy tale (simple models), but also for the novel and for poetry; and also, whether they are not simply paraphrastic transcriptions of original texts based on the very same unexamined sociocultural norms those texts propound — a good case in point being van Dijk's uncritical use of such notions *as norm* (1972: 199), *narrative competence* (1972: 284), *degrees of well-formedness* (1972: 277).

NOTE

1. Note the controversy provoked by Roland Barthes' *S/Z* (1970) and the poststructuralist position in favor of the plurivalence of texts (Kristeva 1969).

3

From Narrative Signs to Descriptive Signs: The Problem of Style

The world is full of narratives. All that we know, do or imagine can ultimately be reduced to a string of narrative sequences. And the point could even be made that any discourse, be it creative or critical, literary, philosophical, scientific, or even artistic (the discourse of the art critic on painting and sculpture), can, irrespective of its particular semantic investment, be articulated, first, *as a story*. Even the mathematician who orders the world in terms of numbers and figures, functions and equations, can be thought of as the author of an ongoing narrative, since mathematical symbols and figures often represent nothing more than a mere formalization of choices between various logical or time sequences basic to any narrative.[1] In addition, any text where the use of scientific concepts lends an anthropomorphic representation to an operating subject can readily be assimilated to a narrative. Such are the texts written by philosophers of science (see Chapter 6).

In all *basic* narratives, however, the narrator's primary concern is with articulating data or facts in a logical and chronological perspective. Anything that might be interpreted to convey more than data or facts; anything that could be construed as not directly related to the development of the action, such as contextual indications of time and place, of the milieu in which the characters evolve, would be considered as extraneous to the narrative itself, and routinely referred to as *description*, while the core of the narrative would be defined as *narration*. Now the line between narration and description is difficult to trace, and is perhaps an imaginary one. In fact we might argue there is no such thing as an objective narrative, that narration proper does not exist. The author, however impartial and detached he may want to remain from the temptations of interfering with his story and of mastering in his writings the glut, what Hegel (1970: 16) would call "den Reichtum der Substanz" [the wealth of the substance] or Joyce (1961, 168) the "wealth of the world", will always imperceptibly infringe upon his subject and make his point of view explicit. In other words any narration always incorporates a certain amount of description, because, as long as a narrating subject makes his presence felt, the narrative partakes of an intentionality, a desire to communicate which goes beyond the communication of a clear message, based on the understanding of a mere class of data or a typology of actions. It is as though the narrator wanted to make us aware of the specific *mimetic* quality of the story he is putting forth. Aristotle laid the foundations to a theory of *description*, when he insisted that the poet differs from the historian in that he represents actions, not as they actually happened, but as they *might have happened*. I am not merely suggesting that acceptability and probability are the only two criteria which enable us to define description, but I am saying that there is in almost any narrative a descriptive intention or attitude on the part of the narrator which can be reconstrued by the reader and whose signs and significance, if properly assessed, will stimulate our imagination and satisfy our unconscious need for appropriation and recognition. I am also suggesting that there is inherent in any narrative process, and specifically in historical narratives, however objective they purport to be, a process of description (and of fictionalization) which is unavoidable and is in turn responsible for our determination of the reliability or the unreliability of straight narrative. Or to push it even further, whereas for most semioticians any narrative complex (narration plus description) can be justified by the categorial functions of narrative alone and description ends up being some sort of optional addition to the significant core of narrative, I am proposing that the common denominator for all narratives is not the order, type, or value of their strict narrative system, but their universal share in a descriptive universe.

Description then offers three avenues of interpretation, three ways in which it can be studied. *First*, it always begins as a matter of pure stylistic investigations: a writer charges his narrative with a certain number of stylistic devices, whose effectiveness is determined by the correlation that can be established between the predictability of a particular audience reaction and the interest of the writer. The problem of description thus appears essentially as one of *indicators*, or better, of the place and the recognition one is to give to the non-purely-narrative signs in any discourse. If one can determine that a particular text contains descriptive signs and which kind, one can offer a classification of texts according to their sign potential: that is the domain of stylistics, or rather, as stylistics continues to have a bad name (Fish 1973: 109-152), the field of application of a new theory of *semiostylistics*. *Second*, because descriptions always give the impression that one is going to relax, and abstract oneself from the narrative for a moment (with an introduction, a commentary, or any other form of authorial intrusion), one may assume that a descriptive passage corresponds to a different kind of authorial consciousness or *intention*. And the task of the critic is then to assess the display, the appearance of this intention (the hero's or the narrator's own) in the text. This particular way of studying descriptions is a phenomenological one. What is at stake is the possibility of communicating the simple idea of existence; of making sure that the simple statement is an act of significance, better, of existence. *And then there is a third way*: this space of description, which is indicated (*signs*), which is lived and made existent (phenomenology) is not only thus indicated and delineated by an *objective consciousness from inside*; it is also sensed as the area where our language ceases to be able to formalize and reduce everything to the simple syntactic model. Description is the area where the dialectic of *language and desire* is most noticeable. Whereas narrative (narration) always strives toward the buildup of a conflict and its subsequent *denouement* (passage from a state of tension to a state of relaxation), description attempts to solicit desire through the manifold manipulation of the signs of display precisely in order to avoid building a model of conflict resolution. Avoidance however, does not always mean rejection. As we shall see, the method introduced here to isolate discrete features of description in three separate areas will enable us to study nonnarrative blocks of description proper, but it will also give us an insight into descriptive processes of manipulation which contribute to the masking of existing narrative processes, or even to the production of an unsuspected *histoire*. In the following chapters, using a stylistic and semiostylistic perspective, I shall be examining the interrelation of narration and description in texts of prose and poetry.

NOTE

1. It is a little more complicated than that. One should say, instead, that if it is agreed that mathematical symbols signify nothing unless they are organized into series, those series themselves are predicated on the adoption of a linear model, where time (chronology and possibility) is inherent to the performance of the model, whether the specific series be eventually considered infinite, circular, recurrent, or any other. On this and related problems, see Serres (1968: 11-35).

4

Narrative and Descriptive Signs in Prose

Let us first remember that our study will involve written literary texts which differ from a Jakobson *passe-partout* discourse by the poetic self-reference of their message. We are speaking now of *literature,* completely accepting Derrida's reservations, according to which all reference to a written language is a disguised reference to a spoken language (φονή). Besides, as we shall see, all stylistic investigation becomes semiological in nature and meticulous about the φονή as soon as it applies itself to the conditions of elocution of the message and the relation of diverse linguistic functions in the elaboration of the message (Jakobson 1960 : 353 ff): always searching beyond the text proper, referring itself to a metatext (the cultural tradition, the lexicon, even the personal experience of the stylistician), stylistics constitutes in fact a return to the authority of the φονή and the conditions of auditory perception of the message (Chatman 1971a: 399-422). A stylistician like Riffaterre, claiming to work only with the code-message relation, may strive to develop the least subjective stylistics possible. He will, nevertheless, remain, like everyone else, dependent on a subjective appreciation of the φονή in the decoding. Let us take as an example the analysis that he gives of the cliché *voix tonnante* in several literary texts, particularly in a passage from Victor Hugo's *Les Misérables*:

Marius "regarda fixement son aïeul, et cria d'une voix tonnante: — A bas les Bourbons et ce gros cochon de Louis XVIII!" Louis XVIII était mort depuis quatre ans, mais cela lui était bien égal (Hugo, quoted by Riffaterre 1971:165).

Marius looked straight at his grandfather and cried in a thunderous voice: "Down with the Bourbons, and the great hog Louis XVIII". Louis XVIII had been dead for four years; but it was all the same to him (Hugo 1931: 544).

With Hugo, the excess of *voix tonnante*, and by the same claim, the excessive affront made to Louis XVIII, express a young republican's angry outburst against his Legitimist grandfather who has just insulted the memory of his Bonapartist father.

One should appreciate here the inability of one generation to comprehend another, the dilemma in which the insult of a respected grandfather places the young man (Riffaterre 1971: 165).[1]

How does one otherwise comprehend this affront that Riffaterre is talking about than in the context of its elocution, *in vivo?* Even so, we must remember that we are studying literary texts, and not painting or music, and remain agreed that style is to be determined in the context of this literature and in relation to a semiology particular to literature (Riffaterre 1971: 269). The function of stylistics, then, is to establish and define clearly the *literariness* of a literature that is itself a typological representation of the ability of a language — and therefore of the world in which we live — to function. This, in effect, is exactly what Barthes does, when, in spite of himself ("la connotation tout de même") and against the *new semioticians* and some of the poststructuralists, he defends the system of connotation:

. . . for if there are *readerly* texts, committed to the closure system of the West, produced according to the goals of this system, devoted to the law of the Signified, they must have a particular system of meaning, and this meaning is based on connotation. Hence, to deny connotation altogether is to abolish the differential *value* of texts, to refuse to define the specific apparatus (both poetic and critical) for the readerly texts . . . (Barthes 1975: 7-8).

Up to this point, there seems to be no problem. Following Barthes one can allow two large areas proper to literary criticism:

. . . the first will include signs *beneath* the sentence, such as old figures, the phenomena of connotation, the 'semantic anomalies' etc, in short, all the features of poetics in its entirety; the second will include signs *above* the sentence, parts of discourse from which one can infer a structure of the narrative, the poetic message and the discursive text, etc. (Barthes 1966a: 62-63).

One will also readily admit that these two areas are closely interrelated: the "signs *above*" may not be studied without the "signs *beneath*." Unfortunately, it is this *without* that poses a problem. In giving a detailed reading to Barthes' treatment (1970) of Balzac's *Sarrasine*, one is impressed with the meticulous attention paid to stylistic codes and rhetorical procedures. For all the abundance of rhetorical terminology, however, one must admit that Barthes' decoding has in the end no other function but to permit the purely lexical denotation of the text, which in turn allows the establishment, outside the text and at a purely semantic level, of a structure (the signs *above*) of the narrative which it is impossible to perceive on a first reading. In the following passage, the hasty rendering of a text into a model soon dilutes the

effects of a style which a rigourous and clear-sighted decoding had
initially revealed:

[Balzac's text:] Les arbres, imparfaite-
ment couverts de neige, se détachaient
faiblement du fond grisâtre que formait
un ciel nuageux, à peine blanchi par la
lune. Vus au sein de cette atmosphère
fantastique, ils ressemblaient vague-
ment à des spectres mal enveloppés de
leurs linceuls, image gigantesque de la
fameuse *danse des morts* (quoted by
Barthes 1970: 30).

The trees, partially covered with
snow, stood out dimly against the
grayish background of a cloudy sky,
barely whitened by the moon. Seen
amid these fantastic surroundings,
they vaguely resembled ghosts half
out of their shrouds, a gigantic
representation of the famous *Dance of
the Dead* (quoted by Barthes 1975:
23).

[Barthes' commentary:]* SYM. [symbolic code] Antithesis: A: the outdoors. —
**The snow here refers to cold, but this is not inevitable, it is even rare: the snow, a
soft, downy cloak, rather connotes the warmth of homogeneous substances, the
protection of a shelter. Here the cold is created by the partial nature of the snow
covering: it is not the snow but the partialness that is cold; the sinister form is the
partially covered form: the plucked, the skinned, the patchy, everything left of a
wholeness preyed on by a nothingness (SEM. [semantic unit] Cold). The moon, too,
contributes to this deficiency: frankly sinister here, forming a defect in the landscape
it lights; we will come upon it again endowed with an ambiguous softness when, in
the form of an alabaster lamp, it will illumine and feminize Vien's Adonis (No. 111),
a portrait which is the (explicit) reflection of Girodet's Endymion (No. 547). The
moon is the *nothingness* of light, warmth reduced to its deficiency: it illuminates by
mere reflection without itself being an origin; thus, it becomes the luminous emblem
of the castrato, a deficiency manifested by the empty glitter he borrows from
femininity while young (an Adonis) and of which nothing remains but a leprous
gray when he is old (the old man, the garden) (SEM. Selenity). Furthermore, the
fantastic designates and will designate what is outside the limits of the human:
supernatural, extra-terrestrial, this transgression is the castrato's, represented (later)
as both sub-woman and sub-man (SEM. Fantastic). ***REF. [reference] Art
(The Dance of the Dead) (Barthes 1970: 23-24).

To perceive the importance of the "partialness" (*partially covered*, and so
on) and the *lack* (*dimly*, and so on) is entirely correct; but this alone will not
be sufficient to justify a passage to the signified "castration" for the very
good reason that a semiological reading of the text, which must generally
entail the perception and the internalization of a stylistic structure, here
consists merely in intensifying the self-referential value of the structure. In
other words, what is very clear here is a certain hidden quality, latency, of
the text. The scenery described by the narrator only holds our attention
because it is *partial*, that is to say, because there is something missing. This
imperfection, which represents a certain manner of not-being-in-the-
normal-world, constitutes the semic axis with which our reading defines
the absence. But nothing authorizes us to explain this imperfection away (to
fill this void), without risking the violation of the bizarre and *fantastic*

closure that the text imposes. Balzac soon reminds us of this closure with a stereotypic wink: the Dance of the Dead — which is later revitalized in the form: Dance of the Living: "then, turning in the other direction, . . . I could admire the *Dance of the Living!*" (quoted by Barthes 1975: 24).

In fact, the problem of decoding calls forth another problem which is fundamental — that of the importance of stylistic investigation itself. Is stylistics a semiotic *system*, or is it only a *process*, which would, before any systematization can take place, permit a translation of the literary text at the level of *passe-partout* discourse, thus making possible a specific determination of the proper register and context to be applied to a purely denotative reading?

One may respond that this depends on what brand of stylistics one practices. One can adopt a normative (Bally 1951) or a genetic (Spitzer 1948) stylistics. Or one can reject either and maintain the principle of a formal imperative at work in the text with but minimal reference to a context. Or one can entertain the possibility that the signata or signified in the text contaminate and crossbreed each other, producing not one, but various layers of heterogeneous meaning. However, the hazards of a systematic polysemism have just been exposed here and it has also been shown elsewhere (Riffaterre 1971: 284-286) that certain formalists readily fall into the trap of normative stylistics, as soon as they begin to entertain an unquestioning confidence in the application of their paradigms of substitution and equivalence: how — since certain of the correlations they establish are hardly perceivable and therefore rarely verifiable — their analyses paradoxically seem to justify the illusion of a stylistic norm and the concept of an author's language. The theory and practice of stylistics (*semiostylistics*) developed here, on the other hand, will attempt to avoid the pitfalls of both normativism and polysemism.

Meanwhile, for the form of a particular stylistic theory to appear clearly, it must now be decided precisely *when* the decoding of a specific and definite *surface level* implicates, with an overall modification in the general narrative structure, an integrative transcoding to a deeper level. It is extraordinary that, on this point, the methodology or pragmatics of reading still awaits its theoretician. Usually, and here we join Derrida's criticism, it is far too often by virtue of a preordered signified structure that the *readerly* (*lisible*) signifier of the text under consideration is arranged.

On the basis of the old distinction made by Barthes in *Communications*, between level of *function,* level of *action,* and level of *narration* (Barthes 1966b: 6), I will now take three examples from Saussurean and Hjelmslevian research in semiology and I will try to approach problems in the text which until now have been examined from a theoretical angle. These three examples will permit me to reconcile semiotics and stylistics, to arrive at a *semiostylistics*, the epistemological foundations of which I propose to establish.

I. At the level of the *functions* of the narrative, that is to say, the rules which govern a narrated universe, the definition of elementary types of narratives — which correspond in other respects to the most general forms of human behavior—does not seem to require any sort of stylistic predetermination. The study of what Brémond calls the conventions of a particular universe, characteristic of a culture, a period, a literary genre, a story-telling style, or in rare cases, of characteristics unique to the specific narrative, goes back in fact to the delimitation of a series of choices in the organization of psychological processes. But as Brémond explicitly leaves aside the "analysis of techniques of narration," *we are told nothing about the actualization of these choices in the text*:

Our endeavor is to proceed with a logical reconstitution of the starting points of the narrative network. Without meaning to explore each itinerary to is finest divisions, we will try to follow the principal arteries, recognizing, along the course of each one, the subtypes. We will thus construct a plan of sequences of models certainly less numerous than one might think, from which the story-teller must necessarily choose. This plan will itself become the foundation for a classification of roles assumed by the characters in the narrative (Brémond 1966: 62).

Now it seems evident that such a systematization is not entirely separate from the coding of the text which it renders visible and without which it would only be able to constitute the mentalist representation of a process that is essentially stylistic. Because Brémond, starting with his studies of formulaic texts (1973)[2] limits his work to the elaboration of a meta-text, I will try to show, with a strictly textual example, that the functions of the narrative have meaning only inasmuch as they can be integrated into a meticulous decoding.

Let us take Prosper Mérimée's *Mateo Falcone*, and begin to analyze it following Brémond's method. The tale is simple: the father leaves; the bandit arrives; there is the trial and contract of honor with the son (promise and delivery of the money, the hiding place); the arrival of the soldiers and their officer; trial and contract of dishonor (promise and delivery of the watch, disclosure of the hiding place); return of the father and redeeming of the wrong contract by the trial of the son's execution. Again, following Brémond, this whole succession can be formalized in the following manner:

father's departure: possible degradation
                      ↓

bandit's arrival: process of degradation = imporvement to be
                                      sought
                                          ↓

                                   process of improvement
                                          ↓

           degradation avoided = improvement achieved
                      ↓

officer's arrival: possible degradation
                      ↓

           process of degradation
                      ↓

           degradation affected
                      ↓

father's return: improvement to be sought
                      ↓

           process of improvement
                      ↓

           improvement achieved

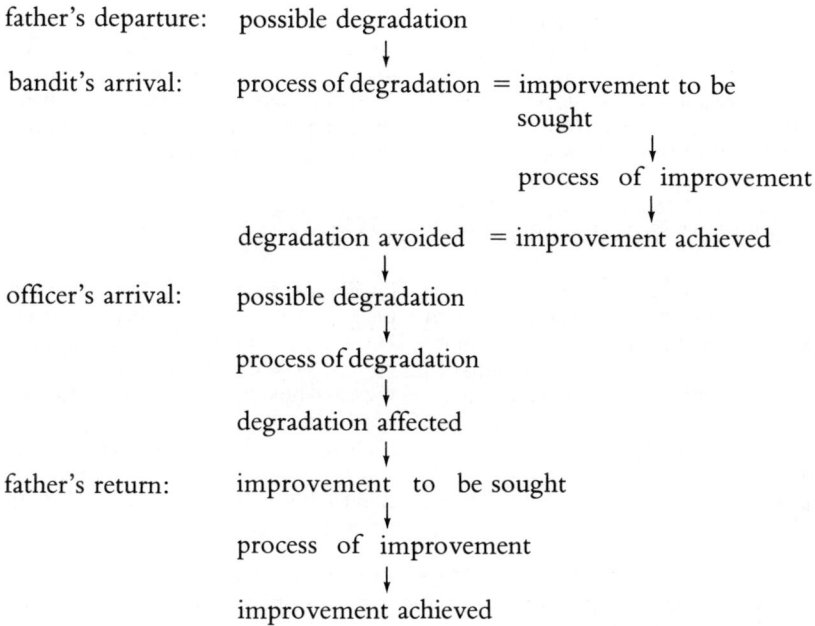

Let us look at the pertinence of stylistic features to the development of logical process in the text's semiotic system. We will immediately notice that an interruption of the stylistic pattern corresponds in fact to each of the developments with a transformation in the code. The father's departure is made in the context of a somewhat apprehensive description of the heath at the border of which the house of the Falcones is perched:

Le maquis est la patrie des bergers corses et de quiconque s'est brouillé avec la justice . . . Si vous avez tué un homme, allez dans le maquis de Porto-Vecchio, et vous y vivrez en sûreté, avec un bon fusil, de la poudre et des balles (Mérimée 1951: 225)	The heath is the home of the Corsican shepherds, and the resort of all those who have come in conflict with the law . . . If you have killed a man, go into the *maquis* of Porto-Vecchio, with a good gun and powder and shot, and you will live there in safety (Mérimée 1966: 33).

The catastrophe is predicted: "Le petit Fortunato voulait l'accompagner . . . le père refusa donc: on verra s'il n'eut pas lieu de s'en repentir" (1951: 226–227) ["Little Fortunato wanted to go with them . . . so his father refused. We shall soon see that he had occasion to regret having done so" (1966: 35)]; then it is announced, with the sequence of *imparfaits* cut by a *passé simple*:

Il était absent depuis quelques heures, et le petit Fortunato était tranquillement	He had been gone a few hours, and little Fortunato was quietly lying out in the

B

étendu au soleil, regardant les montagnes bleues, et pensant que le dimanche prochain, il irait dîner à la ville, chez son oncle le *caporal*, quand il fut soudainement interrompu dans ses méditations par l'explosion d'une arme à feu (1951: 227).

sunshine, looking at the blue mountains, and thinking that on the following Sunday, he would be going to have dinner with his uncle, the *corporal*, when his meditations were suddenly interrupted by the firing of a gun (1966: 35).

The bandit's arrival confirms the degradation:

. . . enfin, dans le sentier qui menait de la plaine à la maison de Mateo, parut un homme coiffé d'un bonnet pointu comme en portent les montagnards, barbu, couvert de haillons, et se traînant avec peine en s'appuyant sur son fusil . . . il avait peu d'avance sur les soldats, et sa blessure le mettait hors d'état de gagner le maquis avant d'être rejoint (1951: 227).

Finally, on the path which led from the plain to Mateo's house, a man appeared. He wore a pointed cap like a mountaineer, he was bearded and clothed in rags, and he was dragging himself along with difficulty, leaning on his gun . . . He had only a short start on the soldiers, and his wound made it out of the question for him to reach the maquis before being overtaken (1966: 35-36).

The improvement *to be achieved* is clearly marked by the trial: " 'Cache-moi, car je ne puis aller plus loin'. 'Et que dira mon père si je te cache sans sa permission?' 'Cache-moi vite; ils viennent . . . Allons cache-moi, ou je te tue'. 'Que me donneras-tu si je te cache?' " (1951: 227) [" 'Hide me, for I cannot go any farther'. 'But what will my father say if I hide you without his permission?' 'Hide me quickly: they are coming . . . Come, hide me, or I will kill you' 'What will you give me if I hide you?' " (1966: 36)]. The *improvement achieved*, on the other hand, is clearly suggested (= degradation avoided) by the following context, where a succession of *passés simples* certifies a completed sequence and a return to the calm of the meditation period:

Il alla prendre une chatte et ses petits, et les établit sur le tas de foin, pour faire croire qu'il n'avait pas été remué depuis peu. Ensuite, remarquant des traces de sang sur le sentier près de la maison, il les couvrit de poussière avec soin, et, cela fait, se recoucha au soleil avec la plus grande tranquillité (1951: 228).

He fetched a cat and her kittens and put them on top of the haycock to give the impression it had not been touched for some time. Then, noticing some bloodstains on the path near the house, he carefully covered them with dust, and, this done, he lay down again in the sun with the utmost sang-froid (1966: 37).

The degradation begins immediately from the arrival of "six hommes en uniforme brun à collet jaune, et commandés par un adjudant . . . c'était un homme actif, fort redouté des bandits dont il avait déjà traqué plusieurs" (1951: 228–229) ["six men wearing brown uniforms with yellow collars and under the command of a sergeant-major . . . he was an energetic man, greatly feared by the

bandits, several of whom he had already hunted down" (1966: 37)].
Notice the importance of adjectives (*brun . . . jaune . . . actif*) connoting
an upset in the plot. The process of degradation is long and
complicated, as the new trial of Fortunato suggests: "Ah! petit drôle,
tu fais le malin! . . . que la diable te confonde! . . . Peut-être qu'en te
donnant une vingtaine de coups de plat de sabre . . .' " (1951: 229-230)
[" 'You're making fun of me, you rascal . . . The devil take
you! . . . Perhaps . . . when you've had a thrashing with the flat of a
sword' " (1966: 37-38)]. It is prolonged to the extreme with the
paradigm of the cat:

Un soldat s'approcha du tas de foin. Il vit la chatte, et donna un coup de baïonnette dans le foin avec négligence, et haussant les épaules, comme s'il sentait que sa précaution était ridicule. Rien ne remua; et le visage de l'enfant ne trahit pas la plus légère émotion. . ."Eh bien, la veux-tu cette montre?" . . . Fortunato, lorgnant la montre du coin de l'œil, ressemblait à un chat à qui l'on présente un poulet tout entier. Comme il sent qu'on se moque de lui, il n'ose y porter la griffe . . . Cependant la montre oscillait, tournait, et quelquefois lui heurtait le bout du nez. Enfin, peu à peu, sa main droite s'éleva vers la montre. . . Fortunato éleva aussi sa main gauche et indiqua du pouce, par-dessus son épaule, le tas de foin auquel il était adossé (1951: 230-232).

One soldier came up to the haycock. He looked at the cat and idly stirred the hay with his bayonet, shrugging his shoulders as if he considered the precaution ridiculous. Nothing moved, and the child's face did not betray the slightest emotion. . . "Well, would you like this watch?" . . . Fortunato ogled the watch out of the corner of his eyes, just as a cat does when a whole chicken is offered to it. It dares not pounce on the bird, because it is afraid a joke is being played on it . . . All the time, the watch dangled and swung around, and sometimes touched the tip of his nose. Finally, little by little, his right hand rose towards the watch . . . Fortunato raised his left hand too, and pointed with his thunb over his shoulder at the haycock against which he was learning (1966: 38-40).

Notice here the importance of a correspondence between human and
animal gestures. It is precisely because of an association between Fortunato,
the cat (remember the cat and her kittens) and the chicken that the *silent*
progress of the plot is made so striking (*main droite . . . main gauche . . .
pouce*).

However, when the father returns, this slow process of degradation is
suddenly brought to completion by a simple, almost ritual gesture:
"Quand il [Gianetto] vit Mateo . . . cracha sur le seuil en disant: 'Maison
d'un traître!' " ["When he saw Mateo . . . spat on the threshold, saying:
'This is a traitor's house!' "] which establishes, through the insertion of an
unexpected occurrence, the complete reversal and closure of narrative
choices. Through this occurrence, then, the logical sequences articulating
the elaborate processes of hiding, concealment, and recovery have been
plainly superseded. The progress of the tale has been made *contingent* on the

perception by the reader of the negative impact of the father's return upon the course of the narrative. In order to maximize this impact, Mérimée feels compelled to use an *exemplum*, substituting with the interpretation of a cultural, an anthropological reference (destruction of the watch as representing the wages of treason; punishment of the traitor, albeit with preservation of his soul), a *discourse* of point of view for the *story* of a faceless narrator (Benveniste 1966: 237-250):

Giuseppa s'approcha. Elle venait d'apercevoir la chaîne de la montre, dont un bout sortait de la chemise de Fortunato . . . Falcone saisit la montre, et la jetant avec force contre une pierre, il la mit en mille pièces. "Femme," dit-il, "cet enfant est-il de moi?" . . . "Qu'as-tu fait?" s' écria-t-elle. "Justice". "Où est-il?". "Dans le ravin. Je vais l'enterrer. Il est mort en chrétien; je lui ferai chanter une messe" (1951: 235-237).

Giuseppa came over to him. She had just seen the end of the watch-chain hanging outside his shirt . . . Falcone seized the watch, and threw it against a stone with such force that it broke into a thousand pieces. "Woman", he said, "is this my child?" "What have you done?" she cried. "Justice!" "Where is he?" "In the ravine. I am going to bury him. He died like a Christian. I shall have a Mass sung for him" (1966: 45-46).

Notice how the closure of the story is both understated and overstated in the ironic mode through the paradoxical display of a dual cliché: "Justice!. . . Il est mort en chrétien." At the level of decoding, it is the reader's identification of the stylistic structure which closes the logical sequence and also directs his interpretation to a recognition of the ritual involved in that closure ("Justice . . . en chrétien"). In this tale by Mérimée where the delineation of choices is, as in all folktales, relatively uncomplicated, the elaboration of a *logique des possibles narratifs* has meaning only inasmuch as it makes symbolic the opening and the closure of choices at the level of decoding: in the expression-form. To say that the tale has been completed because the villain has been punished at the end of a tightly ordered series of peripeteias might satisfy a folklorist's obsession with logical sequences, but it leaves unanswered the question of why the *form of that logic* is so successful in the tradition and so attractive to the public. A stylistic approach to the problem of narrative functions permits, not only the demonstration, but also the experience of what it is that makes the text interesting: the very mystery of its necessity.

II. At the level of actions, the work of Greimas, where the emphasis has been moved from the *form* of expression and content to their *substance* (from semiotics to semantics) in order to derive concrete representations from abstract concepts, seems, upon first examination, to provide the appropriate context for the study of a semantics of style missing in Brémond's model.

Although a theory of *actants* was first developed by linguists like Tesnières (1969: 105–107), Greimas was the first to integrate the actantial model into both a semantic and syntactic perspective. I shall leave aside here the syntactic reduction of Propp's chronological model (thirty-one syntagmatic functions now covered by three pairs of syntactic-semantic operators known as *actants* or acting matrixes) in order to concentrate on the study of the stylistic problems presented by a semantic (ideological and axiological) investment of the actants.

Let us now look at the model-analysis which Greimas gives of the work of Bernanos (1966: 222-256). Beginning with a lexical decoding based on word-units (life/death), he constructs an actantial life/death model which is supposed to function throughout the work and in the context of a fundamental (semantic-syntactic) narrative unit — what he calls an *isotopy* of the type: [E (to be, man, beast = (life + death)]. This implies that, as soon as he has defined his *corpus*, the semiotician must first apply himself to a statistical study of the vocabulary, although Greimas does not indicate how this should be done. Is it because *decoding* operations are always sensed as subjective, that is, depending on the field of reference of the decoder? Is it because the semiotician, who is committed to the study of deep-structure, that is, conceptual *vs.* representational or referential investments, is ashamed to admit that he has to deal, first, with surface-structures? Whatever the reason, this statistical operation will soon lead him into a lexematics (study of clusters) which permits the determination of the *sememic* level of the text, the *sememe* suggesting a transformation of the lexeme by contextualization. At this level of the *sememe*, the semiotician can use the methods of syntagmatic and metonymic analysis. For the sememes produced by the lexeme *life*, he will, for instance, find the following occurrences: *change/ light/warmth*, whereas, for those produced by the lexeme *death*, he might encounter the sememes: *immobility/shadow/coldness*. From the sememic level, he will then proceed to the semic level. The seme, representing in the semantic realm what the actant is in the syntactic realm, makes possible the definition of a semantic context and authorizes sememic classifications according to the rules of cuturally established interpretation. For example, the sememe *change* is made possible by the semes *alteration/rise*, for which it defines a specific (here, historical or moral) context. Let us note that the complexity of what Greimas calls the *palier sémique* [semic threshold] depends on the choice of a specific field of reference at the level of the sememe.

To respect the purely diachronic character of all analysis, and also to simplify my description of a complicated procedure, I have chosen, in this brief summary, to reverse the Greimasian process. But, in the overall perspective of a *Sémantique structurale*, I believe that Greimas and his associates are quite ready to consider the phases of their model as simple hypostases of a fundamentally actantial model, that is, that their theoretical posture is actually predicated on the somewhat Platonic assumption that surface structures are mere expansions or variations — one would almost like to say *imitations* — of universal syntactic and narrative concepts or ideas operative behind the images of the text.

Now it is precisely here that the shoe pinches the semanticist. Even if structural semantics admits, without ever clearly stating it, the usefulness of a stylistic investigation, the conditions of the semic analysis undertaken require less the participation of the reader in the elaboration of an inductive model such as above, than the deduction from the actantial structure of the deductive model of the variations (subtypes or subclasses) possible within each representational class. Only in this way can Greimas really start with the actants to arrive at a study of their investments. But in doing so, he reduces the literary text to a mere program, whose various and refined selections he never bothers to examine.

Let us take, for example, the table of a *Marxist-idealistic thematics* constructed with the actantial model derived from Propp. For idealism, Greimas gives us the following table:

Subject	Philosopher
Object	World
Addressor	God
Addressee	Mankind
Opponent	Matter
Ally	Mind

And for the Marxist model, he gives us:

Subject	Man
Object	Classless society
Addressor	History
Addressee	Mankind
Opponent	Bourgeois class
Ally	Working class (Greimas 1966: 181).

What these tables imply is the use of a *deductive* or *descending* procedure of description applied to the study of the submodels, and which takes the productivity of the higher-ranking structures into account (see Greimas 1966: 166) — from "Subject" to "Philosopher"/from "Object" to

"World," and so on, and not the reverse. In this procedure then, stylistics comes only *a posteriori*: it is purely for purposes of deductive classification. The hierarchical arrangement of the higher-ranking structures is not made at the level of a stylistic function observed in context, but at the purely semantic level of vocabulary; in other words, the determination of actants is *not* stylistic, but syntactic and lexical. One is readily convinced that this is the case when one sees that the author, throughout his model-study of Bernanos, did not cite a single sentence from Bernanos' book, did not refer to a single discourse. The postponement, or worse, the dismissal, of textual analysis, at the very moment when it is admitted that only a thorough examination could aid in defining the *semantic potential (sémanticité)* of certain fields (1966: 231), hardly seems justified. The truth is, the study of stylistic features might lead to the specification of semantic contexts purposely left as nonspecific to facilitate an actantial reduction, and might thus introduce fundamental variations into the model proposed: "Warmth combines with fire, while water allows a *variable paradigm* — water can be cold, warm, or hot" (Greimas 1966: 231; emphasis added). Greimas does not elaborate on this *variable paradigm* nor does he deal with it as a stylistic pattern in its appropriate individual context. Now it should have been very easy for Greimas to deal with it; he could have taken, for instance, this very simple passage from Bernanos:

Les géologues nous apprennent que le sol qui nous semble si ferme, si stable, n'est réellement qu'une mince pellicule au-dessus d'un océan de feu liquide et toujours frémissante comme la peau qui se forme sur le lait prêt à bouillir . . . Quelle épaisseur a le péché? A quelle profondeur faudrait-il creuser pour retrouver le gouffre d'azur? . . . (Bernanos 1961: 1090)

Geologists teach us that the very ground which seems so solid is in reality only a thin film over an ocean of liquid fire, for ever trembling like the skin of milk about to boil . . . [What is the depth of sin?][3] How far down would one need to dig to rediscover the blue depths? . . . (Bernanos 1962: 70)

In this passage from *Journal d'un curé de campagne*, a young priest is observing his new parish. He has just spoken to us about some of his parishioners, in particular, the *petits* [the little ones], who come to confession with "their droning voices, too often a mere repetition of phrases picked out of the prayer book examination of conscience" (1962: 69); he feels toward them a mingling of pity: "May our Lord love and protect these little ones!" and disgust: "Such scarcely veiled animality!" (1962: 70). In the lines immediately following my citation, he worries about the state of his own health, which continues to deteriorate: "I am seriously ill." One clearly recognizes here the categories presented by Greimas (*sememe*) — *water* and *fire* — in a thematic (organic) context (liquid more or less dense, skin–earth, air, fire, vapor), and in an ideological (or religious) context (sin, blue depths). One will accept without difficulty the suggestion of the actants *life* and *death*:

$$\frac{\text{``thin film''}}{\text{``ocean of liquid fire''}} \rightarrow \frac{\text{``[that forms on]''}}{\text{``milk about to boil''}} \rightarrow$$

$$\frac{\text{``[sin]''}}{\text{``blue depths'' (``gouffre d'azur'')}} \rightarrow \frac{\text{``monotonous purring''}}{\text{``confession''}} \rightarrow \frac{\text{life}}{\text{death}} .$$

The problem then is not one of knowing if the content proposed by Greimas permits the verification of these various cases in which a formalization allows the retrieval of the fundamental actantial model, since a quick sketch indicates that this retrieval is to a large extent possible. The problem lies rather in the agent-locutor, and through him the reader, determining for himself the pertinence of the code to the message:

Je suis sérieusement malade. J'en ai eu hier la certitude soudaine et comme l'illumination. Le temps où j'ignorais cette douleur tenace qui cède parfois en apparence, mais ne desserre jamais complétement sa prise, m'a paru tout à coup reculer dans un passé presque vertigineux, reculer jusqu'à l'enfance . . . Voilà juste six mois que j'ai ressenti les premières atteintes de ce mal, et je me souviens à peine de ces jours où je mangeais et je buvais comme tout le monde. Mauvais signe (1961: 1090).

I am seriously ill. Yesterday I was suddenly sure of it — the knowledge seemed to light up my mind. The time when I knew nothing of this relentless pain which sometimes appears to slacken without ever really loosening its hold, suddenly seemed to slip away into the past, slip away into an almost dizzy remoteness, right back to childhood . . . It is just six months ago that I felt the first warnings of this trouble, and now I can hardly remember those days when I ate and drank like everybody else. A bad sign (1962: 70).

One will have noticed the transition from the children of the confession to the childhood of the locutor himself and the relation established between the "blue depths" and the "dizzy remoteness," the "thin film" and the appearance which the pain sometimes gives of slipping away. What the *Journal* brings the *curé de campagne* with this episode of the children's confession, itself another proof of God's mercy, is the revelation of his illness (*certainty* and *sign*), which will be a new occasion for him to experience his own faith. It is through this perception (perceptibility ⇒ stylistic function)[4] that the symbolic relevance of the message is guaranteed.

Now what Greimas' model, applying only to a *formalized* text, does not yield, is exactly the threshold of this perception, which is, first and foremost, sememic (contextual). It is by the game of comparisons and figures that the locutor actualizes the *existential relation* that he establishes and maintains with his own message.[5]

III. Let us pass to the third level; that of *narration*. Todorov, in a practical analysis (1969), developed the principles revealed in his article on the "Catégories du récit littéraire" (1966). Taking his distance from Brémond, who studies "the laws governing the narrated universe" and reflecting on the logical constraints to which all narratives must be subject lest they become unintelligible, Todorov studies the actions as they exist in the narrative discourse — "the structure of the language being confronted not with the structure of the world, but with that of narration which is a type of discourse" (1969: 16). What he gives us, then, is a theory of the semantic and syntactic correlations of narrative. The interest of this study in relation to the two preceding ones is that, by examining the grammatical covering of a text (Boccaccio's) at the level of the semantic substance, it completes the presentation of Brémond's logical models on the one hand, and of Greimas' semiolinguistic models on the other. Without really becoming involved, like Brémond[6] or Greimas, in the formalization of some sort of traditional common sense uniformly derived from syntactic *and* semantic constraints, Todorov approaches the crucial problem of the relation of surface-structures to deep-structures by taking as a point of departure a *distinction by Propp between semantics and syntax* as:

> That which permits us to identify an act, and as a consequence, to affirm the identity of two acts, is the task of semantics. That which permits us to speak of its signification *for the narrative*, of its function, pertains to syntax (Todorov 1969: 21).

Todorov's distinction is between what he calls *meaning* (syntax) and *reference* (semantics). For example, in Boccaccio's work, the syntactic predicate *such an act is a misdeed* can produce the following semantic variations: *such an act is a theft/an adultery/a murder,* and so on. In doing so, he projects a new opposition onto the syntactic and semantic plans, and can pursue his investigation at the level of subgroups in the microcontext of the proposition and the macrocontext of the sequence of propositions. On the one hand, the reduction of the groups (agent-noun/verb-adjective) permits a classification into primary isomorphic (noun/verb/adjective) and secondary ismorphic (negative/opposition/comparative/mode, and so on) categories, where the relationship of *meaning* to *reference* can be either monovalent or plurivalent.[7] We shall note in passing that the use of a new terminology clearly emphasized a departure from the pure syntactic categories to which traditional grammar has us accustomed. On the other hand, the construction of a sequential (syntactic) model on the basis of a causal relation which is obligatory also allows the creation of a certain number of *optional* relations (emphasis, repetition/result, redundancy), and of at least one alternative relation (e.g., reversal of property attribute). This whole model is designed to permit the generalization of a semantic structuring of the text at each particular syntactic level.

Let us take an example from the study of attributive sequences (Todorov calls *attributive* the alternative sequences where the relationship is constituted by a reversal of attribute):

From the semantic point of view, the attributive sequences represent the story of a conflict in the existing equilibrium. The world described at the beginning of the tale is in balance, there is no internal cause for an intervening change. It is an individual desire that provokes its commencement, and which, at the same time, introduces another equilibrium. The tale relates the transition from the first to the second . . . This is the case in *Decameron* I, 9. A lady from Gascony is assaulted by several young rogues during her stay in Cyprus. She wants to complain to the island's king, but is told that it will be a waste of time as the king remains indifferent to insults made even unto himself. Nevertheless, she meets him and addresses a few bitter words to him. The king is touched by this and abandons his lethargy (Todorov 1969: 61).

I will not insist on the fact that the absence of a lexematic analysis deriving *semes* and *sememes* from the formation of an actantial model prevents the serious development here of the proper semantic construction. Todorov is most vague:

What is most important again is that the *Decameron* is not content with describing an already existing system, but that it always takes the system as a base, a point of departure in order to report, in fact, its transgression, and by this obviously, a new system of exchange (1969: 81).

One might wish to inquire about the nature and function of this exchange, but the fact is, because this analysis is limited to the integration of semantic and syntactic relationships in a *grammar* of the narrative, it deprives itself of the examination of a concrete referential. In other words, and most disappointingly for our purposes, stylistics is not relevant to *narratology* defined as the science of the narrative — "our object will be the universe evoked by the discourse, and not this discourse taken in its literalness" (1969: 10).

It seems to me, however, that the simplest approach to the study of narrative procedures in the *Decameron* would have been to define in Boccaccio's text a conventional folklore *pattern* (the procedures of the novella, the fabliau, the tale, and so on), and then to examine the variations and violations of this pattern. But a study of this nature would have required that the critic combine a knowledge of fourteenth-century clerical and oratorical modes with a *reading in the original language*. Todorov, however, expressly rejects this in the name of an ahistoric structuralism, each particular tale being but the "manifestation of an abstract structure, a realization that was included at the latent stage in a combination of possibilities . . . a sort of arch-novella" (1969: 17-18). Yet, when he says that it is "in fact within the *écriture* that the unit is created; the motifs that the study of folklore reveal to us are transformed by Boccaccian writing" (1969: 12), we would certainly like to know at what level we should take this *écriture*. Does he mean the mere text, subject to decoding, or the organization of grammatical relations in this text? And is the latter possible without the former?

Now the *Decameron* is a series of tales presented to persons "foregathered for the purpose of devising together" (Boccaccio 1947: 25). In it, the themes treated, the manner in which they are treated, the tone with which each tells his story, the *elocutio*, are all equally important. It is therefore not without interest to show that a syntactic-semantic reference must include the perception of a stylistic structure.

Let us take a first example (*Decameron* 6: 4). Todorov gives the following summary of the story:

Chichibio offered to his beauty the leg of the crane he was roasting for his master; the latter notices the asymmetry but Chichibio assures him that cranes have only one leg. The master, furious, takes him the next day near the lake to prove him wrong. Chichibio sees, to his delight, several sleeping cranes, perched on one leg; he shows them to his master, but it is only necessary for the latter to give a shout for the cranes to extend their other leg (1969: 62).

"Come diavol non hanno che una coscia e une gamba? non vid'io mai più gru questa?. . ." Chichibio quasi sbigottito, non sapiendo egli stesso donde si venisse, rispose: "Messer sì, ma voi non gridaste *ho ho* a quella di iersera; ché se così gridato aveste, ella avrebbe così l'altra coscia e l'altro piè fuor mandata, como hanno fatto queste" (Boccaccio 1960: 146).

"What a devil?" cried Currado in a rage. "They have but one thigh and one leg? Have I never seen a crane before?" . . . Chichibio, all confounded and knowing not whether he stood on his head or his heels, answered, "Ay, sir; but you did not cry. 'Ho! Ho!' to yesternight's crane; had you cried thus, it would have put out the other thigh and the other leg, even as did those yonder" (Boccaccio 1947: 405).

Todorov gives this story as an example of a semantic variation in a syntactic model recurrent throughout the *Decameron*. The syntactic model is: "to modify the situation," or more precisely, "to perform an action, the goal of which is to modify the situation"; as for the semantic variation here, it consists in substituting for the modifying sequence proper a story which is a pun, or a paradox. Now this substitution represents in itself a procedure on which the storytellers are already in agreement (the sixth day is consecrated to the success of these *bons mots* which constitute its *topos*). The modification, then, is perceived in the specific context of these *bons mots*, as is made clear by Boccaccio's text: "Neifile being silent and the ladies, having taken much pleasure in Chichibio's reply . . ." (Boccaccio 1947: 406) and his previous comment "quasi sbigottito, non sapiendo egli stesso . . . si venisse" ["all confounded and knowing not whether he stood on his head or his heels"], which shows Chichibio feigning to be as subjugated by the process of his own mind as by the anatomy of the cranes. As the editor Vittore Branca remarks, "sapiendo egli stesso . . . si venisse" is actually a condensation for "sapiendo egli stesso da che parte (del cervello, della mente) gli venisse quella risposta" (1960: 146, note 8). The emphasis has therefore been moved from the syntactic meaning to the semantic referent. This is a shift familiar to writers of the Middle Ages and the Renaissance: the moralizing content that the syntax articulates is discharged through a rhetorical apparatus. Todorov suggests that the story is only interesting in relation to a syntax of action: it crystallizes a static fable (in the Russian formalist sense where "fable" is distinct from "subject") in such a way that, by the paradox of a nonaction (*parole*), the situation is resolved. However, because this shift of emphasis from syntax to semantics implies, as we have seen, that the semantic variation preempts (connotes with a *bon mot*) the syntactic modification, we can say the that *locus* of the overall narrative (syntactic+semantic) transformation is no longer semantic, but *stylistic*. We must then conclude that, even in a story as elementary as this one, the incidence of a play on the form of expression (the rhetorical *topos*) compels us to examine the stylistic function at work in the grammatical structuring of the text.

Let us take another example from Todorov: "On the eighth day is discoursed of the tricks that all day long women play men or men women or men one another" (Boccaccio 1947: 491). The syntactic transformation is simple. It is a matter of an alternative sequence with a reversal of attribute. The action designated as modification of an object $X[XA]$ by an optative verb beginning with an agent $Y[(XA) \text{ opt } Y]$ entails the reversal of an attribute originally attached to the object $[XA \rightarrow X—A]$. It must be understood that this scheme of Todorov is only partial and can be developed in several ways. Thus, it can happen that the indication of a specific attribute (B) being conferred upon the agent will emphasize the inevitable character of the modification: in YB, B can be *angry*, *unhappy*, and so on, and take a personal interest in carrying out an act previously considered innocuous — or it frequently arises that the desire (optative) of this modification is made explicit by a redundant proposition which characterizes it: see, for instance, the case (XA) opt $Y + Ya$, where a represents a particular action (*to remonstrate*, *to humiliate*, and so on), through which the subject consciously carries out a whole program designed in advance. Partial as it is, however, this exposition of Todorov's narratological system will suffice. Let us now examine its possible applications in detail by studying in this eighth day the specific tale selected by Todorov in which one Gulfardo

receives a loan from Gasparruolo. The wife of his lender has agreed to sleep with him upon the receipt of a sum equal to Gasparruolo's loan. He promises to keep the arrangement secret. But, in the presence of the couple, he pretends that he reimbursed the wife; she must admit that it is the truth (Todorov 1969: 61).

According to the model proposed by Todorov, the exchange (reversal of attribute) is accomplished by change of vision: to the sexual dissatisfaction corresponds a cancellation of the debt by a retransfer of money. As above, in the story of the lady of Gascony, the tale represents an imbalance introduced in the existing equilibrium by an individual desire. But, there again, a *topos* conceals from the critic the dynamism of the stylistic function. Throughout his narrative, Boccaccio is not secretive of the fact that it is not so much love or the sexual act (which are the *motifs obligés* of the *Decameron*) which interest him as it is avarice and money. One reads in the first lines of the tale:

Fue adunque già in Melano un tedesco al soldo, il cui nome fu Gulfardo, pro della persona e assai leale a coloro ne' cui servigi si mettea, il che rade volte suole de' tedeschi avvenire: et per ciò che egli era nelle prestanze de' denari che fatte gli erano lealissimo renditore, assai mercatanti avrebbe trovati che per piccolo utile ogni quantità di denari gli avrebber prestata (Boccaccio 1960: 303).

There was, then, aforetime at Milan a German, Gulfardo, in the pay of the state, a stout fellow of his person and very loyal to those in whose service he engaged himself, which is seldom the case with Germans; and for that he was a very punctual repayer of such loans as were made to him, he might always find many merchants ready to lend him any quantity of money at little usance (Boccaccio 1947: 492-493).

In the beginning we have the good faith and reputation that merit Gulfardo his good credit. At the end we have a Gulfardo who has recovered the money "by enjoying his sordid mistress without cost" (1947: 494). In contrast, Ambruoggia, the corrupt spouse, appears the villain, the evil woman, whose extravagance (two hundred gold florins must serve to guarantee Gulfardo's noble sentiments) merits punishment and who is indeed punished in the end. Gulfardo's desire, which becomes the vehicle of morality, is used by Boccaccio in order to punish Ambruoggia by taking her lightly; she is forced to return the money that was paid to her for her pleasures. The transfer of modification then consists in making Ambruoggia's punishment contingent upon the satisfaction of Gulfardo's desires. There lies, from a semic point of view, the true sleight of hand that Boccaccio performs. The deserving Gulfardo obtains her favors for nothing, and the wife finds herself obliged to pay for what she believes to have sold. In fact, the whole narrative rests on an exchange: " 'Gulfardo, io son contento: andatevi pur con Dio, che io acconcerò bene la vostra ragione' " (1960:306) [" 'Gulfardo, I am satisfied; get you gone and God go with you; I will settle your account aright']. "Gulfardo gone, the lady, finding herself cozened, gave her husband the dishonourable price of her baseness; . . ." (1947:494). Sexual satisfaction paradoxically brings with it the guarantee of a topical morality (for instance, avarice is always punished: *set a thief to catch a thief*) that it mediates and restores by using a subterfuge. The interpretation, suggested by Todorov, is not satisfying, because it does not take into consideration the stylistic relation of the fable: development of the *topos* of chastised avarice to its motifs (amorous adventure). And the grammatical model, the scheme of which was outlined above, and which Todorov details as follows, appears incomplete:

$$X - A + (XA)_{\text{opt }Y} + (YB \Rightarrow XA)_{\text{cond}} + Ya' \Rightarrow X(YB) \Rightarrow XA + Ya'' \Rightarrow$$
$$Y - B$$

where X = Ambruoggia
         Y = Gulfardo
         A = to have sexual intercourse
         B = generous, paying
         a' = to mask   [cond: optional relation = redundancy]
         a'' = to unmask

(Todorov 1969: 62).

The attributive reversal, modified by a subordinate sequence a'/a'' (mask/unmask) through which Gulfardo attains his ends $(X - A \rightarrow XA)$. loses all its importance if one does not take into consideration the context of the particular *semiostylistic* investment. It is this investment alone which can account for the play in the exchange of semantic values $(YB \Rightarrow Y - B/X - A \Rightarrow XA)$, by connoting the *faire (performance: ⇒)* *syntaxique* with a double, yet false, hyperbole. That Gulfardo found a way to be reimbursed for a (sexual) act for which he did not pay is something extravagant, yet in keeping with his honesty; that Ambruoggia finally had to accord her favors for nothing is also an extravagance, but in keeping with her avarice. But the two actions are also coded in the same rhetorical context where a clear equivalence is established between debt of money and debt of love on the same account ("ragione"), so to speak. It is this amphibology (hyperbole in the strict microcontext of the two actions in question, but nonhyperbole in the macrocontext of a traditional *topos*) which reveals unexpectedly, albeit pointedly, the grammatical structure of the exchange. The essentially syntagmatic perception $[XA + Ya' \Rightarrow Y - B]$ of a narrative transformation, then, is not sufficient to explain the metaphorical integration of the actants. To do that we need a scheme like the one I am suggesting here, where the symbol $\bigcirc$ would represent the only possible (*stylistic*) place for a (syntactic and semantic) structuring of the discourse in the narrative.

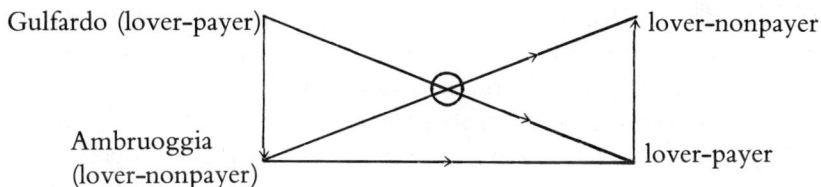

Let us summarize the argument. For semioticians such as Greimas and Todorov, all stylistics is accessory. However, we can now say that, at an initial, purely lexematic level, which is not that of the narrative function, it aids, by the inventory of lexemes into sememes and semes, in determining a fundamental semantic *isotopy*:

... permanency of a hierarchically organized classematic [classeme: group of sememes] base which permits, thanks to the opening of the paradigms into classematic categories, varieties of units of manifestation—variations which, instead of destroying the isotopy, on the contrary, only serve to confirm it (Greimas 1966: 96).

Only if the isotopy is defined by taking into account stylistic criteria can the problems raised by the idiosyncrasies in the decoding be solved. At a second narrative level, once the actantial model is established, a stylistics helps to specify the different investments (metonymy/metaphor) in each of the classes and subclasses of this model and authenticates the model by facilitating the elaboration of a *grammar* (syntax and semantics) of the type Todorov seeks to establish.

The examination of Greimas' and Todorov's method, then, has shown us that a semiological level of analysis could be attained through a reading of the stylistic context. However, this is not to say that, in order to make a semantic analysis complete, it suffices to add to the construction of an abstract model an inventory of the stylistic figures, tropes and different *topoi*. Stylistics and semiotics do not function independently, in sequence or by a redundancy of process; they are inseparable, and require integration into a new program which remains to be defined, the basis of which I am attempting to establish here.

Before proceeding, however, I would like to consolidate my position by showing that a reversal of perspective in no way changes the problem. As a reversal of a semiotics without stylistics (Brémond, Greimas and Todorov), we will now see that a *stylistics without semiotics*, of the sort a dedicated stylistician like Riffaterre suggests, seems just as incomplete.

Let us first note that his method presents obvious practical difficulties as soon as it is applied to the analysis of entire works, because the specifications prescribed by Riffaterre for model of the *arch-* or *super-reader* (1971: 46 ff) seem to retain their relevance only within the framework of a limited corpus. Beside the fact that the interpretation of a stylistic feature may sometimes be problematic, it is also striking to see the stylistic method he defends often leading to nothing other than a rhetorical and compositional structuring of the text under examination. This is the case, for example, with the *Anti-mémoires* of Malraux, on which Riffaterre focuses in his *Essais* (1971: 286-306).[8] The search for a semiological perspective and the preparation of a hermeneutics have little room in a study limited to affirming the presence, at the level of expression-form, but not content-form, of a system of analogical references structured by the use of the verb *filtrer* [to filter]. Now this type of *explication* should immediately invite the criticism of a Greimas, by instituting, after the fact, a vague semantic isotopy that the text seems to verify without actually having structured it. Riffaterre justifies his interpretation by referring himself, albeit questionably, to a thematics of Malraux:

We must suppose that in the *Antimemoirs* we have a variant, perhaps unconscious, of the 1927 image. In *Royaume-Farfelu* the song of the damned is undoubtedly a kind of metaphysical Internationale; it proclaims the rising of the world's oppressed. The recurrence of this structure in the Nuremberg reminiscences changes their meaning: the contrast now signifies the great historical constant of man's humiliation and of man's hope in its despite. This is Malraux's other basic obsession. This has filtered the mimesis of the Nuremberg decor (Riffaterre 1968: 35).

Let us check the detail. The above text refers to the conclusion of the passage of the *Anti-mémoires* in which Malraux superimposes on the memory of Hitler's chamber in Nuremberg in 1945 that of the Pyramid of Cheops. In studying the passage, Riffaterre shows that this room has become the meaningful double of the pharaoh's tomb, and that this double can in effect be detailed in the text, imposing on the reader, through intertwined descriptions, a double reading of the Nuremberg passage as both pictur-esque and symbolic. I am in agreement with this study, insofar as it purports to render explicit a self-referential structure already implicit in the book:

> This is the constant phenomenon that makes *Antimemoirs* as different from memoirs as a poem is different from the most brilliant narrative. Where memoirs would explain and describe the author through the settings in which he appears, through his voice, his actions, antimemoirs refashion memories to the shape of his mental contours, and deflect the meanings of words in accordance with his inner rules. He does not write about a reality remembered; it is rather that reality, filtered by his mind, becomes the symbol of that mind (1968: 35).

But it appears incomplete to me insofar as it reveals but little about the *sémanticité* Greimas was discussing. In the *Anti-mémoires*, for instance, the theme of the voyage is of paramount importance; it is related to a fundamental *bi-isotopy* (distancing in space/proximity in time/journey to an end–journey without an end). And Riffaterre says nothing about this.

It could indeed be shown without difficulty that in the *Anti-mémoires*, the journey and its attributive forms (ascent, descent, and so on) is exactly what permits a relationship to be established between what appears to be ephemeral (the journey measures a distance made of loss and ruin) and what is imposed as eternal (once completed, the journey causes us to discover that this loss is the only thing left to enjoy). In its chronic and achronic polarity, this (bi-)isotopy of the journey then constitutes quite clearly, to go back to Greimas' terms, the formalized scheme of a plurivalent discourse. And it is inasmuch as it can be perceived in relation to this isotopy that the stylistic structure of the filtering (*filtrage*) pointed out by Riffaterre takes all of its value: it ensures the communicability of the narrator's experience; it displays the text's semiotic structure.

Returning now to the passage examined by Riffaterre, let us notice the importance of the seme of the exploratory movement (sememes: *ascent/ descent/flight/navigation*). Riffaterre says only:

> Hitler's lair and Cheops' cenotaph are both reached by way of a narrow initiatory descent into the depths, that both are so locked up inside their architecture that the closure takes on a maleficent symbolism, that both are haunted by baleful shadows (1968: 35).

But what appears, in light of our isotopy, is less a significant double, which, again, is but poorly defined, than the continuity of a semic axis. Malraux sees himself advance (ascend: pyramid; descend: Hitler's chamber), in both expeditions, toward a funeral naos, and through time in the company of many others whose experiences he has read about or shared, he familiarizes himself with the mystery of this advance. Death is at the same time the place of the ephemeral (negative) and of the eternal (positive). In both cases, this revelation appears slowly and painfully at the end of one single journey whose semiotic function is neglected by the critic impatient or himself deceived by the writer: "It matters not that there may be a real architectural filiation between the two actual buildings" (1968: 35):

Mais le chemin qui conduit au tombeau du Pharaon n'a rien de commun avec celui que jalonnaient les piliers géométriques de Nuremberg (Malraux 1967: 54).	But the path which leads to the pharoah's tomb has nothing in common with the path marked out by the geometrical pillars of Nuremberg (Malraux 1969: 33-34).

In truth, the approach to the pharoah's tomb is made through the "complex labyrinth uncovered by the tomb-robbers" (1968: 34), and that to Hitler's chamber, through a "shattered Nuremberg, where our tanks could not even find the central squares" (1968: 35). Further ahead, what the explorers are greeted by is, in one case, the skeletons of the robbers, and in the other, those of the Museum of Natural History, "blown over a balcony by shrapnel" (1968: 35).[9] To allege a connotation in order to establish a *double* between the two episodes *at the level of the signified*, resolves nothing because it is only *in the interrelation of the signifying forms* that one can find the traces of an *ungraspable* content which Riffaterre, understandably then, sees no reason to define. *It is because they lead, properly speaking, to nothing, that this ascent and descent are significant.* The treasures of the pyramids have been stolen, the bodies of the pharaohs have disappeared:

Le sacrophage a été détruit ou dérobé jadis; son absence, proclamée par la cuve ruinée, s'accorde mieux à ces murs incorruptibles que ne ferait sa présence. On pense au conte de l'Inde dans lequel un prince fait construire pendant tant d'années, après la mort de la femme qu'il aimait, le plus beau tombeau du monde. Le monument achevé on apporte le cercueil, qui détruit l'harmonie de la chambre funéraire. "Enlevez cela . . ." dit le prince (Malraux 1967: 56).	The sarcophagus was destroyed or stolen long ago; its absence proclaimed by the ruined casing is more in accord with these incorruptible walls than its presence would be. One is reminded of the Indian tale about the prince who, after the death of his beloved wife, labors for years to build the most beautiful tomb in the world. The monument completed, the coffin is brought in, but it destroys the harmony of the burial chamber. "Take it away," says the prince (Malraux 1968: 35).

So is missing, in the imitation of Hercules' body on the pyre and the bodies of the Jews in the camps, the very body of Hitler: "as the patient pyre awaited Hercules"/"roar of a baker's oven"/"we had opened up extermination camps" (Malraux 1968: 36). The essential truth, a composite of presence (eternal/positive) and absence (ephemeral/negative), which is something other than the mere opposition of life and death, can only be revealed *en route*.

It is the same route Arnauld and Malraux follow in the sands of Mareb, Mayrena and Clappique, in the Moi high country, Mao, in his Long March, and Gandhi, in his famine.

Elsewhere in the *Anti-mémoires*, Malraux, who describes his journey following the tracks of the nineteenth-century French explorer Arnauld, reminisces:

L'arbre à myrrhe, devant le musée, se mêle au palmier en zinc qui était lors du départ de notre avion le seul arbre de Djibouti—c'est une ville, maintenant . . .— avec ses troupeaux de chèvres et ses bergers noirs sur la blancheur des salines, un dernier reflet de soleil sur le fer de leurs lances. Voici le Négus dans le guébi royal. Il est assis sur un canapé des Galeries Lafayette, devant ses dignitaires en toge. Pendant que l'interprète appelle Corniglion-Molinier: M. de La Molinière, parce que le Négus au sourire triste a reçu l'avant-veille quelques junkers, entre par les fenêtres le rugissement des lions de Juda. Leurs cages bordent depuis des siècles la grande allée du palais des Négus, qui tiennent les reines de Saba pour leurs ancêtres légendaires (Malraux 1967: 104-105).

The myrrh tree in front of the museum merges into the zinc palm tree, which, when our plane took off from there, was the only tree in Djibouti (now it's a town) with its flocks of goats and its black shepherds in the whiteness of the salt pans, a last glint of sunlight on the heads of their spears. Here is the Negus in the royal guébi. He is seated on a Galeries Lafayette sofa in front of his toga-clad dignitaries. While the interpreter calls Corniglion-Molinier "Monsieur de la Molinière" because the Negus with the sad smile had received some Junkers two days earlier, the roar of the lions of Judah can be heard through the windows. For centuries, their cages have lined the great avenue of the palace of the emperors of Ethiopia, who number the queens of Sheba among their legendary ancestors (Malraux 1968: 68-69).

Contrasts of idiolectal content, in the obvious opposition of the clichés (for instance "the roar of the lions of Judah" *vs* Junker aircraft), manage to free an actantial energy of a dialectic structure of the ephemeral and the eternal, as the only reality which transcends nothingness, and which the *flowerless terraces* of Arnauld's lost town of Sheba symbolize quite well:

. . . car il est sûrement de ces aventuriers sans tombe, fascinés par la seule passion du hasard et retournés au hasard — il

— for he is surely one of those adventurers without a grave, passionately caught up in the fascination of the chance, and

joue, comme jouent les morts qui tout le long de leur vie furent courageux et frivoles, avec ses terrasses sans fleurs, ses observatoires en poussière, ses entrepôts de parfums et ses ruines qui semblent frémir de solitude sous la tache silencieuse des oiseaux; pour que nous tenions tous deux en nos mains d'ombre un des derniers mystères, qui nous sera fraternel dans l'ennui sans fin de la mort (Malraux 1967: 104).

returned to the realm of chance — he may play, as those dead men play who were brave and frivolous throughout their lives, among its flowerless terraces, its crumbling observatories, its perfume stores, and its ruins that seem to quiver with solitude under the silent blur of birds; so that together we may hold in our ghostly hands one of the last mysteries, which will be a boon to us in the endless boredom of death (Malraux 1968: 68).

We have here perfect examples of a stylistic variation that the stylistician immediately places at the lexematic level of semantic substance (clichés), but whose function is rather to underscore a semiotic structure at the level of form. We only perceive the eternal in its relation to the ephemeral, and all signification is for us only a *double*, a *difference* of signification, symbolized by the difference and the opposition of the stylized actants. Admitting that each of these texts is emblematic of the book, one could extend this model to the entire *Anti-mémoires*. The stylistic structures are at the same time structures of the opposition and transformation of the actants. Malraux's book is a narrative of journey to places where the ephemeral is transformed into the eternal. It is, therefore, a *ritual*, a game where contents solidified and stylized by a culture (see the oppositions of clichés above) become movable, displaced again like the famous ruins of the imagination "that seem to quiver with solitude under the silent blur of birds."

In a conclusion, which now becomes a *postface*, let us now retrace the plan of our study, and restate the conditions of our reading.

Let us remember that we are attempting to isolate a stylistic feature in a text, whose overall semiotic system is self-regulating and predictive and where the stylistic features are encoded and decodable from the marks or perceivable *stimuli* in it. A system of contrast-references helps decode these features through two kinds of contexts (microcontext and macrocontext). The microcontext is limited to the immediate constituents of the passage under consideration. The macrocontext, which can be defined as the *semantic field in which the perception of a stylistic feature remains constant*, is determined, for parts of texts, by deriving additional meaning from references to the complete text, and for longer passages or entire works, by isolating the ongoing feature which increases their coherence by making the display of that coherence an integral part of their semiotic system.[10]

An analysis of this nature, which adopts several criteria proposed by Riffaterre (1971: 105 ff), is in fact, a *composition* of the text: it permits one to retrace the path which leads to a semic and actantial structure of the narrative. However, the next operation should be less the exploration of *latent* content, the *transcoding* of the structuralists, than the interpretation, the *semantization*, so to speak, of a purely formulaic process. In other words, it is not a matter, at this stage, of considering our stylistic analysis as a way *to normalize* literary discourse, to prepare it, as Greimas and Todorov do, for an abstract linguistic structuring. Nor is it a matter of claiming that a simple *thematization* of the lexematic contents (isolated by the stylistic analysis of a Riffaterre) can rationally account for this analysis. Thus, in the text above, the affirmation of the survival of Arnauld and Sheba no longer corresponds to anything when one arrives at the *flowerless terraces* of Sheba, or when one realizes that Arnauld is only alive in the strictures of Malraux's mental landscape. But, to the extent that a stylistic feature increases the perceptibility of a text, one must be prepared to admit that it is this valorization which suggests a possible seme. And indeed we saw that the interesting point in the *Anti-mémoires* is less the reconstitution of an analogical structure in the construction of the memory; less the release of a theme outside the construction than it is the figure of the path, itself a semic axis, the course of which is marked off by stylistic elaboration. By an equivalence between expression-form and content-form, this marking off (stylistic events, motifs, clichés and so on) takes on, in the end, a ritual value (emphasis, signification) in its recurrence and automatism. A structural tie is established between the diachrony of the path and the achrony of the motifs. Indefinitely recurring in the course of a constantly changing path, the motifs themselves are eternal. Less "decorative" than functional, they are an integral part of the semiotic system. Even when they lack or deny a concrete reference (the *flowerless terraces* of Sheba), they retain their significance as motifs. In Boccaccio, it is by a game of form that Neifile keeps the listeners under the spell of her discourse. With Bernanos, it is the process of writing (of editing) the *Journal* which releases, one by one into the text, the secrets which systematically consume the country priest. And in *Mateo Falcone*, it is the recurrence of stylized anthropological features which allows us to verify, through the witnessing of a ritual in the text, the transformation of the functions in the narrative and the advent of the sacrifice. In each case, the mystery lies in a possible, but not yet elucidated, relationship between a level of perceived expression and a level of latent content. To this relationship of variable coherence, which constitutes the veritable operational structure of the literary text, and whose study remains to be done, I give the name of *semiostyle*. Throughout it, the Hjelmslevian semiotic functions of form and content are finally integrated, and reading a text may truly lead to the lost discourse, the *mythos* which literature pursues with itself, and whose study it is now proper to restore to literary criticism.

NOTES

1. Unless otherwise noted, all translations hereafter are mine.
2. In Chapter 6 a more complete account of Brémond's latest theories is given. Here I shall be limiting myself to a purely metasemiotic perspective, without going into the detail of alternate stylistic selections.
3. This short, albeit crucial, sentence was edited out of the Morris translation.
4. The ⇒ sign denotes an implication.
5. In his analysis of Maupassant (Greimas 1976), which appeared too late for me to do it justice, Greimas seems to have tackled the problem of style and description by studying more precisely the mechanisms which seem to index a shifting in the purely narrative, that is, nondescriptive, text. These mechanisms, which are all part of a new concept of *strategy* congruent with the current development of studies on *pragmatics*, on the one hand, and on the other hand, with the growth of a *linguistics of the speaking subject* (*linquistique de l'énonciation*), are categorized according to their *shifting value*. Thus we have *débrayeurs* and *embrayeurs* (*outshifters* and *inshifters*), whose function it is to facilitate the insertion of the descriptive sequence into one of the areas of competence of the subject (*to know, to be able, to want to*). Several problems, however, remain. (1) A concept of *strategy* does nothing to semanticize a word, a sentence or a group of sentences. It only accounts for its syntactic necessity. We are brought back to the *a posteriori* schema exposed above. (2) A meticulous account of *embrayages* and *débrayages* does not account for the effect produced on the narratee, nor does it explain the real consequences of a fragmentation or infinitization of narrative sequences (annulment of differences, mirror effect, and so on). On some of these problems, see parts 2 and 3.
6. For a critique of Todorov by Brémond himself, see Chapter 6.
7. *Monovalent*: for example, all adjectives, although semantically distinct, have an *identical* syntactic (attributive) function. *Plurivalent*: for example, to verbs whose (syntactic) meaning is: *to perform an action leading to an overall modification of the current situation* corresponds a semantic variation of the type: *to tell a story which modifies the situation*; to verbs whose (syntactic) meaning is: *to express a desire* correspond two variations in the semantic reference, the obligative or the optative, and so on.
8. Although Riffaterre's article is readily available in his *Essais* (1971), I shall be quoting here from the original version in English, which appeared in *Columbia University Forum* (Riffaterre 1968).
9. This is in effect a dramatization of past events, which Riffaterre finds strange, because he did not perceive its structure: the skeletons blown over the balcony are reminiscent of the skeletons of the tomb robbers.
10. For a discussion of the theoretical context of this display, see parts 2 and 3.

5

Narrative and Descriptive Signs in Poetry

Most studies in poetic semiotics avoid referring to a poetic narrative for fear of indulging in extratextual considerations.[1] However, such a negative approach, if it has at least the advantage of avoiding the pitfalls of psychologism and literary aesthetics by suggesting a model of description based either on the isomorphism of expression and content, or on the simple homology of content alone, *always neglects two essential aspects of the poetics — of the making — of the text: (1) the relevance of linguistic oppositions and their stylistic function in the integration of a cursory reading; and (2) the semiological aspect of style and the properly mythical and ritual value of the content exposed.*

I began to examine this dual problem in Chapter 4. Concerning the myth, however, let us be reminded that a myth is a conscious form of artistic, literary or folklore expression, by which a society attempts to resolve forgotten and, most often, repressed conflicts. Thus, it is not only a way to record history through legend, it is also a way to project a vision of the world onto a behavioral pattern (see Lévi-Strauss 1966: 1-33). As for rite and modes of ritual, it is essentially this behavioral pattern or this action, whose ramifications are extraempirical (*magical*) and which, self-referential and necessary, is forever protected from change and the future by the exercise and repetition of the same. Whatever Lévi-Strauss may have said elsewhere, a poem written on a page, collected in a definitive version of the critical edition destined to a public of chosen readers, is quite different from an oral myth whose every version is far from being known, and whose reading is never possible outside the ritual behavior that illustrates it (Jakobson and Lévi-Strauss 1962).[2] Yet, the thought of reading a poem as a myth and at the same time as the expression of a behavioral pattern seems an interesting one. The literary critic turned anthropologist would have then only to follow the thread of a dual text, which, in its elaboration, its production, would suggest its own reference and display its own logic. On the one hand, this text considered only in the perspective of its production, would be closed upon itself, but on the other hand, presented and articulated in the mode of a narrative (Rimbaud, Eliot, Pound, or Dylan Thomas), even though the narrator might have wished to remain hidden, the same text would remain open and solicit the reader, so long as he was willing to associate himself with the process of the text without reducing its meaning to the predeterminations of a narrative signatum. His reading would revive the tensions of the text being written and would thus become itself some sort of initiation: a rite. There would remain three problems, however. The first would be to define this individual product of the text, depending on the mobility of the signifier and representing a new, albeit fundamentally antilinguistic pattern (in the sense that the system of Saussurean *langue* is a product of the *masse parlante* escaping individual control and the poem is essentially self-referential and unique).[3] The second would be to justify the notion of narrative in a context no longer prosaic but poetic. It would be a question of finding out whether a poetic text relates anything, and whether poetic function and narrative function can be integrated. The third, then, would be to define what is meant by *rite of writing and of reading*.

Now because it is with a poet like Rimbaud that the temporal and referential illusion is the most tenacious (one wears oneself out, with the dates, letters, and testimonies, reconstituting a Rimbaud-*poète-d'état-civil*), and because Rimbaud is perhaps first a great storyteller (for example "Le Bateau ivre", "Une Saison en enfer", "Après le Déluge", "Conte"), it is with him that we will examine these problems, beginning with the problem of narrative.

POETIC FUNCTION/NARRATIVE FUNCTION

If we truly believe, as does Jakobson, that it is not possible to restrict the operation of the poetic function, whose definition is semiotic and metasemiotic (overdetermination of code and motivation of message) to the phonological area (the poetic text – with its rhythms, its rhymes, and so on), it remains no less true that the poetic function is always fundamentally distinct from the narrative function, and that the boundary between verse and prose often being less than clear, we must eventually resort to other marking devices. As Jakobson himself points outs:

Old Indic and Medieval Latin literary theory keenly distinguished two poles of verbal art, labeled in Sanskrit Pāñcālī and Vaidabh and correspondingly in

Latin *ornatus difficilis* and *ornatus facilis*, the latter style evidently being much more difficult to analyze linguistically in such literary forms verbal devices are unostentatious and language seems a nearly transparent garment . . . "Verseless composition", as Hopkins calls the prosaic variety of verbal art – where parallelisms are not so strictly marked and strictly regular as "continuous parallelism" and where there is no dominant figure of sound – present more entangled problems for poetics, as does any transitional linguistic area. In this case, the transition is between strictly poetic and strictly referential language (Jakobson 1960: 374).

Here, however, Jakobson, who goes on to point out that the work of Propp or Lévi-Strauss is useful for establishing a classification of traditional actions and in tracing the confusing laws that underlie their composition and selection, is simply evading the issue. He abandons his original argument about the poetic function to invite us to follow the semiologists of narrative, as if the study of the former (the poetic function) inevitably should lead to the study of the latter (the narrative function).

In fact, the current poetic semiology, based on the work of the Prague School, then of the Generative School (Levin/Ruwet), is overwhelmed by the problem of the relevance of narrative transformations to the poetic text, as much at the level of chronology (the referential illusion, that it has superbly and perhaps a little too quickly discarded) as at the level of a logic of possibilities and performances (in the pragmatics of Brémond, for instance, or in the symbolic logic elaborated by Kristeva). And the reason seems to be *an initial confusion between poetic function of the message, which, by constituting the text-object as its own end, excludes any consideration of narrative relevance to the poetic quality of the text itself. It is this poetic quality or "poeticity" which informs through the writing a new and ambiguous concept of narrative, producing this narrative as a myth and at the same time setting the stage for its production.* While the poetic function defines the difference between poetic language and nonpoetic language in the context of linguistic communication (axis of continuity-axis of simultaneity/monovalent and conventionalized signifier/signified correspondence), the *"poeticity" of writing* suggests, at the level of writing (strictly speaking, the act of writing), the possibility of an opening, spanning, of the signification process, no longer as a monovalent one-to-one (one signifier to one signified) correspondence, but as an exchange between signifiers, to which Kristeva (1969) gives the name *signifiance*. This new exchange, insofar as it is designed to elude the restrictions of a predetermined signified, is characteristic of any poetic text, as a text committed to founding its own language, its own codes. In the first case (the poetic function), it is not clear what a theory of narrative can bring to the study of poetic texts; in the second case (*poeticity*), if a theory of narrative seems excluded at first from poetic semiotics by the very constraints of narrative monovalence, it appears, later, to be essential to a study of the exchange between signifiers *before* they are arranged to match a narrative signatum.

One will better understand the reason for all these contraditions by looking at a specific text. Let us take "Aube" from *Illuminations*. It is clear that we have here a statement implying the representation of a specific time-sequence, a *narrative*, as the perfect of the first sentence signifies the present result of a past action. Because the whole sequence includes a narrative resolution ("L'aube et l'enfant tombèrent"), certified as narrative *signified* by the use of the *passé simple*, it usually triggers in the critic a delirium of symbolist inquiries (Was it a dream? A hallucination?). I will try to avoid this delirium, however, by investigating what, in the narrative statement, belongs to *narration* proper and what belongs to *description*:

J'ai embrassé l'aube d'été.

Rien ne bougeait encore au front des palais. L'eau était morte. Les camps d'ombres ne quittaient pas la route du bois. J'ai marché, réveillant les haleines vives et tièdes, et les pierreries regardèrent, et les ailes se levèrent sans bruit.

La première entreprise fut, dans le sentier déjà empli de frais et blêmes éclats, une fleur qui me dit son nom.

Je ris au wasserfall blond qui s'échevela à travers les sapins: à la cime argentée je reconnus la déesse.

Alors je levai un à un les voiles. Dans l'allée, en agitant les bras. Par la plaine, où je l'ai dénoncée au coq. A la grand'ville elle fuyait parmi les clochers et les dômes, et courant comme un mendiant sur les quais de marbre, je la chassais.

En haut de la route, près d'un bois de lauriers, je l'ai entourée avec ses voiles amassés, et j'ai senti un peu son immense corps. L'aube et l'enfant tombèrent au bas du bois.

Au réveil il était midi.
        (Rimbaud 1960: 284, "Aube")

I have embraced the summer dawn.

Nothing yet moved at the head of the palaces. The water was dead. The shadows were reluctant to leave the road in the forest. I walked, waking quick warm breaths; and the gems stared at me, and the wings took their flight without a sound.

My first adventure in the path already filled with fresh pale glimmers was a flower who gave me her name.

I laughed at the blond wasserfal unfurling amidst the pines: on the silver summit I recognized the goddess.

Then one by one I lifted her veils. In the lane waving my arms. Across the plain, where I reported her to the cock. To the big town she was fleeing among the steeples and the domes; and I, running like a beggar on the quays of marble, I was chasing her.

At the top of the road, near a laurel wood, I wrapped her 'round with her gathered veils and I did feel a bit of her vast body. Dawn and the child fell down the bottom of the wood.

As I awoke, it was noon.
        (Rimbaud 1960: 284, "Aube")

We quickly discover that the narration proper is constituted only by the series of simple pasts: "et les pierreries regardèrent, et les ailes se levèrent . . . enteprise fut . . . Je ris au wasserfall blond . . . Je reconnus la déesse. Alors je levai un à un les voiles . . . L'aube et l'enfant tombèrent", contrasting with a descriptive series of aspectual imperfects: "Rien ne bougeait . . . L'eau était morte . . . il était midi", or imperfects of intensity: "A la grand'ville elle fuyait . . . je la chassais". All this leads to a series of constative declarations: "J'ai embrassé l'aube . . . je l'ai dénoncée", which picks up two separate series: "En haut de la route, près d'un bois de lauriers, je l'ai entourée . . . tombèrent au bas du bois." Rimbaud's *histoire* then seems only to be the report of this hunt and capture.

Here, an actantial analysis could illuminate, through the dialectics of a subject–object and an isotopy *death/birth*, the extraordinarily intense character of the poem (*death and birth/flight and capture/dawn and noon*).[4] It would, moreover, lead us to postulate a functional evolution — each stanza representing one episode of the action which in general retains all the characteristics of a microepic, due not only to a strict syntagmatic process, but also to a representation both referential (physical geography: mountains/city) and allegorical (Biblical or Iliadic sources?).

This strictly narrative analysis would, however, fail to integrate several elements essential to the poetic function. First, even if it managed to take into account the transformation of meaning, that is to say, in the case of an actantial model, the general effect of the passage from *death* to *life*, *childhood* to *adulthood*, from *dawn* to *day*, it would still leave out that which, for the poet and reader, constitutes a continuous process of metonymic and metaphorical investments, all the more precious that they are often only disguised or nascent:

Metonymy:	"les ailes se levèrent sans bruit . . . sentier déjà empli de frais et blêmes éclats"
Metaphor:	front des palais. L'eau était morte . . . les pierreries regardèrent."
Spun metaphor:	"wasserfall blond qui s'échevela."

Now, it is this process of investments which really makes possible the narrative transformation: for the narrator, *to embrace the dawn*, is, at the end of a long march ("je la chassais"), to surround the goddess with her own veils and to feel her body (of which one has only seen the *silver* crown); it is the beginning of calling things by their names ("Alors je levai un à un les voiles"), substituting reality for fantasy (L'aube et l'enfant tombèrent . . . il était midi"). What is evident at the semantic level appears just as quickly at the stylistic and phonological level. The spun metaphor is in fact a metonymy; it is detailed by a change of both rhetorical position (topotrope: *enfant/aube → adulte/jour*) and semiotic position (index: *cime argentée →* referent: *déesse*), and it is furthermore activated by a syntactic chiasma ("Je ris au wasserfall . . . à la cime argentée je reconnus"). In addition, one notices a general diagrammatization of the vowels and consonants, by which the text manages to reflect or mirror its own representation. Whence comes this constant return of auditive signs to visual ones, and vice versa (Jakobson 1971: 344–359). For the consonants, the flow powerfully suggested by liquid group [1] in the fourth verse ("Je ris . . . "): [faḷ], [bḷo], [eʃəvəla], falls cataract by the two lines with splendid ease: [ri o vasɛ:rfal blõ a travɛ:r le sapē a la sim arʒãte]. For the vowels the sequence by anaphora, substitution of variant and/or metathesis, registers the echo of a melodic line to our eyes and ears:

/a/ɛ/	vasɛ:rfal a travɛ:r
/e/ə/	eʃəvəla
/a/ã/e	arʒãte
/a/i/	a la sim
/a/ɛ̄/	sapē
/i/o/	ri o
/e/o/u/	rekonu

Let us finally remark that [dees] admirably represents the cumulative indexation of the image in the group of sibilants (/vasē:rfal/ki se/le sapē/dees/), and its reinforcement by the ultimate redundancy of the vocalic support [ees].

To be sure, this is only a partial analysis; one could have expanded on the constant metonymization of the modes of perception (four senses): tactile/auditory — ("les haleines vives et tièdes/sans bruit") and visual/olfactory — ("frais et blêmes éclats/En haut de la route . . . j'ai senti") — to the extent that it represents a form of *écriture automatique*: see for instance, "un mendiant sur les quais de marbre", where the original oxymoron has become a cliché. But it is already sufficient in that it points out the link between the *process* of a *parole poétique* (expression-form) and its system (content-form) in the general narrative context. Rimbaud's poem represents a metonymic course ("En haut de la route . . . au bas du bois"), by which the author and reader find themselves literally and figuratively transported into another world: it is not dawn, but noon; time flows through the space of the poem, but this noon is also the present which bears witness to the profound transformation of the text and its writer, its *je-écrivant*. The mystery of this "Aube" and of any *aube*, is the mystery of the birth (of *l'aube*) of the text to its author.

PRODUCTION OF THE TEXT

The establishment of a relation between *récit* (narrative function) and poetic function — by reinvesting, or at least, trying to reinvest, semantic models in the syntactic and phonological text – does not explain the *poeticity* of Rimbaud's language. To explain phrases like "au front des palais. L'eau était morte. Les camps d'ombre ne quittaient pas . . . mendiant sur les quais de marbre"/"wasserfall blond" by the use of a deviation, a derivation from the norm indicating a poetic message, puts us, to be sure, on the path of an interpretation that might be figurative, associative, and so on. But, as I have said, it also leads is very quickly onto the path of the poetic cliché. From "au front des palais" it is indeed a simple matter to argue an automatism of the poetic text, based on a decodable series of clichés which one can follow, as soon as one has been able to establish the proper register of the text (Riffaterre 1971: 64-94), or as soon as the microcontext permits a plausible reference: thus, "palais", "eau," "camps," "J'ai marché" suggest a military and majestic context that foretells an important mission: "La première entreprise". Such a reduction to a system of cause and effect which seems rather simplistic is only the result of a structural analysis combining poetic function and narrative function.[5] It is a superficial analysis, because it explains about Rimbaud only the construction of a text–object artificially isolated for a transparent reading, where the critical eye wishes itself impersonal or transcendental; because it prolongs the ambiguity of a poetic communication, whose form continues to be appreciated, paradoxically, as a function of an aesthetic and ornamental tradition of poetry: the cliché (see Chapter 3).

To say that "au front des palais" is a metaphor supposes not only a definition of the metaphor limited to an intuitive or aesthetic grasp of the peom, but also, and mostly, a conception of a metaphorical elaboration based not on the signified message alone, but on its coding by the poetic narrator and its decoding by the reader. As Meschonnic says:

The working hypothesis is no longer the definition by Jakobson of the poetic function . . . but rather the hypothesis of a text as a language system in relation to an unconscious as a system and transformer of ideology — an undefined I-Here-Now. Today, Jakobson's conception appears as a reaction, necessary but dated, to an instrumentalist theory of *language*. In the same way . . . it denies itself the possibility of investigating linguistic value [*valeur*], this value being the measure of the identification in language . . . It is not a question of *appreciating*, but of constructing a theory of value (1973: 214-215).

To understand Rimbaud's original design, one should not have to reduce his texts to a system of *passe-partout* expression, in order then to show that this system is firmly attached to the general system of *langue*. Rather one must approach the text in an entirely different way, introducing, in the study of the relation of the poetic word to the speaking or writing subject, an ideology of this relation.

However, to enter such an investigation implies that we ask, first, whether there is any linguistic rule for distinguishing between the signs of *narration* and those of *description*. Since, for Saussure, any sign is defined by the concept of linguistic difference (*bat/cat*), does this mean that the difference of narration is distinct from the difference of description? Does it mean that we thus might have two kinds of linguistic signs? Now, if we take the case of Rimbaud's poetry, we shall see that it provides an unexpected answer to our questions. For it seems that in Rimbaud the *poetic*, that is, the non-purely-narrative, representation displays a paradoxical specificity, in that *each difference can readily be exchanged for another one* (see Chapter 7). Whence comes the importance of the articles, "l'aube/l'eau" in a text ("Aube") practically organized around the definite article. Dawn is defined in its greatest generality, and according to a system which, all the while striking us with its force, its expressiveness, leaves us with the feeling of weakness, a certain evanescence of the deixis.[6] The semantic references of the text imply less the designation of referent than a return to the original signifier. It could be said, in more precise terms, that Rimbaud uses the weakening of our code of normal perception (it is not the reference, but our *perception of the reference* which seems to be the same) in order to impose on us another system of representation, based on what appears to be a third *articulation* — this one being more semiotic than properly linguistic, to the extent that Rimbaud's *parole* does not wish itself subject to the homologation of an anonymous *masse parlante*.[7] Suzanne Bernard has commented on the *wasserfall blond*:

Wasserfall means *chute d'eau* [waterfall] in German . . . one would have difficulty explaining the presence of such a word in this text, if it had been written in London . . . when Rimbaud was learning English and did not yet know a word of German. Notice in any case that *wasserfall* permits the felicitous adjective *wasserfall blond*, impossible with *chute d'eau* (Bernard in Rimbaud 1960: 509, note 5).

This comment would have us see the poetic phrase "wasserfall blond" only in the transparency of the semantic form *chute d'eau*, while it is in the substance of the word that the secret of the verse resides. There is no doubt that upon hearing the word *wasserfall*, the suggestion of the German term is just as present in our minds; but this suggestion, insofar as it is pure semantic form, is only indexical (moreover repeated in *blond* which evokes locks — *échevela* — of German hair amid German spruces). What is striking is that, at the level of substance, these indexes become icons, and more precisely, *diagrams* (/vasɛ:rfal/). Appearing intralinguistically in the form, the body of language, as it were, we have there another language not yet completely formalized, and whose characteristic is to exist *between* our perceptions, at a level which renders it irreplaceable because it is practically undefinable. From this comes, for the most part, the mystery of Rimbaud's vocabulary, the abundance of rare phrases, of *hapaxes*, such as the famous "vacheries hystériques" (1960: 129, "Le Bateau ivre") or the "mouches qui bombinent" (1960: 110, "Les Voyelles").

Let us rid ourselves of this obsession to explicate: it is through its own elaboration that the text attempts to escape the destiny of its predetermination, its representation. And the revolution of Rimbaud's text is that it permits us a glimpse of the mechanism of this escape and the conditions under which it was originally performed.

THE POETIC MYTH AND ITS RITUAL INVESTMENT

To define poetry as myth is actually to postulate that it implies a violent confrontation with another reality which cannot be understood in the context of a referential discourse. What reality? It is, first of all, a process of delay. Let us take each of the *Illuminations*: the mark of a difficult beginning can always be seen there. The initial sentences are either very long or very short. Most often when quite long, they try to set a narrative in motion by dint of successive descriptions:

De détroit d'indigo aux mers d'Ossian, sur le sable rose et orange qu'a lavé le ciel vineux, viennent de monter et de se croiser des boulevards de cristal habités incontinent par de jeunes familles pauvres qui s'alimentent chez les fruitiers.
(Rimbaud 1960: 290, "Métropolitain")

From the Indigo strait to the seas of Ossian, on the rose and orange sand which the wine-colored sky has washed, crystal boulevards have just risen and crossed, occupied immediately by poor young families who get their food at the fruiterers' shops.
(Rimbaud 1973: 153)

When very short, they are nominal, exclamative or constative: "Pitoyable frère!" ("Vagabonds"); "O *mon* Bien! O *mon* Beau!" ("Matinée d'ivresse"); "Assez vu" ("Départ"). This discrepancy points to the difficulty of constituting the *objet poétique* through an integration of form and content. In the poem "Les Ponts", for instance, external considerations about the weather lead to an ironic display of an inner poverty: "notre jeune misère" "indigents absurdes"; while in the same poem, designs of bridges seem to appoint a world without fixed reference and in perpetual motion:

O cette chaude matinée de février. Le Sud inopportun vint relever nos souvenirs d'indigents absurdes.
(Rimbaud 1960: 272, "Ouvriers").

O that warm morning in February! The unseasonable south wind came to revive our recollections of ridiculous paupers, our youthful misery.
(Rimbaud 1973: 131).

Des ciels gris de cristal. Un bizarre dessin de ponts, ceux-ci droits, ceux-là bombés, d'autres descendant ou obliquant en angles sur les premiers, et ces figures se renouvelant dans les autres circuits du canal, mais tous tellement longs et légers que les rives chargées de dômes, s'abaissent et s'amoindrissent.
(Rimbaud 1960: 273, "Les Ponts")

Crystalline gray skies. A strange pattern of bridges, these straight, those arched, others descending obliquely at angles to the first, and these configurations repeating themselves in the other illuminated circuits of the canal, but all so long and light that the shores, laden with domes, sink and diminish.
(Rimbaud 1973: 133)

These variations make it impossible to think of a precise reference, because it is less the form of the content than its substance which is troubling. How then to explain this imagery which escapes reference? Far from being transparent, it arrests us because it is elusive and obscure. Now if it is true that one's speech is only affective to the extent that he says something different and distinctive, it is also true that the signification of any *parole* is always established in the context of a common culture, a common *langue* and that this signification is also governed by a context of previous signified. The problem, then, for Rimbaud, was to work out a select method of deciding himself the code-context of a representation which would appear completely unique and original, while remaining *interpretable*, if not readily understandable: a new mimesis based on a reconstruction of the sign. A good example of Rimbaud meeting this challenge is a poem like "Les Ponts", the beginning of which I already quoted above:

Des ciels gris de cristal. Un bizarre dessin ponts, ceux-ci droits, ceux-là bombés, d'autres descendant en obliquant en angles sur les premiers; et ces figures se renouvelant dans les autres circuits éclairés du canal, mais tous tellement longs et légers que les rives, chargées de dômes, s'abaissent et s'amoindrissent. Quelques-uns de ces ponts sont encore chargés de masures.

Crystalline gray skies. A strange pattern of bridges, these straight, those arched, others descending obliquely at angles to the first, and these configurations repeating themselves in the other illuminated circuits of the canal, but all so long and light that the shores, laden with domes, sink and diminish. Some of these bridges are still encumbered with hovels. Others support masts, signals,

D'autres soutiennent des mâts, des signaux, de frêles parapets. Des accords mineurs se croisent, et filent; des cordes montent des berges. On distingue une veste rouge, peut-être d'autres costumes et des intruments de musique. Sont-ce des airs populaires, des bouts de concerts seigneuriaux, des restants d'hymnes publics? L'eau est grise et bleue, large comme un bras de mer.

Un rayon blanc, tombant du haut du ciel, anéantit cette comédie.

(Rimbaud 1960: 273)

frail parapets. Minor chords interweave, and flow smoothly; ropes rise from the steep banks. One detects a red jacket, perhaps other costumes and musical instruments. Are these popular tunes, fragments of manorial concerts, remnants of public anthems? The water is gray and blue, ample as an arm of the sea.

A white ray, falling from the summit of the sky, reduces to nothingness this theatrical performance.

(Rimbaud 1973: 133-135)

Phonological level. From "Un bizarre dessin de ponts" to "chargés de masures", the sequence [tu:s], [tɛl,mã], [leʒe], [lɛ(riv)]/[dədo:m]/ [sabɛse . . . samwɛ̃drisə] is heterophonic. Far from communicating a definable impression, such as *légèreté* for example [/tɛl/leʒe/lɛ] — an impression which moreover would immediately be contradicted by the resonance of the [dədo:m . . .] group — it shocks us by its diversity, indeed, its *bizarrerie*. As has often been remarked concerning Rimbaud, musical quality is weak, while semantic connotation is intense.

Syntactic level. One notices the almost total absence of syntax, and the recurrence of gerunds or perfect participles. The general effect of noun formations (no main verb) imposes on the reader a relationship which seems to defy logical interpretation.

Semantic level. By placing his noun formations in a historic context (the phrase: "ces ponts . . . chargés de masures" actually refers to edifices which disappeared from London in the seventeenth century), Rimbaud does not proceed as a writer, searching for nuances in an already culturalized signified. By the bias of a bold *sémémisation* (isolation and representation of a semantic unity in context), he presents a new possibility of code and culture. Let us take the expression: "Des ciels gris de cristal". One notices the opposition of *gris* and *cristal*; *ciel* is concrete, but truly exists in our mind only through the immediate mention of color (*ciel bleu, couvert*, and so on), so that one can say *ciel* is in itself transparent (→*cristal*). Now *gris* is hardly in accord with transparent, and in our culture, *ciel gris* is synonymous with *ciel couvert* [overcast]. The only remaining possiblity, then, is to assimilate the group *ciel gris de cristal* as a catachresis in which *gris*, a nondescript color, applies equally to *ciel* or *cristal* through the use of a code still considered *bizarre*.[8]

Bizarre is the metalinguistic mark of a language conscious of itself. The "bizarre dessin de ponts", unexpectedly announced is soon developed in the lines that follow: "ceux-ci . . . ceux-la" and the anteposition of the adjective can be interpreted not only as emphasizing the modification introduced, but also as a mark of exclamative or phatic value (cf. the phrase: *c'est bizarre!*). "Bizarre" would then be on the same level as "cette comédie," which is openly critical. If this is so, it is permissible to think that Rimbaud plays actor and spectator at the same time, confirming in such a case the presence of a *scene of the text* which he deems external to his writing consciousness, but whose ultimate significance escapes him in part, since he qualifies it as "comédie", with the grace of an anticlerical ridiculing religious rites. *Yet this scene is from him; it is his work.* It is only through ridicule that he can become conscious of it, sublimating, albeit poorly, his desire to communicate what remains inexpressible due to the restriction of the signified message (for another aspect of ridicule and irony in communication, see Chapter 7).

One has often tried to explain this sudden change by taking a rather simplistic psychological approach. Rimbaud is pure, but he is afraid of this purity, and goodhearted truant that he is, he tarnishes it (Richard 1955: 187-250).[9] But let us return to our text, and postulate that the staging there is purposefully artificial. The description of the bridges is poetically motivated: the text attempts to justify the *bizarre* character of all these edifices by resorting to derivations from a recognized semantic and stylistic norm. But although the derivations are supposed to produce special effects, the private language they intimate can only be identified by reference to a code of common usage. It is thus in constant danger of being overlooked, and Rimbaud, exerting his irony, demonstrates its fragility. This entire scene, staged by derivation, *is only a comedy*, destroyed in a twinkling by a shaft of light from the heavens.

Here the cliché *c'est un comédien/quelle comédie* is symptomatically appropriate: it announces to the reader with an emphasis on the phatic function that the language takes turns playing with itself, that it tricks itself. Rimbaud uses elsewhere a process specifically different but functionally identical; for example, at the end of "Ouvriers": "Je vaux que ce bras durci ne traîne plus *une chère image*"; and at the end of "Ville": "la Mort sans pleurs, notre active fille et servante, un Amour désespéré et un joli Crime piaulant dans la boue de la rue." Because externalizing the poetic object can only be done at the price of losing its specificity, perhaps the author has no other choice but to efface himself from the scene of its utterance. *Therein lies the rite of writing destined to safeguard for each reading the irreducibility of the poetic object.* These *bizarreries* are there only as reminders that we must look twice: under the text is hidden the myth of the origin, the function of which cannot yet be discussed, only suggested and disguised by a punning gesture, a humorous and sacred rite.

What is then conveniently called the *myth of Rimbaud* defies generations of those who apply themselves to interpreting, lexicalizing, and giving it reference. But this myth does not exist without the rite of *protection/ destruction*, honored by generations of readers who, in this, have only followed Rimbaud himself as the primary guardian of a text which speaks and describes the world as if it had created it, and which disappears as soon as it attempts to represent its own *installation*. Now it is true that, in this, as in all texts, representation is made possible only by an order of linguistic difference. But the linguistic hypothesis of functional differences recovers a fundamental problem of consciousness which can only be surmounted in the process of a philosophical dialectic. As Kristeva showed, the *parole*, the expostulating of this contradition, the act of speaking (and here of writing) excludes the possibility of intrinsic reality, existing independently within language:

One makes a statement when in a procedure of negativity (of differentiation) one comprehends in the act of signification that which does not exist in the logic and which is the negation (point of departure in signification). It is a major difficulty in the context of the *logos* (logic) to introduce into language that which does not exist in speech, since the latter marks it by the sign *no* (Kristeva 1969: 250).

However, if we want to tighten this hypothesis of a nascent language which is paradoxically never better justified than when it is about to disappear, in which direction must we advance? Neither the poetic model nor the narrative model appear sufficient. As for the model proposed by Kristeva, in the context of a materialist gnoseology, it is indeed quite attractive, since it combines a Saussurean interest in the pertinence of negative processes (opposition and difference) to the constitution of the concept of sign with a radically new approach, where the conventions guaranteeing the signified context of the subject being exposed, the unity of this subject is then destroyed by what Kristeva calls a *collision of loose signifiers* (*sujet zérologique* and *collision de signifiants*). This new phase in the production of meaning is called *semiotic* and *nonsymbolic*, in contradistinction with the *semiological*, *symbolic* phase which preceded it, and it is the purpose of Kristeva's *sémanalyse* to investigate its *signifiance*. [10] But is it possible to construct a *semanalytical* model that would not be metatheoretical, and does not the application of this metatheory to a specific text place the critic himself under the very authority of a process of negation and difference which he has been trying to reject? And as far as Rimbaud is concerned does not *semanalysis* risk missing both the mythical and ritual context which is the cradle of the poem? Kristeva (1974), going back to the hypotheses already put forth in *Séméiotiké* (1969), attempted to base a part of the description of her *dispositif sémiotique du texte* (phonetic and phonological level) on something other than the permanence of a logical contradiction: a network of rhythmic constraints, grounded on unconscious drives, and constantly short-circuited by the resistance of a monovalent metrical tradition in the speaking subject. The endeavor soon leads to the postulation of a *rythme sémiotique* or *chora* "which remains latent to the text, but which pads it with a semiotic outer form susceptible to becoming actualized into diverse significations through displacement and condensation".

At the syntactic level, the freeing of a semiotic rhythm seems to entail for Kristeva a questioning of the very principle of the syntactic links between linguistic statements and the possibility of dissolving all those links (*déchaînements*) in the text (1974: 209–263). All this leads us to the reinsertion of the principle of *signifiance* into its historical and social context: the political revolutions of the nineteenth century. In short, the mystery of the text lies in the contradiction between the cultural tenets of a bourgeois society seeking to cover up its greed and its guilt and the startling pronouncements of a poetic text asserting its own authority. To be sure, hypotheses such as these, adapted to Rimbaud's text, could well aid us in solving at a deep level the classical problem of Rimbaud's involvement, his *engagement*. However, even if we accept this integration of the text in the perspective of a Marxist dialectic, there remains yet to be solved the general problem of how to read this *signifiance* into the text, *without blocking it* into the time and space of a narrative. The construction of a semanalytical model is valid in that it denies (provisionally or permanently?) the poem its own teleology. Yet, to base an interpretation of the poetic text on the criticism of unconscious drives, themselves in conflict with the ego of a particular historical class, tends to make the literary object the area of conflict, while at the same time moving the stake of this conflict outside the composition of the poem. This leaves unanswered the question of knowing exactly *what, at the surface of the text, grounds our conscious reading of the* Illuminations *onto a deep unconscious structure, and ultimately permits us to use this structure to construct a "signifiance."* It is here that the use of the concept of semiotic production must be modified to account for the *ritualizing* of poetic communication. Because the text resists any contextualization not directly related to its production, it subjugates the readers, and introduces them, as if by magic, to the poetic transformation (*poiein*) par excellence: the passage from a simple elocution to the poetic act giving it its representation and thus making it performative.

Let us consider "Après le Déluge", for example. In this text that received, as Suzanne Bernard likes to remark, a *deluge of interpretations*, deconstruction of the narrative and production of the text are intimately tied to the elaboration of a model of creation:

Aussitôt que l'idée du Déluge se fut rassise, un lièvre s'arrêta dans les sainfoins et les clochettes mouvantes, et dit sa prière à l'arc-en-ciel, à travers la toile de l'araignée.

As soon as the idea of the Flood had subsided, a hare paused among the sainfoins and the swaying bellflowers, and said his prayer to the rainbow through the spider's web.

Oh! les pierres précieuses qui se cachaient, — les fleurs qui regardaient déjà.

Oh! the precious stones that were hiding, — the flowers that already looked around.

Dans la grande rue sale, les étals dressèrent, et l'on tira les barques vers la mer étagée là-haut comme sur les gravures.

In the filthy main street butchers' stalls rose, and barges were tugged toward the sea rising up in tiers as in engravings.

Le sang coula, chez Barbe-Bleue, — aux abattoirs, dans les cirques, où le sceau de Dieu blêmit les fenêtres. Le sang et le lait coulèrent.

Blood flowed, at Bluebeard's, — in slaughterhouses, — in circuses, where the seal of God whitened the windows. Blood and milk flowed.

Les castors bâtirent. Les "mazagrans" fumèrent dans les estaminets.

Beavers did their building. Glasses of black coffee steamed in the cafés.

Dans la grande maison de vitres encore ruisselante, les enfants en deuil regardèrent les merveilleuses images.

In the still dripping big house [sic] with glass panes, children in mourning looked at the marvelous reflections.

Une porte claqua; et, sur la place du hameau, l'enfant tourna ses bras, compris des girouettes et des coqs des clochers de partout, sous l'éclatante giboulée.

A door slammed, and, in the village square, the child waved his arms, understood by weather vanes and cocks on steeples everywhere, under the glittering downpour.

Madame * * * établit un piano dans les Alpes. La messe et les premières communions se célébrèrent aux cent mille autels de la cathédrale.

Madame * * * installed a piano in the Alps. Mass and first communions were celebrated at the hundred thousand altars of the cathedral.

Les caravanes partirent. Et le Splendide-Hôtel fut bâti dans le chaos de glaces et de nuit du pôle.

Caravans departed. And the Hotel Splendid was erected in the chaos of ice and of polar night.

Depuis lors, la Lune entendit les chacals piaulant par les déserts de thym, — et les

From that time, the Moon heard jackals howling through the wilderness of

églogues en sabots grognant dans le verger. Puis, dans la futaie violette,
bourgeonnante, Eucharis me dit que
c'était le printemps.

thyme — and eclogues in wooden
shoes grumbling in the orchard. Then,
in the forest, violet-hued, burgeoning,
Eucharis told me that it was spring.

Sourds, étang;—Écume, roule sur le
pont et passe par-dessus les
bois;—draps noirs et orgues, éclairs
et tonnerre, montez et roulez;—eaux
et tristesses, montez et relevez les
Déluges.

Gush forth, pond; — Foam, roll above
the bridge and over the woods; — black
palls and organs, — lightning and thunder, — rise up and roll; — Waters and
sorrows, rise up and release the Floods
again.

Car depuis qu'ils se sont dissipés, — oh,
les pierres précieuses s'enfouissant, et les
fleurs ouvertes! — c'est un ennui! Et la
Reine, la Sorcière qui allume sa braise
dans le pot de terre, ne voudra jamais
nous raconter ce qu'elle sait, et que nous
ignorons.

For since they have vanished, — oh! the
precious stones burying themselves,
and the opened flowers! — it's a nuis-
ance! and the Queen, the Sorceress who
kindles her coals in the earthen pot, will
never be willing to tell us what she
knows, and what we do not know.

(Rimbaud 1960: 253)

(Rimbaud 1973: 109-111).

We notice first the *après* and *depuis*, the simple past, and then, the "toile de
l'araignée", the "pierres précieuses qui se cachaient, — les fleurs qui
regardaient déjà." And we are struck by the extraordinary dessemination
accomplished between "Après le déluge" of the title and "Aussitôt que" of
the first line: all the simple past tenses articulated in the succession to explain
the *après* are in fact locked in a paradigm, a "horizontality" which draws
them together. The hare is on the same level as the beavers, not to mention
the jackals or the moon that hears them howling. But there is also a bizarre
series of performances (*faire*) which apparently contribute in no way to our
comprehension of the text and which the critics have, moreover, had
extreme difficulty justifying:

> Historical performances: "Madame * * * établit un piano . . ."
> Anthropological performances: "Les caravanes partirent."
> Ritual performances: "Le sang et le lait coulèrent."

And others, hard to place, such as "Une porte claqua". "l'enfant tourna ses
bras", "se dressèrent" "célébrèrent." And what is this "les 'mazagrans'
fumèrent" instead of *se mirent à fumer*, that one would expect; and
"bâtirent" instead of *se mirent à bâtir*? (The necessities of metrics are
not sufficient to justify the absence of the inchoative auxiliary).

Due to the system of the simple past tenses, by which the text highlights
the return to life, the representation takes an obvious performative value,
which contrasts with the illocutionary incapacity of speaker turned inter-

locutor ("Sourds, étang. . . nous ignorons"). The simple past is clearly the form of recounting for most narratives, with familiar logical connectives such as *après, aussitôt (que), depuis.* But the relations of the simple past tenses among themselves in the poem are heteromorphous: the diversity and the length of the description in all its successive strata can hardly be reduced to the mere synchronicity of the "Aussitôt que" introducing the whole poem. As for the semantic reference, the absurd diversity of the semantic categories gives the reader the feeling that the text presents a mysterious zoology fit to entertain Borges, but which has little to do with that of the biblical deluge. It is something, rather, in the style of Bosch or Breughel ("la mer étagée. . . comme sur les gravures"). A study of the patient ordering or reordering of sequences (the blood and the milk flowed, twice) only confirms that Rimbaud wanted to avoid imitating the Bible and attempted an autonomous formulation of a magical life renewal. At the level of content-substance, a text full of humor and almost in the style of La Fontaine ("Un lièvre s'arrêta dans les sainfoins"), suggests a different existence, at the same time new and indefinitely repeated: a ritual. *Life then has a character as meagerly significant, as mysterious as a door flapping in the wind or slammed shut ("Une porte claqua").* Its very existence, its substance, is predicated, as it were, on this simple ritual. At the level of expression, the diversity and occasional bizarreness of *sémémisations* implies a reorganization of the classifying ability, of the very discourse that allows us to classify and as Meschonnic saw, a reorganization between cultural forces.

If we now question ourselves about the meaning to attribute to Rimbaud's postdiluvian genesis, we may conclude that the secret of the *Reine*, the *Sorcière*, is none other than that of a narrative where the ritual attention paid by the narrator (the speaker) to the poetic act fulfilling its desire to communicate can give him the illusion of a well-performed fiction. However, any loss of the attention entails, with the abandon of the production of the narrative, failure for the interpreter, the metalinguist.

Let us summarize. The approach proposed here and for which the name *semiostylistics* is suggested, allows for:

1. The multivalent relation of a narrative function and poetic function in the framework of a production of narrative;
2. Under the only condition of a conjoint study of this production and of its reinvestment at the surface level, the perception, beneath the guise of the poetic object, of a rite of protection of the signifier. One should be able then to extend the hypothesis of this rite of protection to the whole of literary and artistic processes, since it is predicated on a semiotic

contradiction fundamental to the making and communicating of all poetic utterances;

3.   On the basis of the data acquired in 1 and 2, the establishment of fruitful relationships between a typology of literatures and a typology of cultures;

4.   In a perspective which remains to be elaborated, the general system of these relations.

NOTES

1. For a good presentation of the problem, see Charolles (1973).

2. "In poetic works the linguist isolates those structures whose analogy is striking with that which the analysis of myths reveals to the ethnologist . . . Could it be that the two problems are only one?" (Jakobson and Lévi-Strauss 1962). But the question remains as to whether the passage from myth-occurrence to mythological discourse postulated by the ethnologist's research is truly equivalent to the passage of the poem to the poetic discourse marked by the *poetician*.

3. To the extent that the metalinguistic or scientific discourse strives to denote strict limits for the signified and to reduce continually the *"part flottante"* of meaning (see Lévi-Strauss 1950).

4. Following Propp, Greimas, and Brémond, it could even be said that it is a tale complete with *contract*, *alliance* and *trial* stages.

5. The constant oscillation between the essence (inscape) of poetry and its contextual referents is particularly evident in the Riffaterre-Jakobson controversy.

6. The deixis is weak, because the *designata* cannot be said to belong all to the same class, nor the designator to a class with them. For a distinction between *endophoric* and *exophoric* deixis pertinent here (Rimbaud uses the former at the expense of the latter), see Brecht (1974).

7. André Martinet (1960: ch.1) distinguishes between two *articulations* or levels of language analysis: the first level or *première articulation* is composed of *monèmes*, that is to say, *morphemes* without phonological or phonematic traits corresponding to basic semantic choices imposed by the competence of the linguistic subject. The second level or *deuxième articulation* of phonematic criteria. A third level or *troisième articulation* would thus conceivably include all *morphemes* further defined with stylistic or semiostylistic criteria. For an hypothesis on a third *articulation* in another context, see Eco (1972: section B.1).

8. For a systematic study of catachresis in poetry and an extended use of endophoric deixis, see Blanchard (1973).

9. Jacques Derrida has given a critique of the Richard position in "La double séance" in his book *La dissémination* (1972: 200-317).

10. As in the case of Greimas's *Maupassant* (1976), Kristeva's latest book *Polylogue* (1977) appeared to late for me to be able to do it justice here. However, an incomplete reading of it suggests that the problem of the *grounding of the conscious reading onto an unconscious structure* remains obscured by that of the literary or artistic fiction, and by the difficulty inherent in the distinction between theory and practice and experience and fiction. Poetry and poetic language would appear to be one of the avenues taken by those who

fight *l'économic du désir*. But this privilege of poetry, so deftly presented with the help of Bataille (Kristeva 1977: 122) is never seriously taken into consideration, and cannot be, since to study the conventions and the constraints of poetry would be to give some sort of entity to the poetic subject and to dignify its *ego*.

6

Semiostyles: Beyond Narrative Structures

Fifty years after Propp's work on the functions of the fairy tale, narrative studies are now entering a new phase. Beside the ever-recurring studies on themes and values dear to the old school of humanism and literary history and an Aristotelian criticism dealing with the relationship of specific narratives to specific genres or styles in terms of propriety and finality, there is today a structural criticism dealing with the linguistic and semiological aspects of the narrative in terms of systems and structures. The reasons for this development are clear enough. On the creative side, the radical transformation undergone during the first part of this century by the concept of literature in general and that of the novel in particular (Kafka, Proust, Joyce, Thomas Mann) seems to have at least undermined the age-old tradition of oral or written storytelling, complete with plot, characters, and moral judgments. On the critical side, the demise of symbolism in Russia, the writers' involvement with their own narrative selves, and their disenchantment with the traditional hero in the West, must be related, if only very loosely, to the overall development of a formalist criticism both in the East and in the West (from Shklovsky to Lubbock). The New Critics and their disciples approached narrative studies in the context of their relation to a tradition of representation (the dual structure—*showing/telling*—of *mimesis*) in Western culture: in this sense, the *Craft of Fiction* (Lubbock 1931) and the *Rhetoric of Fiction* (Booth 1961) both demonstrate—one near the beginning and the other near the end of the New Criticism and the Chicago School—a clear awareness of the rhetorical implications of story-telling for the narrator and his topic. The Russian formalists, on the other hand, were generally concerned with the purely formal properties of the narrative, its plot sequence, its character system, its style periodization and input. More recently, say, in the last fifteen years, Continental students of the narrative, more concerned with an abstract theory of narrative universals than with a definition of specific surface properties, have combined the heritage of the Russian formalists and the teachings of Saussurean, structural and trans-formational linguistics, in order to isolate what would appear to be the basic narrative (linguistic) structure. However, because there is no marked difference between a theory of human actions and a theory of narrative, and because narratives are, so to speak, everywhere, we are compelled to reflect that there is no theory of human actions which is not first a theory of narrative, and vice versa. Thus, the search for the basic unit cannot depend only on linguistic criteria of selection and pertinence: it must include pragmatic, logical, perhaps even anthropological criteria as well. It is no longer the business of the literary critic turned linguist, but that of the linguist turned semiologist, and interested in all the significant aspects of human behavior. Yet this growing supremacy of semiology raises more than one theoretical question. First, the semiologist, influenced by the enormous development of transformational and generative grammar, searches for matrices, units whose basic pertinence is defined in linguistic terms. But this supposedly clear linguistic scheme requires so many qualifi-cations and adjustments that it becomes either too naive (for lack of refinement) or too obscure (for its excessive complexity). For instance, as Brémond (1973: 103-128) shows in his review of Todorov's work, if the proper noun is just a symbol for the agent as subject and executor of the plot (whose tribulations will only be studied within the linguistic frame of a syntax of exchanges, attributions and reversals), and if the intrinsic proper-ties of this symbol in no way modify the structural function of the agent, there can very well be two names (even perhaps two characters) for one agent. In order to maximize the applicability of the syntactic model, a semantic qualification must then be introduced, and a basic semantic distinction must be made between the concept of subject as *agent* and that of subject as *patient*. Furthermore, since the concept of *patient* usually impli-cates, albeit without including them, those agents, who, without directly affecting the outcome of the action, nonetheless influence it to some degree, and make it take a turn for better or for worse, Brémond also suggests the adoption of the categories of *influencer* and *improver/degrader*. We can take these suggestions even further, and hypothesize that a syntax of the narrative must be complemented with a semantics governed by the rules of logical coherence (principles of identity and noncontradiction), albeit without being subject to the rules of (1) finite state grammars (English, French, and so on), where sentences are derived from other sentences and where such statements as *sincerity knows John* are classified as problematic only because of special restrictions affecting the configuration of a particular sentence; (2) a generative grammar, where, although sentences are not derived from other sentences, translinguistic elements (e.g. narrative kernels or sequences of plot) of the narrative would still be organized on the basis of a mere linguistic competence.

Admitting that such a procedure exists, it would have to meet the following criteria: (1) it must be universal; (2) it must be specific, and because narratives articulate specific qualifications of subjects (*agents/ patients*) in relation to the selection and combination of specific action processes, it must be capable of yielding a classification of those relations in the field of *discourse* (the level of the linguistic *signans*, or its narrative equivalent, the *racontant*, the *telling*) *vs.* story (the *signatum* or *raconté*—to which Brémond expressly limits himself). Brémond believes that only a semantics broadly based on the articulation of logical processes can meet those criteria and solve the problem defined in his foreword: "Is it possible to describe the complete network of options *logically* allowed a narrator at any point in his narrative, to pursue the story in progress?" (Brémond 1973: 8). Whence comes the appropriate title of his book: *Logique du récit*.

Brémond's book is divided in two parts. The first part is a collection of articles offering a critique of some famous forerunners as well as controversial semiologists of the narrative (Propp, Bédier, Dundes, Greimas, Todorov), published from 1964 to 1971 in *Communications, Poétique* and *Semiotica*. The second part is a theoretical sketch of the "principal narrative roles" illustrated with a great abundance of folk and folk-related material. We should remember that the French *rôle* can be translated by *role*, or *part*, or *type*, depending on the amount of emphasis placed on the anthropomorphic aspect of narrative (*role* and *part* connoting a subjective and dramatic process absent from *type*). This two-part division is helpful in that it allows for (1) a situating of Brémond's work in the broad context of narratological studies, and (2) a thorough treatment of the problem outlined in the foreword. The book is remarkable for the flexibility, if not the virtuosity, which the author displays in applying his method to a multiplicity of texts at various stages of the narrative process. In what constitutes a major improvement over Propp's chronological presentation of the narrative functions in the Russian folktale, Brémond's book concentrates on the quasi-behavioral capacity of each function to generate its own subsystem and also to alter the very course of the narrative with each turn of events. Believing as he does that a sequence should be considered neither as an end in itself, nor as a chance occurrence in some drawn-out historical process, Brémond cannot wholly subscribe to Propp's historical coding of sequences. This is not to say that he rejects the idea of cultural constraints: as a matter of fact he does emphasize the necessity for a great variety of subcodes in the close examination of a specific semiotic substance, for instance film as opposed to literature. Yet, because he is reluctant to move from Propp's strict deductions to the sweeping reductions of Greimas or Todorov (according to whom all modifications can be translated into a system governed by the implications or contradictions between two subjective statements), he is not prepared to accept what grammarians of the narrative have to offer. His own system is based on the principle that a one-way plot complete with its established cluster of sequences does not exist.

What underlies Brémond's whole system is a dual structure, which can be formalized in the following manner: (1) a syntagmatic structure in which every action can be defined in principle with reference to a three-stage process— the possibility or likelihood of action, the action in progress, and the action accomplished and results achieved— with the specific indication that, at any of the stages, the action can indeed progress or be stopped; (2) a paradigmatic structure in which every action can also be defined with reference to the fact that, at each stage of the process, it can take a turn for the better or the worse, thus working to the advantage or to the disadvantage of the *agent/patient* and/or the people around him. In the section on the *patient*, under the subsection entitled "the patient exposed to an impending modification which ultimately will not take place", Brémond gives the example of the queen who is expected to give the king a son and who will suffer a miscarriage instead. The great advantage of such a descriptive system is, of course, that it will register elements of narrative, previously unregistered because of their virtuality, yet playing an effective part in shaping the expectations of the narratee and thus contributing to the dramatization of the narrative. To be sure, neither Propp nor any of the other formalists, who believe that each function can only be defined by its results and achievements, will be able to register such alternatives. Since they are obsessed with chronology, not only can they not code virtuality *vs.* reality, but they must also dismiss all *dual morphological functions* and split them successively on the syntagmatic axis, in an analysis which fails to accredit the strength of the narrative. When Dundes, for instance, codes a narrative unit (what he calls a *motifemic sequence*) as *Lack→Assignment of Task→Task Completed→Lack Liquidated*, he does miss, as Brémond shows, the opportunity to order sequences according to the:

specific character of the mediations which ensure the liquidation or creation of the lack. The motifeme *Lack Liquidated*, logically implied in the motifeme *Task Com-*

pleted, is not given next to its correlate in the text, in the manner of an effect next to its cause, but *perceived* through it, as a genre is perceived through species. A bi-dimensional graphic expression becomes necessary, in order to transcribe these parallel series of motifemes, some of which simultaneously imply the rest. Instead of Propp's unilinear sequence, we shall have the following scheme:

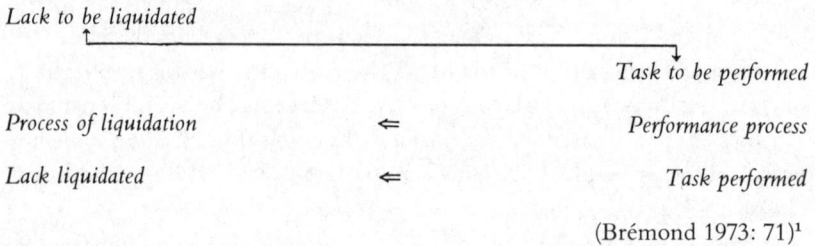

Lack to be liquidated

⌐——⌐
                                          ↓
                                          Task to be performed

Process of liquidation   ⇐   *Performance process*

Lack liquidated   ⇐   *Task performed*

(Brémond 1973: 71)[1]

Now, to understand the structure formalized above, we must define the mode of its utilization and the field of its application.

BRÉMOND'S LOGICAL MODE

1.1. By *logic* and *logical mode*, we might want to refer, first, to those constraints which any narrated series of events must obey in order to remain coherent, constraints which are radically different from those by which a narrative is invested with specific cultural or moral values — consider, for instance, the Aristotelian rule of unity of plot and time, later expanded to include unity of space (Barthes 1966b). All such constraints entail a clause of noncontradiction and exclusion, so that the two statements "Peter was poor; he is not poor any longer" and "Peter was not rich; he has become rich" cannot be said to be logically coherent: there is no necessary relation, no logical coherence between *poor* and *not rich*. As Brémond shows in his discussion of Greimas, the relation of one statement to the other is purely a matter of lexical and stylistic choice (Brémond 1973: 81 ff). The adoption of Greimas' minimal constraints would not enable us to produce a model powerful enough to generate and articulate narrative structures.

1.2. If we wanted to select a more powerful model, we might try to define logical coherence in terms of causation. Thus, for an action to be coherent in relation to another one, it would suffice for it to be brought about by another one in direct sequence. But this would not be satisfactory either, as we have already seen that too much reliance on the concept of causation could only lead to an excessive syntagmatization of the narrative and also result in a serious loss of pertinent information.

1.3. There remains what Greimas himself refers to as Brémond's *logique décisionnelle*, where the terms and value of the concept of causation are to be redefined within the scope of that of *implication*. This is accomplished, first, by a return to an age-old precept (Aristotle *Poetics* 9), that is, that the function of the poet is not to describe, as a historian, things that did happen, but the kind of things that might have happened, or to put it another way, "that which is possible as being probable or necessary". The precept, refined by two Chicago critics, Crane (1957) and Goodman (1954: 1-25), is not only that fiction must be distinguished from reality, but also that narratives are made to work by combining *probable implications*: confronted with a series of alternatives, the skillful author always manages to select, for each stage of the plot, the one that will contribute the most to unifying the whole plot. On the other hand, to be fully effective, a system of probabilities must also contribute to the *dramatization* of the plot. Barthes, commenting on a systemic logic of actions (1966b: 14), indicates that this *dramatization* is the result of a tension between a *logic a minimo* (at each stage of the process, there is a possibility of meaning, which can be, or not be, actualized: thus, in a specific sequence of one of Ian Fleming's novels, James Bond, wanting to light his cigarette, does not respond to the offer of a light, because he instinctively fears it may contain a trap) and a *logic a maximo* (closed upon itself, actualized or not, the sequence is always ready to function as the first subsequence of a broader system, to become, in Pike's or Dundes' ter-minology, linked to the *motifeme* through a particular feature or distribu-tional mode, for instance in Fleming's books, a particular mode of initiating a new Bond mission). Now this kind of *intension* must truly be universal, because, however much we may want to reduce it to a pure meta-language for our own critical purposes, we have to admit that it *speaks* to us, readers or spectators, in a very forceful, albeit undefinable manner: it corresponds to the kind of interior knowledge the characters, and we through them, have about a certain finality of the text. At each stage of the action, there are possibilities of meaning, which become, so to speak, available to us in their totality. These possibilities, in turn, we project in our mind, in a series of paradigms which we then constantly try and reduce to a simple syntagma-tic line. That we understand this process as *logical* does not entail any contradiction with the fact that it is indeed fundamentally related to a structural view of language, based, since Saussure, Hjelmslev and Jakobson, on the dual principle of *presence (identity)/absence (difference)* and *succession (syntagm)/substitution (paradigm)*, and to a generative or transformational syntax, whose parsing and stemming procedures might indeed be very helpful in determining the range of all implications. But *logical* it must remain, if we are to take full advantage of the notion of *implication*, and understand it in terms of its *narrativization* in the course of the story process, that is, in its relationship to the concept of role and its dramatic resources.

2.1. The question of human reference. In his critique of the *constitutional model*, Brémond (1973: 81-102) particularly objects to Greimas' concept of *faire anthropomorphe* as an unnecessary stage between the abstract level of deep syntax and the manifestations of a surface grammar. In his review of Todorov's *Grammaire du Décaméron*, he again attacks the anthropomorphism latent in the categorization of the proper noun: (1) to posit a category of the proper noun without real grammatical properties is tantamount to assuming that the proper noun is itself nothing else but a cover for the substance of the person, and leads to the subsequent proposition that: (2) a narrative which does not deal with animate subjects or objects is not really a narrative, unless it specifically humanizes them: e.g. a science book which tells the *saga of the atom* or the *epic of electricity* by treating physical elements as if they were human variables. Brémond adds that the only correct criterion of coherence in the narrative is not that it is human, but that the subject of the actions remains identical and consistent through the sequence of episodes: such a narrative is the *minimum narrative*, which consists in a string of events arranged in a mere chronological sequence, and discussed from an outsider's point of view (Brémond 1973: 111-112). This ongoing critique of the question of human reference should not be dismissed as an academic debate of ethics and value judgments; indeed, its outcome is likely to affect our outlook on the narrative in a very fundamental way. While in his now classic 1966 *Communications* article, Brémond had come out in favor of the *vision anthropomorphe*, in the *Logique* (1973), formalizing a trend that had long been obvious in articles published since then, he definitely rejects it. An anthropomorphic rule which would make the supremacy of the acting subject bound only by obstacles to his will or his desires as essential to narrativity as, say, the overall emphasis on the code of the message is to *literariness* in Jakobson's poetic function, yet would provide no criteria to define the concept of *humanness* (which must thus remain as vague as that of *literariness*), cannot be of any help in the linguistic determination of an arbitrary set of (narrative) structures. With Brémond, there is no need to invoke such a rule, since narrativity is not tied to modifications effected only by the acting subject or *agent* (a thesis with which structuralism unwittingly shows what is perhaps too much respect for the old humanistic tradition of the hero), but also depends on the reactions of a *patient*, variously affected by the progress of his or the other characters' actions, and even perhaps, on the manifestations of the other functions directly related to that of the *patient*: the *influencer* and the *improver/degrader*.

This means that even the *minimum narrative* is endowed with role potential. Because, irrespective of the number of characters in the story or of its complexity, its coherence is not defined by the mere succession or combination of sequences, but rather by the relation of these sequences to the various types of *simulacra* they constitute.

Let us pause for a moment and ponder this concept of *rôle*. First of all, let us notice that the 1964 *Communications* article, "Le Message narratif" devoted to a review of Propp's work, and later included in *Logique* (1973), in the context of a critique of folk-narrative studies, does not, in any way, refer to a theory of roles: Brémond is merely interested in making Propp's system more flexible by suggesting that one should, wherever possible, take advantage of the *dual morphological function* manifested by any text (each process can or cannot be completed, in a way that is beneficial or detrimental to the *patient/agent*). In the 1966 article, however, Brémond is edging toward a theory, when he suggests that the model of the *dual morphological function* be made more specific, by registering:

(1) three modes of connection available between sequences:

(a) *the end-to-end connection*
   villainy to be committed
   ↓
   villainous act
   ↓
   villainy committed   =   villainy to be punished
                                    ↓
                                    judicial procedure
                                    ↓
                                    punishment administered

(b) *the enclave connection*
   task to be accomplished   =   means of accomplishment

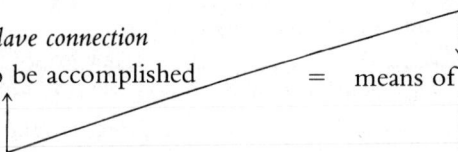

   procedure of accomplishment   putting the means
                                        into operation

   task accomplished   success of the operation

(c) *the joining connection*

damage to be inflicted   =   villainy to be committed

damaging procedure   villainous act

damage inflicted   villainy commited

(2) three phases (included in the above);

(3) three perspectives, through which the concepts of separate *dramatis personae*, of one hero and/or one heroine, are absorbed into the larger concept of separate or concurrent roles:

> This singleness disappears, when the improvement, instead of being creditable to chance, is credited to the intervention of an agent, endowed with initiative and undertaking to achieve it on the grounds *that it is indeed a part of a task to be performed.* The process of improvement is then organized as behavior — which implies that it becomes structured into a network of goal-means that can be filled ad infinitum. Furthermore, this transformation introduces two new roles: on the one hand, the agent, who undertakes the task for the benefit of a passive beneficiary, plays, in relation to him, the part of a means, no longer lifeless, but endowed with his own particular interest and initiative — he is thus an *ally*; on the other hand, the obstacle encountered by the agent can be incarnated in an agent, also endowed with his own initiative and interests — this other agent is an adversary (Brémond 1966: 65).

Thus, inasmuch as the text makes possible a pair of alternatives at each stage of its narrative process, and inasmuch as these alternatives are incorporated into the narrative to make it more tense, more interesting, the text literally produces roles which help the narrator establish a value system applicable to his story, and very soon gives us the illusion that he or his characters have suddenly developed a point of view. Let us note in passing that *alternatives* are an integral part of the concept of a *dual morphological function*, where each feature mode, for instance, is usually defined as the result of a choice between two (alternate) possibilities: the term *alternative* makes this selection a function of both form and content, so that any stylistic choice which does not radically alter the content is simply not registered as *alternate*. We shall see later that this simple restriction is actually of such importance that it does reduce the effectiveness and the applicability of the whole model. For the moment, however, let us continue our presentation of the *logical mode*.

2.2. *Roles and actants.* In his 1964 article, Brémond suggests that his analysis makes possible the building of an integral model capable of producing "those *simulacra* of events and characters (*dramatis personae, actants, roles,* whatever one may wish to call them) required for a semiological analysis of narrative structures" of an indefinitely growing complexity. The simulacra are semantic investments of abstract concepts, whose combination is designed to illustrate, through the use of a binary scheme, the transformation of basic logical constraints inherent in any *signatum* (primary contradictory relations of the type *white vs. nonwhite* and adversary relations of the type *white vs. black* with derived secondary adversary relations of the type *nonblack vs. nonwhite*) into basic discursive, narrative functions. By reducing Propp's sequence of thirty-one syntagmatic functions to six, and casting these six, first, into a primary couple of contradictives, Greimas establishes the basic *couple actantiel subject/object*; then, by driving two secondary adversary couples from the first one, he establishes the other two couples of *actants*: the *addressor/addressee* and the *ally/adversary* (or *traitor*). These narrative functions are, again, no more than the superficial *loci*, the semantic *topoi* corresponding to logical constraints, where the specific *actors* (S_1, S_2, S_3; A_1, A_2, A_3, etc.) are located and from where they can move and can be moved through operations of *disjunction* and *conjunction*. For instance, the Fair Princess, who belongs in S and A (along with her father the King, the Court and the Kingdom), is disjoined into O and moved to T by a mischievous traitor cousin. The hero (S_2) will attempt to retrieve her in turn and bring her back to her parents, thus effecting a conjunction. In the Russian folktale, as in most other narratives, it can therefore be stated that the narrative process is activated by a disjunctive conjunctive relation between the *actants*, which usually leads to an inversion of the semantic content, according to Greimas' *dialectic algorithm*,

$$\frac{X-1}{Y-1} \simeq \frac{X+1}{Y+1}$$

where X and Y represent two types of actions: positive and negative.

Still, because the appreciation of the *actants* depends on the actualization of the semantic investment in a linguistic substance (proper noun, adjective, verb, and so on) and on its pertinence (relationship of each of the specific *actors* to the *actants*), their interrelation can only be traced satisfactorily when the analyst takes into account the level of a *superficial* or *surface grammar*, that of semantics and style in particular. This, in turn would require a definition of the criteria of selection and pertinence applicable in surface analysis, which Greimas does not want to undertake. Brémond, on the other hand, appears to have avoided the dilemma by opting for a semantic mean between structure and texture. Avoiding reductive abstractions as well as stylistic analyses, he provides an intermediate level, which he calls the *precoding of the narrative* (the coding taking place at the level of the literarary text only), and which enables him to perceive the investment of a pragmatic and motivational context as directly constitutive of a set of narrative roles. The perception of the role, therefore, does not hinge, as is the case for the *actant*, on the relation of an investment to a deep-structure modification in what Brémond calls the *Haven of ideas* (1973: 84), because, as Brémond's own analysis shows, *it is the investment which directly constitutes the role*; then, and only then, can we resort to the models of formal logic and/or stylistics.

2.3. Phases of the model: an example. Along with each phase of the reconstituted process, and to emphasize the relative flexibility of his model, Brémond usually gives one or more examples of *role phase*, and, sometimes, even the summary precoding of a full-length tale episode. Yet, because the book makes, as we have seen, no distinction between *human* roles and *narrated* roles, he rightly assumes that there is no need for him to offer the reader a step-by-step analysis of an entire work, say, an epic like the *Iliad*, a play like *Hamlet*, or a novel like *Madame Bovary*: the closure of a literary work is nothing more than the termination of the role process by elimination of all possibilities available at a given moment. *Logique du récit* only strives to provide a chart of all those possibilities, leaving for the end a table of relations (1) between roles, and (2) between the level of roles and the other levels in the narrative. In the chapter devoted to the *patient*, for instance, Brémond selects two levels of inquiry, corresponding to the two types of action discernible: (1) a subjective level, where the *patient* reacts to the situation according to his knowledge of it; and (2) an objective level, where the *patient* is the beneficiary of an evolutionary process or the victim of a counter-evolutionary process. Now, at each stage of the situation, provision is made for a set of alternatives, where the selection of one of the alternatives will help define the specific conditions to be fulfilled so that an action ceases to be a virtual alternative and becomes an actual fact. At the subjective level, the *patient* can:

(1) be exposed to an actual process of (positive or negative) modification, without specification in the text as to whether the *patient* is actually affected by this process in his mind, and whether he is reacting or not;

(2) be exposed to an actual process of (positive or negative) modification, with specification in the text as to the *patient* being or not being affected:

(a) (with specification that) the *patient* has no knowledge of being affected, in which case the *patient* is exposed to one of several information processes, leading him to the truth or, on the contrary, to a countertruth;

(b) (with specification that) the *patient* has knowledge of being affected, but that this knowledge, which helps form an opinion in the matter, is going to be lost because of the initiation of certain counter-evolutionary processes (distraction, refutation, dubitation);

(c) (with specification that) the *patient* has knowledge of being affected, but that this knowledge may have been lost; that it can, nonetheless, be retrieved under certain conditions;

(3) derive satisfaction or dissatisfaction from the process;

(4) anticipate deriving satisfaction or dissatisfaction from the process (Brémond 1973: 139-173).

Then, and only then, can we go on to the objective level, where the *patient* is thought to be either the victim or the benficiary of a particular process. If the process is completed, the *patient* can be the beneficiary of a process of *improvement* or the victim of a process of *degradation*. However, if the process is interrupted, the *improvement* takes the form of a *protection*, and the *degradation*, the form of a *frustration*. In each case, the *protector* or the *frustrator* can be one or several persons. They can be the same as (or different from) the victim: in Act 4 of *King Lear* there is a good example of the two being performed as subroles (Edgar or Gloucester) of a single *patient*-victim (Lear).

2.4. *Pertinence of the model.* Having abstracted his complete register of roles from the examination of specific narrative units, conversely, Brémond now ends with an examination of how this register will, in turn, help define relative criteria for the constitution of narrative units in the pragmatic and motivational context ("Le codage du récit"). He offers four relative criteria, which he enters into a table with the functions of *patient* and *agent*:

(1) syntax (which formalizes implicatory relationships between processes);

(2) process (process of improvement, degradation, information, and so on);

(3) phase (mere possibility, in progress, completed);

(4) voluntary or involuntary aspect.

He then concentrates on what happens to the rest of the elements in the table, each time one or two criteria change. At the end, Brémond gives us a separate table for the classification of all *syntactic links* used in the syntax column, claiming that only through this classification can one get the synthetic picture of the relations of the *patient* and the *agent* and also be ultimately guaranteed an equivalence between logical and linguistic structures (1973:321). This last part of the book is perhaps the most interesting, as it justifies Brémond's work on three grounds, by responding to a series of anticipated objections:

(1) *Is not the book really incomplete, since it studies only one element in the narrative* (roles)? No, because roles are the fundamental and constitutive element in the narrative. In this respect, the book offers a complete semiology of roles, and, perhaps, although Brémond never actually suggests it, the only complete semiology of narrative available today.

(2) *Is not the book irrelevant, since it does not use a linguistic model?* No, because, in its process, it still considers modifications and transformations performed on the two linguistic universals of narrative, the subject and the predicate.

(3) *Is not the book based on the predication that a particular system of roles works better than another?* No, because there is, again, no difference between narrated roles and human roles in general: the apparent anthropomorphic quality of roles merely results from the humanization of processes performed by the narrative itself, and understandably maximized by the narrator. Brémond thus goes so far as to suggest that the problems of point of view, and more generally, of a teleology of the narrative, which are usually considered to fall within the province of the theorists of the *narrating* (the *racontant*) are actually textualized, one is tempted to say, *somatized*, at the level of the *narrated* (the *raconté*).

After this review of Brémond's *Logique*, I would now like to discuss the pertinence of his model, not in the restricted context of a semiology of the *narrated*, but rather in the general context of a semiology of the total narrative and the relations between narration and description.

In the last part of his last chapter, Brémond asks himself: "Do the criteria of plot analysis selected for our coding of roles yield an essential part of the signification of the narrative text?" (1973: 324). And he answers:

> We do not believe that one can approach the meaning of a narrative without constantly referring oneself to a system of roles. He who chooses to do without it is condemned to the following alternative: either he applies to the text categories of analysis where the notion of role does not obtain— but what one can grasp by means of an analysis of this type has nothing to do with the narrative: it is an enclave in the midst of the narrative, or a message paralleling that of the narrative proper— or the seemingly nonpredicative or achronic concepts which he applies to a structuring of the plot camouflage personal subjects and predicative processes, i.e. *roles* (1973:327).

He adds that these enclaves (the parts of the narrative— read: *descriptions*— not concerned with roles) have no bearing on the coding of the roles, which are already *preset* or *precoded*, so to speak. In a total semiology of the narrative, then, it is this *precoding* which should be studied first, as *the sole determinant of a form,* whose particular *substance* can be examined later. In the end, however, and as to the question whether such precoding does make the text genuinely more significant, or on the contrary, whether it obscures other meanings, which must thus remain partially latent in the course of the interpretation, Brémond finds himself hard pressed to answer and would rather not comment.

I in turn would like to offer a critique of Brémond's position on the following grounds (which I shall indicate in general form and then discuss in some detail):

1. By further distinguishing those processes that belong from those that do not belong in his study (e.g. the above discussion of the enclaves), Brémond does indeed clarify his argument; yet, by the same token, he also imposes great limitations on the scope of his study. By defending a primacy of the narrated over the narrating, without bothering to establish a relational model for their integration, on the one hand, he fails to assess, through a paradigmatic analysis, the semantic value attached to a particular alternative, and, on the other, he isolates himself from the context of today's integrative semiology, from Barthes (1970) to van Dijk (1972).

2. In fact, the claim to the establishment of narrative universals transcending genres or modes and aspects or voices (which commit the particular *phonè* of a narrator to his text) in oral literature, where it is easy to reduce a work to a sequence of motifemes with a subsequence of allomotifs, may not prove successful in the context of more highly sophisticated processes, where the configuration of the *narrating* has an impact on the structuring of the *narrated*.

3. If one admits, as Brémond does, that *narrated roles* and real life roles are one and the same, because, in any event, a role is always related to a narrative which describes it and articulates it, then we shall have serious problems every time we encounter a work where the behavior of the characters depends on roles which are designed to put us in touch with reality precisely through the extravagant fiction in them (*Don Quixote*, for instance).

To begin with, even if we admit that there is no difference between a theory of actions and a theory of narrative, and if we allow for the constitution of a reductive model of roles, we still face the question of knowing what to do (1) with texts essentially produced by a series of enclaves, where the narrator's own slant is fundamental to the proper understanding of the *story* developments; and (2) with texts that are essentially not narrative in the usual sense of the term, including highly stylized poetic genres. Again, what is at stake here is the pertinence of role analysis to a general semiology of narrative.

In the first case, even if, as Brémond suggests, we do keep in mind that a logic of roles still has to undergo further testing and evaluation, it is disturbing to me that a theory, which continually builds its model from the narrative of numerous folktales and folk-related works, offers almost no example from the novel narrative, nor from the very specific context of the folk-related novel: the novel of adventure, say, Jules Verne's *Around the World in Eighty Days* with its quest-type hero Phileas Fogg (Brémond 1973: 216). Indeed, most of the quotes used relate to fairy tales, epics, or, occasionally, drama, and since they are not arranged following an individual work, but according to a system of logical alternatives, we may find it difficult to extrapolate from them a whole model which could be applied to something as complicated and sensitive as a novel by Stendhal or Flaubert, or as deceptively simple as Camus' or Sartre's stories. There, a form of logical analysis would yield very little of interest.

Which is to say, in so many words, that the novel is a specific genre, not in the classic sense of the term, because of aesthetic or psychological considerations, nor in a more Proppian sense, because of a particular sequence of functions, but in a very structural sense, because of a narrative structure which has become too sophisticated to be coded or pre-coded primarily as a role structure. Once this becomes clear, what had appeared before as a textural or cultural variable in a system (the novel genre complicating, yet accountable in terms of, roles) now seems to constitute a functional problem in its own right, and also to raise fundamental questions about the effectiveness of a semiology of *narrated* narrative in general and of Brémond's model in particular.

To be sure, Brémond's tacit disqualification of the novel as genre has its precedent elsewhere in structuralist criticism. In almost every case, the model functions at such a level of linguistic abstraction, and the field of applicability is so narrow, that the results are disappointing. Thus, the *Decameron* is only a collection of microtales (Todorov 1969), and Laclos' *Les Liaisons dangereuses* only an epistolary novel (Todorov 1966); that is, in each case, the narrative instance affords sequences easily reducible to pragmatic criteria, while the patterns (*parole*) of the characters are but the dramatic variations of a single narrative language (*langue*). Other critics, following Todorov, have recently attempted a delineation of the concept of character. Philippe Hamon (1972a) and Sorin Alexandrescu have both suggested criteria for a possible typology of characters. Hamon adopts a linguistic distinction between *referential* characters (historical characters or characters related to a historical context), *shifter* characters (mouthpiece characters, messengers, author's representatives, and so on), and *contact* characters (characters of a pure anaphoric function). Alexandrescu, for his part, follows a purely logical configuration of character classes based on inclusion and exclusion. Yet, although both studies assuredly deserve full consideration on their own terms, they still fail to answer the basic question of how a specific character (a character *substance*) can be derived from a particular role (a semiological form or *seme*). Furthermore, and as far as logic is concerned, even assuming the process underlying an episode ends once the premises have been carried out, and the identification and classification of the episode pose no serious problem, it does not automatically follow that this logical process truly corresponds to a distinct stage in the dramatic progression of the entire story. For instance, when Rodomont in Ariosto's *Orlando furioso* (Brémond 1973: 288) discovers, too late (after he has beheaded Isabel) that her philter will not work, can we properly restrict our enquiry to the situation involving Isabel and Rodomont? And are we not oversimplifying the implications of the story by coding something like "Isabel afraid of being raped" with "patient attempting to frustrate a possible degrader"/ "patient unable to frustrate his degrader"? In the end, considering all these and Brémond's studies together, we may just have to ask ourselves whether the implicit reduction of a *class episode* or *narrative frame* to that of *rôle* is really a productive one.

So far, I have only mentioned genuine narrative texts. But what are we supposed to do about nonnarrative, poetic, philosophical and/or dogmatic texts? What about Plato's *Republic*, where the account of the building of the city-state has more to do with the clarification of the concept of justice than with the description of any particular class of people? What about the account of life in Atlantis in the *Critias*? What about Eliot's *The Waste Land* or Ezra Pound's *Cantos*? In any event, even if we were to dismiss this last group of texts, there would still remain another problem, which has been with us since the beginning, that is, the basic ambiguity of linguistics and semiology in any narrative study. On the one hand, the basic narrative structure is translinguistic — although one could conceivably account for one-sentence-narratives in strict linguistic terms, where the narrative statement would not be different from a linguistic statement; this, however, would be very simplistic. Yet, on the other hand, narrative studies, and Brémond's in particular, do take for their basis the linguistic principle of difference between *langue* and *parole*, between, as we have seen, the idiosyncrasies of a character and the general constraints of his role, and concentrate on the abstract *langue* aspect of the text. All this means a constant interplay between an arbitrary set of rules and surface manifestations that can only be assessed empirically. On the one hand, consideration of surface content is preempted by the establishment of syntactic relations; on the other, an examination of that content is required to ensure a correspondence with those relations.

This might explain why Brémond, who manages some sort of mean by working on specific examples, while dismissing the thematic content in each narrative, cannot finish his book (afterthought? awareness of a lack?) without paying at least lip service to a stylistic criticism, whose subtleties and distinctions on semantic investments he otherwise finds not pertinent to a study of roles. Taking the example where one character signals to another by coughing, he asks himself whether the critic should not pay attention to the substance of the message (the semiotic relation of *cough* to *speak*) and its referential context (the semantic value of the signaling act). His answer is quite ambiguous: if, at the level of a general logic of actions, the semantic investment is irrelevant, it may be that, in the tradition and the context of a particular narrative, it is the key to our understanding (Brémond 1973: 323-324). Evidently, the answer could be made easier and clearer by suggesting a better case in point: something more substantial and more dramatic, involving a whole literary work, like the impressive account of physical postures and object locations in Robbe-Grillet's *La Jalousie*.

The problem, however, is one of theory, and we would need more than practical answers. So now is the time to suggest that this and other problems above cannot actually be resolved without the help of a *semio-stylistic* theory, whose specific purpose it is to study relations between the semiotic and the linguistic level.

I will not deny that any narrative can indeed be charted according to Brémond's specifications. But I shall insist that a logical coding can only be elaborated *in relation to a particular process obtaining in the text and regulating its message*, for example, making possible the translation of narrative units into narrative or dramatic roles, and authorizing their subsequent classification. Thus, whether two texts appear to have been structured by identical or different roles, those roles are actually secondary codings of a primary perceptual process which relates a linguistic substance to a semiotic form in the specific context of a stylistic analysis, and makes it possible for us to acknowledge identity or difference. A *Logique du récit* can only be useful if it is based on the discovery of those processes which I call *semiostyles*, and whose theoretical context I established in Chapter 4.

Let us now take an example given by Brémond to illustrate identity or difference in what he sees as an original precoding of roles. He likens a situation in the *Odyssey*, where Ulysses, having put wax into the ears of his sailors, chooses instead to have himself tied to the mast of the ship, to another in Eastern European folk literature, where the hero, however hard he may try, never manages to know fear (Brémond 1973: 159–160). Brémond charts the two roles as:

(1) "Patient exposed to an actual process of influence (seduction); being influenced; experiencing something (desire)" and

(2) "Patient exposed to an actual process of influence (fear); remaining uninfluenced; not experiencing anything (no fear)."

Yet, if the stories of Ulysses and the fearless hero are thematically the same (both yearning to go home and return as heroes, both yearning for that last experience which still eludes them), their situation cannot be compared: the approximation of desire and fear as two psychological motivations functioning identically is quite vague, and any criticism of Propp's chronological sequence notwithstanding, too little attention has been paid to the lack of contextual correspondence between the two stories. Not only is Ulysses going home, while the other hero's quest has not even begun, but the Greek is conscious of his experience, while the Lithuanian must be asleep. Indeed, it is through a play or a trick on the theme of desire, that both heroes appear as such: they both want to know what (a deathly desire, on the one hand; a crippling fear, on the other) would prevent them from being what they are. Accordingly, it is the writing of the texts themselves which should be examined. They should both be seen as testing their own workability by making a trick, a subterfuge, possible: Ulysses, who cannot surrender to the Sirens, lest he cease to be a hero, has himself tied to the mast of the ship, so that he may still hear their song, and the other one, who cannot be overcome by fear, lest he too cease to be a hero, must be surprised during his sleep. Eventually, one might be able to show that, if the two heroes' experience appears similar, of the agents give us the impression of having acted the same part and come out with different results, the reason is that the narrative itself is the product of a semiostylistic process which guarantees its effectiveness both at the semiotic level—relation between *to know* and *to do*—and the semantic level—relation between different forms of knowledge (*deaf vs. asleep*). The *topos* of the impossible deed is also that of the impossible thought.

Not only does it enable two heroes to play identical roles with what, according to Brémond, would only be a slight semantic modification in the end (*nondeaf/awake*), but also, *prior* to any consideration of *agent/patient/influencer*, it constitutes the narrative kernel of their action by issuing the predicative content through a stylistic display of the terms of the impossibility, the *adunaton*: the fearless hero able to hear the unheard and live, on the one hand, and the fearless hero able to sleep and wake up unstartled, on the other. In the *Odyssey*, it should have been easy for Brémond to detect this transformation in the play on the verb ἀκούω [the series "to hear" → "to listen" → "to listen to" actually intersecting with the series "to hear/not to hear"]:

ὅς τις ἀϊδρείῃ πελάσῃ καὶ φθόγγον ἀκούσῃ
Σειρήνων, τῷ δ' οὔ τι γυνὴ καὶ νήπια τέκνα
οἴκαδε νοστήσαντι παρίσταται οὐδὲ γάνυνται,
ἀλλά τε Σειρῆνες λιγυρῇ θέλγουσιν ἀοιδῇ,
ἥμεναι ἐν λειμῶνι· πολὺς δ' ἀμφ' ὀστεόφιν θὶς
ἀνδρῶν πυθομένων, περὶ δὲ ῥινοὶ μινύθουσι.
ἀλλὰ παρὲξ ἐλάαν, ἐπὶ δ' οὔατ' ἀλεῖψαι ἑταίρων
κηρὸν δεψήσας μελιηδέα, μή τις ἀκούσῃ
τῶν ἄλλων· ἀτὰρ αὐτὸς ἀκουέμεν αἴ κ' ἐθέλῃσθα,
δησάντων σ' ἐν νηῒ θοῇ χεῖράς τε πόδας τε
ὀρθὸν ἐν ἱστοπέδῃ, ἐκ δ' αὐτοῦ πείρατ' ἀνήφθω,
ὄφρα κε τερπόμενος ὄπ' ἀκούῃς Σειρήνοϊν.

(Homer 1964: *Od.* 12. 41–52; emphasis added).

. . .and that man who unsuspecting approaches them and *listens* to the Sirens singing, has no prospect of coming home and delighting his wife and little children as they stand about him in greeting, but the Sirens by the melody of their singing enchant him. They sit in their meadow, but the beach before it is piled with boneheaps of men now rotted away, and the skins shrivel upon them. You must drive straight on past, but melt down sweet wax of honey and with it stop your companions' ears, so none can *listen*; the rest, that is, but if yourself are wanting to *hear them*, then have them tie your hand and foot on the fast ship, standing upright against the mast with the ropes' ends lashed around it, so that you can have joy in *hearing* the song of the Sirens; but if you supplicate your men and implore them to set you free, then they must tie you fast with even more lashings (Homer 1967: book 12, 186, 40-54; emphasis added).

Now one could object that: (1) roles are already constituted before the *topos* of the *adunaton* takes effect — yet this is not really the case, because the acceptance of the narrative is predicated on the acceptance of the stylistic figure which subsumes it, and not the reverse. To reduce, as Brémond does, both the Lithuanian and the Greek narrative to the performance of a trial process is simply to void it of the semiostylistic feature which makes it possible and gives it meaning; (2) in any event, a narrative only begins when a role structure has appeared, so that the actualization of the *topos* depends on it — but this is not true either, as the roles are bound themselves by the built-in transformations of the *topos*: what if Ulysses had *listened to* the Sirens?

We can then conclude that a logic of roles is but a dramatization of basic constraints already at work in any given corpus. As such, it is, no doubt, an extremely valuable attempt at exploring and formalizing the dramatic potential of narrative. It does not, however, permit us to consider texts where this dramatization is weak or complicated by the accumulation of textural devices. On the other hand, we could also extrapolate from the above examples, and state that: (1) *semiostylistics* is an effective tool of investigation; (2) it offers more possibilities than a logic of roles through the establishment of a list of *semiostylistic* processes with reference (A) to a particular work, (B) to a group of works, which could then be identified as *semiostylistically* similar and (C) to an entire body of works, so as to constitute a new (*semiostylistic*) history of literature: it could be shown, for instance, that, in times of revolution, most artistic productions utilize the *cliché* as *semiostyle* (see Chapter 4). This may read like an invitation to practice Russian formalism all over again. Yet *semiostylistics* has one feature Russian formalism does not have: it is mostly relational, and stresses correspondence between all levels of the texts. It is thus an ideal common ground for all structural studies of literature.

To suggest what the procedures of a *semiostylistics* might be in this case, I shall offer some final remarks.

Semiostylistic Structure vs. Logical Sequence

Let us assume that a logical sequence has been established; in this case, a particular phase of the *patient* process illustrated by a La Fontaine fable, *Phébus et Borée*, where the Sun and the Wind compete with each other in trying to inconvenience a traveler:

. . .; le Vent perdit son tempts	. . .; the Wind wasted its time:
Plus il se tourmentait, plus l'autre tenait ferme.	The fiercer it would rage, the firmer the other would stand.
(La Fontaine *Phébus et Borée* 31-32)	

Brémond codes:

Possible patient of a possible modification of his state; possible patient of an actual process liable to modify that state; patient maintained in his initial state, because of the noncompletion of the process liable to modify that state (1973: 141).

Yet, if we look closely, we shall see that the logical process delineated by Brémond is actually inverted from the original one. The descriptive notation of failure does precede that of the narrative modification process itself: "Le Vent perdit son temps". We shall also notice that the fable features a translation from *story* to *discourse*, where the use of the imperfect indicates an aspectual shift in the narrative (*wasted* → *would rage*). Now, I am suggesting that the perception of a nonmodification of the original state is related to, better, depends on, the perception of a stylistic opposition between a reversed order of imperfect and simple past, linked to a shift from *story* to *discourse* and from narration to description. It is mainly through the unusual collocation (the imperfects—"tourmentait" and "tenait ferme"—follow the simple past—"perdit"—instead of the usual sequence, where the simple past breaks the imperfect) that we can be convinced of the vanity of Borée's efforts and thus perceive the process of noncompletion registered by Brémond. In this case, actually, the selection of the process of noncompletion is made absolutely necessary by the phrase "perdit son temps": the negative reverse (*ne perdit pas son temps*), which could have conceivably determined that the choice of the other alternative (that is, completion), would idiomatically be inappropriate here, as the French *ne pas perdre son temps* is always used in another figurative and expletive fashion (English: "to waste no time"). Finally, a simple look at the rest of the text would also confirm my interpretation, as, in the lines following the couplet hastily isolated by Brémond, the use of the present indicative will clearly underwrite, through a decisive shift, the subsequent choice of the other alternative, and thus expose the linear development of a role structure through the successive stages of (1) noncompletion, (2) completion of the initial modification process:

Sitôt qu'il [Borée] fut au bout du terme	As soon as he had reached the end of the time
Qu' à la gageure on avait mis	Prescribed for the wager,
Le Soleil dissipe la nue,	The Sun dissipates the clouds,
Récrée, et puis pénétre enfin le Cavalier,	Recreates and then eventually penetrates the Cavalier,
Sous son balandras fait qu'il sue,	Through his mantle makes him sweat,
Le contraint de s'en dépouiller	Compels him to divest himself of it.
(*Phébus et Borée* 33-38)	

All this particular detail takes on special significance when one wants to understand why Brémond's analysis never offers any logical criteria for selecting one or the other alternative: it is because there is nothing in his stemming that permits him to mandate this selection without relying on a surface procedure. According to his model, a Patient X in a State A and a potential patient of a modification process X can *either* remain in A *or* be changed to xA. And this is precisely where *semiostylistics* is indeed useful, because it can help determine the writer's commitment to one or the other alternative as a matter of textural procedure, where a logical model could not be specific enough. It is thus the tool required to effect a translation from virtuality to actuality, and guarantee that a logical model is truly operational.

Stylistics and Semiostylistics: The Styletic and Stylemic Aspects

The criteria for *semiostylistic* analysis are, first and foremost, stylistic, aiming at defining a (macro and micro) context, as proposed by Riffaterre (1971) and others. They are (together or separate):

Derivation: the contextual pattern is broken.

Convergence: there is a contextual relation between linguistically unrelated elements; for example, expletives and nongrammatical statements can still make a sentence connoting surprise, and so on, while, on the other hand, the rhymes and the verbal structure of a sonnet can also concur in creating meaning.

Redundancy: the context is activated by an anaphoric system.

This context, however, is not interesting in itself. It only serves to alert us to the possible activation of a *semiostylistic* process, through the application of the above criteria in the field of phonology, metrics, syntax and/or morphology, where appropriate. The *semiostylistic* process thus contemplated has two main aspects:

(1) On the one hand, it consists of a structure of reading, where meaning is assessed in terms of value, quality, intensity and time, e.g. in the La Fontaine episode, the pair *simple past/imperfect*. This aspect I call the *styletic aspect*.

(2) On the other hand, it also comprises a structure of semiotic coherence, by helping bring about the particular mode of a deep-structure implication related to a surface modification, that is, by *making it manifest*. In the *Odyssey*, for instance, every time Ulysses is about to enter a danger

zone, the poet makes him, almost ritually, pull out his sharp sword alongside his thigh: παρὰ μηροῦ (see *Odyssey* 10. 294; *Od.* 11. 231, and so on). This implication may belong in Brémond's system of alternatives, with a shift from *patient* to *agent*: Ulysses will not be changed into a pig by Circe's wand; on the contrary, he will use his sword and Hermes' plant to subdue her. Likewise, it may be specified in relation to any other semiological model: in Todorov's table of syntactic transformations, with an inversion of attributions (the object, Ulysses, becomes endowed with the attributes of the subject); in Greimas' model of semantic opposites (the subject, Ulysses, with the help of an ally, Hermes, retrieves his lost strength and his disjoined companions). This particular aspect I call the *stylemic aspect*.

This distinction, adapted from Pike's *etic* and *emic* contexts (1954: 8–28) — the behavioral context is restricted to the reader's perception of the text — has the advantage of stressing *integration* as well as *distinction* proper. For instance, a modification in the intensity of the styletic aspect, that is, a change in the stylistic register, would be in direct relation to a modification in the logic of the *stylemic* aspect, that is, a choice between two alternatives. It has the other advantage of playing down the subjective factor involved in any stylistic analysis, and, accordingly, of eliminating some of the vague criteria proposed to regulate this subjectivity (Riffaterre's *superreader*), by allowing a constant check of the *styletic* against the *stylemic* and vice versa. In conclusion, I can summarize my position in the following way:

1. Brémond's *Logique du récit* appears to offer valid criteria for the study of narrative at the level of the *narrated* and in the form of a general theory of roles and role playing.

2. However, neither this theory nor any other theory of narrative should be considered apart from the stylistic processes, which it implies, and on which it eventually becomes dependent for its elaboration and its application, as the narration proper turns into description.

NOTE

1. The sign ⇐ denotes an implication in a dual morphological function.

Part Two : Self

7

Phenomenology of Literary Experience and Fiction of the Sign

A great deal has been written about the phenomenology of the literary experience, and following the achievements of the Geneva School and the Heidelberg Circle, the critic finds himself at a loss to say anything of import. However, looking over ten years of the structuralist controversy, now that the movement seems to have been totally appropriated by traditional histories of literature, while also to be succumbing to the attacks of poststructuralist critics, one feels it is right to ask what has become of the literary experience of the subject after years of benign neglect. I am thinking not only of the semiotics of narrative, where the various choices of syntax and semantics are referred, less to a particular, an empirical subject, than to a transcendental subject postulated by narrative universals, but also of post-structuralist analyses, where the concept of subjective consciousness is played down so that differences in and among signs can be interpreted exclusively in terms of the displacements of an anonymous desire (Lyotard 1971: 73-89). Actually, the question is not whether the imperialism of the sign preempts the examination of consciousness or whether the consideration of the thrusts of desire forbids the constitution of a thinking subject, but whether either of these enterprises automatically voids our concern for the integrity of an autonomous self-consciousness. One can certainly agree with Roland Barthes' statement that:

the goal of literary work (of literature as work) is to make the reader no longer a consumer, but a producer of the text. Our literature is characterized by the pitiless divorce which the literary institution maintains between the producer of the text and its user, between its owner and its customer, between its author and its reader. This reader is thereby plunged into a kind of idleness— he is intransitive; he is, in short, *serious*: instead of functioning himself, instead of gaining access to the magic of the signifier, to the pleasure of writing, he is left with no more than the poor freedom either to accept or reject the text: reading is nothing more than a *referendum* (Barthes 1975: 4).

One can also decide that the age when each text defines a one and only type of consciousness has passed, mainly because there no longer is any such thing as one text — or rather, because texts are *woven* from concurrent codes which parallel, overlap, and feed each other what is to constitute, in each case, new relevant information (the concept of relevancy changing with the semantic choices made at the outset or in the course of the reading). But the concept of semantic choice itself cannot be understood without the prior acceptance of an identical consciousness surveying the various possibilities of *meaning*. What is perhaps confusing in the *weaving approach* to the text is the implicit presupposition that all choices are indeed equal, that no text really propounds one idea— and concurrent with it, the suggestion that we, the readers, remain at all times conscious of the possiblilities of these contradictory choices (see Chapter 6). In other words, a critical attitude such as Barthes' actually implies the ongoing activity if a synthetic conscious-ness comprehending all these choices, what Starobinski (1970a: 154-169) calls the *hermeneutic circle* and which is the very locus of all subjective experiences, authorizing each and every one of them in their distinctive variety. As Barthes himself suggests:

the *writerly* text is *ourselves writing*, before the infinite play of the world (the world as function) is traversed, intersected, stopped, plasticized by some singular system (Ideology, Genus, Criticism) which reduces the plurality of entrances, the opening of networks, the infinity of languages (Barthes 1975: 6; emphasis added).

But the suggestion is only made in passing and is of no methodological consequence for the writing of *S/Z*. The fact is, the decision as to *which* choice should be made is only possible if the synthetic consciousness of the subject surveying the entire set of possible narrative choices is actually affected by the specific choice he is making. That is, if it is possible for the subject (the interlocutor/the reader) to take responsibility for the choice and to actualize it himself: to view himself as being both himself and one in a series of possible others (locutor/interlocutor; narrator/reader; hero/reader). Then, and only then, can he properly understand what he hears or what he reads and respond accordingly. To investigate such a possiblity is to seek to determine how the selection of a specific semantic context, origi-nally suggested in the synchronicity of all possible contexts considered together, affects the image the subject has of himself in the process of understanding. Now is the time to question the simplistic reduction effected by semiotics from a synthetic consciousness to the transcendental subject posited by linguistic and narrative universals. And the first point to be made is that, in semiotic studies, all narratives are always programmed *routinely*, without any consideration given to the programming activity itself: how the conscious mind actually creates significance out of the collection of a few data, and how the structures of form and content are nothing without the presence of a consciousness enacting them, of an act, an intention bringing these structures into existence at the time they are used and applied to a specific text (Starobinski: 1970a: 154-169).

To try and justify such a position may seem particularly hazardous after the blows handed to phenomenology in general and to the specific phenomenological method of J.-P. Richard by Derrida (1972). Grounding his whole analysis on a critique of the origin, the initiation of consciousness in Husserl's distinction between external *indication* (*index*) and internal *meaning* (*expression*), Derrida attempts to demonstrate how even *expression*, which is in no way supposed to be indexed by, or related to, any gestural element, nor to imply a context of outside reference, is only conceivable, in fact, in the context of a reference to its own expression, its own mode of being made noticeable. It requires the metaphysical assumption of an existence beginning with the voice that always *speaks* (however silent the speaker might have wished to remain) in the heart and in the mind of each of us: the voice: the φονή (Derrida 1973: chs. 2 and 3). Derrida further remarks that it is no accident that in his notes on language, apparently inspired by the desire to put an end to a long tradition of historicism and metaphysics and later to become the *Cours de linguistique générale*, Saussure actually refers to the authority of spoken language and considers written language as a mere derivative (an *expression*) of the spoken. From there on, the deconstruction of phenomenology as a metaphysics of presence is, of course, easily understandable: the search for an original consciousness stems from the desire to account for a beginning and represents nothing else for Derrida but an attempt to appropriate that which cannot be appropriated, except marginally, as it were, in the very sign eliciting the appropriation. In sum, the attempt to arrest and solidify the semiotic game by ascribing it to a beginning or a beginner can only appear symbolic of the fact that, in reading texts, one is essentially *deceived* by the illusion, the *mimesis* inherent in the idea of sign. One believes, not only that an acoustic image corresponds to a conceptual image, that there is an adequation of form and content, of texture and structure, that a cause always creates an effect, but also that this relation is itself to be mandated at once as an objective correlation *and* as a subjective determination that existence simply follows, or rather, flows, from one to the other (Derrida 1973: ch. 4). This criticism could be extended to all forms of phenomenological criticism: from Richard's *consciousness of experiential patterns*, to Poulet's *empathetic awareness* (1950) to Starobinski's *hermeneutic circle* (1970a) and even to Ingarden's *Triangle of interest* (1965) between the work, the

author, and the reader. Is this to say that phenomenological criticism is doomed?

Let us look more closely. The first thing that should be said about and for a phenomenological approach to literature is that it proposes a unified theory of the reader and of the author-narrator-creator. Far from believing that there is, on the one hand, a process of writing and, on the other, a process of reading, which are as separate as *writing creatively* is from *writing criticism*, a phenomenological approach substantiates a unity, a monad, which incorporates into the written text the two processes of writing and reading. No doubt reading a text is very different from writing it; but, when considered in the context of the *meaning* of a text, the two processes are concurrent. I am not suggesting that they are coterminous; rather that they supplement one another in a perspective where the awareness of a difference in the very signs of language, which is constitutive of meaning and confronts the writer as he elaborates his text, is compounded by the difference, the otherness of the writer to himself and to his reader. Anyone who writes knows that the consciousness of what he is writing is dependent on the consciousness of himself as other, at the same time that the constitution of a universe through denominations, verbs and deictics, entails the negation of worlds *other* than the one immediately called forth in the specific representation.

In this sense, most fictional narratives demonstrate *the possibilities in the play on symbolic otherness*. The use of "he" or "they" to refer to a hero or to heroes suggests both the presence of a speaker and a reference to a world to which he is supposed to be only a spectator. In the case of a first person narrative, however, the experiment is more daring because otherness is an explicit feature, as it were, of the person being and writing about himself. Let us take a specific example from Augustine:

Voluptates aurium tenacius me implicaverant et subjugaverant, sed resoluisti et liberasti me. Nunc in sonis, quos animant eloquia tua, cum suavi et artificiosa voce cantantur, fateor, aliquantulum adquiesco, non quidem ut haeream, sed ut surgam, cum volo. Attamen cum ipsis sententiis quibus vivunt ut admittantur ad me, quaerunt in corde meo nonnullius dignitatis locum, et vix eis praebeo congruentem. Aliquando enim plus mihi videor honoris eis tribuere, quam decet, dum ipsis sanctis dictis religiosius et

I used to be much more fascinated by the pleasures of a sound than the pleasures of smell. I was enthralled by them, but you broke my bonds and set me free. I admit that I still find some enjoyment in the music of hymns, which are alive with your praises, when I hear them sung by well-trained melodious voices. But I do not enjoy it so much that I cannot tear myself away. I can leave it when I wish. But if I am not to turn a deaf ear to music, which is the setting for the words which give it life, I must allow it a position of some honour in my heart, and I find it

ardentius sentio moveri animos nostros in flammam pietatis, cum ita cantantur, quam si non ita cantarentur, et omnes affectus spiritus nostri pro sui diversitate habere proprios modos in voce atque cantu, quorum nescio qua occulta familiaritate excitentur, sed delectatio carnis meae, cui mentem enervandam non oportet dari, saepe me fallit, dum rationi sensus non ita comitatur, ut patienter sit posterior, sed tantum, quia propter illam meruit admitti, etiam praecurrere, ac ducere conatur. Ita in his pecco non sentiens et postea sentio (Saint-Augustin 1961: 276).[1]

difficult to assign it its proper place. For sometimes I feel that I treat it with more honour than it deserves. I realize that when they are sung these sacred words stir my mind to greater religious fervour and kindle in me a more ardent flame of piety than they would if they were not sung; and I also know that there are particular modes in song and in the voice, corresponding to my various emotions and able to stimulate them because of some mysterious relationship between the two. But I ought not to allow my mind to be paralyzed by the gratification of my senses, which often leads me astray. For the senses are not content to take second place. Simply because I allow them their due, as adjuncts to reason, they attempt to take precedence and forge ahead of it, with the result that I sometimes sin in this way but am not aware of it until later (Augustine 1961: 238).

The appeal of this text is due to the dramatic, almost theatrical quality of the narrative displaying various layers or periods in the history of the narrator's self, while the same narrator's active consciousness embraces them and incorporates them all together into one single *persona*: the *I* which stands behind all the operations in the text, as well as in the rest of the *Confessions* ("I used to be... I was enthralled... I admit that I still find..."), and which seems to underlie, better, to support, each specific statement with somewhat of a blanket guarantee of the indestructible *presence* of the narrator. Actually, this guarantee of presence, which is most apparent in first person narratives, but which is also built into every narrative, goes beyond a mere certification of the narrator's existence. It represents an attempt to ascribe to the hypothetical identity of a single person the different *voices* enacted in the course of the narrative and thus gives the illusion that this identity remains forever safe, protected from the vicissitudes of time and speech, albeit only produced by them. In Augustine's text, this identity is experienced in the form of a trinity. There is one person making the statements, looking over the actions of another person in the past. And then there is also a third person putting everything in perspective ("with the result that I sometimes sin in this way but am not aware of it until later") and whose confrontation with the past allows him to realize who he really is ("I can leave it *when I wish*"). But no amount of linguistic evidence can account for the effects of this varied experience. For suppose we attempted to base our distinction of each of the above *persons* on a classification of their statements as code-restricted utterances, for example "I used to be much more fascinated" ("Voluptates tenacius me implicaverant") = *statement of fact relating to a particular state of the speaker combined with an explicit judgment*; "you broke my bonds and set me free" ("resoluisti et liberasti me") = *statement of fact with intensification of the reference to the subject as object* (use of the perfect), we would only be able to prove that language formulates identity as a function of difference and opposition (for example present/perfect; *I/you*) and that the *other*, therefore, is but the expression of this difference as it relates to the process of the subject becoming conscious. God is precisely this *other* who allows the speaker (Augustine) to become conscious of himself by causing him to review his change from past to present, from an (old) life of sin to a (new) life of Christian virtue, and even if God can see and hear all that man does because nothing is ever hidden from Him, man-the-sinner still has to speak forth: *he must accomplish the confession*, so that the ears of God will listen to him (*audiant aures templi tui*). But such a reductive view of the divine presence would not really help us understand the experience of the *Confessions. It is the very substance of that experience which must now be elucidated.*

And the experience comes in two stages. First, there is a statement of recognition, *in time and place*, of how the subject is affected by the external world ("implicaverant . . . Nunc . . . adquiesco"). This realization, which is partially judgmental, is expressed in various degrees of semantic investment— from "fascinated" ("implicaverant") to "enthralled" ("subjugaverant"). Second, there is the consideration of how this experience relates to the rest of the subject's life— "But I do not enjoy it so much that I cannot tear myself away" ("non quidem ut haeream"). In between, there is the reality of an emotion which remains too precious for words — "a greater religious fervour than if they were not sung" ("religiosius et ardentius . . . quam si non ita cantarentur"), and which, because it is too precious for words, often passes unnoticed, until the subject recognizes it for what it is and experiences guilt—*"not aware of it until later"* (*"postea sentio"*). In other words, for all the efforts of the zealous Christian, who believes in the perfect adequation of what will be termed later *adequatio rei and intellectus*, there remains something unexplained, which Augustine ascribes to an overfilling of the senses and which Saint Thomas will see as proof of the sacred, indeterminate specificity of each individual human being (Bobik 1965: 137-138). In this passage, as in many others, Augustine displays great caution: he is aware that emotions do escape definition and that simply to force them into a concept of the intellect might restrict their flow and do more harm than good. As he remarks:

Aliquando autem hanc ipsam fallaciam inmoderatius cavens erro nimia severitate, sed valde interdum, ut melos omne cantilenarum suavium, quibus Davidicum psalterium frequentatur, ab auribus meis removeri velim atque ipsius ecclesiae (Saint-Augustin 1961: 277).	Sometimes, too, from over-anxiety to avoid this particular trap, I make the mistake of being too strict. When this happens, I have no wish but to exclude from my ears, and from the ears of the Church as well, all the melody of those lovely chants to which the Psalms of David are habitually sung (Augustine 1961: 238).

The fact is, something remains unexplained:

Aliquando enim plus mihi videor. . . et omnes affectus spiritus nostri pro sui diversitate habere proprios modos in voce atque cantu, quorum nescio qua occulta familiaritate excitentur (Saint-Augustin 1961: 276).	and I also know . . . that there are particular modes in song and in the voice, corresponding to my various emotions and able to stimulate them because of some mysterious relationship between the two (Augustine 1961: 238).

The awareness of a correspondence between the *song, voices* and the *emotions* does not include the experience. It simply recognizes the lack of nomination based on difference: *some mysterious relationship.* The absolute gratification of the senses goes beyond words, and Augustine invites his readers to empathize with him ("weep with me and weep for me"), because, not knowing whether or not to hold back his senses, *he has become a problem to himself.* What is meant by this *problem to himself* is that there remains in his consciousness a side of his existence unexplained, and it is this remainder, much more than the rest of the *Confessions* (the joy to feel with and inside God; the desire to bring the entire world to God, and so on), which gives them their true meaning as confessions. Not only does Augustine have to confess his past errors, his life of debauchery, but he also has to admit that, for all his progress, there is still an important part of him that does not conform to God's desire and his own sense of perfection: that which is mentioned here with respect to the magic of music reappears time and again throughout the tenth book in the general context of an overactivity of the senses (see also *Confessions* 1 and 2). To come out, however, and *confess* (in the original sense: *to converse with God*), this very fact atones for its strangeness, and it is precisely the imperfection remaining in the *otherness* of the narrator himself and ascribed to the omnipotent presence of the Creator in the speech of the confessant which ensures that the latter is totally forgiven, whether or not he can spell out his sins. In fact, he can even ask to be forgiven for all the other sins he may have committed, but which he does not remember. The presence of God provides the subject with the totality of consciousness which he himself lacks. In cases where he is missing something, the simple confession of it effectuates this totality ("But I beg you, O Lord, my God, to look upon me and listen to me").

The point here is not simply to suggest that the discourse of the believer is based on the fiction of a total and transparent consciousness which, modeled on God's, rejoices in knowing its limits and transcending them at the same time, something akin to what Merleau-Ponty describes as the liberating function of a synthesis between the *in-itself* and the *for-itself* (1962: 453–456). It is, rather, to suggest the double goal of the *Confessions*: (1) to bring God into the circle of one's existence as it appears, represented to itself— the concept, so to speak, to vouch for the truth, the reality of one's own image. What comes out of this somewhat circular quest is the verification that, in the latter case, the meaning of language lies beyond the grasp of language—a paradox which Augustine attempts to expose. This discovery, which had long ago been made by the mystics is, of course, threatening to those who believe in the order of signs and symbols and shy away from unmediated contact with the world because, in the tradition of the Bible and the Church, the absence of clearly identifiable signs of medication can only be a *sign* of the Devil. Otherness then is required as presence in, or rather to, consciousness, while it remains well beyond the understanding of reason. This is to say that the ideology of the sign can only justify itself by limiting the mind's ability to *comprehend the presence which helps substantiate it*. This presence, however, the ineffable sponsor and guarantor of the sign, remains a fictitious dogma, only so long as one does not see that language is not only a system of signs, *but also, and primarily through speech, a phenomenon*. Following Merleau-Ponty (1964: 84–97), one could say that because we can only objectify language as a system through the operation of a speaking subject, language as the Saussurean *langue* can only exist in relation to a particular speaker. Which is to say three things at once: that it is the phenomenon of this particular speech which establishes the sign; that this sign is only a sign because it is also a phenomenon; and finally, what semiotics is totally incapable of accounting for, that this phenomenon is essentially significant at the moment of, or in conjunction with, its appearance, its beginning: *it is* — and yet, this existence is never explained.

From what I have been saying about Augustine in particular, it is obvious that the effectiveness of autobiographical texts *depends* on the effect created by the constant use of the first person. Because this first person can only be defined through the otherness inherent in the self, it graces communication with the sophistication of yet another subjectivity, as each and every time the past is relived, experienced again through a different present, the speaker (the autobiographer) refers to a different image of himself, to a different *persona*. Much has been written on the modes of autobiography and this is not the place to argue the merits of phenomenology as the mode of personal inquiry par excellence. My purpose in using the instance of the first person was to introduce some of the phenomenological implications of a structural approach to language. Let us now expand our discussion.

From Saussure and structural linguistics, we have learned that language is essentially to be studied, not as knowledge oriented toward the discovery of a beginning and determined by a proximity to these origins — Hebrew, for the Port-Royal grammarians; Sanskrit, for the nineteenth-century comparatists — but rather, as communication, thus substituting a horizontal reference (between addressor and addressee) for a vertical one (between God and the various forms of Babel). Instead of leading to a general consideration of the substance of linguistic messages, this emphasis on communication has generally served as a convenient framework, if not an excuse, for the specific study of the various causes and effects, agents and patients, parts and subparts of the linguistic exchange, without much attention being paid to the nature of communication and its signs. Thus, if we take the scheme proposed by Jakobson to account for the six functions of language (Jakobson 1960: 353ff), it is immediately obvious that (1) his thesis is in line with other attempts to avoid the hypothesis of a monolithic structure of language — one where contexts (those of the addressor, of the addressee, and of their common reference), do not in any way interfere with or modify the account that can be made of any communication; (2) the substance of the argument is to point out, not so much the peculiarities of language as modes, but as interrelated functions, where no message can be elaborated, much less communicated, without all or almost all of the functions involved, including those of referential context, of code, contact and message; (3) finally, if communication is at all to be evaluated, it is through an assessment of the proper hierarchy of the various functions involved, for example the emotive function corresponding to the activity of the speaker (the addressor), or the conative function corresponding to the activity of the receiver (the addressee).

On the first point, it is clear that there is in the attack against the monolithic structure of language an attempt to take one's distance from all restrictive definitions of language (transformational grammar limited to the sentence structure; stylistics limited to consideration of how form in effect regulates content; even a psycho- or sociolinguistics where nonlinguistic considerations are allowed to regulate linguistic concepts). This attempt is well in line with the structural attitude that a work, a sentence, a text, are not to be studied from the mere classification of linguistic data, but that these data are actually organized, that is, they function, on the principle that every linguistic communication is goal-oriented, and not the representation of a fixed, immovable scheme. In every case, however, even if we admit that the orientation of a message is determined by an emphasis on any one or two or three of the six functions combined, we must notice that what Jakobson calls *emphasis* is less an emphasis *per se* (which would bring it within the realm of the speaking subject), than the *direct result of an emphasis*. Which means that the linguist is actually translating in the objective terms of the whole linguistic system differences in the specific orientation (expectation/volition/wish, and so on) of the addressor or the addressee. And this specific orientation, which Jakobson urges us to read after the model of a simple emphasis, escapes the purview of the linguist, because what really strikes us in a communication process is not the typicality of a message, what would be called its *reductive commonalty*, but the fact that I or somebody else conveys it, and that it is assimilated by the receiver (and sometimes even by the speaker) as pertaining only to his personal situation, as belonging to his own field of reference. Each message is thus given a new goal which makes it different indeed from any other. For instance, in the above example, where the conative and the emotive function coincide, the meaning of Augustine's statements becomes clear *only after* this coincidence (Augustine talks to himself through God) has been established and the message is perceived as precisely dependent on this *mysterious* coincidence. We then have to revise our statement that language is goal-oriented, *to read that it is the consciousness of language which is goal-oriented*, and that the meaning of a message is dependent on the apparent realization of the consciousness of that goal.

Which brings us to the next point: it is the appearence, the conscious realization of meaning which certifies the sign, and not the reverse. In other words, *signs appear as the results of intentions*. In this sense, Jakobson's emphasis on the code (message → code = poetic function) and his privileging the poetic function (of all the functions of language, it is the only one to operate in a closed circuit between code and message) represent an attempt at correcting the failure of linguistics in the area of the expressivity in language. Indeed, they imply a capability of language to deliver more than one could ever hope to account for by studying the specific contexts of communication (context of the speaker, of the receiver, of their common phraseology); and as was made clear by the example of Augustine, it suggests that language can set itself on stage and display the surplus or the *supplement* which it acquires in this manner.[2] It could also be suggested that Jakobson's theory is related to the whole Russian formalist tradition, where the perception of stylistic effects is explained by the principle of *foregrounding*: it is the consciousness of a difference as against the background of commonly used and expected sociolinguistic structures which authenticates the ongoing literary process. But the point is: it is precisely because there is such a consciousness that a work actually communicates something special to us every time we read it. For in addition to a sequence of actions which can easily be charted on a semantic or syntactic model and which would seem to make a specific narrative totally congruent with dozens of others, in terms of its relationship to an overall language of narratives and its dependence on narrative universals, the reading of a narrative always suggests to us more than a repetition or a modification of existing contexts and relationships. It brings us something new in the form of what could now be called *the presence in the representation.* Now, Greimas and others have proposed that the structure of any narrative is like a dramatic scene or a spectacle, where linguistic functions (of subject, object, attribute) *behave* like the signs or the indexes of physical space (Greimas 1970: 157-183). The action unfolds as the plot takes us from one space to another: the hero (the subject), deprived of a part of himself, sets about to retrieve it, generally by retrieving a lost lover or parent taken away and detained in another place. Such a theory, however, merely *dramatizes* what remains on the whole a symbolic reduction. What I mean by *representation* is something else. Every narrative not only offers a scene which can be staged or dramatized in various ways, *but it is itself that scene.* It carries with it the subliminal message *that it is indeed a story* and that this story functions, that it is successful, because of the translation of an authorial interest into the narratee's own. In other words the staging process functions not only at the level of a signified, of a referential context (to which Greimas' syntactic and semantic categories pertain), but also at the level of a signifying process, where the display of signs is preceded by a display of the narrator's involvement with actually delivering the narrative, and implies the recognition of this involvement by the reader.

Until recently, however, structuralists and poststructuralists have ignored this involvement and have reduced it to the mere presentation of narrative choices — thus merely indexing the narrator's own discourse in the sequence of historical facts and assessing his reliability in the process (see Genette 1972; Booth 1961). Since it is the involvement which illuminates the choice and makes it significant, and not the reverse, it appears to lie beyond the reach of structural analysis, even beyond the reach of words. It could, in fact, prove to be silent, and thus be impossible to define clearly. Yet, I am not advocating a criticism of the ineffable, which would amount to nothing else but a return to the psychologisms of the old school of literary aesthetics. The silences are traceable in the text, not in the form of rhetorical devices, nor in the terms of universal, albeit anonymous, narrative structures, for instance the logic of our daily life or that of the prevailing ideology or counterideology, but outside the path of signification proper, in the margin, so to speak. In other words, in order to be communicated, the intent to communicate must be given form and substance in the universe of our knowledge, of our culture: it must appear an integral part of the narrative *exemplum* (see Chapter 10). However, to reduce this intent to the representation of the action (the *exemplum*) designed to illustrate it and to relate it to our context without examining it for what it is, would be to disregard how the text solicited our attention in the first place (see Chapter 6). To put it more simply, perhaps: all narrative texts perform two distinct functions which we must consider separately. On the one hand, their function is to inform us of a determinate sequence of actions, and thus to record various kinds of histories; and on the other hand, their function is also to appear as communicative acts: they must make themselves understood by superimposing, as it were, on the reference in the anonymous narrative structure another special representation of *what it is the narrator is talking about*.

Let us pause for a moment. In the process of elaborating yet another theory of phenomenological criticism, it might appear as though I were suggesting that we go back to the unexpressed or unconscious intentions of the author and that we explore hidden or subliminal material underlying the text; so that my phenomenological critique of structuralism and semiotics would rest on nothing but a thinly veiled psychocriticism with Freudian or Lacanian undertones. But this is not the case. What I have in mind is to explore in literature and literary criticism the points where language and consciousness intersect, and *prior to the time when a consciousness* (any consciousness — the writer's, the reader's, or the critic's) attempts to contextualize a text, to make it familiar in order to cope with the estrangement produced by the confrontation with another subject's consciousness. In other words, I would like to suggest that not everything in a text can be justified in terms of pragmatic choices based on linguistic criteria of commutability or noncommutability (if the hero does A, he does not do *B* and must proceed to *C*) or logical criteria of noncontradiction (if *A* entails *B*, the hero cannot choose to do *A* and not do *B*). The issue is not commutability *vs.* noncommutability — an issue which would bring us back to a universe defined in terms of conscious choices already made and allow us, therefore, to disregard the problem of what precisely constitutes the choice for consciousness. It is whether there is room in criticism for a critique of intentions, in relation, not to choices already made, *but to choices in process, before they are actualized*: for a critique of language as appearance (see Lewis 1966).

This would seem to suggest that I am identifying with the critical heritage of Mallarmé and Hopkins and following those critics who maintain that literature always falls short of what it really has to say, because it remains caught in a circle, resulting from the Hegelian *impossibility of saying things as they are* — the mere act of writing *about* something precluding the possibility of writing the thing itself (Merleau-Ponty 1948: 125–167). But I would like to take my distance from these critics as well, because I am not interested in ineffable realities, but rather, in the consciousness of existence, as it appears at the beginning of writing. To this, however, one can also object that the attempt to describe *the phenomenon in the sign and to communicate the presence of it*, apart from the narrative that certifies it, is doomed to failure because even in trying to approximate what precedes articulated, organized language, we are governed by the very rules of articulated, organized language, and the only avenue left open to us is to write a text that offers its own commentary — a text which deconstructs itself in the Derridean fashion of *Glas* (Derrida 1974). But I would further respond by pointing out that such words as *presence, appearance, representation* and even *energy* are proof indeed that our attempt to postulate an entity *before* the sign can only lead to confusion, and that the conventions of semiotics and linguistics do not provide us with the means successfully to challenge language on its own terms, since language *is master of everything*. In other words, I am contending that approximation and confusion of the unsaid is what most every criticism avoids, and what I intend to tackle. I am not suggesting that this unsaid is already said elsewhere, in the unconscious, and that it is occulted by the restrictive mechanisms of conscious language; nor am I suggesting that it exists somewhere as the-Thing-which-never-gives-itself alluded to in Freud's *Interpretation of Dreams* (1961: 509–622). *I am suggesting that most texts, and especially narrative fictions, generate the sentiment of a form of existence, the hope of a reality unmediated by words.* This reality, however, is nothing but a *representation*, a duplicate, the product of a process in which signs simultaneously suggest and deny a presence. As the French philosopher Emmanuel Lévinas states:

> Every sign is, in this sense, a trace. In addition to what the sign signifies, it represents the passage of him who delivered the sign. The meaning [*la signification*] of the trace duplicates the meaning of the sign emitted for communicative purposes (1967: 200).

In texts where a narrator *points out* to a particular world in which to involve us (a fiction, a novel), in the mere operation of *pointing out*, the reader's attention is called twice, as it were, and he is invited to contemplate something he has never seen before: objects, things and people, *ek-sisting* out of the grille of organized signs and now making these signs necessary to their existence. We shall later see how practically all descriptive processes issue from this experience in literature. But, for the moment, let us just continue to investigate the experience by taking a specific example from *Madame Bovary*:

La chambre, au rez-de-chaussée, la seule du logis, avait au fond contre la muraille un large lit sans rideaux, tandis que le pétrin occupait le côté de la fenêtre, dont une vitre était raccommodée avec un soleil de papier bleu. Dans l'angle, derrière la porte, des brodequins à clous luisants étaient rangés sous la dalle du lavoir, près d'une bouteille pleine d'huile qui portait une plume à son goulot; un *Mathieu Laensberg* traînait sur la cheminée poudreuse, parmi des pierres à fusil, des bouts de chandelle et des morceaux d'amadou. Enfin, la dernière superfluité de cet appartement était une Renommée soufflant dans ses trompettes, image découpée sans doute à même quelque prospectus de parfumerie, et que six pointes à sabot clouaient au mur (Flaubert 1966: 126).

The ground floor bedroom — the only bedroom in the house — had a wide uncurtained bed against its rear wall; the window wall (one pane was mended with a bit of wrapping paper) was taken up by the kneading-trough. In the corner behind the door was a raised slab for washing, and under it stood a row of heavy boots with shiny hobnails and a bottle of oil with a feather in its mouth. A Mathieu Laensberg almanac lay on the dusty mantelpiece among gun flints, candle ends and a bit of tinder. And as a final bit of clutter there was a figure of Fame blowing her trumpets — a picture probably cut out of a perfume advertisement and now fastened to the wall with six shoe tacks (Flaubert 1957: 105).

In this true picture of destitution, where Emma Bovary's appearance seems totally incongruous ("Leon walked around the room; it seemed to him a strange sight, this elegant lady in her nankeen gown here among all this squalor"), Flaubert has managed to convey the impression of utter poverty through a paradoxical crowding of information. We understand that the room is bare, because the text is filled with its space ("the ground floor . . . rear wall . . . window wall") and devoid of all the objects that usually fill a room — where are the usual table, chair, dresser, mirror, of bourgeois rooms? The impression, the representation, of empty space is attained through the marking, the designating of areas of the room and the filling of those areas with single objects which barely have anything in common and whose relation to, and function in, the room is sometimes hard to establish ("Fame", "heavy boots . . . a bottle of oil with a feather in its mouth"). In a sense, much of the narrator's energy is bound in the process of designating and indicating, as if what the room had to offer was precisely empty space, against which to project various plane figures. What has happened?

To answer this, we must take a look at the way in which the designating process is articulated. In most texts, this process is only a small part of the overall signifying process which ends in the completion of a satisfactory reference (the objects pointed out only *carry meaning* if they refer us to an already known context). In this passage from *Madame Bovary*, however, it seems that the designating process (notice the deictics: "*in the corner behind . . . under*") stands alone and that it is alone responsible for meaning. The perception of the objects actually in the room is made totally contingent upon an almost gestural process of designation by the narrator's insistence that their ancillary capacity (their function as objects or instruments) not be understood by a reference to their use in daily life, but only fictitiously, as it were, by the mere reference to their position in the room — to the very locus of their designation. Which leaves us uncertain as to their function at all. For if their function is simply to fulfill the designation of the descriptor, without reference to their function in daily life (in the proper world of reference), then are they not superfluous? Flaubert himself seems to admit this, when he decides to cap his description with "la dernière superfluité" ("Fame"); the baroque picture of a cheap "Fame" has apparently nothing to do with the rest of the scene; and besides, it comes from an advertisement for perfumes. But, in effect, because of the way it has been presented to us, everything seems superfluous. The only objects whose reference to the world of daily use is automatic (the bed and the kneading-trough) are purposefully devalued: their presentation is almost accidental, as the areas designated for them could have been occupied by almost anything else. The "window wall" is taken up with "the kneading-trough" and the bed is *without* the customary curtains. The wall is like any other, except that one pane is *missing* (or the resident is too poor to replace it). As for the *shoes*, they have been placed "under" the sink, as if the location itself expressed a negative connotation. Finally, the almanac, the *Mathieu Laensberg* (another typological, albeit meaningless, object), "lay" ("traînait")[3] in the midst of other objects — "des morceaux d'amadou," and so on. In sum, the feeling of

irrelevancy— which we immediately *interpret* as pertinent to the representation of poverty — is caused, *first and foremost*, by a system of designation
which undercuts the fiction of the proper reference. Because the objects
described in the room lack substance and function, the lack itself is what
gives them meaning. What we have here is a true picture of poverty and
destitution.

Pulling our threads together, we can see in this passage the duplication at
work in representation. First, the fact that objects are ostentatiously located
in the room Emma is entering ("come in. . . your little girl's asleep inside")
suggests a rule for all descriptions: in order simply to appear, reality must
first be set and indicated before it is referenced and made wholly meaningful.[4] Let us make our rule more precise: although usually considered to be
inextricably linked in the linguistic process, designation and reference must
remain distinctly separate for a descriptive context simply to appear as
against the narrative context. Here, for instance, the deictics designating the
walls ("the rear wall. . . the window wall") can easily be distinguished from
a qualifier like "wide uncurtained" referencing the bed where one expects to
see the baby Emma has come to visit and perhaps retrieve. Making our rule
even tighter, we could say that any description entails a division of space and
cannot do without the deictics which are the prime markers of space.

Second, objects and persons so located appear different from one another
only because of an ongoing process of dividing and locating inherent in the
designation (the wide uncurtained bed against its rear wall . . . the
kneading-trough against the window wall) and not because of any symbolic
meaning of their own. This ongoing process which articulates the reader's
vision, as he follows the narrator and adopts his character's (Leon's) point of
view, determines a representation where objects and persons are less
referenced to a pragmatic narrative context. (What is this beautiful lady doing
in a hovel like this? She has come to fetch her baby), than *designated* to
live-for-our-consciousness, that is, to play a part on the stage which has
been assigned to them and where the spectator, at a loss precisely for
reference, for meaning, cannot fail to denote dramatic irony: "taken up. . .
with a feather . . . lay". The irony is, moreover, totally explicit and
unmistakable in the image of a "figure of Fame blowing her trumpets"
("une Renommée soufflant dans ses trompettes"). What does Fame have to
do with anything here? A poetic abstraction in a room so painfully, so
concretely bare? But the answer is that Flaubert wanted this to appear as
symbolic of the reality confronting Emma and Leon upon their entering the
room: a reality so unreal that it appears to raise the question of its own
existence. Flaubert's detractors, however, defending, like the *Procureur de*

l'Empereur, the canons of established morality, all the members of the *Tribunal Correctionel* where *Madame Bovary* is being tried, feel justified in attacking what they see as *le tour de phrase le plus équivoque*: the *perverse* way in which *excesses* in the description, due to an expert manipulation of the designating process, suggest the narrator's contempt for the vacuousness of the bourgeois referent implied in his presentation of the other side of Romanticism. The room is as empty as Emma's heart. Naturally, the critics are on safe ground, criticizing the narrator for excesses of form (*le tour le plus équivoque*) rather than excesses of content. Soon, however, their argument turns to the impropriety of the material itself. They move from a discussion of *the intent to signify* to *the value of the sign itself and its referents*: that is to say, from the criticism of the implicit provocation in the *tour équivoque* to that of the *"réalité sans voile"* subsumed in it:

Jusqu'ici, la beauté de cette femme avait consisté dans sa grâce, dans sa tournure, dans ses vêtements; enfin elle vient de vous être montrée sans voile, et vous pouvez dire si l'adultère ne l'a pas embellie (Flaubert 1966: 378; "Réquisitoire").	Up to now, the beauty of this woman had consisted in her gracefulness, her posture, her clothing; in the end, she has just been shown to you *without veil,* and you can say whether adultery has not increased her beauty.

But let us not forget the intent behind the representation: the *tour équivoque.* The *tour équivoque,* by placing a wedge between designation and reference, subverts the presentation of *things-as-they-are-supposed-to-appear* and exposes an ideology where the relation between things and their signs is predicated on the occultation of the true reference in the designating process. It is because in Flaubert's description the mere naming and placing of persons and things takes the place of interpretation that Emma's presence in it — as incomprehensible as the shabbinness of the room itself — can become symbolic of the avarice of the bourgeois class in its attempt to treat men like commodities, or of the price the innocent and the oppressed must pay for the silly dreams of their masters (Emma, who spends all her money and time on her adventures, cannot take care of her own child). The bourgeois view of the world, exemplified in the speech of the *Prosécuteur* at Flaubert's trial, is jeopardized by its being set on stage and exposed for what it is, a fiction. The fiction maintained by the prosecution that signs, which are supposed to be universal and arbitrary, are actually bound to the communication of certain, limited signified or signata, is now clearly exposed:

Cette morale stigmatise la littérature réaliste, non pas parce qu'elle peint les passions: la haine, la vengeance,	This morality indicts realist literature, not because it depicts passions: hatred, vengeance, love; the world lives only

l'amour; le monde ne vit que là-dessus, et l'art doit les peindre; mais quand elle les peint sans frein, sans mesure. L'art sans règle n'est plus l'art; c'est comme une femme qui quitterait tout vêtement (Flaubert 1966: 388 "Réquisitoire").

from these and art must depict them; but when it depicts them without restraint, without measure. Art without laws is no longer art; it is like a woman shedding all her clothes.

But as soon as the narrator engages in descriptions which will jeopardize this principle, as soon as he attempts to go beyond the accepted presentation of the referent and expose, through a carefully orchestrated designation, the fiction that it is, then his representation is sensed as dangerously true, as true as the poverty of the house to which Emma's·baby has been relegated.

After having shown that it is only by becoming conscious of the *representative value* of the sign that we can transcend the limitations of an objective communication, I would like to conclude with two remarks: one pertaining to the collusion of the sign with a referential system of (economic) production underlying it, and the other, pertaining to the role of irony in a return to the phenomenality of the sign.

    One of the reasons why semiotics has been unsuccessful in accounting for instances of representation in the narrative is that it is itself but an expression of the ideology of a constant, albeit uncritical, representation. In other words, in a context where literature and art are expected to render reality *only up to a point*, the presentation of this reality will be limited to an exchange of signata, firmly anchored to, and limited by, their designation. Because, in the designating process, one is less concerned with experiencing reality than with indicating it and locating it, any overemphasis on the designating process will lead to the production of *clichés* of the sort to be found in *Madame Bovary*: representations whose meaning is only in their production and accumulation. Thus, again, the use of persons and things as mere designata, in a text where the accumulation of *tours équivoques* bares a reality never *sans voile*, offers an insight into the covert ways an economic system (capitalism) designates persons and things as empty commodities in its ongoing search for profit. The fiction of a *veiled* reality defended by the *Procureur* and exposed by Flaubert is as alienated as the world of bourgeois capitalism it stands for. Now, because semiotics has been attempting to structure a world where subjective differences can all be resolved into a supposedly objective and arbitrary system of designation, it has been playing the part of the prosecution and performing a repressive task, which will always keep it from investigating specific differences in the speech of the person. Indeed, as a part of bourgeois ideology, it has been articulated

on the assumption that there is in the world of communication an established commonalty of signs, that their signata are indeed equivalent: ready
to be exchanged, and their referents, relocated. It matters little what is depicted, provided that the object or the person depicted is reducible to basic
features which make that exchange possible (see Baudrillard 1976: 309-321).

This is where one can appreciate the importance of irony in the constitution of representation. One could pursue the above critique from a
Marxist point of view and work toward the elaboration of a historical
dialectics and its integration to the semiotic process. Or one could
propose that the limits of semiotics are determined by its rejection of the
speaking subject as the locus of a speaking desire, and suggest with
Deleuze and Guattari (1972) that one must follow the manifestations of
desire through systems of production and consumption that are endlessly
interrelated (the *machines*). Or one can decide that semiotics fails the test
of description because it is caught in the multiplication, the proliferation,
of the sign without ever managing to relate sign and person; and that
what is needed instead is to develop a critical consciousness which can
conceive of differences as *essential* to the constitution of the subject and
understand that in order to proceed to a state of meaningful objectivity it
needs to accept the process of those differences as a game. *It must be
ironical*.

Irony is that which enables us to take stock of all our communicative acts,
and at the same time, to stand back in the realization that our relationship to
the world is both one of the articulation of those signs and one of the
consciousness of the role, of the fiction, of those signs. Irony, which is
Flaubert's true weapon and one misunderstood by the prosecutor, thus
appears to function at the level of semiotic form. Through the description of
things *only as they are supposed to be*, it exposes the fiction which is a part of our
sign production, while it also plays on the idea of a reality *sans voile* itself as
the ultimate fiction: that which is of little substance as it can only be grasped
through the excessive designation and display of a *veiled* reality. While
appearing to denote an extremely pessimistic view of the world and a
concept of the writer as peddler of dreams and fantasies, this fiction, which
Nietzsche would have ascribed to an extramoral sense, is actually necessary
to expose the ways in which we are stuck in our modes of reference.[5] To be
sure, this reading differs from traditional readings of Flaubert's works as a
monument to *realism*. But it is in accordance with Flaubert's own reading of
himself as an author constantly searching for words, for signs, which would
enable him to write "a book *on nothing* . . . holding itself together by the
internal strength of its style" [un livre sur rien . . . qui se tiendrait

lui-même par la force interne de son style"] (Flaubert 1926: 345).[6] It has, moreover, the advantage of emphasizing the artifice of literature: an artifice which can in turn be experienced as inherent to the phenomenality of the sign and be of interest to the semiotician to the extent that it helps him understand how we are bound by the limits of our communication and must become aware of our own activity as we go on building sign systems.

NOTES

1. The edition quoted actually follows the custom of printing *v*s as *u*s. For the convenience of the reader this has been changed.
2. On the theory of the *supplement*, see Derrida (1976: 141-164).
3. The French word *traînait* indicates human negligence; and the nonverbal English phrase "with a feather" renders the French "portait une plume", which suggests a masquerading mood.
4. For a theoretical discussion of designation *vs.* reference, see Chapter 12, note 5.
5. The most seminal reflections on irony can be found, albeit elaborated from a totally different point of view, in Nietzsche's "Gay Science" 354 and 356 (Nietzsche 1910). There, arguing against the possibility of ever knowing ourselves as individuals in a world (*a herd*) of communal signs, Nietzsche suggest that most of Western culture's weaknesses can be traced to the unqualified acceptance of signs as *media* and to their use in bad faith to confer an appearance of existence to functions in the community and thereby develop a dominant ideology based on *role faith*. But it might very well be that, any abuse of role consciousness notwithstanding, *comprehension* of the world of signs (whose possibility Nietzsche denies) can only be gained through an ironic acceptance of our fictitious posture in the field of knowledge and (the game of) communication. For the context of this debate see *Poétique* 5 (1971).
6. For classical interpretations of Flaubert see Brombert (1966) and Hemmings (1974).

8

Daphnis and Chloe: The Story of Mimesis

Daphnis and Chloe today belongs to Maurice Ravel. Longus has been forgotten. His text is of interest only to specialists.

This pastoral work is not unique. Without knowing its date, one sees clearly that it has something of the bucolic and Alexandrine idyll: for poets, Daphnis is the ancestral patron of shepherds and Longus' text allows a glimpse here and there of the influence of Theocritus and Virgil,[1] and also something of the Greek romances of Chariton and especially Heliodorus. Even if Daphnis and Chloe never leave their island of Lesbos, the role of pirates and soldiers, the function of money in an essentially capitalist society under the inane appearances of the pastoral, and a certain conception of love triumphant remain the elements common to the picaresque and the pastoral. One can also see, as in Apuleius, the heritage of the Milesian Tales, where the gods of magic fight over the heroicomical destiny of the characters: in Longus, the god Eros and the god Pan seem to initiate two rustic lovers to the rites of a complicated biology and physics. One may want to find an echo of the orators of the Middle and Late Roman Empire, of the authors of *Quaestiones* and *Suasoriae* who encode the elements of the game, the hunt and custody of love into a system of rhetorical probabilities:[2] with Longus it is only under certain conditions that Daphnis and Chloe can be together and consummate the act of love, and his text defines their movement according to these probabilities. One also rediscovers in this pastoral the programmings of the new comedy, where abductions and the abandonment of children are only the prelude to opportune meetings: both Daphnis and Chloe are rich and from good families, and it is a bit on the model of Menander and Terentius that their real origins are finally revealed, making possible the happy accomplishment of their sylvan destiny.

All that has been said so far is only a matter of conjecture. There remains the work itself, with its pastoral imitation of life: a *mimesis* where characters derive their own self-image from the functioning of an elaborate narrative system displaying an ideology of the pastoral genre, while also suggesting the reality of the historical drama concealed in the fiction.

1. THE SYSTEM OF MIMESIS

Longus begins his story of love by reminding us that it is entirely contained in the space of a certain *fiction* (painting) that he purports to have seen himself at Lesbos ("εἰκόνα γραπτὴν ἱστορίαν ἔρωτος"). The reference to an earlier *mimesis* — instead of historical, daily reality — is certainly a usual procedure for the storytellers of that time, but here it takes on a particular importance.[3]

Daphnis and Chloe is the story of the birth of the emotions, feelings, and finally, of the gestures of love between two foundlings, the shepherd Daphnis and the shepherdess Chloe. The two young people, after many tribulations— herdsmen's jealousy, invasions by pirates, their discovery by their natural parents, who are of the rich bourgeoisie of Mitylene — can finally taste of the mutual happiness they long for; and they choose to return to the country. At the very moment when they have the possibility of being integrated into a story, into a given society, at the moment the satisfied reader could consider that *fiction* gives way to reality, the author takes his characters and returns them to their sheep: Daphnis and Chloe will live happily ever after in the country. The tale closes in upon itself. Nothing out of the ordinary here. Propp (1958: 107 ff.) and Lord (1965: 242-259) have already shown that the end of the tale or the epos is marked by a return to, and a confirmation of, a prenarrative situation through various devices (punishment of the villain, reward of the hero, marriage of the lovers, and so on). Let us now see how this representation is detailed in the fictional world of Longus.

The development of the intrigue is interrupted four times by the insertion of an exemplary narrative, which is supposed to bear some relation to the action in progress. There are three narratives concerning Pan and the Nymphs on the one hand,[4] and one narrative involving the discovery of Love-Eros on the other. Because the three narratives concerning Pan are reversed representations of the fourth concerning Eros, the double image of a pursuing(Pan)-pursued(Eros) cannot be reduced, neither can the *mimesis* be integrated without the aid of an operator as competent as he is undisputed: Dionysophanes — observer-observed — who appears at the end of the story and whose discovery foretells that of Daphnis' and Chloe's.[5] Love pursued surrenders to Love pursuing, according to the Dionysian rite. We shall have the opportunity to return to the religious and economic significance of these variations later.

1. *Love pursuing (Pan)*: (A) Daphnis' narrative "Pan and Pine":

There was once a maiden, a very fair maid who kept many cattle in the woods . . . she would sing of Pan and the Pine, and her cows would never wander out of her voice. There was a youth that kept his herd not far off, and he also was fair and musical, but as he tried with all his skill to emulate her notes and tones, he played a louder strain as a male, and yet sweet as being young, and so allured from the maid's herd eight of her best cows to his own. She took it ill that her herd was so diminished and in very deep disdain that she was his inferior at the art, and presently prayed to the Gods that she might be transformed to a bird before she did return home (Longus 1962: 51).

The theme of pursuit and metamorphosis (Pine transformed into a bird to escape Pan's embrace) is clearly suggested.[6] But it is done indirectly: the god and his nymph are for Longus only an emblematic reference here. The theme of the musical context (song or instrument) and metamorphosis of the female character[7] is found in other narratives concerning the god Pan (Syrinx becomes the reed of a flute, Echo, the acoustic phenomenon that bears her name), and even appears in the narrative concerning Eros, where the shepherd Philetas shows us the god Love, fluttering in the garden and "singing in a voice more lovely than that of the swans", to escape the pursuits of his admirers. The story told by Daphnis is of a young shepherdess like Chloe ("$\mathring{\eta}\nu \ldots, \pi\alpha\rho\theta\acute{\epsilon}\nu\epsilon \pi\alpha\rho\vartheta\acute{\epsilon}\nuo\varsigma, \ldots$"), who in order to restrain her cows, must compete with the voice of a young shepherd-herdsman watching his steer "not far off" ("$o\mathring{v} \mu\alpha\kappa\rho\grave{\alpha}\nu \nu\acute{\epsilon}\mu\omega\nu \beta o\tilde{v}\varsigma$"). And as he recounts this story, he naturally incarnates the young man and Chloe, the young girl. Having become the hero of a mythical discourse (the legend of Daphnis and Chloe) which sets itself on stage, as it were, he is unbeknownst to himself and to the reader, his own mythologist, by the *mimesis* of a more ancient myth (here: "Pan and the Pine") hidden in the depths of the written text.

(B) Lamo's narrative "Pan and Syrinx".

This pipe was heretofore no organ, but a very fair maid, who had a sweet and musical voice. She fed goats, played together with the Nymphs, and sang as now. Pan, while she in this manner was tending her goats, playing and singing, came to her and endeavoured to persuade her to what he desired, and promised her that he would make all her goats bring forth twins every year. But she disdained and derided his love, and denied to take him to be her sweetheart who was neither perfect man nor perfect goat. Pan follows her with violence and thinks to force her. Syrinx fled Pan and his force. Being now aweary with her flight, she shot herself into a grove of reeds, sunk in the fen, and disappeared. Pan for anger cut up reeds, and finding not the maid there, and then reflecting upon what had happened, joined together unequal quills, because their love was so unequal, and thus invented this organ (Longus 1962: 115-116).

The pursuit and metamorphosis theme, perhaps the expression of a sexual taboo (Pan will never possess Syrinx), is taken up again in the episode where Daphnis, having decided to act out the shepherd Lamo's tale ("ὁ Δάφνις Πᾶνα ἐμιμεῖτο" — the form of the verb emphasizes the relevance and responsibility of the action), pursues Chloe who is *playing* the exhausted Syrinx ("ενέφαινε την κάμνουσαν"). One notes the detail of the metonymy and the veiled metaphor: Daphnis' flute becomes Chloe's, and Daphnis, without realizing it, plays with the beloved object ("he wooed her and she delighted in it"), a game quite different from the one he plays with animals he calls and sends away at will.

(C) Daphnis' narrative "Pan and Echo"

. . . She was educated by the Nymphs, and taught by the Muses to play . . . the pipe, . . . and, . . . she sung in consort with the Muses; but fled from all males, whether men or Gods, because she loved virginity. Pan sees that, and takes occasion to be angry at the maid, and to envy her music because he could not come at her beauty. Therefore he sends a madness among the shepherds and goatherds, and they in a desperate fury, like so many dogs and wolves, tore her all to pieces and flung about them all over the earth her yet singing limbs. The Earth in observance of the Nymphs buried them all, preserving to them still their music property, and they by an everlasting sentence and decree of the Muses breathe out a voice. And they imitate all things now as the maid did before, the Gods, men, organs, beasts. Pan himself they imitate too when he plays on the pipe; which when he hears he bounces out and begins to post over the mountains, not so much to catch and hold as to know what clandestine imitator that is that he has got (Longus 1962: 161–163).

This time the pursuit and metamorphosis theme is played to an impossible, aporetic conclusion. The nymph instead of escaping, dies according to the ritual mandated by an Orphic or Dionysiac tradition (she is torn to pieces by animals) and a scenario Daphnis recreates after he himself has received his first amorous initiation at the hands of a country wench named *Lycenion, the little wolf*. The tale, indefinitely replayed by Echo (echo) every time she (it) repeats "more or less what has been said" in the world ("μικροῦ γὰρ καὶ τὰ αὐτα εἶπεν ἡ Ἠχώ"), enables Longus to connote his original fiction

(*Daphnis and Chloe*) with the *mimesis* of another symbolic tale (*Echo*) which only amplifies it because it is already lodged in the linguistic universe of the text. This is made clear by the phrase "her yet singing limbs" — the Greek *melè* (μέλη) applying both to *parts of the body* and to *parts of harmony*.[8]

Summary

A love pursuer never attains his goal, unless it is by murder, and even then it is only an illusion: in the last narrative, Pan, bewildered, knows not what mysterious musician continues untiringly to play. The secret of the *mimesis* seems indefinitely protected, reinforced by its very representation, but never revealed or explained.

2. *Love pursued (Eros)*: Philetas' narrative:

As I went in there to-day about noon, a boy appeared in the pomegranate and myrtle grove, with myrtles and pomegranates in his hand; white as milk, and his hair shining with the glance of fire; clean and bright as if he had newly washed himself. Naked as he was; he played and wantoned it about, and culled and pulled, as if it had been his own garden. Therefore I ran at him as fast as I could, thinking to get him in my clutches. For indeed I was afraid lest by that wanton, untoward, malapert ramping and hoity-toity which he kept in the grove, he would at length break my pomegranates and myrtles. But he, with a soft and easy sleight, as he listed, gave me the slip, sometimes running under roses, sometimes hiding himself in the poppies, like a cunning, huddling chick of a partridge . . . I asked him therefore that he would give himself without fear into my hands, . . . With that, setting up a loud laughter, he sent forth a voice such as neither the swallow nor the nightingale has, nor yet the swan when he is grown old like to me: . . . "I am not a boy though I seem to be so, but am older than Saturn and all this Universe . . . And now I take care of Daphnis and Chloe . . ." (Longus 1962: 71–75).

The representation of Love pursued goes beyond a mere cultural reference: designed as a challenge to the signified in the reference, it is no longer the representation of a character in love, but of Love-Eros himself, who escapes embrace and whom no more *Philetas (lover — of Eros?)* than Psyche in her palace of clouds holds the power to capture. This object then, every one continually pursues everywhere — and the text covers all the common places of Epicurianism and Orphism: Love, order of all things, youth and energy of the world, and so on,[9] — is never assignable to any one place, whence comes the listeners' perplexity: "having for the first time heard the name of Love, they found themselves in greater distress than before" (Longus 1962: 79). Indeed, in this garden where "all the flowers appear so beautiful to the eye", the tremulations of the bird–god who sings better than the most famous of birds soon jeopardize the order of nature.[10] At this point, Philetas' tale continues to be a mystery which the old fellow's argument cannot possibly explain to listeners unfamiliar with the *brigandage of love*: "For there is no medicine for love, neither meat, nor drink, nor any charm, but only kissing and embracing and lying side by side" (Longus 1962: 79).

Summary

Love pursued is never attained. As in the preceding sequence, the secret is all the better kept as neither Daphnis nor Chloe understood Philetas' tale. Heroes of a pastoral, genuine "stage shepherds", they are the prisoners of a *tableau vivant*: the description of Love in the garden is a famous *topos* of rhetoricians and artists. But this *topos* so clearly destined to them, they cannot grasp. *They do not know what role to play.* They would have to learn the forms of love, what it means to be in love, to make love.

Between the fable of Pan and Eros, both identifying a pursuer and a pursued, but neither of them yet understood, the pastoral releases an entire series of intermediary representations, where Daphnis and Chloe slowly learn to act out their own story. For example, in the scene of Daphnis bathing, Chloe compares herself to the *Other* and becomes conscious of herself:

. . . to Chloe's eye he seemed of a sweet and beautiful aspect, and when she wondered that she had not deemed him such before, she thought it must be the washing that was the cause of it . . . "Would to God I might have been his pipe that his mouth might inspirit me, or a goat that he might be my keeper! Thou cruel water! thou hast made Daphnis beautiful, but I for all my washing am still the same" (Longus 1962: 27-31).

There is also another scene where a stray grasshopper gives Daphnis the courage to touch Chloe without fear, and in a manner which is, to say the least, highly suggestive:

. . . a grasshopper *that fled* from a swallow took sanction in Chloe's bosom . . . The grasshopper *sang out* of her bosom, as if the suppliant were now giving thanks for her protection. Therefore Chloe again squeaked out; but Daphnis could not hold laughing, nor pass the opportunity to put his hand into her bosom and draw forth friend Grasshopper, which still did sing even in his hand. When Chloe saw it she was pleased and kissed it, and put it in her bosom again, and it prattled all the way (Longus 1962: 49).

Other gestures of love then follow by imitating the animals: "And therefore he asked of Chloe that she would lie by his side . . . that he might try the only canon, the only medicine to ease the pain of love" (Longus 1962: 149). This, however, proves unsuccessful because of the inexperience of the lovers. The situation will only be changed when Daphnis receives his instruction from Lycenion and finally from Dionysophanes, the permission to wed Chloe in a proper marriage. The Pan-Eros ambiguity is henceforth resolved; the fables are given a satisfactory ending (Daphnis catches Chloe) and their meaning is understood. Daphnis and Chloe have recaptured their image.

2. THE IDEOLOGY

At another level of the text, this game of illusion is possible only under the condition that it remain faithful to an ideology of the pastoral.

Norm: The pastoral text covers, in spite of the brief mention of Lesbos and Mitylene, only one area. Even the *bergers* who visit Daphnis' and Chloe's countryside (Astylus, his father Dionysophanes and his mother, Clearist) belong to this bourgeoisie rich enough to enjoy rustic pleasures:

Astylus . . . went a-hunting the hare; for he was rich, and given to pleasure, and therefore came to take it abroad in the country (Longus 1962: 205).
Dionysophanes . . . for his riches few came near him; for honest life, justice, and excellent manners, scant such another to be found. He . . . offered the first day to the president Gods of rural business . . . (Longus 1962: 209).

The ideology constitutes itself on this side of a perfect world, filtering down and making possible the subtle reality of the pastoral. The reader need not even imagine the Arcadian world to accept and understand it. It is already there, laid down in its principle, *in its norm*, throughout:

Mytilene is a city in Lesbos . . . great and fair . . . From this Mytilene some two hundred furlongs there lay a manor of a certain rich lord, the most sweet and pleasant prospect under all the eyes of heaven . . . the valleys with orchards and gardens and purls from the hills; . . . the sea-billows, swelling and gushing upon a shore which lay extended along in an open horizon, made a soft magic and enchantment (Longus 1962: 11).

Moreover, because they are incapable of satisfying this norm, the intruders, pirates, thieves and other evildoers, never succeed in truly occupying the pastoral scene. In the first book, Daphnis, taken prisoner with his cows, escapes the sinking of the pirates' ship carrying him because he is "without breeches and scantily clad," whereas his kidnappers, all heavily equipped, as is natural for true pirates armed to the hilt, can do nothing but drown. Seized by a great inspiration — or is it, using his shepherd-herdsman instinct? — he clings to the cattle and escapes with them, while, called to the shore by Chloe's enchanted flute, they jump off and cause the ship to capsize. Longus comments that: "Now an ox or cow swim so well that no man can do the like, and they are exceeded only by water-fowl and fish" (1962: 57). Elsewhere, in the second book, Chloe, who has also been kidnapped, is freed through the agency of Pan and immediately, the sound of the pipe "began to be heard again, not martial and terrible as before, but perfectly pastoral, such as is used to lead the cattle to feed in the fields" (Longus 1962: 107).

This norm finally becomes a certain notion of propriety or impropriety, implying with it the mere adequation of words and things in the language of fiction. Thus, the servant who carries news from the country to his master in the city is called *Eudromos* [fine runner].

Symmetry: The story is that of Daphnis *and* Chloe. The entire text is symmetrically ordered in relation to these two characters: that which is given to Daphnis is also given to Chloe. He is a shepherd; she, a shepherdess. He is a foundling; she, too, is a foundling — both are adopted by shepherd couples in identical circumstances. Chloe barely escapes an attempted rape by the herdsman Dorcos, and another of her wooers, Lampis, tramples upon the master's garden in the hope that Daphnis will be punished for it and that the marriage will thus be prevented. Daphnis, for his part, proves himself in the "brigandage of love" with Lycenion, and then finds himself exposed to the eager desires of the parasite Gnathon. In another episode, Daphnis is taken by the young Methymnaeans, furious at having lost their boat (that a peasant inadvertantly unmoored), while Chloe is later in turn kidnapped by Bryaxis, captain of the same Methymnaeans renewing their attempt. In Daphnis' case, Dorcos, who has now reformed, lends his flute to Chloe and helps her lead Daphnis and all his cattle back to shore, while in Chloe's case, Pan himself, who plays the seven-reed flute at Daphnis' request, succeeds in rescuing Chloe by having her surrounded and protected by a multitude of ewes. Finally, by a double discovery, the two lovers are reunited. Daphnis' father, Dionysophanes, immediately recognizes his son from the 'signs' which were expected one day to permit the boy's identification, and allows him to marry Chloe, while Chloe is herself recognized at her bridal feast by her father Megacles.

This ideology of norm and symmetry is borne out by the Greek text, as the romance weaves ("*μέν/δέ*") the parallel stories of Daphnis and Chloe, each *echoing* the other:

> It happened that Daphnis was not then with his goats, but was gone to the wood, and there was cutting green leaves to give them for fodder in the winter. Therefore, this incursation being seen from the higher ground, he hid himself in an hollow beech-tree. But his Chloe was with their flocks, and the enemies invading her and them, she fled away to the cave of the Nymphs . . . (Longus 1962: 95)

Program: The terms of the narrative, while unknown to the hero and the heroine, are clear to the reader from the beginning and long before the *apocalypse* which reintegrates the characters into their historical past. Even chance is foreseen. The denouement is that of a new comedy. Menander in Greece, Plautus and Terentius in Rome, had cultivated the device of comic recognition in depth. By using it, Longus plays a double deck. On the one hand, he takes his child characters, and, from their adoption to their marriage, he makes them follow a well-worn path; the dynamism is almost organically constituted by the growth of Daphnis and Chloe and the maturing of their emotions. On the other hand, he gives his reader the illusion that the programming of these very characters is not arbitrary. Their past is placed in parentheses, confined in a writing, until the moment their existence has been established, and the text yields a destiny whose revelation is perfectly opportune for them. Never having known the anguish of their beginnings (it is the others who impatiently await their apocalypse), it is still possible for them to learn about their past, their families, to obtain the agreement of their parents to enter into an adult life, to receive the fortune to which they are heirs, and finally to confirm their adulthood through their first act of independence (they return to the country).

To be sure, the denouement of the pastoral is ambiguous. On the one hand, it is programmed as on the stage of comedies, where one expects the *unexpected* to present itself at any moment. On the other hand, it is itself rejected or denied from the moment of its advent. By a subtle trick and the unveiling of some traditional deception Longus reaffirms the existence of the pastoral world as both an eternal illusion: "And thus they did not only then for that day; but for the most part of their time held on still the pastoral mode" (Longus 1962: 245); and the only reality:

> And when they came near to the door, they fell to sing, and sang, and with the grating harsh voices of rustics, nothing like the Hymenaeus, but as if they had been singing at their labour with mattock and hoe (Longus 1962: 247).[11]

But this ambiguity is also transparent. The text prepares the disclosure of its preface, of its prehistory, that is:

When I was hunting in Lesbos, I saw in the grove of the Nymphs a spectacle the most beauteous and pleasing of any that ever yet I cast my eyes upon. It was a painted picture, reporting a history of love . . . I had carefully sought and found an interpreter of the image (Longus 1962: 7).

Once this prehistory is restored, the text is firmly established, innocently but certainly, in the city where it was first conceived: ". . . Dionysophanes [bid] him *first* relate the exposing of the child . . ." (1962: 241; emphasis added). *However,* by next returning Daphnis and Chloe to their coun-tryside, Longus not only proclaims the superiority of country life over city life, but at the same moment, unveiling the convention that founded his judgment, he frees the pastoral from it. The story, like the children, has matured:

But Daphnis and Chloe lying together began to clip and kiss, sleeping no more than the birds of the night. And Daphnis now profited by Lycaenium's lesson; and Chloe then first knew that those things that were done in the wood were only the sweet sports of children (1962: 247).

The programming is not only that of the denouement. It is also that of chance. The author uses chance in his text each time he wants to introduce strangers into the quasi-sacred world of his characters.

Let us take the most flagrant example: the episode with the Methym-naeans. Having already devised a pirate invasion, Longus, who now wants to bring in other intruders, must, in order to maintain the credibility of his story and present this intrusion as an unexpected, unplanned occurrence, resort to yet another device. He fabricates an incident between two groups, the Methymnaeans and the shepherds, who apparently were not destined to meet at all: on one hand, Daphnis and Chloe, who: ". . . upon the trunk of an old oak, and having tasted the sweetness of kisses were ingulfed insatiably in pleasure . . ." (1962: 83); and on the other, the rich youths of Methymna, who:

thinking to keep the vintage holy-days and choosing to take the pleasure abroad, drew a small vessel into the water, and putting in their own domestic servants to row, sailed about those pleasant farms of Mytilene that were near by the seashore. . . (1962: 85).

Here we have these same Methymnaean youths in love, like the author, like his two pastoral heroes and the reader, with a pastoral peace which, by definition, they could not possibly want to disturb: "The ship therefore passing along and from time to time putting in at the bays, they did no harm or injury to any . . ." (1962: 85); but who are presently going to bring chaos to the universe of the *bergerie*:

. . . a country fellow wanting a rope, his own being broke, to haul up the stone wherewith he was grinding grape-stones, sneaked down to the sea, and finding the ship with nobody in her, loosed the cable that held her and brought it away to serve his business. In the morning the young men of Methymna began to enquire after the rope, and (nobody owning the thievery) when they had a little blamed the unkindness and injury of their hosts, they loosed from thence, and sailing on thirty furlongs arrived at the fields of Daphnis and Chloe, those fields seeming the likeliest for hunting the hare. Therefore being destitute of a rope to use for their cable, they made with of green and long sallow-twigs, and with that tied her by her stern to the shore. Then slipping their dogs to hunt, they cast their toils in those paths that seemed fittest for game.

The deep-mouthed dogs opened loud, and running about with much barking, scared the goats, that all hurried down from the mountains towards the sea; and finding nothing there in the sand to eat, coming up to that ship some of the bolder mischievous goats gnawed in pieces the green sallow-with that made her fast. At the same moment there began to be a bluster at sea, the wind blowing from the mountains. On a sudden therefore the backwash of the waves set the loose pinnace adrift and carried her off to the main . . . Therefore the Methymnaeans, . . . looked for the goatherd, and lighting on Daphnis . . . (1962: 87-89).

Notice the extraordinary story of the Methymnaean boat's mooring cord ("τὸ πεῖσμα"). While the offhandedness of the peasant ("τις ἀγροίκων") holds no consequence at first, Longus plays with his chance occurrence, and duplicating it with the incident of the goat gnawing the replacement cord, he manages to bring in the unexpected catastrophe. Chance has now been programmed into an incredible streak of bad luck. The Methymnaeans, who hold Daphnis responsible for the loss of their boat, get into a scuffle with the peasants, leave and return with a whole army. It is then necessary for Pan himself to intervene lest the Mitylenians be crushed, and above all that lovely Chloe be kept hostage.

It is thus clearly by a subterfuge that Longus succeeded in integrating chance into his narrative — but the subterfuge was necessary for the completely accidental character of the event to appear. If someone was responsible, it was the first peasant and he disappeared in the night; it was the starving goats who cared little of the boat. The story, unassignable, incomprehensible, has now taken on the proportions of destiny.[12]

3. THE REFERENT

Religion: Chalk (1960), in an article on the role of Eros in *Daphnis and Chloe*, has emphasized the religious and especially the ritual context of the pastoral. Whatever the exact date of composition, the Love-Eros theme is not only a simple mimesis of the love story of Daphnis and Chloe, it is also symbolic of a ritual evolution in a triadic Pan-Dionysos-Eros system throughout the Hellenistic period.

Pan (et al): In this story, Pan is the most easily recognizable figure. He is the god who, at least three times, pursues a frightened heroine. But he is also the warrior who causes the Methymnaeans to flee by signaling to them that Chloe is consecrated to him:

"O ye most unholy and wickedest of mortals! . . . you have driven away herds of cattle, flocks of sheep and goats that were my care. Besides you have taken sacrilegiously from the altars of the Nymphs a maid of whom Love himself will write a story. Nor did you at all revere the Nymphs that looked upon you when you did it, nor yet me whom very well you knew to be Pan. . . . I will drown you every man . . . unless thou speedily restore to the Nymphs Chloe . . ." (1962, 105-108).

Finally, at the end of the pastoral, the young couple construct an altar to Pan the soldier ("$\sigma\tau\rho\alpha\tau\iota\acute{\omega}\tau\eta\varsigma$"), who wins battles (of love) (1962: 247). All this is somewhat ironic since in mythology Pan is always the unhappy lover: would the sylvan god then do for the shepherds what he never knew how to do for himself? But let us return to our text. Several other minute details further denoting a Panic ritual also appear elsewhere. Thus the description of a relationship between Pan and three Nymphs ("I drew these four books, an oblation to Love and to Pan and to the Nymphs . . ." (1962: 7), far from being gratuitous, is related to the iconography of the period, as demonstrated by a relief from the Acropolis, where Pan appears to three frightened Nymphs. Actually, there seems to be little difference between these three Nymphs, the Nymphs of "the Nymphs' grotto" in the prologue and the three Nymphs to each of whom the mythological text reserves an ambiguous end beyond the reach of gods and men, Pine, Syrinx and Echo. And to the extent that Chloe escapes Daphnis, as she does all her suitors, she is then truly, even if paradoxically, under the protection of Pan — who never catches his Nymphs: devoted to his cult, faithful to his music, she takes on the sacred character of the Nymph no one can catch, and three times put through a mimesis of pursuit, she escapes until the very end her "capture" by Daphnis, the only man with whom she will consummate her love. In fact, from narrative fiction to pastoral ideology and now to religious ritual, it is all sacred mystery, the beginnings of which Longus traces for us:

Then she told him everything one after another; how the fresh and berried ivy appeared on the horns of all the goats, how her sheep howled like wolves, how a pine sprung up upon her head, how all the land seemed on a fire, what horrible fragors and clashings were heard from the sea; with the two tones of that pipe from the crag of the promontore, the one to war, the other to peace, the terrible spectres of the night, how she not knowing her way had for her companion and guide the sweet music of that strange invisible pipe (1962: 109).

The rite is confusing, since it retrieves several mixed traditions from before the imperial era (Roscher *Lex*. 1419. s.v. "Pan"). The theme of the (panic) pursuit of the frightened Nymph is compounded by a whole ancient tradition, not only Panic, but also Orphic in character: "the terrible spectres of the night" ("*νύκτα τὴν φοβεράν*"), the "for her companion and guide the sweet music" ("*καθηγήσατο τῆς ὁδοῦ μουσική*") recall the *mystes'* trials of Eleusis where the spectators participated, among other things, in a sacred drama of quest and pursuit: Demeter searching for Korè; Orpheus for Eurydice.

Eros: In the first book, Eros is introduced as the love story's secret agent in the dream shared by Lamon and Dryas, the adoptive fathers of Daphnis and Chloe:

They thought they saw those Nymphs, the Goddesses of the cave out of which the fountain gushed out into a stream, and where Dryas found Chloe; that they delivered Daphnis and Chloe to a certain young boy, very disdainful, very fair, one that had wings at his shoulders, wore a bow and little darts; and that this boy did touch them both with the very selfsame dart, and commanded it from thenceforth one should feed his flock of goats, the other keep her flock of sheep (1962: 17-19).

In the second book, we saw Philetas retell the primeval history of Eros and present the god as the demiurge of natural beauty. In the fourth book, Eros inspires Dionysophanes in a dream and convinces him to give Daphnis and Chloe a wedding feast, during the course of which the mystery of Chloe's birth will be solved. Finally the two contented lovers erect an altar to the god next to the one they have already built for Pan (1962: 247).

Eros, who clearly appears as the spiritual or "Platonic" counterpart (cf. Plato's *Symposium*) to Pan, and whose legend emphasizes the inaccessible character (who is rarely seen, who imprisons, but is never imprisoned), is, in Greek religion and literature, the master (*τύραννος*), the demon (*δαίμων*), while at the same time the demiurge. In the Orphic system, Eros is the "first to appear" (*φανής* or *πρωτοφανής*)—see below under "Dionysos", he whose vision is given in secret, or in a dream.

Dionysos: In the fourth book, one notices the temple's paintings dedicated by Dionysophanes to his patron god:

And in the more inward part of the fane were certain pictures that told the story of Bacchus and his miracles; Semele bringing forth her babe, the fair Ariadne laid fast asleep, Lycurgus bound in chains, wretched Pentheus torn limb from limb, the Indians conquered, the Tyrrhenian Mariners transformed, Satyrs treading the grapes and Bacchae dancing all about (1962: 193).

To be sure, Dionysos only appears late in the book. But his presence is no less certain than that of Pan and Eros, as numerous symbolic references demonstrate from early on. Thus Doros (a spiteful lover), disguised as a wolf better to abduct Chloe, makes one think of the ritual hunters in the Bacchic mysteries; thus Daphnis escaping the pirates on the backs of the cattle who swim so well is a *mimesis* of Dionysos escaping the sinking of his mutinied ship. In the second book, there is even a pure and simple cult transposition. When, after having been separated during the bad season, the two lovers are reunited and Daphnis joins Chloe's family to celebrate the new year, we are reminded that in Greece both the mystery of the new year and the appearance of Dionysos were celebrated together with great pomp:

Now when they had made a libation from the bow to Dionysos, they fell to their meat, with ivy crowns upon their heads. And when it was time, having cried the Jacchus and Euoe, they sent away Daphnis, his scrip first crammed with flesh and bread (1962: 145).

In truth, Dionysos recaptures the flight-pursuit of Eros-Pan: he catalyzes their dual energy and, at times, their violence. He *reveals* it. But, in a sense, he also acts as the mediator between them. A relief, today in the British Museum, shows Dionysos courting Ariadne, and encircled by Eros and Pan. Now, if in Longus' text, the representation of this triad is not made fully coherent, if throughout the entire pastoral, Daphnis is seen assuming at times the character of Pan, at times that of Dionysos, and Chloe sometimes that of the Muses, sometimes of Eros, these variations, this confusion, are themselves the consequences of real historical developments in the Roman Empire: the dissolution of the Greek pantheon, making possible the integration of heterogeneous rites into a unique mystery which remains to be taught, and whose rules the protagonists learn as they go along at the mercy of circumstances or with the aid of a guide, an interpreter.

Economics: *Daphnis and Chloe* would not exist without *money*. Money permits the amassing of land by Dionysophanes, the increase of its value with slaves, and the creation of the framework of a pastoral— a literature of diversion for the comfortable classes who choose to live in the city, but *read* in the country, as it is historically true that most landowners, by then, had allotted their land to sharecroppers. Because Daphnis and Chloe are found-lings promised a better destiny (the discovery of the foundlings is based on deciphering the signs of a secret past), the pastoral finds its auspicious denouement thanks to the discovery of wealth and the restoration of monied values. Chloe finds that her father is rich and Daphnis, whom the Nymphs send rummaging for a treasure in the wreckage of a boat, ends up being an acceptable suitor. Finally, it is also because of money that Daphnis and Chloe can *return* to the country. Having proven that they have means, they can genuinely play at being shepherd and shepherdess.

The commercial world of cities needs its antithesis, a world without money. The pastoral, with its story of Eros and Pan, constitutes the magical financial operation: to all the Dionysophanes of the world—those who have money, but who want, like the god, that is to say *ex officio*, to appear amid splendor and delight — it restores the land in a rustic fashion ("πάντα γεωργικὰ καί ἄγροικα"), in a country festival atmosphere where the gold from commerce and trade has actually disappeared: "possessed of sheep and goats innumerable, and nothing for food more pleasant to them than apples and milk" (1962: 245).

That we have found an improbable romance to be patterned on the model of both an ideal logic and the reality of a true historical context only points to the contradiction between narrative and descriptive processes in *Daphnis and Chloe*. Dedicated to preserving its characters from the strictures of reality, the pastoral uses narrative vignettes as pieces in the reconstruction of a descriptive picture (the painting in the grotto of the Muses). Thus the end of the story (Daphnis and Chloe recognized by their true parents) is not the end of the romance, because the romance is endless (Daphnis and Chloe return to their sheep) and the vignettes point to sets of intriguing reflections, signs ricocheting onto other signs, which seem for ever to protect from all the Flauberts and all the *Prosécuteurs* the myth of a pastoral domain one may call one's own. That the tale ends well this time only proves the narrator's singular commitment to the detailing and preserving of all the facets, all the appearances of that fiction: to its description.

NOTES

1. The sixth *Idyll* of Theocritus is in honor of Daphnis; the eighth and ninth also sing of his exploits; and amply developed in the second idyll is the *topos* of lovesickness. Longus is certainly thinking of Virgil's (*Bucolics* 2.26; 5.20, 25, and so on) and Parthenius' romances (see Daphnis' story in the twenty-ninth romance). Finally, a possible influence of Sappho, the poetess of Lesbos and Mytilene, is still discussed today (see Valley 1926).

2. Plutarch, following the elder Seneca, gives in his *Greek Questions* some examples of this casuistry.

3. From Homer until the Second Sophistic, "to describe" a painting or an object (see Chapter 9) allows the storytellers their favorite introduction. Mittelstadt (1967: 752-761) has shown the influence of post-Pompeian frescoes in the evolution of literary technique, particularly after the appearance of the famous *Imagines* by Philostratus.

4. The number *3*: three trials, three vows, three chances, ends up taking a ritual significance.

5. Here, for convenience's sake, I have studied the three narratives concerning Pan together, but in Longus, Eros' narrative comes second, just after Pan's first narrative, as if better to convince the reader of a Pan-Eros alternation or symmetry.

6. Here, contrary to the original myth, Pine (πίτυς = "pine-tree") is changed into a bird. But the context has determined the form of the *mimesis*: Daphnis' narrative was actually suggested by the cooing of a dove.

7. See below for other signs of an Orphic ritual. Regarding the "double deckers", Chalk (1960) offers other characteristic examples.

8. Note, with respect to this tragic dismembering, that according to the legend, Orpheus' body, torn apart by Dionysos' Maenads, had been transported to Lesbos.

9. Besides the fact that this assimilation is not new (see Lucretius *De Rerum Natura* 1, 1-49), it is so commonly accepted that the substitution of one mimesis for another (legend of Eros/cycle of the seasons, realm of nature) places the Daphnis-Chloe/Eros relation in the context of that of Love and Nature (a theme already outlined in the first scene). Daphnis soon looks for his models among the animals: "Then coming away they looked what became of their sheep and goats, and found that they neither fed nor blated, but were all laid upon the ground, peradventure as wanting Daphnis and Chloe that had been so long out of their sight" (Longus 1962: 59). Anthropomorphism is perhaps a *mignardise* but it still symbolizes the power of natural animation which is Love's.

10. Return to the musical motif introducing the familiar pursuit-metamorphosis theme.

11. One could have supposed that Daphnis and Chloe would return to the city, the author abandoning the illusion of the pastoral world, and satisfying his need for historic versimilitude.

12. For an equivalent progression, see the narrative of the beginnings of the *guerre pichrocholine* in Rabelais, and the first trials of the *fouaciers* of Lerné with the mob of the Capitoly (*Gargantua*, 26).

9

The Eye of the Beholder and the Sophists' Homer

I. As we have seen, the recent development of literary semiotics has been marked by a considerable advance in narrative studies. Following Propp, Greimas, Brémond and others have elaborated and refined the basic logical and semantic functions of narrative, so that we now have, in such areas as the folktale and the short story, a complete and rather definitive system of discrete *narrative signs*. However, and as we have also seen, we are still at a loss when we have to account for some more sophisticated systems, such as the novel or the essay, where the literary text proves too rich or too complex to be effectively scanned or *saturated* by a program of narrative signs only. This is where a theory of semiostylistics, helping define *descriptive vs. narrative* patterns as against a theory of form-free restrictions in the selection of sequences can be useful (see Part 1).

We suggested above (Chapter 7) that a philosophical investigation into the problem of description could complement a semiostylistics proper and thus contribute to expand the field of narratology. Our escapade into the pastoral pleasance of Daphnis and Chloe should now encourage us to investigate the mythical origins of narrative and to examine the early implications of an *intent to narrate*. Perhaps, we shall discover that, from the beginning, man has been attempting to use descriptive patterns in order to define his own place in the world as narrator, as actor, and that these descriptive patterns are a part of an expanded semiosis, incorporating into the experience of writing and reading a text, that of painting and seeing a painting, of relating the space of the body to the time of consciousness.

This chapter then, is devoted to a study of the origins of *descriptive vs. narrative* patterns in literature and in the arts, as evolved in the tradition of the Sophistic *Imago* and of the *ekphrasis* and the *simile* in the Homeric epic. From this study I hope to be able to develop a series of theoretical statements on description proper, the development of mimetic systems and the emergence of point of view, that is the instance of the speaking (describing) subject in the representation of objects, facts and men.

At this point, rather than attempt to say what a *description* is, I will begin by stating that *description* is so much a part of narrative that there really is no narrative which does not include a degree of it. A narrative without any description is not a narrative, but a mere collection of linguistic statements, establishing a relation between a subject and a predicate or class of subjects and a class of predicates, without either one or both of the following elements: (1) the indication (instancing) of an interference by the speaking (narrating) subject; or (2) the representation of time in one statement or in several statements taken as a group. These two elements can then be combined into *modes* of *report/comment/description/speech* (Bonheim 1975: 329–344), with their *subclasses* (*ornamented report/straight comment*). In all these classifications, however, description is mixed, and runs through more than one class. It is very easy, for example, to think of a description as a *speech* or a *report*:

The autumn now being grown to its height and the vintage at hand, every rural began to stir and be busy in the fields, some to repair the wine presses, some to scour the tuns and hogsheads; others were making baskets, skeps, and panniers, and others providing little hooks to catch and cut the bunches of the grapes. Here one was looking busily about to find a stone that would serve him to bruise the stones of grapes, there another furnishing himself with dry willow-wood brayed in a mortar, to carry away the must in the night with light before him. Wherefore Daphnis and Chloe for this time laid aside the care of the flocks, and put their helping hands to the work. Daphnis in his basket carried grapes, cast them into the press and trod them there, and then anon tunned the wine into the butts. Chloe dressed meat for the vintagers and served them with drink of the old wine, or gathered grapes of the lower vines (Longus 1962: 67).

In this chapter, however, I will concern myself with a specific kind of description: *topical description* — that is to say: (1) one that utilizes modes of narrative in such a way as to blur distinctions between those modes or submodes, and to posit the primacy of the relation between modes over their relation to the whole narrative complex; (2) one that utilizes sets of referents (*topoi*), approved and recognized by the culture as pertaining specifically to a particular class of narratives. Thus it could be said that Catullus' piece on the *Wedding of Thetis and Peleus* (Poem 64) is as much a (translated) *exposition* as a *narrative proper*: the wedding itself and the gifts associated with it (the magnificent tapestried bed cover) matter less than the description of the decoration of one particular gift. It could also be said that, in the course of the description, the relation between the actual substance of the woven tapestry and the actions of the mythological heroes is at least as important as the plot sequence itself. Finally, it could be said that the use of the tapestry is a recognized *topos* of classical and Hellenistic poetry, one which has the specific advantage of allowing the exploration of the concept of representation (the *mimesis* of a scene within a scene), and also, as we shall see, of underlining the closure of this *mimesis*. Now, because all these elements are both separate from, and congruent with, the body of the narrative proper, which they enrich and help maintain, I shall call them *paranarrative elements* or *paranarratives* and order them in two classes. First, they can be defined, *negatively*, by their divergence from the original narrative as delineated above: for example in Catullus, the paranarrative is everything that contributes to our impression that the scene described is seen on a tapestry, and that this vision is but the vision of a vision. Second, they can also be defined *positively*: reading them, we are forced to admit that the reference of the narrative is not to reality, but to the cultural *topos* (the use of the tapestry and the exploitation of a series of mythological entries); and we must conclude that this *topos* actually replaces reality itself. Paranarratives thus impose their original difference as the foundation of their own special field of reference. They tend to limit our perception. Or do they?

In effect, they are designed to introduce into the literary work a structure which is essentially self-referential and combines three important properties:

1. *It establishes the literary work in a locus*, which, although referable to reality, remains protected from it, as though the narrator had insisted on locating *his* world outside of reach, not, as in a utopia, *nowhere*, that is, in a place whose reference is only to the syntagma of the discourse, but in a place which, although attainable or forceable, is definitely closed: *hortus conclusus/locus amoenus*. This means that the original form of (pastoral) description can never be modified or displaced outside the closure: representation (*mimesis*) takes for its reference not the real world, but its prescribed absence. I have shown elsewhere (Chapter 8) how it is this absence which is in fact responsible for the distance which, we always feel, separates us from the pastoral world, and how both absence and distance are basic to the manifestation of desire in all representations (see also chapters 13 and 15).

2. Because it only refers to a closure and the tradition of that closure, paranarrative descriptions invite an appreciation based on the avoidance of modifications in the referential content, one that is essentially concerned with *literariness*.

3. Because of its particular character, this traditional closure between the *real* world and that of written fiction can be transposed by simply

displacing and condensing the concept of reference: one simply has to assume that the reference is not to the outside world, but to another sign-system connoting the first, say, painting connoting literature or vice versa. Such is precisely the case with the rhetorical tradition of the *imago*, most clearly exemplified by Philostratus' *Imagines*, Callistratus' *Descriptions*, and much later, by Diderot's as well as Baudelaire's *Salons*, in which the author redefines or pretends to redefine a painter's work in linguistic and literary terms. To this first body of *ekphrasis* can be added the tradition of the description of craft, both in the epic, where it constitutes an expected diversion, a bravura *de rigueur* ("The Shield of Achilles" in the *Iliad*; the tapestry of the Bower of Bliss in *The Faerie Queene*), and in lyric poetry, where it manifests itself in the form of the *epyllion* or the *epithalamion*. In these various forms of *ekphrasis*, closure consists mostly in the delineation and ornamentation of the difference between two sign-systems: thus the poet will report noise or music in the course of a painting description. Finally, there is another tradition of *ekphrasis*, which is less literary and more philosophical, and which tends to dissolve the above difference, by involving the speaking subject (the originator of the *ekphrasis*) into a subjective reflection on his own relation to the world of the *ekphrasis*: such is the tradition represented by Keats' *Ode on a Grecian Urn*. In the space of this chapter, however, I intend to concentrate mostly on the first type of *ekphrasis* above, and I will attempt to derive from its study the first elements of a theory of *mimesis* based on the interrelation of literature and painting.

II. Philostratus' *Imagines* (the tradition mentions at least two Philostrati: the Elder and the Younger, both of whose separate, albeit very similar works have been preserved) and Callistratus' *Descriptions* are supposed to be the transcriptions of actual speeches delivered before an audience, and designed to induce, from the close examination of specific paintings or sculptures, the recognition of a mythological theme ("Amphion", "Phaeton", "Hippodameia"), of an episode from Homer ("Cyclops"), or simply, of a scene from the Hesiodic or Alexandrine table of motifs ("Hunters", "Singers"). Whether the paintings or sculptures are real or imaginary cannot be determined. But we shall see that this indeterminacy is in fact most pertinent to the paranarrative process: because the *imago* is twice removed from reality— the first time, through a dubious reference to a work of art (usually a painting), whose existence cannot be ascertained, and the second time, through an explicit reference to a literary text whose status remains legendary— the scope of the Sophist's description needs to be redefined, and its purpose to be assessed.

In the first *Imago* in the first book by Philostratos the Elder, there is a description of the Scamander river, constructed on an episode of the *Iliad* (*Iliad* 21) where Achilles has risen to avenge the death of Patroklos and makes the river overflow with the blood of the Trojans he has killed. The *Imago* tells how the painter has rendered the story from the *Iliad*. In this particular instance, the illustration has been reduced to only one part in that episode, where "Hephaistos fell upon Scamander with might and main" to keep him from rebelling against the massacre which made it overflow. By selecting one episode in the whole story of the *Iliad*, by emphasizing only a part of the episode and making it the whole story, the painter and his critic cut off the narrative thread of the *Iliad* (the account of Achilles' anger) and they leave us with fragments only acceptable in genre painting. Let us look at the description closely:

Now, look again at the painting; it is all from Homer. Here is the lofty citadel, and here the battlements of Ilium; here is a great plain, large enough for marshalling the forces of Asia against the forces of Europe; here fire rolls mightily like a flood over the plain, and mightily it creeps along the banks of the river so that no trees are left there. The fire which envelops Hephaistos flows out on the surface of the water and the river is suffering and in person begs Hephaistos for mercy (Philostratus 1931: 9; "Scamander").

The Sophist's prose is nothing but *deictic*. It designates what in the space of the painting reminds him of the Homeric text. Usually, a painter who paints a historical scene, say, a battle, will remember the most important spatial features of the story (where the mountain is, where the river, where the battlefield are, and so on); but he may also use his own imagination to structure his space (consider the layered back drops of Renaissance paintings or the architectural compositions of Poussin or Claude Lorraine), and allow his paintings to contribute a new version to the original narrative. With such an occurrence, the primary relation between *text* and painting is reversed, and it is the art critic who can suggest new ways to explore literature (Marin 1971). In the discourse of the *Imagines*, however, the critic's speech is not interpretive. It is not meant to cause a redefinition of Homer's text through the description of the painter's work, real or imaginary. It simply endeavors to give the painted substance its rhetorical equivalent, by emphasizing the *mimetic*, the illusory quality of representation:

The lad is still in the pool, still in the attitude in which he hurled his javelin, while the youths stand in astonishment and gaze at him as though he were a picture [αὐτὸ οἷον γραφέν] (Philostratus 1931: 115; "Hunters"). You might have seen that, hard though it was, it became soft to the semblance of the feminine, its vigor, however, correcting the feminity, and that, though it had no power to move, it knew how to leap in the Bacchic dance and would respond to the god when he entered into its inner being [τῷ θεῷ εἰσιόντι τὰ ἔνδον ὑπήχει] (Callistratus 1931: 381; "On the Statue of a Bacchante").

It is this *deictic* character which makes these *portraits* totally descriptive and nonnarrative.[1] From a theoretical point of view, it might be said that none of the descriptions one finds in the *Imagines* or the *Descriptions* are really diegetic: they never contribute to the development of a story in progress, which is, perhaps, the secret of genre painting: the syntagma, the detail, is valued more for its singularity, its lifelike semblance, than for its contribution to a paradigmatic system through which the narrative could progress. Thus, in the Scamander episode, Philostratus mentions nothing of the symbolism involved in the river's fury, and which is directly pertinent to the narrative of the *Iliad* (Achilles' anger). He only warns us that there are fine details in which the text of the *Iliad* is actually no longer followed. Whereas Homer quite naturally has Scamander-Xanthos *speak* to both Achilles and Hephaistos, Philostratus' alleged painting is silent and must then impersonate, embody, the gesture of the river, ready to address the hero and the god, each in their specific context. Hence the modifications noted by the Sophist, which suggest that the painting has improved on the realism of the Homeric text: Scamander's hair has been burnt off ("οὔτε ὁ ποταμὸς γέγραπται κομῶν ὑπὸ τοῦ περικεκαῦσθαι"); and Hephaistos, who, in Homer, is only described as the originator of the fire that sweeps the river bed, is represented as moving in the center of the flame ("το δὲ ἀμφὶ τὸν Ἥφαιστον πῦρ ἐπιρρεῖ τῷ ὕδατι") and *running* with it, instead of limping along, as mythology usually pictures him ("οὔτε χωλεύων ὁ Ἥφαιστος ὑπὸ τοῦ τρέχειν"). Indeed, "in this Homer is no longer followed" ("ταῦτα οὐκέτι Ὁμήρου"). All this should, perhaps, remind us that the distribution of lexical items in any narrative, be it oral or written, can only be context-free, if every single episode, however singular, contributes more to the appreciation of the whole narrative than to the detailed understanding of a specific situation. Thus, the exchange between Scamander and Hephaistos is only part of a larger testimony to the growing glory of Achilles: Hephaistos' fire allows the poet to purify his narrative of the stench (the guilt?) of the massacres and to proceed unhampered; the enormity of the devastation acknowledged and accepted, Achilles' anger spent, we are now prepared to witness the decisive battle between the son of Thetis and the son of Priam. In other words, the small detail of the encounter between Scamander and Hephaistos is not what matters to Homer; to Philostratus, on the other hand, this small detail is what enables him to phase out the rest of the narrative and establish the primacy of his description, a fully autonomous paranarrative, giving us the illusion, through the use of a genuine Homeric phraseology, that a detail in a part of the story is as important as the whole part, indeed, as the whole story itself, which is another way of saying that narratives can only convey a sense of history in the making if they give up the faithful imitation of every single event in the sequence. This is something that Aristotle had already emphasized in the *Poetics* with his concept of probability (εἰκὸς): the poet writes history, not as it is supposed to have taken place, but as it might have been: "*κατὰ τὸ εἰκὸς ἢ τὸ ἀναγκαῖον*" (Aristotle 1965: 1451a, p. 15) according to pragmatic criteria of selection (character balance, thought clarity, diction propriety, and so on). And this is the reason why he is more of a historian than the historian himself: he tends to give general truths: "*ἡ μὲν γὰρ ποίησις μᾶλλον τὰ καθόλου*" (Aristotle 1965: 14516, p. 15). Someone like Philostratus, on the other hand: "of this battle of the gods . . . ignores all the rest [the context of the whole narrative, which involves gods against gods, and gods against men] . . . but tells how Hephaistos fell upon Scamander with might and main" (1937: 7), and concentrates *on what concrete reality must have underlined the Homeric episode*, because, concrete reality being made of details, there is very little detail that a painter or an art critic can take for granted. What could remain implicit (included) in the narrative sequence, requires special treatment from the artist and almost always entails, through an actualization of the subject in the sequence, the explicitation of *deixis* usually neglected in the text of the original narrative. Thus, instead of issuing a symbolic reference to Hephaistos as the agency of the fire, and to Scamander as the angry patient in *Iliad* 21 (1967: 427): "Hera spoke, and Hephaistos set on them an inhuman fire"/"He spoke, blazing with fire, and his lovely waters were seething"); and because of the actual verbal exchange in the text, *the painting must at least substantiate, that is, embody, the gods: it must make them of flesh*. With this substantiation, the original percepts of the mythological *mimesis* are modified in the microcontext of the episode. Hephaistos appears to be moving in the middle of his fire; and since his fire literally sweeps everything away, he is no longer seen limping, but running. His flames are shining "like gold and sunbeams" ("*χρυσοειδὲς καὶ ἡλιῶδες*"), instead of the "blond" ("red" or "ruddy": "*ξανθὸν*"), which could have been used, considering that Ξανθός is also the epic name of the bloodied Scamander in the *Iliad*:

καὶ τὸ ἄνθος τοῦ πυρὸς οὐ ξανθὸν οὐδὲ τῇ εἰθισμένῃ ὄψει, ἀλλὰ χρυσοειδες καὶ ἡλιῶδες (Imagines 1. 19).	and the flames of the fire are not ruddy nor yet of the usual appearance, but they shine like gold and sunbeams (Philostratus 1931: 9).

Because he pretends to be only a spectator gazing at the painting — an ordinary painting not inspired by the *Iliad*, and only knowable through a reference to nature, not literature — Philostratus cannot see the Homeric formulation: "... ὃ δ' ἐς ποταμὸν τρέψε φλόγα παμφανόωσαν" (*Iliad* 21. 349) [... then he turned his flame in its shining into the river (Homer 1967: 427)] as anything but a cultural cliché: that is, to say the flame is "in its shining" ("παμφανόωσαν") is only a way *not* to say that the fire is visually burning *red* or *ruddy* as fire should be. On the other hand, because the convention of the *Imago* requires that, as a sophist and a stylist, he stay close to the Homeric text and preserve its flavor, and because Homer rarely uses anything but tautological or analogical clichés (his stock of distinct color epithets is almost nil), Philostratus can only suggest a meaningful difference with the original by foregrounding a new cliché: hence the "χρυσοειδὲς καὶ ἡλιῶδες" ["like gold and sunbeams"].

The *imago* thus always stands at a remove. Because the original text (Homer) it is supposed to imitate is too vague, the painting description develops a precise and concrete reference, either directly, by supplying missing or unknown details, or indirectly, by adding new clichés, immediately foregrounded by the context. In any case, it always tends to direct our attention away from the sequence of the plot and onto the side picture constituted by the paranarrative: that of a world still and atemporal, the supposedly nonverbal world of the painted text. To that world, the rhetorical balance of the text is of primary importance.

To begin with, the text of the *Imagines* and the *Descriptions* is essentially oral; the suggestion that the written parts are there to accompany the paintings or the sculptures is merely an illusion. The Sophists are supposed to deliver their speeches in front of a live audience:' "Very well", I said, "we will make them the subject of a discourse as soon as the young men come" ' (Philostratus 1931: 7; "Foreword"). They even use the device of an innocent young boy, whom, like the little slave in Plato's *Meno*, they try to educate in the appreciation of art objects:

The son of my host, quite a young boy, only ten years old, but already an ardent listener and eager to learn, kept watching me as I went from one to another and asking me to interpret them... "Let me put the boy in front and address to him my effort at interpretation" (1931: 7).

Now one could simply reject this as the artifice of a compositional cliché. But since the text is literally sprinkled with allusions to the audience, to deny the importance of an actual rhetorical motive is to discard an important part of the expression: "I will describe the wrestling also, *since you earnestly desire it*" "*And let not the here yonder escape us*, let us join the Cupids in hunting it down" (Philostratus 1931: 25-27); "Cupids"; emphasis added). Indeed, most of the *Imagines* and the *Descriptions* aim not only at *convincing*, but at *persuading*. At persuading of what?

The fact that the *Imagines* and the *Descriptions* are not one text, but many texts, following one another in no particular order, makes it clear that each painting, each scene, is always for the author the occasion of a particular effort. Each one is very much like the subject of a praise, of an *encomium*. Encomiastic literature had formerly been limited to poetry, and especially to religious poetry (the *Homeric Hymns*), and that trend continues during the Classical and the Hellenistic period (from Pindar to Callimachus). However, during that same period, encomiastic literature also appears in prose, mostly in the form of *panegyrics* or formal discourses delivered on events or persons of historical importance. These panegyrics may have been written from a public standpoint, that is, to induce listeners or readers to act (such is Isocrates' *Panegyricus*, which calls for the union of Greece under Athens and against Persia). They may have been written in a more private vein (Isocrates' *Evagoras* is supposed to have been a eulogy of the deceased King of Salamis in Cyprus; his *Helen* and his *Busiris* are criticisms of the Sophists). But the fact that prose works of either type multiply is a clear indication that a discursive encomiastic literature is developing, that the poetic effects of the verse encomium are now being transferred to prose, and that the narrative process is made dependent on rules of rhetorical persuasion instead of euphony and metrics. Indeed, when we come to the period of the Greek and Latin Sophists, especially after the dissolution of city politics through-out the Hellenistic world and the suppression of political thought in Augustan and Post-Augustan Rome, we can see that the encomiastic genre has become almost entirely prosaic and rhetorical: (1) at the level of expression, stylistics and the choice of vocabulary are of utmost importance; and (2) at the level of content, the religious and moral aspects of the encomium having faded, what counts now is the beauty of the topic assessed in rhetorical terms. Unwary of class distinctions, of aesthetic considerations, ignorant of philosophy and lyric poetry, rhetoric is the new bond of a classless Hellenistic culture, the cement of popularized romances, whose plot can be reduced to a game of *Suasoriae*, of questions and answers (Seneca the Elder).

In the narrative of the romances, time is jumbled, and the narration is organized around the alternation or the reversal of logical choices. When, in the *Aethiopica*, Theagenes, after countless adventures, finds himself a spectator in the Olympic stadium, he catches sight of his lovelost Charicleia carrying the prize of the race about to be run. He cannot resist, and he decides to jump into the arena, to have his name entered into the drawing. He runs and wins. Heliodorus gives the tenor of the passage:

The nexte day Apolloes games did ende, but Cupid youthfull disportes began, Cupid (in mine opinion) moderatour and Arbiter thereof, beeing in ful determination to declare his force, in most ample wise, by these two champions, which he had set together. Such was the sight. All Greece looked on, and The Amphictiones sate in judgement (Heliodorus 1895: 99).

and then he elaborates on his *topos*:

. . . the crier called for some man, to be runne with that other. Theagenes saide to me: This man calleth for me. For me, quoth I, what meane you by that? It shalbe so, father (quoth he). For none but I, if I be in presence, and looke on, shal receive reward of victorie at Cariclias hande. Do you neither care for, nor esteeme the shame that ensueth, if you be overcommed, sayd I. What man, said he, will look on Cariclia, and approch to her so hastily, that he can get before me? to whome can her eies give like wings, as to me, and cause him flie so faste. Knowe you not, that painters make love with two winges, declaring, as by a Riddle, the nimblenesse of those that be in love? And if I must needes boast, beside that I saide already, hetherto never anie man vaunted, that he out ranne me. When he had said thus, he lepte foorth, and went downe, declared his name, and countrie, and wente to the listes ende, and when he put on his armoure, stoode at the place appointed, panting, for great desire he had to runne, and was very willing, and had much a doe to tarrie the sounde of the Trumpet. It was a goodly sight and worthie to be looked on, much like that wherein Homer *bringeth in Achilles, as he ran at Scamander*: all Greece was much moved at this deed, which fell contrarie to their expectation, and wished the victorie to Theagenes, as hartily as if everie man had runne himselfe (Heliodorus 1895: 100; emphasis added).

With this triumph, however, the romance does not end, because Charicleia had, during her long separation from Theagenes, been made to exchange vows with someone else. They will have to flee. Meanwhile, she falls ill.

What is particularly interesting in the passage just quoted is that it is a reported speech: a narrative made to someone else about the heroes, and thus emphasizing, through the instance of a staged speaker, the rhetorical aspect of the descriptions. A few lines later, this continued emphasis produces again, through some kind of metamimesis, the possibility of yet another *topos*, another adventure:

I also sleapt but litle, for considering, whether we should goe to conceale our flight, and into what countrie God would have the young couple caried, and I conjectured that we must take our voyage by sea, by the Oracle where it saide

   and sailing surging streames:
   Shall come at length to countrie scortchte
   with burning Phoebus beames [Ethiopia].

But whether they shoulde be conveyed, I could finde but one way to knowe, if I could by any means gette the fascia which was laide outwith Cariclia, wherein

Caricles saide, that he heard say, all the maydes estate was notified (Heliodorus 1895: 102).

With this discussion of the topicalization processes in the Greek romances, it may appear as though we digressed from our subject and became inadvertently more involved with narration or diegetic description than with description proper. But our excursion may have helped us understand the function of rhetoric in the production of paranarratives. For in Greek romances, indeed, there is very little sense of a complete narrative from beginning to end; rather it seems that the whole work is made up of juxtaposed paranarratives, each attempting to present, as if under a magnifying glass, the solution to a passing problem. The whole system thus appears based on a principle of constant juxtaposition: first, to a historical reality which it aestheticizes and romanticizes; and second, to the narrative context itself, as constituted by the report of the speaking subject. In the end, the incredible success of the genre may have been determined by this juxtaposition, which gloriously effects narratives as descriptions (see *Daphnis and Chloe*) and reduces an incomprehensible history to thousands of intricate vignettes which the narrator carefully seals off one at a time. Now, to understand the function of this closure, we will go back to the origins of paranarrative, where the *topos* of the microcosm imposing the closure is already inscribed within the text of the Homeric epic. We will also go back to the origins of rhetoric, and we will be able to see later (mostly in Sections IV and V) that the rhetorical format of the *Imagines* and the *Descriptions* is part and parcel of the Homeric heritage. We will be able to see how, through the incorporation of a metamimetic system such as the episode of the shield of Achilles within a narrative (the *Iliad*) which it is supposed to emphasize and illustrate, the poet develops a whole paranarrative system, designed to test, not the substance of the *mimesis* (for example whether the two cities on the shield are or are not to be seen as representative of Troy and Sparta or Argos), *but rather, through the use of similes and the instigation of a point of view, the role of the subject in the construction of history.*

III. What a study of the ὁπλοποιία ("the poem of the arms": *Iliad* 18) will teach us is that the poet finds it very easy, indeed, to become involved with the serene description of *objets d'art* in the midst of a battlefield narrative already filled with actions and peripeteia.

As one of the operators of the battle, Achilles' shield has a magic value, which is expressed symbolically: far from being a simple object in the world, it encompasses the whole world within itself (a tale of two cities, the

Ocean, and so on). It fascinates the narrator, who sets about describing it, following the patterns of the craftsman, and thus also underlining the general importance of decorative content (history, culture) in the production of objects in the ancient world. This fascination can best be characterized as an experience in the fetishization of the object, which is probably indicative of a stage where semiotic processes are subordinated to a symbolic order (Gernet 1968: 93–137): a stage where the object, even if a simple tool considered pragmatically in the perspective of its usage (here, as a part of the warrior's equipment), cannot, phenomenologically, be voided of its objectal content. We are thus asked to consider the shield of Achilles, *before it is ever used.* When the time for battle comes, this same shield, which took so much of the time and the energy of the poet, will hardly be mentioned again, except at the end of the nineteenth book, when Achilles puts the armor on and checks how it feels before going into battle. During the battle, the shield, sometimes qualified by one or two adjectives, but never fully described again, becomes a tool. Now this preoccupation with a useful object precisely before it is put to use, in other words, the development of its intrinsic as well as ornamental qualities, is characteristic of paranarrative description and the pastoral genre in general. With it, the emphasis is not on usage, but on the transformation of the tool into an *objet d'art.* In the context of literature, the "Shield of Achilles", which shows how an episode can be excerpted from an action narrative to be considered in and for itself; that is, how it can be denarrativized, dehistoricized to accommodate a casual spectator or reader, is an excellent example of this transformation.

The first step in this transformation is a suspension of narrative time. To the narrative having reached an impasse (Achilles has lost his armor to Hector), will succeed an intermission, during which the missing object will be produced or reproduced. But the production of this object immediately becomes the occasion for an encomiastic description, which praises it in a most special way: by attempting to communicate to us the concrete feeling of its existence, it is as if the poet also took the opportunity to assess, not the pragmatic importance of the shield in war operations, not, as has so many times been suggested, the symbolic (synecdochic) value of the shield in regard to the whole poem, to life and death, joy and work, and so on, but the nature of the very description which features the object. Because Achilles' destiny was cast at the time of his birth, and later sealed in the promise of an interesting narrative (he went to war with the rest of the Greeks, thus relinquishing his claim to a long but inglorious life, in order to die a hero), the production and the acquisition of this new set of arms does more than simply fill a gap in the narrative continuum. It takes a metaphorical value: it represents the assimilation of discourse to life, and thus makes any communication, any semiotic operation more than the mere relation of a word, a noun, to a thing, a referent; it makes the text of the ὁπλοποιία the locus of the very description of the narrative process itself. The "Shield of Achilles", therefore, is the perfect introduction to the end of the *Iliad*: it solves the question of narrative continuum, and at the same time, it offers a series of statements on the nature of that continuum.

One could show that the ὁπλοποιία actually represents a late inclusion in the Homeric fiction. A purely linguistic analysis, for instance, would show that much of the shield's description uses somewhat more individualized epithets than the mere stock-drawn qualifications for places and things used in the rest of the poem (Gray 1947). Such a discrepancy, in turn, could authenticate a difference in the date of composition between the two, and imply a difference in the artistic purpose as well (the *ekphrasis* could very well have become the cliché that it is *only after* the vogue of the epic had passed). But this is for the philologists to decide. Whether contemporary with the rest of the narrative or not, the shield episode is still very much a part of the whole epic *as well as* the first in a series of genre tableaus of mixed media, highlighting the influence of an iconic tradition on Western linguistics and literature. If it appears to fill a gap in the narrative, it may be that it does indeed blend the epic with a more subtle form of poetry, celebrating between scenes of life and death, of prosperity and poverty, of peace and war — seemingly abstracted from the contextual epic — the glory of artistic creation, and beyond the poet's own encomiastic myth of the maker, the growing importance of descriptive processes in the constitution of a narrative *mimesis*. Finally, it may explain how the ambiguity of description proper (artistic and literary, historical and symbolic), its uniqueness (once it is finished, the narrative will simply resume its epic form), are linked to a growing process of dissociation between the historian and the novelist.

Because the model of the work of art (Hephaistos' shield) is nowhere to be found (it is divine, and the whole work is accomplished by a divine agency), the description of the shield seems to suggest itself as an invitation to fantasize, while also raising the question of how to regulate the fantasy. For instance, Homer will never let us forget that we are witnessing: (1) the making of the shield ("he made"/"on it he wrought"/"the reknowned smith of the strong arm"); and (2) with it, the collocation of a certain space, which is the space of representation ("He made upon it a soft field, the pride of the tilled land"). But he never really tells us how this operation comes about: most of the technical detail is merely implied in the cursory description:

> He made on it a great vineyard heavy with clusters,
> lovely and gold, but the grapes upon it were darkened
> and the vines themselves stood out through poles of silver
>
> (Homer 1967: 390)

—or brought in under the guise of a simile:

> At whiles on their understanding feet, they would run very lightly
> as when a potter crouching makes trial of wheel, holding
> it close in his hands, to see if it will run smooth.
>
> (Homer 1967: 391)

Now because the emphasis is not on technicalities, and the description is self-teleological, in contradistinction with, say, in the *Odyssey*, the description of the making of a raft, or of the hauling and tempering of the pole before it is used to burn out the Cyclops' eye, the reader is left with the impression that the shield is, first of all, an object of wonder:

> . . . [Hephaistos] such as another man
> out of many shall wonder at, when he looks on it.
>
> (1967: 387)

Moreover, this feeling that everything depends *on the appearance* of the work, can also be internalized. The external vision of the spectators then becomes the vision of a group of characters, whose actions are fully inscribed within the shield:

> But, apart from those, were sitting two men to watch for the rest of them
> and waiting until they could see the sheep and the shambling cattle
> who appeared presently . . .
>
> (1967: 389)

or simply reduced to a point of view:

> The earth darkened behind them and looked like earth that has been ploughed
> (1967: 369)

or even made to coalesce with the substance of the material itself, to offer a poetic grasp on reality:

> There, they sat down in place shrouding themselves in the bright bronze.
> (1967: 389)

Finally, the skill and sophistication in the detail help bring out into the field of vision elements which, although not directly visual, may nonetheless be related to visual percepts:

> He made upon it a soft field, the pride of the tilled land,
> wide and triple-ploughed . . .

(1967: 389)

The "soft field, the pride of the tilled land ("νειὸν μαλακήν, πίειραν ἄρουραν," [*Iliad* 18. 541]) is in a sense, no more than a connotation derived from the observation that the field was "wide and triple-ploughed" ("ευρεῖαν, τρίπολον" [542]) — and that statement itself functions as an equivalence between the space of representation, which is that of the spectator, and the space of creation, which is that of the craftsman.

In essence, then, although much of the description is geared to an interpretation which would seem to transcend the limitations of the visual sense (as when the poet, describing a move on the mimetic space of the shield, interprets it as an ambush and sets the scene accordingly), at no stage of that interpretation is there any mention of an event, of a place, a character, of an intention, which does not coincide with the stages in the production, as ascertained through the visual sense. And since there are no dialogues, and characters are not here, as in the epic, to speak, to exchange discourses (they are never named, never heroicized: who are these people described as dancing, reveling, fighting?), the author rounds their action at his leisure, and attempts to weave them into the loom of the epos, in a manner that is exactly the reverse of the one used in the rest of the poem. There, description is but accessory to the narrative, and simply an adjunct to it; here, it is the only factor regulating the narrative form and eventually responsible for articulating its relevance to the main plot of the *Iliad*. Let us take a specific example:

> On it he wrought in all their beauty two cities of mortal men.
> And there were marriages in one, and festivals.
> They were leading the brides along the city from their maiden chambers
> under the flaring of torches, and the loud bride song was arising.

(1967: 388)

In this instance, any observer would have been able to determine that what the painted text represents is actually marriages and/or festivals, and if one checks the Greek, one finds that this determination can indeed by verified by the "νύμφας . . . ἠγίνεον" (494) ["they were leading the brides"]. Nothing then, so far, which does not square with a purely objective description based on the visual sense. However, when we come to:

"πολὺς δ ὑμέναιος ορώρει·" (495) ["the loud bride song was arising"], we are faced with an obvious modification of the *mimesis*; and yet there is nothing in this which stands out as what we would characterize today as an obvious *intrusion of authorial discourse*. The flourish of Lattimore's translation is simply misleading us. The poet has merely drawn from his own religious and cultural context, to round up his description of the classic *epithalamion* scene; and there is nothing in ὀρώρει (ὄρνυμι [to arise]) — also used a few lines later: "ἔνϑα δὲ νεῖκος/ὠρώρει" (Il. 18. 497-498) ["where a quarrel had arisen"] which could pass for a metonymy. As for "πολύς", which Lattimore translates as "loud", it is no more than the accepted quantification in descriptions of this type. All this then to show that Homer, while continuing to use a typically *Homeric* language, subtly develops his own description into something different from the epic narrative, by contextualizing a proven theme.

Let us take another, more sophisticated example:

> But around the other city were lying two forces of armed men
> shining their war gear. For one side counsel was divided
> whether to storm and sack, or share between both sides the property.
> But the city's people were not giving away, and armed for an ambush.
> Their beloved wives and their little children stood on the ramp
> to hold it, and with them the men with age upon them, but meanwhile
> the others went out. And Ares led them and Pallas Athene.
> . . . .
> These, when they were come to the place that was set for their ambush
> in a river, where there was a watering place for all animals,
> there they sat down in place, shrouding themselves in the bright bronze
> But, apart from these were sitting two men to watch for the rest of them,
> and waiting until they could see the sheep and the shambling cattle
> who appeared presently, and two herdsmen went along with them,
> playing happily on pipes, and took no thought of the treachery.
> Those others saw them, and made a rush, and quickly thereafter
> cut off on both sides the herds of cattle and the beautiful
> flocks of shining sheep, and killed the shepherds upon them.
>
> (1967: 389)

Here, it seems that the poet wanted to tell a story similar to the account of the incursion of Ulysses and Diomedes into the Trojan camp (*Iliad* 10), or to the raid of Hector and the Trojans upon the Greek fleet (*Iliad* 15). And since the whole presentation is obviously reminiscent of the conflict in the *Iliad*, many scholars, taking advantage of this parallelism, have chosen to make this passage alone symbolic of the ὁπλοποιία, even to consider it as an emblem for the whole epic.[1] What interests me here, however, is the *mode of relation* between narrative information and descriptive information. If we look closer at the above episode, we shall see that what Homer has added to the description of the besieged city—it did not seem as though it would have required more detailing than the other one, the peaceful city— generates a narrative which goes beyond the need for casual identification. The poet, for instance, talks of *division of counsel* — and here again, the translation does not render, with the insertion of a point of view, the aspectual change in the Greek: "δίχα δέ σφισιν ἥνδανε βουλή," (*Il.* 18. 509), which really means: "a decision was attracting them [the besiegers] in two directions" and shifts the convention of the pure description into the more subjective realm of the account. This type of presentation, combined with the use of registered stock phrases: "ἄλοχοί τε φίλαι καὶ νήπια τέκνα" (*Il.* 18. 514) ["their beloved wives and their little children"], tends to give the modern reader the impression that Homer, while indulging in passing details, has indeed modified the structure of his text, moving it away from the identification of objects and men, and using it to elaborate a representation based on the development of a subjective input.

This argument, derived from the linguistic analysis of a *painted text* like the "Shield of Achilles", becomes, as we shall see, more convincing when made in the context of Greek art and painting proper. The "Shield of Achilles" might actually be the earliest criticism of a work of art we have, and something, perhaps, like the first *imago* in Western culture. It also marks the first time in our poetic tradition that the concept of craft and craft production, which can easily be incorporated within the perspective of the epic narrative (the craftsman makes the object which is indispensable to the accomplishment of the heroic task), is modified to the degree that the *mimesis* itself becomes as important as its material support. This occurrence, which can be amply documented from a historical point of view — see, in Hesiod's Prometheus myth, the passage from a didactic discourse treating the object as a means to an end, to a paranarrative involved with the idealization of that same object (Hesiod *Opera et Dies* 50ff.) — is of great import to semiologists. Beginning with a study of the transfer of one semiotic substance to another (from the written to the painted), and proceeding with a review of new mimetic forms related to this transfer (the scenes of daily life claiming as much "representativeness" as the battle scenes), he will arrive at the definition of a new value for descriptive, nonhistorical, topical narratives.

IV. When one studies the "Shield of Achilles", one cannot just assume that the patterns of description are simply between those of writing and those of painting. There is a transfer of semiological substance between the two, and it is a complex one.

First, and as we have seen, the shield episode is easily woven into the plot sequence. Since Achilles needs a new set of arms to avenge the death of Patroklos, it seems perfectly natural for Homer to describe the shield *at the time it is being made.* On the other hand, one could have expected the description to be directly related to the war purpose and to enhance, magically as it were, the power of the shield: it could have, for instance, focused on the dramatic (bellicose or awe-inspiring) quality of the design: Gorgon's heads, wild animals, and so on. Such a description would have been totally referential, and it would have contributed to the building up of our emotions, as we are waiting for Achilles to rejoin the battle at any moment. Had Homer used this device, we would have felt no significant change in the system of the *mimesis*: the description of the shield would have been directly related to the war narrative.

The change actually occurs when the text chooses to use the ancillary function of the object-tool (the shield as the primary instance of combat) to promote a description largely unrelated to it, which, because it is carefully organized and pursued along the lines of spatial exposition natural to painting or design, seems to suggest a real interchange between the static figures and scenes of the description and the narrative background of the *Iliad*. This interchange is either very precise, as when Homer describes two cities, one at peace, and the other, at war, or very general, as when he describes the order of the cosmos. Between two stages of the war narrative (Stage 1: Achilles needs a new armor; Stage 2: Achilles has now received his new armor), a symbolic episode has been inserted, emphasizing the polysemy, the versatility of poetic representation. This representation monopolizes the object and displays in it the possibility of a variation in the use of the semiological substance. Either the indication of substance works to reinforce the totally ancillary nature of the object: whatever descriptions there are merely emphasize that the shield's material has been worked on, and the report of this work, presumably, will enhance our perception of the shield. Or conversely, that same substance is utilized *to deemphasize* the ancillary nature of the object, and the object, deprived of reference (if the object is not a tool, what does it mean?), and with it, of the possibility of an immediate *signatum*, requires what Hjelmslev (1961: 47-60) would have called a new *purport* and Husserl (1952: 234-241) a new *horizon*. However, because of the requirements of narrative continuity and the importance of the context of craft in Homer's time (the shield is the work of the Artisan-God), and as we shall see in a moment, because of the general semiology of the epic world (the agency of Hephaistos makes the shield one of the operators of the narrative), the time is not yet come when a Philostratus can describe a painter indulging in the separate representation of a short mythological piece. In Homer, this ancillariness of the object cannot be lost. It must be reasserted; and it is, by being hypostatized as *a mimesis of ancillariness* into the scenes of daily life inscribed on the shield.

All this should help us draw some conclusions about the semiology of paranarrative descriptions.

Semiologically, the ambiguous status of paranarratives is due to a confusion over two functions of the object: a primary function, which is ancillary, and a secondary function. Although related to the first one, the secondary function implies a modification of the total sign-function— with the result that the *signified* or *signatum* is only loosely associated with its referent (it is difficult to relate the figurative detail on the shield to *specific* instances in the epic narrative of the *Iliad*). We must now inquire how this new sign system functions, especially in a context (the epic) where relationships between men and men and between men and objects are regulated by a single principle of war and illustrate a praxeology based on tightly ordered exchanges (communication is always direct and specific).

Let us examine, for instance, how the whole world of the *Iliad* revolves around signs of war. There are many *ekphrases* where this is made quite evident. Let us remember the description of the chariot and the aegis of Athena (*Il*. 5. 719-751) or that of Agamemnon's armor (*Il*. 11. 15-46), both much less extensive than that of Achilles' shield, and of the catalog of ships (*Il*. 2. 484-779). Not to mention, of course, the innumerable instances where characters are in situations of conflict, and where the poet often underlines the significance of a particular act by issuing a metonymical reference to the means or the end of that act: thus Paris' boastful manner, subtly characterized by Homer's description of his arms, is contrasted with his actual behavior in a one-to-one battle with Menelaus (*Il*. 3. 15–37). In this respect, one could say that the "Shield of Achilles" not only symbolizes the way in which the whole sign system for actions and things in the *Iliad* is related to the war referent, but that it also indicates how the whole world of the *Iliad* is entirely and immediately significant: *it makes sense*. Men engage in actions which require just the outlay of energy and the use of tools that Homer is prepared to allow. And the gods, of course, are there to lead and substantiate the action, to intercede and generally to facilitate the formation and the circulation of meaning. They move with the heroes, they send messengers, or they simply manifest their will: thus Zeus, through his oracle at Dodona, grants to Achilles that Patroclos may beat the Trojans back, albeit at the cost of his life (*Il*. 16). In short, there is a sign for everything, even for that which has no sign: destiny is represented by scales that Zeus, as the simple mediator or midwife of meaning, will hold far above the melee at the appointed time. And so, when the poet begins his description of the shield by noting the design of the sky and its constellations, as opposed to that of the earth and its rivers, he in effect gives us as much as a review, a redeployment of the whole sign system of the epic.

Let us look at this semiosis more closely yet. In the fourteenth book, Hera borrows Aphrodite's zone, in order to seduce Zeus, so that during his sleep, the Achaeans may move against the Trojans and thus retake the advantage:

> [Aphrodite:] "Take this zone and hide it away in the fold of your bosom.
> It is elaborate, all things are figured therein. And I think
> whatever is your heart's desire shall not go unaccomplished."
>
> (1967: 300)

Nothing very special about this embroidered kerchief, except that its use is very representative of the Homeric praxeology: actions are always mediated by the intervention of the proper agent, be it a god or an object. In that perspective, the *Iliad*, or for that matter, the *Odyssey*, remains a testimony to an age of heroes, where men were still close to their gods, and where the constant recourse to divine power or to magic devices by the narrator simply indicates that the completion of any task, in a world where there is no room for chance, is entirely conditional on the use of the proper agency. There can be no mystery, no secret, in a narrative *whose function it is precisely to display as a rational explanation* the restoration of the missing link in a sequence of actions, albeit without ever explaining the agency behind that restoration: for example Paris is saved from Menelaus by Aphrodite, Zeus is seduced by Hera, and so on.[2]

Now, in order to understand this process of *display*, we must not concern ourselves with referential problems (that the epic world of gods and heroes might or might not appear, through the proper decoding— Gods $\Rightarrow$ Nature — as a mere figuration of our own, is not for us to decide here); rather, we must try to examine how this display is produced and how it functions in the text.

There are two classes of *display-operators* in the Homeric text: first, the gods; and second, magic or ritual objects. I am using the term *display-operators*, and not *shifters*, because the instance I am studying, while certainly representative of a form of *discourse* in the narrative (*discourse* being opposed to *story*), still does not imply a specific variation in the context of the speaking subject (the narrator, the bard). The class of the gods is clearly defined, and will not detain us here. Any time the narrative is concerned with a hero, it will sooner or later incorporate a reference to a specific action, and that action will often, as is the case for Paris or even Hera, require the mediation of a god. Gods are as close to men as their favorite fantasies or wishes:

> As the thought flashes in the mind of a man who, traversing
> much territory, thinks of things in the mind's awareness,
> "I wish I were this place or this", and imagines many things;
> so rapidly in her eagerness winged Hera, a goddess.
>
> (1967: 311)

The class of magic or ritual objects, on the other hand— to which both the zone and the shield belong— is much more complex and interesting, and we shall spend more time with it.

In the zone episode, the display feature is essential. First, Hera has already done much to make herself more attractive to Zeus: she has bathed, dressed and perfumed herself; now, she only wants Aphrodite's zone, to improve her chances of seducing her husband. Second, her whole recourse to Aphrodite in a matter of the heart and the senses makes it easier for her to receive, and for us to accept, what she has requested. What she has been requesting is not merely help, but also the gratification of her wish, the fulfilment of her desire (that Zeus be seduced). The agency of Aphrodite thus becomes particularly appropriate in a situation, where the *display* of her agency coincides with Hera's own gratification — even if we later realize that Hera sleeps with Zeus, only to make him unaware of the progress of the Achaeans and the break of the ceasefire he had ordered. In a sense then, this zone is the ideal object, containing, much like the *fascia* (the headband) of the unconscious Charicleia above, a promise of mediation in a matter directly related to questions of want, desire and possession:

> She spoke, and from her breasts unbound the elaborate pattern-pieced
> zone, and on it figured all beguilements, and loveliness
> is figured upon it, and passion of sex is there, and the whispered
> endearment that steals the heart away even from the thoughtful.
>
> (1967: 299)

Now that we have understood the role played by *display-operators* in the semiosis of the epic, we can return to our discussion of the semiotic status of paranarratives, and we can say that in a sense the shield is just another zone, like it, artistically designed and decorated. It has the same function: it displays the agency of Hephaistos, as the zone displays the agency of Aphrodite. In another sense, however, it is different, as it becomes clear that Hephaistos' agency, by helping insert the ὁπλοποιία into the main body of narrative, does, at the same time, allow the description of this insertion to remain *frozen* on the threshold of the epic and causes the transformation of the *display-function* into a function of another (*paranarrative*) kind. The shield is thus both narrativized (integrated with the rest of the epic) and displayed (offered as a separate representation), and this relation between *narrative* and *display* is reciprocal. If it were now possible to put this relation in focus, and to determine the point at which a *narrative* becomes a *display*, and vice versa, we would not only be able to point at a *terminus ab quo*, where paranarratives can be constituted (the *Imagines*, the *Descriptions*), but we could also determine the *terminus ad quem*, where paranarratives dissolve into pure narratives. In the next stages of our research, therefore, we shall find that the study of the Homeric *simile*, and particularly, of its modes of insertion into the epic narrative, can suggest a very helpful model.[3]

V. Arrested in the present tense, inspired by scenes of daily life, the Homeric simile has one main function, which is to allow the narrative to refer one of its particular processes to a specific manifestation of the natural order:

> As among cattle, a lion leaps on the neck of an ox or
> heifer, that grazes among the wooded places and breaks it,
> so the son of Tydeus hurled both from their horses . . .
>
> (1967: 132)

In spite of this natural link, however, a culturalization has taken place. Whether the simile displays the current reactions of a man or the reflexes of an animal, whether it shows simple cutouts from a panorama of daily life, or reflects on man's general destiny, it obviously uses the medium of the narrative, to introduce into it, in pseudo-narrative form, fragments of other narratives which only become understandable and contribute to the understanding of the main narrative ("so the son of Tydeus . . .") because they are juxtaposed with it. These fragments of other narratives effect the naturalization of the epos, while also becoming culturalized by contamination with it. In the next comparison, for instance, the description of the two armies pitted for battle gains from the association with the two lines of reapers facing each other:

οἱ δ', ὥς τ' ἀμητῆρες ἐναντίοι
  ἀλλήλοισιν
ὄγμον ἐλαύνωσιν ἀνδρὸς μάκαρος
  κατ' ἄρουραν πυρῶν ἤ κριφῶν
  (*Il.* 11. 67-69)

and the men, like two lines of reapers,
  who facing each other
drive their course all down the field of
  wheat and barley
for a man blessed in substance . . .
  (1967: 236)

War appears ingrained in the patterns of daily life, and our view of the harvest, on the other hand, is modified, foregrounded, so to speak, by this analogy with the war heroes. In other words, war appears as perfectly natural, and the harvest, through the poet's figuration, something strange and forceful, as though we had never seen the real harvest. Here, one could say that the function of the epic is to serve as general purveyor or mediator for the crowds which like to have it recited to them. They like to contemplate an ideal structure of society which, in the case of the Homeric poems, coincides with a nostalgic past (the Mycenaean age); but they also want to see it contextualized in, and measured with, the representation of their own daily life. Now, if we concentrate on the latter aspect, we will see that the above simile contains all the ingredients of the scenes on the shield of Achilles. Although the scene in the simile is not really a narrative one (the teleology of actions in the main body of narrative is already perfectly clear: the men will go to battle, whereas, in the simile, it remains undefined: who are these reapers? what are they doing which needs to be told?), it does nonetheless contain the lineaments of a narrative. There are two lines; they are facing each other, and they drive their course all down the field ("ὡς τ' ἀμητῆρες ἐναντίοι . . . / . . . ἐλαύνωσιν . . . κατ' ἄρουραν"): the functional character of daily life begins to appear. On the shield, scenes were limited to a pattern by a curvature or a plating in the metal. Here, it is the main body of narrative which limits the expansion of the simile. The progress of the action of the combined reapers-warriors (the Achaeans and the Danaeans) brings, within a few lines, another situation, crystalized by another simile:

> But at that time when the woodcutter makes ready his supper
> in the wooded glens of the mountains, when his arms and hands have grown weary
> from cutting down the tall trees, and his heart has had enough of it
> and longing for food and for sweet wine takes hold of his senses;
> at that time the Danaeans by their manhood broke the battalions.
>
> (1967: 236)

We can notice in passing that we have moved from one locus to another (from the fields of the harvest to the woods of the mountains — a transfer somewhat equivalent to the one we have in the shield, when Homer moves from the city to the country). But the real difference is, while the expansion and the articulation of the simile is tied to that of the narrative text and vice versa (the move from the fields to the woods is justified by the fact that we are now at another narrative stage where the battle is breaking), the organization of the scenes on the shield is not simply dependent on the progress of Hephaistos who fabricates his object as the poet fabricates his narrative and plots the appropriation of space on the metallic substance as the poet plots the appropriation of time in the written substance of his narrative. It is also regulated by the connotative sign system Homer wants to introduce with it: war and death, peace and life, and so on. Paratactically juxtaposed with the making of the Iliadic war, the making of the shield as a whole emphasizes as much the possibility of autonomous narrative meaning, which the simile lacks (the shield tells a story of its own), as that of diegetic meaning, which it shares with the simile (the shield tells the story of the *Iliad*). To put it another way, the episode of the shield demonstrates that the existence of paranarratives is contingent on their not being reducible to mere similes, where the sense of the semiotic substance and the self-teleology of the object would be lost to an ongoing plot. Arranged through the operation of the Signifier-Hephaistos, the scenes on the shield can indeed be considered a part of the Homeric *signatum* (two cities like Troy and Sparta; the ambushes of the *Doloneia*, etc). However, it is, perhaps, more interesting to see them as representations or *signs* of that *signatum*, referred, not to the outside historical world, but to a *mimesis*-producing system, where the artist, in the triple instance of the blacksmith, the painter and the poet, attempts *to create reality* out of the imitative process itself. Thus, depending on how one chooses to look at them, paranarratives appear either as the outer lining of the narrative corpus, or, conversely, as its core.

If we choose the latter, how shall we explain a system where signs themselves are representations of signs? Shall we say that signs are in fact always covered by their *interpretant*, and that this covering represents a constant challenge to the (descriptive) artist? But this would not take us very far, as the concept of *interpretant* in Peirce (1931: 141–145) only applies to the mere referring act between two signs as a part of the total referring act involved in the sign (not only from sign to thing represented, but also from sign to sign), and does not tell us anything about the function of systems like the Homeric and Sophistic paranarratives. We must therefore move from the field of semiotics into the field of interpretation, where we will discover that the *paranarrative model of a sign of a sign* is actually central to the development of what we usually consider to be the full-fledged narrativity of *point of view*.

VI. Paranarratives are indeed an integral part of the development of narratives. Following and adapting Gombrich (1960), we shall say that there are no paranarratives in Egyptian paintings, where the artist, who is mostly interested in communicating the irreducible opposition of life and death,

Plate 1. *Heracles slaying Busiris*

Plate 2. *Alexander and Darius at Issos*

Plate 3. *Detail of Plate 2*

presents his picture as the very symbol of that irrelation. In Egyptian *texts*, however, and in the Homeric epic as well as in Mycenaean and later Greek art, what begins to appear is a sense of reference which pervades the artists's space and opens it to interpretive manipulation. Gombrich gives two striking examples.

In the first one, a vase painting of Heracles slaying Busiris and his followers (1960: 134; see Plate 1) an Egyptian influence is definitely marked. But whereas the model for Heracles (the many pictures of Pharaohs massacring their enemies begging for mercy) was gigantic, because it symbolized something altogether different from his opponents, the Greek Heracles appears more of a giant, simply because his opponents have been made to look like pygmies. This means that the way the Greeks translated the Egyptian influence was to transfer the radical, unstructurable, difference between a god and his enemies, into a system where it would begin to be structurable, that is, a giant among pygmies. In this instance, the detail of Heracles is opposable to the detail of his opponents, and each of the two groups in the painting acquires a separate existence, which is the result of their being opposed, albeit not unrelated. The narrative (Heracles defeats Busiris) depends, for its full realization, on the perception of the discrete character of the message in its dual context (Heracles/Busiris).

The other example is a Pompeian mosaic of 100 B.C. describing Alexander's victory over Darius at Issos (see Plate 2). To quote from Gombrich:

The despairing gesture of the defeated King may ultimately derive from those tokens of helpless surrender we know from the chronicles of the Ancient East— but in the context of the eye witness account, it gains a new meaning; it compels us to look at the scene of slaughter not only through the eyes of the victors but also through those of the man in flight. We feel how he looks back in agony at the young Alexander, who has just run his lance through a Persian noble; panic has seized the Persian army, the warriors have fallen, the horses shy. The bold foreshortening of the foreground figures, the frightened horses, the fallen Persian whose face is reflected in his shield, all draw us into the scene. We are forced to sort out the puzzling shapes to build up the image of events in our mind, and in thus lingering on the situation we come to share the experience of those involved. I believe that the one response cannot be separated from the other. Once we are "set" for this kind of appeal to our imagination, we will try to look through the picture into the imagined space and the imagined minds behind its surface (1960: 115-116).

What Gombrich's analysis shows is the discovery of the reference function in space, and as in this case, the possibility of doubling or reversing the representation: the battle can be seen from either point of view, Alexander's or Darius'. And this is exactly what enables us to establish the radical difference between narratives and paranarratives. Without the dual reference that Gombrich underlines, we would have nothing else but a narrative

F

statement of Alexander at the battle of Issos, emphasizing (the painter was probably a Greek anyway) the Greek and Macedonian victory. A narrative of this sort would suggest token representations of the winner and the loser ("tokens of helpless surrender"), only to enhance the historical importance of the subject. In other words, it would simply provide for the identification that goes with the decrypting, the decipherment of representation itself (for example, "this is a battle scene"; "this is Alexander's victory"; "there is Darius", and so on). However, paranarrative elements begin to appear (1) when the reader or spectator begins to realize that the scene can be viewed from more than one angle, and that it is possible to conceive the representational effect of the painting, its *mimesis*, as actually contingent upon the discovery and the implementation of this dual vision: how Alexander won, how Darius lost, and how their visual exchange is readily inscribed in the conjunction of their action and reaction (one charges; and the other retreats) as the double mark of victory and defeat; (2) when the reader is able to integrate purely descriptive elements *both* as organizing *percepts* of narrative continuity *and* as pure *phenomena* — details he cannot help noticing because they contribute to the whole, just as peripheral vision always contributes to straight vision, and because they also stand out from the rest as indexes of the narrative underlying the work. This would suggest that the appearance of paranarratives is linked to an awareness of the fiction— shall we now say *representativeness?*— built in the representation of reality itself. Whether our eyes move from a title, and a title often accompanied by the name or signature of an author, or whether they look at the painting without first looking at the title, we organize the *signatum* of a scene as much from the interpretation of purely descriptive elements as from our understanding of the context. In actuality, we always read a painting twice.

In literature, because space is imaginary, the process of reading is internalized. Instead of shifting our vision from one point toward another within the space of the painting, we merely scan the text, until it offers us those alternatives which can help us transcend the limitations of syntagmatic (successive) discourse and enjoy, with the experience of a paranarrative process, the feeling that communication is open, that language and the world it stands for are indeed more than the tools or the reference of that discourse: something rather like an object of wonder. This is what Philostratus and Callistratus attempt to convey to us, when they give us a rhetorical treatment of painting subjects and propose to incorporate the space of reference within the space of representation. Their works are to be enjoyed much in the same manner as paintings themselves, not because we can see what they mean (that is, what they refer to), rather because we can afford merely to see them, to look at them. In the epic, where the narrative is hurried and careful of its own progress, this sort of reflectiveness is too much of a luxury: an experience which the poet can only afford, if he clears it first through the established sign system. So it is that Homer makes a shield for Achilles to be able to resume the narrative of his exploits, or uses similes to show the acts of god and heroes to be both as simple and as inexplicable as the whims of nature itself. Reality has become the mirror of fiction.

VII. In order to study the *archaeology* of paranarratives and thus attempt to shed some light on the relations of narrative and description, we retraced our steps from the Sophistic treatment (the *Imago*) of literature and the arts, back to the Homeric concept of *ekphrasis* and we learned how the mechanisms of this *ekphrasis* develop into those of historical narrative with the insertion of similes into the corpus of an ongoing narrative. We can now say that the simile fully represents the first type, and the primitive form, of a paranarrative process, which later develops into (1) the epic *ekphrasis* and (2) the Sophistic *Imago*, thanks to the maturation of a rhetorical *technè* and the growing awareness of specific audience reactions. We also learned that the investigation of narrative and descriptive processes cannot be conducted without a degree of interest in the concurrent development of the fine arts and a study of the principles regulating the exchange of semiotic substance (for example between literature and painting).

As we are drawing to a close, our experience may ultimately suggest that the system of literary discourse is more dependent on that of other discourses than usually appears. This dependency, which only becomes of interest to literary critics when the poet leaves literature proper to become an occasional art critic (Diderot, Lessing, Baudelaire, Bataille), needs to be reasserted in a perspective where correspondences, established at the level of form (for example the relation between the structure of Homer's text and its illustration by the Sophist) or at the level of substance (for example the relation between the context of a color and that of a word), can lead to philosophical considerations about the role of a subject reading a text and seeing a picture based on those correspondences. Through the study of *painted texts* appearing at various times in the history of Western narrative, we have found the hero in that narrative to be struggling to establish and maintain the proof of his existence. But whereas the pastoral made it easy for him to be fascinated with the endless reflections of romance, now he seeks a definite association with the world of reality, the historical world, and he discovers that to be oneself, *one must also be another*; that it is not enough to produce beautiful images: one must also look at them and find oneself in them. Where would Alexander be without Darius?

NOTES

1. See Mazon (1959: 209-212). More interesting, however, are the attempts of archaeologists to anchor the mimesis of the shield in a specific period (see Fittschen 1973).
2. On the display-function, see Chapter 12.
3. Although I am aware of the existence of Michael Nagler's book (1975) on the Homeric simile in which he attempts to use structural principles to explain the generation of Homeric formulas, I feel that its objectives are quite different from the ones I have in this chapter. Nagler is essentially concerned with establishing a sound theory of *motifs* at the level of the Aristotelian plot and character; I am concerned primarily with that which makes plot and character possible.

10

Montaigne's Preserve of the Self

Montaigne writes neither a journal nor chronicles; even less a novel or an invented fiction, the *Essais* are neither an autobiography nor are they confessions. And it is obscuring the plan of the book to see the completed painting of a historically determined and philosophically examplary man, properly represented by the author on all points. In considering the work only in its relation to literary history and the history of ideas, one risks losing the time (the story and the history) of the writing: one is forgetting the subject involved in the writing process.

Montaigne warns us himself that the consubstantiality of the author and the book will not be able to guarantee a foreign and anonymous public the right or even the possibility to reconstitute the character of the writer through his work: posthumous, the *Essais* are a familiar book only for those, parents and friends, who knew Montaigne during his lifetime. They alone can compare the model offered by the book with the reality that they knew, and only for them will the being fixed within these pages coincide with the historic anecdotic man and not with the writing subject. For such readers, indeed, the author is first the parent or friend they knew, and everything in the style, the manner of presentation, the object of reflection, authorizes them such an identification, since, putting aside all literary consideration:

En mon climat de Gascongne, on tient pour drolerie de me veoir imprimé. D'autant que la connoissance qu'on prend de moy s'esloigne de mon giste, j'en vaux d'autant mieux. J'achette les imprimeurs en Guiene, ailleurs ils m'achettent (Montaigne 1962: vol. 2, p. 227).

in my region of Gascony they think it a joke to see me in print. The farther from my lair the knowledge of me spreads, the more I am valued. I buy the printers in Guiene, elsewhere they buy me (Montaigne 1965: 614).

The writer is no longer anything but the speaking front, the mouthpiece for a man who is now forever silent.

Always concerned with the subject (of Montaigne), but clearly incapable of restoring the writer (*écrivain*) suspended from the book of his life, we have henceforth only one resource left, that of the "writer-writing" (*écrivant*) in his subjective existence, not in the structuralist sense where the writer is merely the operator of a narrative which does not concern him (for instance the newspaperman), but in the sense that the projective perspective of the one (whoever he may be) who writes can be discovered through the examination of what was once *being* written.[1] The *writer-writing* represents this progressive aspect of writing of which we must attempt to partake through the operation of our own reading. We should substitute, then, the traditional *writer-reader* couple of the *Essais* a *writer-writing/reader-reading* couple, whose function would be to guarantee the textuality (or textual possibility) of the *Essais*. Thanks to the *writer-writing/reader-reading* couple, the presence of an *I-writing*, not captured by an organized text, would acquire, in the very process of this organization, a new dimension: an existence, the trace of which would be precisely the work of the stylistician to detect in fiction of the text being written. The writer-writing would be established as author, and we, as readers, in a perspective which would be hence truly that of a pro-ject (a Sartrian *pro-jet*), an essay, without reference to outside norms of any sort.

Let us say at once that a simple analysis of Montaigne's style, whether it be purely functional and apply itself to structuring his text without concern for an I-writing, or whether it be more traditionally descriptive or genetic— as for example with Gray (1958) , Auerbach (1953: 285-311), or Baraz (1968: 169-208), cannot, in my opinion, clarify the radical problem of the beginning, the origin of the *Essais*. Let us also note that most historians of Montaigne's style always appear to be caught between two equally undesirable alternatives: sometimes they drown in ideological speculations; sometimes, overwhelmed by the prestige of autobiographical fiction, they become stuck with the image of the man and not the writer. Thus, to study something like the perfect coordination of form and content in the pages of Montaigne, and to suggest as Floyd Gray (1958) has, that in the dual context of the sixteenth and twentieth centuries, the style of the writer is both realistic and naive and/or poetic, renders nothing precise, because a stylistics of this nature, in spite of its meticulous analyses, is only the instrument of an aesthetic and moral criticism and in the end, remains prisoner to the traditional relationships between form and content, language and style. It results only in the retrieval of the familiar commonplaces of literary history: Montaigne-humanist, -independent, -flowing, -diverse.

What we need is a stylistics, free from historical as well as formalist obsessions, which will reanimate the subject, the original "I" of the writing in the inanimate text-object. And it is this method which I will try to use here.

My approach will be somewhat different from that taken by George Poulet, his friends and disciples. Poulet (1950: 1–15) endeavors to delimit the length of time that the literary creation incorporates, and his study of Montaigne's creation, by the definition that it gives of the *engagement* (*prise*), the possession of the instant through a rational consciousness, seems to neglect two points: (1) the constant movement of the reader–reading, and the integration of writing and reading; and (2) the theory of a phenomenological stylistics, which, by the practical study of the organization of the writing, narrates this creation. We encounter here Starobinski's preoccupations (1970b) in attempting to link the *autobiographical-I* to a form of private writing, the *discourse-story* (intermediate between the narrative in the third person and the pure monologue). Elsewhere he gives a further illustration of this relation by indexing certain stylistic deviations in a passage from Rousseau's *Confessions* (Starobinski 1970a: 83–169). But while Rousseau, above all preoccupied with guaranteeing the veracity of his *récit*, takes his reader from the very first as a witness, as did Saint Augustine elsewhere with God himself, Montaigne *takes* no one as his witness. His advice "Au Lecteur", the unconstraint of which is most obvious, constitutes more an *admonition* than a preface, more a retreating than an offering. We are taken unawares by a book which, by denying categories and the norms of tradition, by denying a moral or artistic plan, by even refusing a coherence in content (in spite of Michel Butor, one still debates the place to give the "Apologie de Raimond Sebond" in the *Essais*), appears to want to escape all concrete objectification.

This writer-writing we seek lies in the depths of the text, and as Hugo Friedrich (1968) clearly showed, he is masked by culture: a Latin culture, a Latin language.

Erstwhile, long before the *Essais*, and by reason of a harmonious and private education, Latin could be for young Michel a personal and living language, the private and only form of his expression and communication, not only with his German tutor, but with the rest of the world:

Quant au reste de sa maison, c'estoit une reigle inviolable que ny luy mesme, ny ma mere, ny valet, ny chambriere, ne parloyent en ma compagnie qu'autant de mots de Latin que chacun avoit apris pour jargonner avec moy. C'est merveille du fruict que chacun y fit. Mon

As for the rest of my father's household, it was an inviolable rule that neither my father himself, nor any valet or housemaid, should speak anything in my presence but such Latin words as each had learned in order to jabber with me. It is wonderful how everyone profited from

pere et ma mere y apprindrent assez de Latin pour l'entendre, et en acquirent à suffisance pour s'en servir à la nécessité, comme firent aussi les autres domestiques qui estoient plus attachez à mon service. Somme, nous nous Latinizames tant, qu'il en regorgea jusques à nos villages tout autour, où il y a encores, et ont pris pied par l'usage plusieurs appellations Latines d'artisans et d'utils (Montaigne 1962: vol. 1; p. 188).

this. My father and mother learned enough Latin in this way to understand it, and acquired sufficient skill to use it when necessary, as did also the servants who were most attached to my service. Altogether, we Latinized ourselves so much that it overflowed all the way to our villages on every side, where there still remain several Latin names for artisans and tools that have taken root by usage (Montaigne 1965: 128).

But when he has acquired a library filled with books inscribed with quotes, when he begins to write the *Essais*, this is no longer the case. Latin has become the universal instrument of culture. It is no longer a question of a marvelous association between the self and the world, of a language where the locutor, in speaking in his own words, would restore form and function to a language otherwise frozen in the commonplaces of antiquity. The *Essais* clearly mark, with this death of Latin, the beginning of the reading and work. Montaigne becomes prisoner of a norm he can no longer satisfy:

Quant au Latin qui m'a esté donné pour maternel, j'ay perdu par des-accoustumance la promptitude de m'en pouvoir servir à parler: ouy et à escrire, en quoy autrefois je me faisoy appeler maistre Jean. Voila combien peu je vaux de ce costé là (Montaigne 1962: vol. 2, p. 40).

As for Latin, which was given me for my mother tongue, I have lost through lack of practice the ability to use it quickly in speaking; yes, and in writing, in which they used to call me Master John. That is how little I am worth on that side (Montaigne 1965: 484).

And his French is hardly better, "alteré, et en la prononciation et ailleurs, par la barbarie de mon creu" ["corrupted both in pronunciation and in other respects, by the barbarisms of my home soil"]. From the moment he begins to write a book about himself, he discovers that the problem of being an essayist is less one of depth (if it is at all permissible to speak of oneself, Montaigne deals with a subject that he knows better than anyone):

Le monde regarde tousjours vis à vis; moy, je replie ma veue au-dedans, je la plante, je l'amuse là . . . je me considere sans cesse, je me contrerolle, je me gouste (Montaigne 1962: vol. 2, p. 61).

The world always looks straight ahead; as for me, I turn my gaze inward, I fix it there and keep it busy. Everyone looks in front of him; as for me, I look inside of me; I have no business but with myself; I continually observe myself, I take stock of myself, I taste myself (Montaigne 1965: 499).

than it is a problem of form:

J'ay tousjours une idée en l'ame et certaine image trouble qui me presente comme en songe une meilleure forme que celle que j'ay mis en besongne, mais je ne la puis saisir et exploiter (1962: vol. 2, p. 237).	I have always an idea in my mind, and some blurred picture, which offers me as if in a dream a better form than the one I have employed, but I cannot grasp it and exploit it (1965: 482).

And because of this problem of form due to a contradiction between the requirements of a clear rational discourse and Montaigne's complex rhetorical heritage anyone studying the style of the *Essais* cannot be satisfied only with qualifying their expressiveness (the images, poetic or rhythmic effects). He must also isolate the procedures which constitute the message, which assure, by a constant actualization of the "I" in the act of writing (and I give the name *deixis* to this operative identification), the existential, the phenomenal quality of writing and the passage from an objective "I" to a subjective self.[2]

Following this devaluation of Latin, the language that Montaigne spoke so well is henceforth no more than a writing of reference, a normative and ideal code, both superknowledge and superlanguage he no longer possesses, which now symbolizes a marvelous and impossible harmony:

Il m'advint l'autre jour de tomber sur un tel passage. J'avois trainé languissant après des parolles Françoises, si exangues, si descharnées et si vuides de matière et de sens que ce n'estoient voirement que parolles Françoises (1962: vol. 1, p. 156).	I happened the other day to come upon such a passage. I had dragged along languidly after French words so bloodless, fleshless, and empty of matter and sense that they really were nothing but French words (1965: 108).

Montaigne, then, is led to redefine the conditions of his expression. He acknowledges that he is incapable of speaking the words of a clear consciousness. He is aware of the arbitrary and mediate character of signs as well as the impossibility of ever giving meaning to all this lost Latinness that is a norm of language, style and culture. He is even more aware of the impossibility of speaking "good" French, or failing French, of speaking any sort of language well. He must be assured— and this is clearly the basic plan of the *Essais*— of a form of communication with himself and with the reader that satisfies his desire for expressiveness and substantiates his autonomy in a universe which can only remind him of his inability to communicate (*conférer*) the fragility of his self. The "I" of the written text (much more so than that of spoken language) is somewhat lacking in substance: its *deixis* is weak — referential in principle, but referring to a being uncertain and unknown, it is, as Hjelmslev (1961: 33) would say, but a *functive of expression*; it functions as an agent of a universal *langue*, but without ever being able to substantiate the person, the unique being lost in the silence of beginnings evoked by Blanchot (1955: 48). Montaigne *essays* to fill this silence with his voice.

Montaigne always speaks of antiquity, of culture. But it is not the least result of his confrontation with his time that the distance which separates him from this culture has changed. It is no longer possible for him to perceive himself, as Rousseau later in the *Confessions*, on the same level as the Epaminondas and the Catos, the illustrious men of Plutarch. All these men have become characters in a moral gallery: magnanimous heroes and models to whom he compares himself without illusion, whose assocation he continues to seek, because in this relationship— as slight as it may be— which unites him to the exemplary figures of culture, he hopes to be able to read more clearly the outline of his own existence, the style of his own person. This culture, which is essentially Latin, and if Greek, transcribed into Latin or directly into French, continues to represent the aspirations of a whole historical period. It is by *reference* to it that everything is understood and communicated; it is the very foundation of discourse and thought— whence often comes the school of manners in the historians Montaigne reads. He likes them: "ma droitte bale" ["they come right to my forehand"] because as interpreters and moralists, they invite him to read himself into their own texts and not because they narrate faithfully:

Or ceux qui escrivent les vies, d'autant qu'ils s'amusent plus aux conseils qu'aux evenemens, plus à ce qui part du dedans qu'à ce qui arrive au dehors, ceux là me sont plus propres (1962: vol. 1, p. 457).	Now those who write biographies, since they spend more time on plans than on events, more on what comes from within than on what happens without, are most suited to me (1965: 303).

However, the truth is, this culture, this history, have no existence *in themselves: they exist only because they are the norm.* The men of whom they speak and to whom they refer most certainly had a chronological and real existence at some moment in the past. But if their discourses and actions ever came to posterity in the pages of books, it is by caprice of the authors, or of history. For suppose one were to admit that the historian's ambition was to retain everything, to record everything, he, remaining a prisoner of his choices and overcome by the infinity of space and time, could only deal in his book with one particular series of facts among others:

De tant de milliasses de vaillans hommes qui sont morts depuis quinze cens ans en	Of so many myriads of valiant men who have died sword in hand in the last

France, les armes en la main, il n'y en a pas cens qui soient venus à notre cognoissance. La memoire non des chefs seulement, mais des batailles et des victoires est ensevelie. . . Nous n'avons pas la millième partie des escrits anciens: c'est la fortune qui leur donne vie (1962: vol. 2, p. 47).

fifteen hundred years in France, there are not a hundred who have come to our knowledge. The memory not only of the leaders, but of the battles and victories is buried . . . We have not the thousandth part of the writings of the ancients: it is Fortune that gives them life (1965: 475-476).

Modified by tradition and recalled in the style of a particular writer, these lives have become imaginary and exemplary; they have ceased to be personal. A personal relation to the culture, then, cannot be established on the mode of being, since this culture, written and codified, essentially expresses a lack of being; it must first be defined and learned as knowledge. Thus Montaigne attempts to construct a substitute knowledge using the foundations of the primary knowledge which tradition dictates. It is with this *épistémè* and *by default* that he tries to actualize his relation with the world.

A knowledge within knowledge, this *épistémè* attempts to codify itself, it can only actualize itself, by the writing and reading of the practitioner, the apprentice of the book. It is by writing a book, and a book on himself— or rather, by writing himself into a book— that Montaigne, assuming his own emptiness, fulfills the lack of being in the culture. And since the retreat "into the bosom of the docte Muses" coincides not only with a reading and a meditation but precisely with the beginning of a vast process of writing, the book appears in effect to constitute in its writing, in the time and space of this actualization, the author's personal domain.

To him, his writing is not only the activity of his solitary life, it also represents the desire to experience the reality of it at a profound level (see Lejeune 1975). Already long before the book was going to be published, before an actual outside reader was going to be solicited, Montaigne manages to allow himself both the objective and subjective perspective of a writer writing his book, and of a reader "reading-in" the process of his own writing. During that time, he is, like every artist, both within and without; he already wants to see what the finished work reads like and he tries to view his book objectively, as if it were already separate and distinct from its author (see "Au lecteur"). With Montaigne, however, the *reading part* is so important that we might be tempted to say that it is the *reading part* which supports and nurtures the *writing part* through the additions Montaigne makes as he rereads himself. But we must be careful not to invoke the objective historical evidence of Montaigne's additions, as what we are investigating is *not* Montaigne's book, *but the possibility of a subjective reading* of that book. In approaching Montaigne's text, then, we should again be prepared to perform a reading in the form of a *project*, where the progress of the writing is realized only in the fiction of the text being present to itself, soliciting the joint consciousness of the writer and his reader. We should then be able to see this same text, delayed, one would say today, *différ(a)ncié* and *disseminated* by the game of syntax and rhetoric, the combination of topological and semantic places, reabsorb and collect itself in a particular and unique signification which for a while immobilizes it and quite clearly constitutes the engagement (*saisie*) sought by Georges Poulet (1950: 11-12). Now the clues for this reading performance are inseparable from the writing of the text; they are a part of it. They are not in the additions to the first edition, in what some wish to see as a critical reflection on (outside of) the work (a work, incidentally, that Montaigne never finished). We will find them in the body of the text at the moment that our reading rewrites it: a reading which reacts to the *stimuli* of the text without becoming purely formal or formalist by abstracting a system from its underlying project; a reading which has ceased to be purely ideological (by returning the book to the implacable form of a methodical discourse); and finally a reading which, while striving to remain objective, provides us with the subjective image of Montaigne's own essayist writing:

J'entends que la matiere se distingue soy-mesmes. Elle montre assez où elle se charge, où elle conclud, où elle commence, où elle se reprend, sans l'entrelasser de parolles de liaison et de cousture introduictes pour le service des oreilles foibles ou nonchallantes, et sans me gloser moymesme (1962: vol. 2, p. 439).

I want the matter to make its own divisions. It shows well enough where it changes, where it concludes, where it begins, where it resumes, without my interlacing it with words, with links and seams introduced for the benefit of weak or heedless ears, and without writing glosses on myself (1965: 761).

But what writing? Writing *of*, or writing *on*? When we say that Montaigne writes *on* himself, and not on some other subject outside himself, this *on* of our critical grammar is in fact only a redundancy of sign. It emphasizes the difficulty we experience in correctly expressing a reflexive and autonomous (or *autotelic* activity): Montaigne writes himself into the book at the same time he is writing a book, and it is this integration of the man and his book which a reading of the type sought here can help discover.

First, from the point of view of space, we follow the *Essais* in the configuration of their dual text, with on one side, *the text of the "I"*; and on the other, *the text of culture*. Whether we see in Montaigne a writer infatuated with himself and with his own prejudices or on the contrary, a model autobiographer, his book suggests, and often imposes, the association of the *text of the "I"* and the *text of culture* with one another. Does Montaigne experience himself as a subject at the very moment he believes he defines his relationship with the world? Or rather, is his "I" only external: exemplary and constative without any self-awareness? Whatever the degree to which the reference is actualized and the *deixis* is imposed, the presence of the referent in the personal pronoun (or in structural terms, of the *shifter*) plainly and most prosaically underlines the return of the general to the particular, the multiplicity of the culture to singularity and the specificity of the person who animates this "I". The typography which delimits these two texts represents then the place and the point of a reversal:

Les autres beautez sont pour les femmes; la beauté de la taille est la seule beauté des hommes. Où est la petitesse, ny la largeur et rondeur du front, ny la blancheur et douceur des yeux, ny la mediocre forme du nez, ny la petitesse de l'oreille et de la bouche, ny l'ordre et la blancheur des dents, ny l'épesseur bien unie d'une barbe brune à escorce de chataigne, ny le poil relevé, ny la juste rondeur de teste, ny la frécheur du teint, ny l'air du visage agreable, ny un corp sans senteur, ny la proportion legitime des membres peuvent faire un bel homme.

J'ay au demeurant la taille forte et ramassée; le visage, non pas gras, mais plein; la complexion, entre le jovial et le mélancolique (1962: vol. 2, p. 42).

The other kinds of beauty are for women; the beauty of stature is the only beauty of men. Where smallness dwells, neither breadth and roundness of forehead, nor clarity and softness of eyes, nor the moderate form of the nose, nor small size of ears and mouth, nor regularity and whiteness of teeth, nor the smooth thickness of a beard brown as the husk of a chestnut, nor curly hair, nor proper roundness of head, nor freshness of color, nor a pleasant facial expression, nor an odorless body, nor just proportion of limbs, can make a handsome man. For the rest, I have a strong, thick-set body, a face not fat but full, a temperament between the jovial and the melancholy (1965: 486).

It is also the mark of an exchange. Note the relationship between what is "I" and what is "non-I" in the following text:

On dit communément que le plus juste partage que nature nous aye fait de ses graces, c'est celuy du sens: car il n'est aucun qui ne se contente de ce qu'elle luy en a distribué. N'est-ce pas raison? Qui verroit au delà, il verroit au dela de sa venuë. Je pense avoir les opinions bonnes et saines (1962: vol. 2, p. 61).

It is commonly said that the fairest division of her favors Nature has given us is that of sense: for there is no one who is not content with the share of it that she has allotted him. Is that not reasonable? If anyone saw beyond, he would see beyond his sight. I think my opinions are good and sound (1965: 499).

This reversal, or this exchange, can be formulated in the following way: the text of common knowledge, which is not properly Montaigne's own, but that of others, is in such relation with the text of the "I" that it represents more or less appropriately the space (of text) that the author can pass through (write) before being able once again to say *I*.

Historically speaking, we divide Montaigne's work into three or four books or periods. The additions within the books indicate the renewal, at precise moments in the author's life, of his relationship to his culture, and they imply in the perspective of a continuous writing of twenty years (around 1571 to 1591) that the relation between originals and additions is essentially experienced as an ongoing process, in spite of the disconnections of our critical chronology. Expressed by Montaigne's additions and repetitions throughout the space of the book, this ongoing process is made necessary by the writer's need to recommit himself to his writing and to seek in it the image of time passed.

Finally, Montaigne appears sparing of judgment about this culture — he voluntarily offers his preferences of authors, their expression and content, while remaining uncertain that his own good sense, his judgment, really corresponds to a category. Now because a judgment objectivizes, in a category extrinsic to *being*, the life which he never ceases to want to represent, it is rather from the point of view and (in) the form of a person that we can integrate Montaigne into the only culture agreeing with his image.

This person is not yet Montaigne; it only exists inasmuch as it is an image. But being both synchronic and successive, it is close to existing; it truly signifies the extreme collusion of the being and the work in the game of *self-portrait*; the "I"-writing being now endowed with the fiction of its own posthumous existence.

NOTES

1. The use of the term *writing* herein is different from what it was in Part One. There, the emphasis was on the text as communication system. Here, the emphasis is on the philosophical (phenomenological) implications of the attempt to communicate. We encounter here, under the guise of a phenomenological vocabulary, the same problematics defined by Continental linguists in their attempt to distinguish between a "subject-in-the-statement" (*sujet de l'énoncé*) and a "subject-making-the statement" (*sujet de l'énonciation*) (Benveniste 1966: 258 ff.), in order to clarify the relations of a social *langue* and a private *parole* in most linguistic processes. In this chapter, however, I am more interested in defining the philosophical context of a *collusion* between the two: the "I" of commonday language and the "self" of Montaigne's own private essays.
2. For uses of *deixis*, see above p. 54 and chapters 6, 9, 12.

11

Pastoral Style, Pastoral Self

Can the Age of Enlightenment be proud of its pastoral poems? Are they a degenerate yet typical form of the feeling for, and the return to, nature? Or, is the *bergerie* only the pet diversion of serious philosophers? Mornet (1907) and others after him have shown with erudition the importance of bucolic expression[1] and it may be that some sort of link exists between the serious philosophy and physiology of the *Encyclopédistes*; the erotic games of *Anette et Lubin, Estelle et Némorin*, and *Daphnis and Chloe*,[2] and the general movement of the return to nature. It can be established that literary history is not separate from history proper;[3] that, in spite of the contradiction between the feeling of mundane servitude and the desire for a pastoral freedom, the eighteenth century can integrate the heritage of Theocritus and Callimachus, Virgil, and *Astrée*, in the style of a nature that is free from history and at the same time, subject to it.

The philosophers did read and write pastorals and those are not simply erotic pieces. One knows that Montesquieu wrote his *Lettres persanes* to cavort in the seraglio; Diderot, his *Bijoux indiscrets*, Crébillon, *L'Écumoire, ou Tanzaï et Néadané: histoire japonaise*. But few are aware that besides the *Devin du village*, Rousseau set *Daphnis and Chloe* to music, that he claims the *Lévite d'Ephraïm* to be his most cherished piece (Rousseau 1973: vol. 2, p. 360),[4] and that he signed other minor pieces like the *Verger de Mme Warens*. Diderot wrote two pastoral tales to complete the 1773 translation of the second *Idyllen* by Gessner, after he had already contributed to the Huber translation of the first *Idyllen*. One forgets the commentaries, judgments, the tradition and style of the period. The *Encyclopédie* has an article 'Églogue' by Turgot; the *Correspondance littéraire* gives evidence of a constant interest in an ideal countryside (*une campagne*); even Condillac and d'Alembert took notice of the pastoral vogue. In fact, the entire reading public itself welcomed Fontenelle, Gessner, Saint-Lambert, Bernis, Marmontel, Berquin, Léonard, and Delille, who, since Rivarol, has only been scorned, and finally Chenier and Bernardin de Saint-Pierre. The public *read* pastoral verse, rhyming prose, novels. In 1775, the *Nouvelle bibliothè-que de campagne* was established.[5]

How then can one be unaware of the importance of a pastoral literature? The problem here is not how to argue about the masters of sensibility, or some sort of preromanticism, which would only be a device (*l'emboîtage*) used to bury the literary embarrassment of the French Revolution (see Monglond 1966). The problem is rather of asking oneself *why the feeling of nature is manifested in the form of the pastoral, the eclogue or the idyll*, to what degree the constitution of a bucolic writing is part of the rhetorical and mythical invention of the eighteenth century. The problem is to see just what, in the pastoral movement, is a return to nature, to the origin of representation itself, and what justifies this return to the forms of the eclogue, idyll, and Alexandrine poetry.

THE RETURN

The world is discovered, seas are traversed, continents are crossed. The savages of Bougainville are near, and even characters in novels feign a comprehension of the limits of the real world. Saint-Preux writes to Madame d'Orbe:

J'ai vu de loin le séjour de ces prétendus géants qui ne sont grands qu'en courage, et dont l'indépendance est plus assurée par une vie simple et frugale que par une haute stature. J'ai séjourné trois mois dans une Isle déserte et délicieuse, douce et touchante image de l'antique beauté de la nature, et qui semble être confinée au bout du monde pour y servir d'asile à l'innocence et à l'amour persécutés: mais l'avide. Européen suit son humeur farouche en empêchant l'Indien paisible de l'habiter, et se rend justice en ne l'habitant pas lui-même. (Rousseau 1964: vol. 2, p. 413).

I have seen from afar the abode of these supposed giants who are only great in their courage and whose independence is better guaranteed by a simple and frugal life than by their imposing stature. I have stayed three months in the deserted and delightful Isle, sweet and moving image of the ancestral beauty of nature and which seems to have been relegated to the ends of the world to serve as a haven for persecuted innocence and love; but the greedy European follows his aggressive nature in denying the peaceful Indian the right to occupy it and does himself justice by not living there.[6]

While man is traveling to the ends of the earth, he questions the beginnings of his own thought processes. The discovery of discoveries is the origin, somewhere in the past, in an immemorial time. As if the discoveries of the great travelers had in the end brought about one of a different sort: by an internal journey, coextensive to the one on the map, a deepening of self-awareness leads toward the original moments when the world shone by its simplicity and its *naiveté*. Travel to and discovery of distant lands constitute but one of the axes of anthropology. The other remains the study of the foundations of society, and this *connaissance*, an investigation into nonhistory, or at best the beginnings of history, presupposes a guiding mark in the middle of disorder: with Rousseau,[7] with Buffon, with Helvétius and Diderot,[8] the history of species is a pretext to return man to a primeval vision of himself in harmony with the laws of nature.

FIELD OF THE RETURN AND FIELD OF THE CULTURE

In the field of anthropological investigation, the return is in the form of an asymptotic curve toward regions far enough away to appear imaginary, yet close enough (they are part of the planet) to have been reached by the navigators who explored them, the companies which exploited them, and the philosophers who speculated about them.[9] However, in a symbolic sense and *en miroir*, there is also a return in the form of another curve exactly symmetrical to the first one, toward regions as far as Tempe, Gnide or the Tendre, and as close as the Petit Trianon. Between these two curves lies the area we must cover, combining, from *Astrée* to *Paul et Virginie*, a fiction out of a book[10] with the spectacle of a tragic and savage reality.

In a very literal sense, the area is first an agricultural field. It has been said that the return to pastoral literature was only a metaphor for a massive return to the land. And the first few pages of Mornet's work seem in effect to confirm this opinion: "To love nature is not only to read the alternating songs of Tityrus and Meliboeus but also go near it" (Mornet 1907: 19).[11] Interest in the land is expressed not only by the controversy, passed on from the seventeenth century, of the country and city mansions (Mornet 1907: vol. 2, ch. 1), but also, toward the end of the century, in the renewal of agricultural techniques at the behest of several major landowners. Agricultural societies multiply; and although Paris continued to hold the advantage over the countryside, there is no doubt that the primacy of agriculture had been respectfully acknowledged. Must one stop there, as did Mornet himself: "We are not proposing to recover the first manifestations of the feeling for nature" (1907: 19)? Or is it necessary to go even further and claim that his movement to return to the land is interesting only in that it essentially signifies the *idea of the return* to countries which are only those of Greece and Rome?

Those who know how to read, return to the land; those who do not — peasants, serfs, freeholders — never left it. Whence come, no doubt, the incongruities of this philosopher-freeholder, reader of the *Georgics*, and smelling of the rose, who is celebrated *ad nauseam*. And for a La Rochefoucauld, watching over the rise in value of his Liancourt lands, for a Turgot, plowing the rows of his Limousin district, how many thousands of sensitive natures return to the groves of the *belles-lettres*?[12] The land is there, as a reference. To work it, to aid in its productions, to communicate with it, in the *books*, is to permit by this single gesture, the advent of the return, and to feel pleasure by participating in it. From the furrow of the earth, to the trail of the letter, to the thread of the discourse, the line is constant, and Rousseau is not wrong when he has Saint-Preux *recount* to Bomston the organization and agricultural exploitation of the Wolmar estate.

Saint-Preux's letter to Bomston (*Julie ou la Nouvelle Héloïse* 5. 2) is read by all readers. Economics has become a function of literature:

Ces soins que vous appelez importuns sont à la fois nos devoirs et nos plaisirs; grâce à la prévoyance avec laquelle on les ordonne, ils ne sont jamais pénibles; ils nous tiennent lieu d'une foule de fantaisies ruineuses dont la vie champêtre prévient ou détruit le goût, et tout ce qui contribue à notre bien-être devient pour nous un amusement (Rousseau 1964: 549).	These occupations which you call innopportune constitute both our duty and our pleasures; given the forethought with which they are apportioned, they are never painful; they replace a host of wasteful fantasies the taste for which is eliminated, and all that contributes to our well-being becomes entertaining to us.

Bucolic, pastoral, the writer expresses the preoccupations of a *class* whose obsessions with the land can only be satisfied by constant purchase, apportionment, and cultivation. Indeed, the return to the land coincides with the reinforcement of property rights, as is shown by a reaction of the nobility defending its legal privileges on the one side (*réaction nobilière*), and, on the other, by the bourgeoisie continually buying into the estates of the *Ancien Régime*. As Marc Bloch states:

The tradition of these land acquisitions in the families of the *haute bourgeoisie* persists in the seventeenth and eighteenth centuries. It becomes implanted in noble families. To join pastures to tillages, and vineyards to forests, is, for the merchant grown rich, to assure the wealth of his heirs by establishing foundations more solid than those afforded by the pursuit of trade and business (Bloch 1955: 143).

This accrued emphasis on property rights can also be verified another way, by surveying, like Tocqueville (1967: 85 ff.), the registers of the *Ancien Régime*. There one immediately notices the extreme division of the land.

True, some peasants were freed from their servitude to become land-owners, freeholders (*laboureurs*); but many others, burdened by taxes and pressed for money, were led to give up their homeland. It is the rich bourgeois and the nobles who repurchase them. On the whole, in spite of the peasants' acquisitions, it is the upper classes that *return* to the land.

The pastoral is not unaware of this reality; one can join the end of the article "Property" in the *Encyclopédie* and Saint-Lambert's preliminary to his *Saisons*:

Dans les états où l'on suit les règles de la raison, les *propriétés* des particuliers sont sous la protection des lois; le père de famille est assuré de jouir lui-même et de transmettre à sa postérité les biens qu'il a amassés par son travail. Les bons rois ont toujours respecté les possesssions de leurs sujets; ils n'ont regardé les deniers publics qui leur ont été confiés que comme un dépôt, qu'il ne leur était point permis de détourner pour satisfaire ni leurs passions frivoles, ni l'avidité de leurs favoris, ni la rapacité de leurs courtisans (*Encyclopédie* 1954: 192; "Propriété").

In states where one follows the rules of reason, the *property* of individuals is under protection of the law; the head of the family is assured the enjoyment and the right to pass on to his children the wealth he has amassed through his work; good kings have always respected the possessions of their subjects; they considered public revenues entrusted to them only as a deposit that they were not permitted to embezzle to satisfy either their frivolous passions or the greed of their favorites, or the rapaciousness of their courtisans.

Si la poésie descriptive doit émouvoir, elle doit instruire. Il ne suffit pas de répandre dans un poème des senti-ments honnêtes et des maximes ver-tueuses. Il faut lui donner un but moral; c'est lui donner, à la fois, un mérite et une beauté de plus. Il en aura plus d'unité dans le tout et dans ses parties. Je n'ai point perdu de vue le dessein d'inspirer à la Noblesse et aux Citoyens riches, l'amour de la campagne et le respect pour la vie champêtre. Aucune de mes digres-sions, aucun de mes tableaux, ne feront oublier ce but aux Lecteurs. J'ai fait des *Géorgiques* pour les hommes chargés de protéger les campagnes, et non pour ceux qui les cultivent: ce n'est point aux agriculteurs que j'ai parlé, ils ne m'auroient pas entendu . . . il sera utile à jamais d'inspirer à ceux que les lois élèvent au-dessus des cultivateurs, la bienveillance et les égards qu'ils doivant à des citoyens estimables. Il est

If descriptive poetry must move, it must instruct. It is not sufficient to scatter honest feelings and virtuous maxims in a poem. It must be given a moral end, which is to give it both merit and an added beauty. There will be more unity in the whole and in its parts. I have not lost sight at all of the design to inspire in noble and rich citizens love for the countryside and respect for the country life: none of my digressions, none of my tableaux will let the readers forget this. I created *Georgics* for the men responsible for protecting the countryside, and not for those who farm it: iᵗ is not at all for peasants, they would not have understood . . . ; it will always be advantageous to inspire in those that the law raises above peasants the kindness and consideration that they owe to these esteemed citizens. It is especially beneficial at this moment to inspire in the higher classes the

utile, surtout en ce moment, d'inspirer aux premières classes des citoyens le goût de la vie champêtre . . . Peut-être la Noblesse pensera-t-elle enfin, que dans les moments où elle n'est pas nécessaire à nos armées, elle peut employer son temps à éclairer ses vassaux, à perfectionner l'agriculture, et à s'enrichir par des moyens qui enrichissent l'Etat (Saint-Lambert 1769: xxiii–xxv).

appreciation for life in the country . . . Perhaps the nobility will finally think that in moments when they are not indispensable to our armies, they can use their time enlightening their vassals, perfecting agriculture, and in growing rich in ways that will make the state grow rich."

One notices the subtle relation of economy to morality, to literature, and throughout, the presence of money. The *Encyclopédie* ("Property") recognizes the right of the peasant to enjoy "the wealth he has amassed through his work", but is is not unaware that in order to accumulate this wealth, one must already have land, and that this land is in the hands of the rich:

Malheur au pays où il serait vrai que le *laboureur* est un homme pauvre; ce ne pourrait être que dans une nation qui le serait elle-même, et chez laquelle une décadence progressive se ferait bientôt sentir par les plus funestes effets . . . Il faut donc que le *laboureur* soit propriétaire d'un fonds considérable, soit pour monter la ferme en bestiaux et en instruments, soit pour fournir aux dépenses journalières, dont il ne commence à recueillir le fruit que près de deux ans après ses premières avances (*Encyclopédie* 1954: 130; "Laboureur").

Woe to the land where the *freeholder* [laboureur] would be a poor man: it could only be in a nation which would itself be poor and where a progressive decadence would soon be felt in the most destructive fashion . . . It is thus necessary that the *freeholder* be the proprietor of a considerable estate, either to augment his cattle or his implements, or to defray daily expenses from which he begins to profit only past his first two years.

Likewise for the country in literature. As the Abbé Delille recalls in *Jardins*, the aristocratic inclination for the pastoral requires both wealth and leisure:

Que j'aime le mortel, noble dans ses penchants,
Qui cultive à la fois son esprit et ses champs!
Lui seul jouit de tout. Dans sa triste ignorance
Le vulgaire voit tout avec indifférence

How I love the mortal, noble in his inclinations,
Who cultivates both his spirit and his fields!
Only he can enjoy everything. In his sad ignorance
the mob sees everything with indifference

. . . .

Non, ce n'est pas lui qu'en ses tableaux si vastes
Le grand peintre forma d'harmonieux contrastes.

No, it is not for him that in his grandiose paintings
the great painter formed harmonious contrasts.

. . . .

Le sage seul, instruit des lois de
l'univers,
Sait goûter dans les champs une
volupté pure:
C'est pour *l'ami des arts* qu'existe la
nature
(Delille 1833: *L'Homme des champs* 1-20,
emphasis added).

Only the sage, cognizant of the laws of
the universe,
Can appreciate in the field a pure bliss:
It is for the *patron of the arts* that nature
exists.

There is what partially explains the ambivalence of pastoral culture: happiness is nature, but nature can only be found in the books of the rich, the landowners and their friends.

With some rare authors, however — Rousseau, for instance, Mably, and perhaps Turgot — the *true* pastoral return appears less scandalous (it does interest other than the privileged) and more *realistic* (the bucolic consists not of imagining, but of working the land) because the system of private property functions in a utopia. One idealizes a return to a land common to all, in a countryside where everyone works and shares under the aegis of a benevolent figure like Wolmar. Let us consider the system extolled by Turgot in an ordinance which he had published in 1770 together with the one described by Saint-Preux (*Julie* 5). The subject is a paternal world in which a good heart and friendship relieve the suffering of the peasant. There one finds proclaimed the denial of money and that of destitute country life such as it is described by investigators and travelers:

que lesdits propriétaires de biens-fonds partageant avec tous les citoyens aisés l'obligation qu'imposent la religion et l'humanité de soulager les pauvres, cette obligation devient plus stricte encore, et semble appartenir plutôt à la justice qu'à la charité, lorsqui'il s'agit d'un genre de pauvres avec lesquels ils sont liés par des rapports plus particuliers fondés sur les services mêmes qu'ils sont dans l'habitude d'en recevoir: que ces pauvres, au moment où la misère les a frappés, s'épuisaient par les plus durs travaux à mettre en valeur les biens de leurs maîtres, lesquels doivent à ces travaux tout ce qu'ils possèdent; qu'à ces motifs d'humanité et de justice se joint, pour les propriétaires, la considération de leur véritable intérêt, puisque la mort ou la fuite des cultivateurs, l'abandon et l'anéantissement de leurs familles, suites infaillibles de la situation à laquelle ils seraient réduits, priveraient

that the aforementioned property owners of extreme wealth share with all well-to-do citizens the obligation imposed by religion and humanity to relieve the suffering of the poor, this obligation becomes even more strict, and seems to belong to justice rather than to charity, when it concerns the poor with whom they are associated by relationships more particularly based on the very services that they are accustomed to being given: that these poor people, at the moment when misery has descended upon them, exhaust themselves with the most difficult work to increase the wealth of their masters, these masters owe to this work all that they own; that joined to these motifs of humanity and justice, for property owners, is the consideration of their genuine interest: since death or flight of the peasants, abandon or destruction of their families, infallible consequences of the state to which they would be

leurs maîtres des moyens de tirer de leurs terres un revenu qu'elles ne peuvent produire que par le travail (Turgot 1919: 243–244).

reduced, would deprive their masters of the means of producing from their farms a yield that can only be obtained by their work.

'Jetez les yeux tout autour de vous, ajoutoît ce judicieux père de famille, vous n'y verrez que des choses utiles, qui ne vous coûtent presque rien et nous épargnent mille dépenses' (Rousseau 1964: 549).

"Glance about you," added the sensible family head, "you will see only useful things, which cost you almost nothing and save us a thousand expenditures."

But reality is elsewhere. Rousseau is disappointed when he realizes that the shepherds of the Lignon existed only in his imagination; he is furious to discover that everything in the world is not on the model of Clarens: see the stinging commentary after a stop with a peasant terrified by tax inspectors (Rousseau 1973: vol. 1, pp. 216-217). It is even worse when the most celebrated pastoral of the time, *The Death of Abel* (Gessner 1771) announces, with the first crime, the end of the Golden Age. History looms on the horizon. Abel dies at the gates of Eden as will soon Virginie on the shores of the île de France.

But in the meantime, in spite of and perhaps even because of a frightening history, one holds on to the ways of antiquity, *one continues to believe in the shepherds of Sicily and Alexandria* — even if it means ignoring the obscenities of the *Greek Anthology* and visiting once again the Forez in *Astrée* or the Egypt in *Télémaque*. With Theocritus and Callimachus on one side, and d'Urfé and Fénelon on the other, one entertains the illusion of a *mimesis* forever youthful.[13] A wager all the less reasonable that, according to the *Encyclopédie*:

[Ces bergers] ne ressemblent en rien aux habitants de nos campagnes et à nos bergers d'aujourd'hui, malheureux paysans, occupés uniquement à se procurer par las travaux pénibles d'une vie laborieuse de quoi subvenir aux besoins les plus pressants d'une famille toujours indigente (*Encyclopédie* 1755: 426; "Eglogue").

[These shepherds] in no way resemble the inhabitants of our countryside and our shepherds of today, unfortunate peasants, only concerned with obtaining through the toil and labor of a painful life that which can satisfy the most pressing needs of a family forever destitute.

Be that as it may, it is also quite true that "This illusion is more pleasing than reality" and since imagination is closer to the heart than the senses, we are more easily moved by a *painting than by the spectacle of the country*. The most exact reasoning, the most novel observations will never produce the blissful illusion created by these images. In such a case then, why not fill "our mind with these sweet chimeras, and [have] shepherds capable of charming us" (Fontenelle 1968: 59, emphasis added)?

ECLOGUE AND NAIVE PAINTING

The function of the eclogue is (etymologically) to *choose* (*what is pleasing*) without suffering anything that might spoil this pleasure, such as pain of loss or death. In order to attain it, one must only obey one rule: naive painting must be simply derived from nature as *naïf* is derived from *naturel*:

Il ne s'agit pas seulement de peindre, il faut peindre des objets qui fassent plaisir à voir. Quand on me représente le repos qui règne à la campagne, la simplicité et la tendresse avec laquelle l'amour s'y prête, mon imagination touchée émue me transporte dans la condition de berger: je suis berger, mais que l'on me représente, quoique avec toute l'exactitude et la justesse possible, les viles occupations de berger, elles ne me font point envie, et mon imagination demeure fort froide (Fontenelle 1968: 59).

Depicting is not enough, one must depict objects which are pleasing to the sight. When one shows me the peace reigning in the countryside, the simplicity and the tenderness with which love is dealt there, my imagination is moved and puts me in the station of a shepherd: I am a shepherd. But if you show me, even with all the exactness and precision possible, the lowly occupations of shepherds, they do not appeal to me, and my imagination remains very cold.

This derivation is a connotation, which requires that we change our register of reading. The referent (earth, eighteenth-century nature as we know it through chroniclers like Young) has been lost. In the *naïve* world, nature is an image of lovely color, a few formulas. And the value of these formulas can only be appreciated by reference to a code, itself formulaic. Formula means repetition, and repetition, identification. One searches not for mystery, but for convention. A gentle *exordium* is followed by the cliché description:

Les biens qui contentent nos coeurs
Viennent s'offrir à nous sans coûter
　　　　　　　　　　　de larmes;
L'amour le plus heureux a toujours
　　　　　　　　　　　ses alarmes,
Aux innocents plaisirs il ôte leurs
　　　　　　　　　　　douceurs:
Les chansons des oiseaux, les
　　　　　　　　ombrages, les fleurs
Les doux zéphirs ont pour nous tous
　　　　　　　　　　　leurs charmes
(Fontenelle 1968: 125; *Une Nymphe*).

The possessions which make our
　　　　　　　　　　heart content
Come to offer themselves without
　　　　　　　　　causing our tears;
The most joyous love always has its
　　　　　　　　　　　　alarms,
To innocent pleasures, it takes away
　　　　　　　　　　their sweetness:
The songs of the birds, the shadows,
　　　　　　　　　　　the flowers
The gentle zephyrs hold for us all
　　　　　　　　　　　their dreams

Action is nowhere to be found. One speaks, as in former times in the salons, of the possessions which are pleasing to our hearts and of the charms of the zephyrs ("douceurs" of a rusticity "sans . . . larmes" or "alarmes"): it is as though one had never left the Hôtel de Rambouillet.

Even when Fontenelle's *preciosité* has made way for Gessner's realism, the convention is still to present a coding immediately perceivable to the reader, as in the following passage, the biblical episode of Cain and Abel:

Wie ein zottigter Loewe, der an einem Felsen im Schatten schlaeft, (der bange Wandrer geht leise weit neben ihm vor-yber, [denn Gefahr drohet aus der Maehne hervor, die des Schlafenden Stirne dekt]), wie der, wenn er ploezlich die tiefe Wunde des schnell fliegenden Pfeiles in seiner Hyft empfindet, mit tobendem Gebryll schnell aufspringt, und wytend seinen Feind sucht, und ein unschuldiges Kind zerreisst, das nicht weit mit Blumen im Grase spielt; eben so sprang Kain ploezlich vom Schlaf auf; schaeumend; vor seiner Stirne sass tobende Wuth (Gessner 1972: vol. 1, pp. 151-152).

As the fierce lion crouching at the foot of a rock, (who though asleep, freezes with terror the trembling traveller, and obliges him to take a wide circuit to avoid the dreadful beast) if the murder-ous arrow, in its rapid flight, pierces his side, suddenly starts, and, with dreadful roar, seeks his enemy. He foams. He rages. His blazing eyes menace destruc-tion. The first object he meets is the victim of his fury; perhaps an innocent child, playing on the grass with the variegated flowers. Not less terrible rose Cain. His eyes were enflam'd, and rancour sat on his pallid cheek (Gessner 1771: 155).

The reader, who already has a thorough understanding of the story, is first interested in the form. What form does he see? In the overblown English translation "his eyes . . . enflam'd;" *"variegated* flowers"), he sees above all a Homeric comparison in Madame Dacier's or in Pope's manner.[14] In the German text, he notices the redundancy of clichés underscoring an epic disturbance of the pleasance: "zottigter Loewe", "die tiefe Wunde", "tobendem", "Gebryll". Despite all its heroism, the painting of a *Cain macturus* is hardly convincing, and if we were even tempted to see in the *Death of Abel* some omen of a catastrophe on the pastoral horizon, some clear sign that history is indeed menacing the shepherds of the rich, the interpretation would be out of context with the *Zeitgeist*. It is not for naught that the poem's title is not "Cain's crime," but the *Death of Abel (Der Tod Abels)*. The rabid Cain appears hardly different from a naughty faun or an evil satyr, made furious in the agonies of love. The same Gessner who trifles with the Bible recovers the delicacies of Fontenelle rather well:

O wenn die frohen Lieder dir gefielen? die meine Muse oft dem Hirten ab-horcht; auch oft belauschet sie in dich-ten Hainen, der Baeume Nymphen und den Ziegenfyss'gen Wald-Gott und Schilfbekraenzte Nymphen in den Grotten; und oft besuchet sie bemooste

Oh! pleasing to thee be the simple songs my muse has learned among the shepherds; the strains she has listened to in the thick groves where the dryads resort, where wander the wood-gods, and the sedge-crowned nymphs of the stream. Oft has she visited the mossy

Hytten, um die der Landmann stille Schatten pflanzet, und bringt Geschichten her, von Grosmuth und von Tugend und von der immer frohen Unschuld. Auch oft beschleichet sie der Gott der Liebe in grynen Grotten dicht verwebner Straeuche, und oft im Weiden-Busch an kleinen Baechen. Er horchet dann ihr Lied, und kraenzt ihr fliegend Haar, wenn sie von Liebe singt und frohem Scherz (Gessner 1972: vol. 2, pp. 2-3).

cot, where the peasant reposes under the peaceful shade his hand has planted; from thence she brings these tales of simplicity and virtue, and ever frolic innocence. And oft too has she watched the god of love, while he reclined amidst the green bower's interwoven branches, and among the willows which bend over the little stream, he listened to her strains, and crowned her flowing hair with dewy roses, while she sang of love and frolic joy (Gessner 1802: 2).

Here, too, the exaggerated English translation only serves to underline the impact of Gessner's *préciosité* on his European audience: the "fliegend Haar" of the Muse is adorned with "dewy roses". Gessner's "simple songs of shepherds" have made an art of simplicity. It is clear then, that the *only* earthly paradise is at Tempe or Gnide. This is where the folklore aspects of the *bergeries* appear. It is the formulaic description which is pleasing. It is that which is required as a motif. Any pastoral that does not contain these formulas is not a pastoral. Nothing distinguishes these repetitions, these comparisons, from those of Bion or Anacreon:

Nous goûtons une paix profonde,
Venez, venez parmi nous.
Que l'amour au reste du monde
Fasse ressentir ses coups,
Ils n'iront point jusqu'à vous.
Venez, venez parmi nous,
Nous goûtons une paix profonde.
Venez, venez parmi nous,
Nous goûtons une paix profonde,
Venez, venez parmi nous
(Fontenelle 1968: 125; *Chœur des nymphes*).

We enjoy a profound peace,
Come, come among us.
That love to the rest of the world
make his blows felt,
They will not reach you.
Come, come among us.
We enjoy a profound peace,
Come, come among us,
We enjoy a profound peace,
Come, come among us

But culture serves morality and the pastoral return is only one of the forms of a return in time, to the original man and his pure unadulterated ways. The charm is in the tenor, the quality of movement, of gesture, which because it has no other reference but the *mimetic context* into which it fits without difficulty, integrates a moral content (*la grandeur d'âme, la vertu, l'heureuse innocence*) which justifies a worn-out *bergerade*. From Gessner to Greuze, there is only one step. Diderot, before a painting by Boucher (inspired by Fontenelle's pastoral), exclaims:

le tout est fin, délicat, solidement pensé; ce sont quatre petites églogues à la Fon-

the whole is fine and delicate, soundly considered, these are four little eclogues

tenelle. Peut-être les moeurs de
Théocrite, ou celles de *Daphnis et
Chloé*, plus simples, plus naïves,
m'auraient intéressé d'avantage
(Diderot 1965: 463).

à la Fontenelle. Perhaps the ways of
Theocritus or those of *Daphnis and
Chloe*, simpler, more naive, would have
interested me more. (emphasis added).

He even admires *la Jeune fille qui pleure son oiseau mort* by Greuze:

La jolie élégie, le charmant poème! la
belle idylle que Gessner en ferait . . .
Quand on aperçoit ce morceau, on dit:
Délicieux! Si l'on s'y arrête, ou qu'on y
revienne, on s'écrie *Délicieux*! *délicieux*!
Bientôt on se surprend conversant avec
cette enfant, et la consolant. Cela est
si vrai, que voici ce que je me souviens
de lui avoir dit à différentes reprises
. . . (Diderot 1965: 533).

The lovely elegy, the charming poem,
the beautiful idyll that Gessner would
make of it . . . When one discovers this
piece, one says *"delightful!"* If one lin-
gers there, or by chance returns, one
cries *"delightful, delightful!"* Soon one
catches oneself conversing with this
child and consoling it. This is so true that
this is what I remember having said to
her at different times . . .

Drawing support from the constant use of Alexandrinisms,[15] and recalling
the stereotypes of adolescent verses, the poet (the painter) *works on* the
classical, the bourgeois culture, freeing, beyond the already known, the
philosophers' nature, an immense desire for representation, which because
it is with no other reference than that of the return (but return to what?) is
limited to sketching the moral outline of this same culture. Apparently
neither history nor destiny were able to discourage the undertaking: even
the revolution cannot dry up the streams of Arcadia. The writing seems, on
the contrary, to search for, and fixate, the perfect moment, when, from the
ancient or classical book, emerges an *homme naïf*, in other words, not nude,
but clad in the manner of Tityrus and in the style of the eighteenth century,
and who lives not from naught, but on love and poetry. He runs through the
woodlands of literature, he sings for the society that caused his rebirth.
Model to the painter and emblematic form on the canvas from Watteau to
Greuze, the *nativus* smiles without conviction, or laments Abel, Virginie
and Lesbia's sparrow, who never cease to die. It is as though the
philosophers, having just seen themselves in the correct historical perspective, cherished the fiction of the perfect, the eternal moment, which allowed
them to forget it.

NOTES

1. See particularly chapters 1, 2, and 3 of the second book, "L'Églogue galante." Compare
   also Trahard (1931-1933) and Monglond (1966); May (1964); and finally some
   specialized studies: Gros (1959) and Roudaut (1959, 1962). For a bibliography of
   English pastoral literature, see chapter 14. More recently, Riffaterre (1972, 1973) has

given the criticism of pastoral literature some theoretical stature. In this section, however, my purpose is specifically distinct from Riffaterre's and closer to Hartman's preoccupations (1975). I am attempting to go beyond the linguistic structures presented above in Part 1, and to incorporate into a simiostylistic process philosophical considerations of Self and Other totally absent from Riffaterre's surface analysis. Now, while the qualifier *bucolic* should only be applied to the eclogue, here I take it in its most widely accepted meaning (bucolic-pastoral-*bergerie*) – all that can be attached to the Alexandrine pastoral theme (novels, epic, eclogue) with or without shepherds, fauns, or satyrs, which revives the idea of the return (see below). Insofar as these nonpastoral works can be associated with this theme, by an episode, an atmosphere, or indirectly, they will draw my attention (for example, the fifth book of *Julie*).

2. *Anette et Lubin* is a pastoral by Marmontel; *Estelle et Némorin* a pastoral by Florian (preceded by an important *discourse on the pastoral*). As for *Daphnis and Chloe*, Longus' pastoral remained very popular in the eighteenth century: Rousseau created two romances on the subject, and he set the first act of a *Daphnis and Chloe* to music with words by Corancez. The pastoral reached its climax with Gessner, whose work took Europe by storm.

3. See Mornet (1907: preface) and Trahard (1931-1933). Here, perhaps more than anywhere else, is the temptation great to explain the taste for the pastoral by a series of historical coincidences. But this strategy is often counterproductive, as it remains conditioned by socioaesthetic norms, pastoral being a minor genre, from which the eighteenth century must be excused. The phenomenon is never taken seriously.

4. Whether or not the *Lévite* is a pastoral, it is, at any rate, a naive painting of origins.

5. The title is misleading: in reality, it was a portable library. But there as elsewhere the success of the *Nouvelle Héloïse* encouraged the novels-in-the-country: Fanny de Beauharnais's *L'Abailard supposé*; François de Baculard d'Arnaud's *Les Épreuves du sentiment*; and later, Loaisel de Tréogate's *Dolbreuse*, where the forsaken heroine awaits her fickle lover in a lowly cottage.

6. Let us remember the importance of the travel and exploration motif in the eighteenth century (*littérature des voyages*). Rousseau, before writing the above text, was lent the translation of Richard Walter's compilation of the voyages of Lord Anson, *A voyage round the world*. During the same period, Bougainville and Poivre's accounts were extremely popular. One can find all these themes in the *Histoire générale des voyages*, covering 1746 to 1789, which appeared under the direction of the Abbé Prévost.

7. One obviously thinks of Rousseau's venture in the *Discours*, the *Contrat*, and certain parts of *Julie*: "To the extent that Rousseau desires not only to elicit the intellectual support of the hearer, but also to inspire love and admiration, it is toward himself that, through the watching universe he directs the final intent of his *parole*. It is not outside, at the farthest reaches of the world, that the discourse will be lost; the eloquent *parole*, by awakening the reader's passion, by asking him to take Jean-Jacques as the object of his enthusiasm, offers us the image of a circular journey where the beginning and the end coincide" (Starobinski 1971: 325).

8. The works referred to are: Buffon, *Histoire naturelle*: 2 volumes on man; 12 on the *quadrupèdes vivipares*, 9 on *les oiseaux* (the Buffon "second manner" in the *Époques de la nature* clearly perceives the hypothesis of the transformism); Helvétius, *De l'esprit* and especially *De l'homme*; Diderot, *Rêve de d'Alembert* "Qu'était l'éléphant dans son origine? Peut-être l'animal énorme tel qu'il nous paraît, peut-être un atome, car tous les deux sont également possibles" (Diderot 1951: 825) [What was the elephant in its beginnings? Perhaps the enormous animal as it appears to us now, perhaps an atom, as both are equally possible"].

9. "Le voyage de Bougainville est le seul qui m'ait donné du goût pour une autre   "Bougainville's journey is the only one that instilled within me a desire for a country

contrée que la mienne; jusqu'à cette lecture, j'avais pensé qu'on n'était nulle part aussi bien que chez soi; résultat que je croyais le même pour chaque habitant de la terre; effet naturel de l'attrait du sol; attrait qui tient aux commodités dont on jouit, et qu'on n'a pas la même certitude de retrouver ailleurs" (Diderot 1951: 998).

other than my own; before this reading, I had thought that one was nowhere any better than at home; a result I considered equally applicable for each inhabitant of the land; a natural effect of the earth's attraction; an attraction tied to the comfort one enjoys and which one does not feel the same certainty of finding elsewhere".

10. Thus one sees Fontenelle protest against the eccentricities of Sannazar: "Sannazar n'a introduit que des pêcheurs dans ses églogues, et i'y sens toujours que l'idée de leur travail dur me blesse. Je ne sais quelle finesse il a entendu à mettre des pêcheurs au lieu des bergers qui étaient en possession de l'églogue: mais si les pêcheurs eussent été en la même possession il eût fallu mettre les bergers en leur place" (Fontenelle 1968: 58) ["Sannazar introduced only fishermen into these eclogues, and I always feel shocked at the idea of their difficult labor. I do not know what shrewdness he had in mind to put fisherman instead of shepherds, who were masters in the art of the eclogue: but if the fishermen had also been masters in the same art, it would have been necessary to replace them with shepherds"].

11. Unless indicated otherwise, translations in this chapter are mine.

12. "L'illusion et en même temps l'agrément des bergeries consiste donc à n'offrir aux yeux que la tranquilité de la vie pastorale, dont on dissimule, la bassesse . . . il ne s'agit pas seulement de peindre, il faut peindre des objets qui fassent plaisir" (Fontenelle 1968: 59).

"The illusion and at the same time the pleasure of the *bergeries* consist then in offering our eyes only the tranquillity of pastoral life, from which baseness is concealed . . . the problem is no longer to paint, but to paint only objects which bring pleasure."

13. One is aware of the importance of the return to antiquity before and during the revolution (see Bertrand 1968).

14. Homer has become a fashionable author again.

15. The theme of Greuze's painting goes back to Catullus' "Lesbia's sparrow" (*Poems* 2, 3).

12

On Description and Descriptiveness: Further Inquiry

Descriptions are often considered superfluous: something which the reader of a novel can afford to miss on occasion, casually skipping pages here and there without prejudice to his understanding of the plot. Poetry, on the other hand, does not know description as such, except perhaps in the specific genre of pastoral or didactic poetry (for example Thomson and Delille). As for drama, if *dramatic descriptions* (the tale of a messenger, the song of a chorus) usually increase our understanding of the action, they can never take the place of a dialogue or a monologue, nor can they be considered a part of the performative core of the play.

The trouble with a definition of this kind is that it is, of course, much too vague. Not only does it make use of vague criteria (Which reader are we talking about? What is the descriptive genre in poetry? How can description be dramatic?), but it also tells us nothing about the function of descriptions, except perhaps that they exist only as a part of something else: they are the ornament, the exterior, the absence or presence of which enables us to distinguish between literary statements and nonliterary statements. We have learned nothing really positive about description itself, its value, its function, and whether, for instance, it is at all possible to consider description as a function of any linguistic statement, whether it is not in fact one of the functions of language itself. Two things, at least, seem assured: (1) that descriptions are always sensed as problematic: they may or may not be part of something else (a narrative statement)— which might lead us to conclude hastily that they deal with nonessential matters; but this hasty conclusion will automatically compel us to raise the question of truth and untruth in language; and (2) that, while they may still be expendable, descriptions paradoxically underline the value of what they are describing, by stressing a threefold reference: first, to the speaker or the narrator who takes time to *describe*; second, to the world in general, whose presence a description is supposed to render or imitate; and third, through the specific object being described, less to a world that we already take for granted, *the one we know*, then to another one, which we have not noticed *because we have not been able to see it yet: the one we do not know*.[1] It is usually on the basis of this last reference, that is, by summarily equating *descriptiveness* with *newness*, that we tend to evaluate descriptions, thus merely substituting a psychological problem for an epistemological one.

There is, however, one major difficulty in attempting a critique of description, in that there is no other way for us to find out what a description is, *than to describe what we think a description is*. Thus, it seems that, far from being a simple option in the communication process, description is the way in which we must use language if we want to reflect upon its modes. In this sense, the descriptive function in language is a very special one indeed: it is not only a referring or denoting one. It is the only one which enables us to identify a piece of information both as redundant (we know there is something that has been added to the simple perception of an object-in-the-world) and as pertinent (we are sure that this piece of information will immediately or later be part of a larger narrative whole). In other words, there is in a description something like a surplus value, an aura which glorifies narrative discourse and makes it more noticeable. Although descriptions are often viewed as involving the narrator with matters which do not relate directly to the action, and thus appear to derive their surplus value from a real addition to the original reference delineated by the narrative (as when an author writes about the social or cultural context of his hero), they cannot be defined merely by a process of temporal or spatial extension, because it would have to be proven that what they make explicit is not already implicit in any narrative and that they are real additions to the discourse instead of being constitutive of it. Outside literature proper, in philosophy or in mathematics, in various types of scientific discourse, where it is never institutionalized as the privilege of a narrator, a description is a way to ensure the adequacy of an object and a concept: it makes obvious, it exhibits, it underlines, the conditions under which a particular object is to be considered, whether it be inside or outside experience. The problem is thus greatly simplified as descriptions can immediately be classified according to various degrees of truth, according to whether the concept being applied always, sometimes, or never, agrees with its object. In literature and in literary criticism, however, truth is of a different, imitative, kind. In the course of this essay then, we shall have to ascertain how the descriptive process in literature contributes to the establishment of truth in fiction.

I. *Description: describere*. Let us look at the word itself. The prefix (*de-*) implies something like a distance taken from the act of writing (*scribere*). First: *de-scribere*, from top to bottom, as though it were a matter of unfolding, of laying bare the successive stages in the formation of a *scriptum*. Then: *de-scribere*, with a movement from close to far away, in an attempt to move away from that which has already been stated, recorded, and which cannot be changed. In the latter meaning of *de-scribere*, the prefix *de-* stresses not only that the object will be taken apart, that its parts will be examined one by one, but also the idea that this operation could not be completed without a shift, a displacement from the place, the *topos* in which the object was inscribed in the first place. A description then is that system which enables us to modify a common frame of reference and to introduce our own view of the world. One could object that I am making too much of description, and that the simplest way to put conformity to the test is to make not descriptions but judgments. This, however, is not quite true either. If I say: "The house is blue and its roof is red", I have not given a description of that house; I have simply stated some of its qualifications. Or rather, I have truly given a description of the house, if the statement I have made about it being blue and its roof being red has been taken in itself to signify more than the blueness of the paint or the redness of the roof. For instance if the house is indeed simple, and its simplicity, which has already been made apparent in the basic contrast of colors, is a clear mark of its distinctiveness, that is, if this is a house which is distinct from any other, *there is a story behind it*. We can summarize the whole matter by saying that any statement, any judgment, can become a description, when it can be experienced as *being a part of an actual or potential narrative*. In this case, the house is of interest to us because (1) it is perhaps the house where we are going with the hero of the story, or (2) it is the house which the writer has taken for his decription topic at this stage of the narrative. The house, as a familiar concept with which I am used to define my environment, my habitat, is no longer familiar, unquestioned: it has become a sign for something else, which I may not fully understand yet. What has happened is that the object has now been *given*, as through some sort of ritual presentation. Instead of this house being taken for granted in the course of a narrative, I, the reader, am asked to pause and gaze at it. However brief the description (it can even be so brief as to be undistinguishable from the narrative itself), I now have the distinct feeling *that the object is happening. This experience I call the experience of the object being given, or the givenness of the object.*

Now the question is, what are the criteria for establishing and recognizing this *givenness*? First of all, there do not seem to be any proper linguistic criteria for this sort of occurrence. The most a linguist would say is that a description is an *expansion*: that is, aside from a structure which it has in common with all the other statements with which it makes up a text, a description is mainly a development of one or several lexical entries, which would not otherwise receive any special treatment. This is obvious with the novel narratives of the naturalist type (Flaubert, Zola), where an occurrence is always the occasion for a technical or historical explanation, as given by a character whose introduction will justify the occasion. In this sense, a description is nothing more than the unfolding of a *scriptum* or a *scripture*: of that which has already been written in other books and which refers to a world we all take for granted. It is a description merely in the first sense of the term above. And because it is just that, I shall not concern myself with it here. What interests me is description in the other sense of the term: that which is both a shift and a displacement and represents a real modification of the narrative function.

Let us take a case where this modification is so subtle as not to be easily perceived: the first sentence in a story by Joyce ("The Dead") — I am quoting the whole paragraph, to allow us to refer to the context.

Lily, the caretaker's daughter, was literally run off her feet. Hardly had she brought one gentleman into the little pantry behind the office on the ground floor and helped him off with his overcoat than the wheezy hall-door bell clanged again and she had to scamper along the bare hallway to let in another guest. It was well for her she had not to attend to the ladies also. But Miss Kate and Miss Julia were there, gossiping and laughing and fussing, walking after each other to the head of the stairs, peering down over the banisters and calling down to Lily to ask her who had come. (Joyce 1956: 173).

If we consider the first sentence ("Lily . . ."), we can see that it is indeed a description. Let us take two examples.

1. At the very beginning of the text, we find the proper name *Lily*. In common parlance, the function of the proper name is to indicate both a reference and a classification: it is merely a *deictic* or a *shifter*, which can help us relate one code to another (the code *person* or *human being*, *male* or *female*, to the code *Peter* or *Paul*). Now, because we generally use proper names to assign the subject of a particular action to a particular place, that is, this or that person with this or that quality, we lose sight of the fact that their use is based on the understanding of their deictic function, for example, in vocatives ("Mr. Jones . . ."; "Peter . . ."); in forms of social convenience ("Let me introduce Mr. Jones"); in formal addresses ("Will

the true Mr. Jones stand up?"); or in appositive sequences (here: "the caretaker's daughter"). We forget that behind this deictic, the whole story of this or that person lies in a close or larger context of cross-references:[2] a story which narrative discourse will then pick up, explaining, making obvious the information stored in the proper name. In this passage, however, because Lily is mentioned at the very beginning of the narrative, the introduction of a proper name outside a vocative situation (where the context of the introduction would already be known) leaves us perplexed: we have the feeling the narrator acts as if we already knew who Lily was; and because we do not, we expect this person to be more appropriately introduced to us, and the ensuing narrative, to provide us with the missing information. Joyce is eliciting our attention here with some sort of trick, a *captatio benevolentiae legentis* which is a favorite of many writers. This then is the very first descriptive factor, and one, as it were, by default.

2. The second descriptive factor is the "literally" in: "she was literally run off her feet", which, by qualifying the action of "run off her feet", over-determines our perception of the text as a description. In the first sense, *literally* introduces a modification of the action, but this modification is not warranted by the *preceding* context — I say *preceding*, because it is obvious that the lines following this description merely explain why Lily was "literally run off her feet": *literally* could have been replaced by *quickly, suddenly*, or any other modifier of the same type. In another sense, however, *literally* suggests a reflection upon the value of the phrase *run off* (instead of *moved*, for instance). Because it brings the action to our attention, before that action is even mentioned in the order of our reading, *literally* is both an indicator and an amplifier of that action: it authentifies and underscores the importance of the narrative, by setting it in a specific perspective, at a specific distance.

And it is this distance which I would like to discuss now. Whereas in many nineteenth-century novels, a description can be cordoned off from the rest of the discourse, in narratives of the above type, on the other hand, the descriptive function determines the narrative function: it is after the paragraph above that Joyce concludes with what he could have said at the beginning: "It was always a great affair, the Misses Morkan's annual dance" (1956: 173). It is as though he had needed the description of the caretaker's daughter — only a minor character in the story — to give his narrative a place, a frame, a beginning. Interestingly enough, we shall not learn anything about Lily's own physical appearance until later, when yet another visitor has been introduced, who suddenly notices the girl's complexion, as she is taking his coat: "Gabriel smiled at the three syllables she had given his surname and glanced at her. She was a slim, growing girl, pale in complexion and with hay-coloured hair" (1956: 175).

This is indicative of the distancing process inherent in any description. It could be said that, whereas a narrative communicates to us the conditions of a possible experience, it is the business of a description to make us share in that experience itself, in the *givenness* of the world of that experience. Exactly what kind of experience is it? For most of us who can see, it is essentially a *visual* experience. Even though the narrator will often call upon other senses to solicit our imagination, our imagination will itself be visual, that is, we will always *picture* a human reference, most often ourselves, as the receiver of sensory data.[3] And because a visual experience entails a field of vision, the descriptive process will function through the medium of a character, whose sequence of actions serves as a pretext for the description: here, Lily merely attends to the entering guests who are going to contribute to the story; or it will function through the author interposing himself between us and his hero and calling upon us to imagine the scene: thus Balzac announces to us that a specific description of the surroundings would be useful; thus Proust uses the fiction of his own persona to acquaint us with the world of his characters. This whole process of *zooming*, of concentrating on specific details, can range from very slow to very fast, according to whether the narrator will only jot down a few reference points or whether he chooses to deal with, and magnify, only a small section of the scenery at a time. However, and once again, the purpose of a description is not to make us see the place of the action, so that we might be able to juxtapose our understanding of it with our understanding of the action itself. It is, rather, to tell this imaginary vision, as if it were a part of the story as well: not as the story, the plot, to which the description is supposed to contribute a specific, albeit superfluous, illustration, but as a story of the building, the composing of that vision. If we go back to the Joyce text, we shall notice that the sequence of Lily's actions is only significant in relation to the *crowding* of information, which, because it is merely *indicative* of the existence of a party (the distributive "one gentleman" implies repeated scampering along the corridor, to let in the numerous guests), establishes the party as the sum total of all actions suggested by the description. In this sense, the scene described is as far from us, as invisible to us, as it is to Miss Julia and Miss Kate, who have to peer down the banisters and call down to Lily "to ask her who had come". One could say that the place described, the locus of description, is constituted by those very definite areas which Lily has to scamper through in order to let the guests in. But, in fact, the locus of the party, that which enables Joyce, a few lines later, to declare the Misses Morkan's annual dance "a great affair," is *not delineated*, not even visually, although much of the experience is visual (the wheezy hall-door bell's clang is only perceived in association with the immediate motion of scampering "along the bare hallway"), it uses the visual sense to stimulate in us a pleasure of a particular sort.

Beyond the detail of Lily's comings and goings, we are interested in the world defined by her various moves and manifested through the various designations (*"the* caretaker's daughter . . . *the* little pantry . . . *the* wheezy hall-door bell. . . *the* bare hallway"): the world of a joyous party. However, and although linguists will explain the paradigm of the party in terms of a redundancy of pertinent features (the noise/the motion/the crowd), the semantic combination of contiguous elements is not enough to account for what it is that the two ladies are "gossiping and laughing and fussing" over. What we are delighted with, and the two ladies with us, as they are watching the steady flow into their house, is not a party, not even the coming together of a party, but the multiplication and the concatenation of the *signs* of a party, which remain signs, whatever commentary, whatever conclusion the narrator or his characters might want to draw ("It was always a great affair"). These signs are not explicitly decoded into an explanatory metacode, but woven into other signs (for example, after the doorbell has clanged, Lily follows the ritual of allowing the guests into the little pantry behind the office, from where they will presumably join the rest of the party), and we are made to go through some of the routine beginnings of a party, without actually being told at first what kind of party it really is. Joyce's description thus leaves us filled with the anticipation that must also be Lily's; we associate with her, even to the point of lending her the indirect speech of our reliable narrator ("It was well for her she had not to attend to the ladies also"). What I mean to say is that, whether the narrative context is explicit and clear (here, for instance, the beginnings of a party) or simply unclear (in the first stages of a detective novel, for instance), it is the privilege, and perhaps the function, of any descriptive process always to fill us with a certain kind of anticipation. The anticipation of distance and desire that goes with denoting, making objects appear, introducing them, giving them names. One could perhaps express this by saying that any narrative involves us in two different ways: one which is to make us understand a sequence of actions paradigmatically (as constituting one episode or paradigm), which could be defined as the *intelligible function* in the narrative; and another, in which we seek to assess the reality of the sequence, its manifestation, which could be defined as part of the real or *sensible* function. The first function is dependent mostly on the activation of the plot, and in the text from "The Dead", for instance, it determines the total meaning of the scene successively described in the first paragraph: having suddenly been brought to the scene, we merely seek to understand what is happening. The other function causes us to look for that total meaning by identifying, not the significance of such and such an action and its possible integration into the structure of an episode, into the whole design of a story, but the *authenticity* of the sign-process, sign irrespective of its signata. That is to say, we seek to understand these signs by assocation with others we know; we compare the context effected by the narrator with the one we are familiar with.

II. Let anyone who is not familiar with life at sea think of a Conrad novel. He knows he can savor all the descriptive passages, but often without knowing exactly what it is the narrator is talking about. A spate of technical terms, a string of sentences referring to a particular maneuver he does not understand — all these will not diminish his interest in the story, in Conrad. In a description, then, we are not simply concerned with the *signified*, but we also pay attention to the *signs* in their *signifying* process. Now, we have many ways to do this. We can determine for instance that the terminology used means nothing, unless we break up the syntax (see *Ulysses* or *Finnegan's Wake*); or we can decide that this terminology is indeed pertinent and that the question is only one of patience and attention, as the author himself will often provide a glossary or a commentary (see *A Clockwork Orange*). What I mean by authenticity of the signifying process is that the text seems to gain in purpose what it has lost in intelligibility. In following the development of the story, the reader is interested as much in the staging, the construction of a scene, as he is in the scene itself. The intelligible function determines the conditions of a modification of reality; the sensible function, whose importance is paramount to the descriptive process, suggests the process of that modification itself. A description, then, gives us the illusion of having got in touch with, better, of having *appropriated*, the representation of that segment of reality which had been merely implied in the course of the narrative. It is thus inevitable that, in descriptions, the opaque signifier (what we read and whose reference we do not exactly understand) will, at times, obscure the signified (what we think it means), as we, the readers, experience a conflict between our frustration with the meaningless object in the description and our desire to proceed with the course of the narrative, as if we already knew what the narrator was talking about.[4]

For the signifier unlike the signified does not depend on a constituted reference, but on simple designation. We saw the part played by designation in the referencing process with a passage from *Madame Bovary* (see Chapter 1) and we decided that the manipulation of designation is one of the more powerful processes at the disposal of a judgmental novelist. Let us now expand our discussion and explore the relation of designation to the ongoing process of our reading. Whether we understand the reference perfectly, as in "Jungfraud Messonge book" — what *Finnegan's Wake* compounds from the messages and the *mensonges* of Jung and Freud into a *fraud*, the image of a young *Frau*, or a *Jungfrau* of allusions (Joyce 1958: 460), or as in "*Corpus*. Body. Corpse. Good idea the Latin. Stupefies them first" (the scene of the Holy Communion watched by Bloom in All Hallows (Joyce 1961: 80), or whether we do not understand it all, as happens with other passages from Joyce, as soon as we have grasped the design, however, we understand the idea, and we immediately feel in touch with the object. The process of designation, then, is that which sets the stage for the presentation of objects to our perception. Whereas a reference to an object is general and enacts it synthetically, in *toto*, a designation seeks the object out on the restricted basis of one or a few constituent features; and because this presentation cannot take place without some sort of interruption in an ongoing discourse, we must pause from the action and take the time for contemplation.[5] The process thus works essentially to create an ambivalence in the message of written communication, and of prose narrative in particular. Even when the narrator uses a technical language and his designation appears exceptionally complete, he may leave us to wonder what it is he is referring to. Our contact with the object, our *picturization* of it, will remain vague; and because it is vague, we may find ourselves involved even more in the illusion of the text: we are set to dream, to fantasize about the reference, which the narrator has tantalizingly indicated. Let us take the following passage from Conrad's *The Nigger of the Narcissus*:

A breeze was coming. The ship that had been lying tide-rode swung to a heavier puff; and suddenly the slack of the chain cable between the windlass and the hawse-pipe clinked, slipped forward an inch, and rose gently off the deck with a startling suggestion as of unsuspected life that had been lurking stealthily in the iron. In the hawse-pipe the grinding links sent through the ship a sound like a low groan of a man sighing under a burden. The strain came on the windlass, the chain tautened like a string, vibrated—and the handle of the screw brake moved in slight jerks. Singleton stepped forward (Conrad 1974: 26).

In this passage, the accumulation of technical terms should rightly make anyone uneasy ("hawse-pipe . . . windlass . . . screw brake . . ."), as it seems to be the purpose of the narrative itself to acknowledge this uneasiness ("unsuspected life that had been lurking stealthily in the iron"). One would assume that the use of a technical jargon, which is very common in Conrad, is designed to prevent any ambiguity in the reference, and thus to ensure both the complete and exact performance of an action, while, at the same time, suggesting a descriptive context which will not hinder the progression of the narrative. Here, however, this technical jargon has an opposite effect. The punctiliousness of the designation is underscored by the performative content of the reference: a hawse-pipe has a specific function in a ship lying anchored; any motion or noise in that area points to a general motion of the ship no longer lying still (responding, as is here the case, to a heavier gust) — and one could imagine a sailor (Conrad himself) watching the movement of the hawser, as he hears the clink, and debating how the change in the weather or the winds is going to affect the ship the next day, when they are at sea. But as though technicalities were only reducing the field of our perception, instead of further expanding his description, Conrad finds it more convenient to translate these technical terms into an everyday language, by comparing the noise made by the moving links of the steel hawser with the "groan of a man sighing under a burden". This comparison says nothing more specific about the *swinging* of the ship, but in a way negates, or, at the very least, understates, the minute symptomatization of weather patterns, by substituting for it a suggestion of life "lurking stealthily in the iron," and then again, the anthropomorphic fantasy of the "groan of a man sighing under a burden". In other words, signs that were used to determine and expatiate a particular reference ("A breeze was coming. The ship . . . swung to a heavier puff") appear now less interesting, once decoded. They are, therefore, immediately recoded, to substitute for the precision of a technical reference the uncertain analogy of a comparison. What could better demonstrate the prestige of *description*, its capacity both to deliver the narrative (a few lines later, we learn that the whole passage was indeed meant to be a premonition of the sailing of the *Narcissus* out of Bombay: "Next morning, at daylight, the *Narcissus* went to sea") and to hold it, remotely captive of signs as yet unsignified (unsuspected . . . lurking stealthily"): clearly designating, albeit poorly referenced?

III. If descriptions make things more precise, this precision cannot be assessed in quantitative terms. Precision simply denotes a specific quality of our intuitions about time and space.[6] Because language is referential, it is generally assumed that the more exhaustive the reference is, the more expressive language will be: the more we know about the reference (as in a dictionary or a technical manual), the more effective our communication will be. But the effectiveness of language cannot simply be measured by the exhaustiveness of the reference, because a system of complex references can also be used to create in us the *illusion* that we are in touch with reality. In the passage above, we saw that with his technical checklist, Conrad was actually trying to symptomatize in the narrative a change which had occurred in

weather patterns and was meant to be symbolic of a change soon to come in the overall narrative (the ship impatient to sail from its port). But, in the end, this checklist accomplished little to help us realate to the object of the reference: *a motion experienced but not described*. The comparison with the man groaning under the burden, on the other hand, is there to suggest the unsaid, the ineffable, both in terms of the heavier puff of wind previously noted and of the parts of the ship which respond to that wind. The comparison is but a cliché, anticlimatic by technical standards, but very attractive by any other, because it appears more appropriate than the string of technical references preceding it and leaves us under a mysterious spell.

This, then, is the descriptive strategy: to expose us, first, to the very different, the alien, only to confront us later with what was too close and too obvious for us to see right away. While seemingly clarifying references, a description would thus partially obscure them, only to heighten our delayed recognition. Any description, because it is felt to arrest the flow of narrative discourse, is considered as a delay or detour in itself. And the greater that detour, as with Balzac and the naturalists, the greater, in a sense, the necessity for recognition, but also, and in another sense, the lesser the familiarity with the object described. There, description performs a negative (*de*-scription) function: carrying us away on an avalanche of facts and data, it leaves us wanting to reflect upon the experience, to integrate it. It is the tension between what we recognize to be different from our own experience, and what we recognize *of our own* experience in the object, this mixture of the different (the other) and the same (ourselves), which makes our recognition the apprehension, the appropriation of something which a descriptive process cannot define, cannot control, but whose time, duration and actuality it indicates.[7] Whence comes what Roland Barthes calls *l'effet de réel* [the *reality effect*] (1968), the illusion that we know what it is the author is talking about. Zola gives us a magnificent example of this in *Nana* (Chapter 6):

Nana eut, à ce moment, des fantaisies de fille sentimentale. Elle regardait la lune pendant des heures. Une nuit, elle voulut descendre au jardin avec Georges, quand toute la maison fut endormie; et ils se promenèrent sous les arbres, les bras à la taille, et ils allèrent se coucher dans l'herbe, où la rosée les trempa. Une autre fois, dans la chambre, après un silence, elle sanglota au cou du petit, en balbutiant qu'elle avait peur de mourir. Elle chantait souvent à demi-voix une romance de Mme Lerat, pleine de fleurs

Nana in those days was subject to the fancies a sentimental girl will indulge in. She would gaze at the moon for hours. One night she had a mind to go down into the garden with Georges, when all the household was asleep. When there, they strolled under the trees, their arms around each other's waists, and finally went and lay down in the grass, where the dew soaked them through and through. On another occasion after a long silence up in the bedroom, she fell sobbing on the lad's neck, declaring in

et d'oiseaux, s'attendrissant aux larmes, s'interrompant pour prendre Georges dans une étreinte de passion, en exigeant de lui des serments d'amour éternel. Enfin, elle était bête, comme elle le reconnaissait elle-même, lorsque tous les deux, redevenus camarades, fumaient des cigarettes au bord du lit, les jambes nues, tapant le bois des talons (Zola 1967: 150–151).

broken accents that she was afraid of dying. She would often croon a favourite ballad of Madame Lerat's, which was full of flowers and birds. The song would melt her to tears, and she would break off in order to clasp Georges in a passionate embrace, and to extract from him vows of undying affection. In short, she was extremely silly, as she herself would admit when they both became jolly good fellows and sat up smoking cigarettes on the edge of the bed, dangling their bare legs over it the while, and tapping their heels against its wooden side (Zola 1927: 210-211).

The whole paragraph is descriptive. Zola wanted to *specify* some of Nana's fantasies and daydreams, as she is beginning to tire of her prostituted existence (she is still a dancer in the Variétés theatre). These specifications may not be warranted by the course of events so far, but they are required in a naturalist novel to document a *social fact*: how the poor Nana with her sweet *petit* Georges Hugon has become a mere sex object in the eyes of her manager, Steiner, and of her rich admirer, Count Muffat. As Zola dogmatically assert:

Nous estimons que l'homme ne peut être séparé de son milieu, qu'il est complété par son vêtement, par sa maison, par sa ville, par sa province; et, dès lors, nous ne noterons pas un seul phénomène de son cerveau ou de son cœur, sans en chercher les causes ou le contrecoup dans le milieu. De là ce qu'on appelle nos éternelles descriptions (Zola 1968: 1299; "De la description").

We consider that man cannot be separated from his surroundings, that he is completed by his clothes, his house, his city, and his country; and hence we shall not note a single phenomenon of his brain or heart without looking for the causes or the consequence in his surroundings. There results from this what are called our eternal descriptions (Zola 1893: 232).

A description is a help toward determining the *milieu* (the environment and the origins of the hero), the understanding being that there is no hero without a *milieu* of which he is the product. By putting together what happens to Nana herself and to the people with whom she lives, the reader will realize that the real story in someone's life, in a novel, is that of the *milieu*: indeed, in the rustic and peaceful surroundings of a countryside near Paris, the true innocent nature of a simple girl will express itself, free from the pressures of the city.

Now, if one were simply to adopt Zola's theory, one would only see in this text the clear determination in time and space ("in those days . . . one night . . . down into the garden . . . under the trees . . . in the grass," and so on), of the singular moods the character would not have had, had it not been for this *planned* country outing. Here, then, we should find a perfect illustration of the theory that the function of descriptions is indeed to anchor the character in referential reality, by assimilation, or by contrast (the character out of his *milieu*). But let us turn the tables on Zola, and imagine that this text is significant, not so much of Nana's bruised innocence, as of the novelist's attempt at tackling that which, in her character, in her world, in *the* world, usually resists significance. How does non-sense, restriction-free pleasure fit into the *Rougon-Macquarts'* deterministic system? Zola can only say: "the fancies a sentimental girl will indulge in" ("des fantaisies de fille sentimentale"), which is one way of categorizing something that otherwise does not really fit into any definition. What Zola is supposed to want to tell us is the story of Nana, at a time when she has stopped subjecting herself to the degradations of the system and she has become herself anew. But that story is no story: it would be happy and boring; nothing would be happening. One could object that I have purposely selected a passage which is uneventful, in a book where there are so many typically eventful passages, and that naturalistic descriptions are generally designed to facilitate our comprehension of an action in progress, without concerning themselves with fantasies for their own sake. But I think that this one particular description only demonstrates clearly what the others conceal from us, that is, that the process of anchoring a character into his environment creates a semiotic overdetermination, whereby what is described is not supposed to be significant by itself, but in relation to a system which remains implicit: "Never had she experienced this. Country living was soaking her in tenderness". The power of the Parisian *milieu* is underscored through Nana's liberation from it, while this liberation is also enhanced by her realizing how far she is from Paris. In this manner the narrative is fraught with something which does evade the categories of the theorist, *which is difficult to describe* precisely because its latent presence *between* two explicit signata (Paris as against the country/the country as against Paris) is so easily mistaken for something which is indeed absent and therefore incommunicable:

C'était, sous la caresse de cette enfance, une fleur d'amour refleurissant chez elle, dans l'habitude et le dégoût de l'homme. Il lui venait des rougeurs subites, un émoi qui la laissait frissonnante, un besoin de rire et de pleurer, toute une

It was, under the caress of this childishness, a love flower blooming anew in herself, in the midst of her promiscuousness, her disgust with men. She would experience sudden blushings, an excitement which left her shivering, a

virginité inquiète, traversée de désirs, dont elle restait honteuse (Zola 1967: 149-150).

need to laugh and to cry, a whole maidenhood, anxious and riddled with desires, for which she would remain guilty (Zola 1927: 149).

Fortunately, Zola did sense this incommunicability. If we look at the text again, we shall see that Nana's attitudes are interesting, *precisely because they are insignificant*: her moods are spontaneous (Zola describes states rather than actions), to the point of being silly ("In short, she was extremely silly"). The fact that there is no time limit set to those states of mind (as emphasized by the French imperfect of duration) can only underline a difference in pace, even a lack of progression altogether. All these symptoms of Nana's bliss are only noticeable because of the past state of her alienation. But what Zola seems to want to describe, and what he perhaps feels he cannot render because of the overly deterministic structure of his work, is something which clearly looks neither like disease nor good health, *but is simply banal*, and for which there is no room in a novel of this sort where everything is related to everything else and has its own significance parceled out. "She was extremely silly" ("elle était bête") expresses less a judgment than a kind of inner sympathy Nana has for her own actions ("as she herself would admit"): something which cannot actually be judged, because it is all feeling and desire in the nascent stage. Now, we may ask: is there any room for the banal in description, for that which, not being delimited or prescribed, remains undescribed, and if at all described, can only be characterized in terms of undertones ("she would remain guilty")? Actually, there is something here which does escape the grip of the narrator, which he can only retrieve under the guise of a difference, of an opposition with past states in the narrative sequence. But what moves Nana so, is that this existence is totally out of difference, beyond understanding. It could last forever: "It was all so delightful, and Nana was so charmed with her present existence, that she seriously proposed to him never to leave the country". Accordingly, the narrator must struggle with a paradoxical problem: how *not* to overload with meaning something which can only be comprehended as meaningful in the absence of any relational meaning. Apparently, quite a difficult task, since meaning infecting everything, there does not seem to be any way to present as banal what is *to remain* banal or insignificant (in a positive way, that is): Nana is therefore condemned to feeling guilty.[8]

It will be objected that the problem I am raising is pure sophistry, that everything that is incorporated into a narrative is, by definition, noteworthy and significant, because of the differential way language works, and also because the interest of the reader in any narrative is already defined as some sort of *cui prodest*, a narrative always imposing, again, by definition, a narratee. I will respond by emphasizing that there is in the very concept of description something which frustrates this *cui prodest*. I would even go so far as to suggest that in a novel like *Nana*, the obsessive use of descriptive features is one of the ways the narrator can relieve the boredom of a well-planned narration. Instead of insisting that any work of fiction is controlled by a narrative program where the characters' only function is to advance the plot by feeding their moves to a story machine, with only occasional descriptive interludes, what if we suppose that the characters want to be out of the choosing for a while? What if they simply want to be and contemplate what they are? What, as happens so often in real life, if the reader wants to lose himself in the instant? This is, perhaps, the fundamental problem of description, and one that is too often discarded in modern criticism, considering that twentieth-century literature has specifically dealt with it: I am thinking particularly of Joyce and also of the French New Novel. Under the guise of stream of consciousness or that of total objectification (both excluding the format of classic narration), the difference between past and present, fantasy and reality, ceases to be clearly marked, and the descriptive process itself seems to be invested with the task of producing new, unhistorical meaning. This, in turn, causes new problems, as the reader, who cannot count on the world to fit with what he already knows of it, must readjust to a new vision, a new way of seeing things.

IV. Before we go on to these texts, however, I would like to mention a perfect example of the way in which nineteenth-century description attempts to resolve its dilemma: not by insisting on the relevancy of yet another detail; rather, by displaying the irrelevant as an integral part of a series with which we are supposed to be familiar and thus fooling us into accepting that part of the description as significant too. Roland Barthes once gave a very good example of such an occurence in *Un Cœur simple* by Flaubert, where, at the end of a long passage describing the house of Madame Aubin and her servant Félicité, there is the sentence: "an old piano was sustaining, under a barometer, a pyramidal mass of cardboard boxes" (Barthes 1968). The mention of the barometer is justified by nothing except Flaubert's whim. But in a text obsessed with the detail of reality, it communicates the feeling, the illusion that this reality is concrete, that it is simply there, without sign, not as a member of any historical series, but standing for itself, rid, as it were, of its own *representativeness*. There are many other instances of this in Flaubert, as well as in other writers of the period. Take this text by Melville:

And the women of New Bedford, they bloom like their own red roses. But roses only bloom in summer; whereas the fine carnation of their cheeks is perennial as sunlight in the seventh heavens. Elsewhere match that bloom of theirs, ye cannot, save in Salem, where they tell me the young girls breathe such musk, their sailor sweethearts smell them miles off shore, as though they were drawing nigh the odorous Moluccas instead of the Puritanic sands (Melville 1962: 35).

As Melville takes us through the streets of New Bedford, his enthusiasm for the whaling town extends to everything that could attract, fascinate or repel the visitor ("But think not that this famous town has only harpooners, cannibals and bumpkins to show her visitors"), including the women. His remarks are couched in a style that is at once inspired and jocular. What particularly interests me in this paragraph, however, is the allusion to the young girls of Salem "who breathe musk". Obviously, Melville capitalizes on some famous legend or ballad, whereas Flaubert's simple addition of the barometer had been occasioned by nothing more than a passing fancy, and he legitimizes his use of the comparison by a familiar invitation to the reader ("Elsewhere match that bloom"), who suddenly finds himself matching the Puritanic shores of Massachussets with the odorous sands of Indonesia. The comparison is made even more inviting by the suggestion, expressed in Melville's own epic mode ("their sailor sweethearts smell them miles off shore"), that these women of New Bedford and Salem are the epitome of the exotic seductress. But the effect is much the same as in Flaubert. In *Un Cœur simple*, the inscription of yet another object is intended to communicate the feeling of the concrete; here, an exotic comparison is designed to increase our fascination with New Bedford, to the point where we begin to believe in the reality of the fiction. As in the case of *Un Cœur simple* where the *addition* of the barometer is significant, *mostly because the barometer itself is insignificant*, what the descriptor adds in *Moby Dick*, he also takes away, as Melville's *tertium comparationis* is uncertain (it is the bloom of the women which is compared with the perfume of the Salem girls, and Salem is admittedly an exception anyway: "Elsewhere match that bloom . . . ye cannot"). In both cases, the reader is trapped into applying to a denotative series something which does not exactly fit (no more the barometer with the rest of the room — a barometer could be placed anywhere — than the musk with the bloom — how do we match the musk and the rose?), and could only fit, if dismissed as some sort of addition, a *connotation*. But as a connotation, it precisely lacks significance and credence; it is merely the concreteness of an illusion.

Now the question is, what is the effect of such an illusion on the overall narrative? An immediate reply would be that the narrator needs to substantiate his narrative: he needs to make good on the premise that there is indeed a *cui prodest*, an interest on the part of the reader, as clearly indicated by the informal address ("Elsewhere match"). But more to the point: the effect of the above description is to engage the reader into believing that the narrative may not be the fiction he assumed at first, because, while most narrative descriptions are generally closed and limited to a certain number of details which are not in doubt, this particular one affords the opportunity to break the circle and present reality as only vaguely relational, as open and hypothetical (the legend of the New Bedford women is supported by another, even more fanciful, that of the musk-breathing young girls of Salem). The reader then is lost; he cannot reconcile this with expectations of a determinate and realistic narrative, as raised by the narrator himself "taking [my] first stroll through the streets of New Bedford," and fooled by his own obsession with relation and difference and deceived by Melville's conceit, he ends up believing that, precisely because things are no longer clear, they probably are all the more real. By appearing light and fanciful, the novelist has got him hooked: instead of appealing to his knowledge of the context, to this capacity for accepting signs, order and certainty, he tempts him with what lies on the borderline of his discourse, on the outskirts of a world which he had designed as closed and which he now opens to uncertainty. I suspect that it is in this area of fiction that a narrative's most interesting possibilities lie; it is here, when it risks losing its fundamental identity as fictional difference, that fiction holds its greatest promise.

But there is another advantage to this system of description. It modifies our perspective of time and space, by introducing the concept of unfinished duration and that of unlimited space. I think the Zola passage was already a good example of this, and as we discussed the *reality effect* in description, we realized that the modification of time in sequence, of space enclosed, altering the idea of sequence and the concept of limit, was something which haunts description in particular, and language in general. Not only is our time-space reference made up of structures of opposition and exclusion, but the very substance of representation, of novelistic illusion, depends on these structures being switched around and recombined. I now would like to examine what happens to our intuitions about the sensible world in terms of that descriptive time and space. What I am asking, in terms of time, for instance, is whether there is not, in description, the suggestion of a time that not only tends to slow down the pace of narrative, but also to ruin the idea of sequence altogether, by implying that the representation of time itself is a fiction.

There is in description an eternity which is ontologically different from the time that modulates any narrative. First of all, it is true that a picture, for instance, will cause us to linger over it, because of the detail of the composition (Gadamer 1975: 91-127). However, it is not the time we take *to read* a description (for example the picture of a house or the page of a book describing that house) which makes if different from, say, a straight narrative sequence, but the absence of time delimitation in the *designation* of the object (the house) represented. Thus Melville, talking of the women's carnation, delights in the *perennial* character of their picture ("the fine carnation of their cheeks is perennial"). One might object that the shift of *story* to *discourse*, with the voice of the narrator now specifically formulating comments on the course of his own narrative, is actually what suggests to us there the possibility of eternity: the narrator occupying a position which is ever-present (the act of narrating), we are ready to assume that his comments have an ever-present, timeless validity.[9] But I still believe there is in the eternity of description something which is intrinsic, *sui generis*, which does not belong to designation as it is incorporated in the descriptive process. The first clue toward the understanding of this eternity is the fact that a description *makes us contemporaneous with its representation*. What does that mean? It means that, notwithstanding any traces of authorial presence (for example the use of deictics, of the preterit as against the imperfect), most mediation has been removed from the work: no longer do we know who is doing the talking, nor even perhaps, who the character is; we just know that whatever is said, is, exists at the time it is being said, even if we discover otherwise later. Now it is true that the description of any logical series (for example the character slips, slips and eventually falls, or he is so harassed that he finally goes mad) will reasonably fulfill our expectations and thus give us the *illusion* of contemporaneity because we are satisfied that it can happen to us too. But this is only an illusion: contemporaneity is different from universality. Because most mediation is removed or weak (again, do we care, if it is the narrator who sets the stage, when reading the book keeps us from sleeping?), there is the opportunity for the reader to forget that he is watching the representation of an object or an action. There is in any description a modicum of self-forgetfulness that affects him, in terms of the image he has of the object, in terms of the image he has of the author-narrator, and in terms of the judgmental relationship he has with himself. Indeed, what is there to reflect upon or to judge, in the description of the New Bedford women? Nothing: like the rest in *Moby Dick* ("Call me Ishmael", "Some years ago — never mind how long precisely . . ."), it is a case of take it or leave it. We are not asked to relate those roses to our memories of red roses in summer, but to the concept of the quintessential rose, irrespective of distinctions of time and space.[10] We are asked to do exactly the contrary of what Wallace Stevens would ask us to do, when he invites us to contemplate the thirteen ways of describing a blackbird, and thus enacts a description from the very delineations of time and space (Stevens 1954: 92-95). In discussing the *Dubliners* example above, I referred to the immediacy of the experience we might derive from hearing or reading a cliché, or an idiomatic phrase. I would now like to suggest that in the relation we have to a descriptive text, there might also be something which struggles with our sense of, our need for, significance, and which makes us immediately copresent with the representation. This experience encourages us to substitute for the usual reading of contiguous sequences into one single sequence or episode thanks to mechanisms of selection and substitution, a new process based on the unlimited repetition of differences. In this new process, contrary to the traditional assumption that the enumeration of all the parts of a whole can only result in the perfect integration of that whole, we are discouraged from *graduating* too soon from the representation of separate or discrete wholes (individual objects or persons) to organized wholes (those same objects or persons as simply constitutive of the narrative context). It is as though reading a description implied a separate activity of consciousness, which can only be defined as a unique way of being both outside and inside oneself, blending the introspective mode with the mild concern which comes out of being merely curious.

Let us go back to the Melville text: "And the women of New Bedford, they bloom like their own red roses". When I read or hear such a line (again, it might have been drawn from some nice ballad), I am not asked to imagine what the women of New Bedford might really be like, nor should I believe that the line is intended as some sort of classification, although these women are routinely contextualized (Melville is enumerating all the attributes of the whaling town) and placed at the top of a hierarchy (through the comparison with the women of Salem). I should understand that, through the use of the verb *to bloom* as a substitute for the verb *to be*, they are not only endowed with beautiful (flower-like) attributes, but that they also *exist* like flowers through the specific action of *blooming*. In other words, it is not enough to say that the women of New Bedford are described in metaphorical terms — an analysis of the type used, not only by most Melville critics, but, perhaps, by most literary critics obsessed with the symbolic relation between texture and structure.[11] We have to specify that, through the use of a metaphor, subsequently developed into a whole descriptive system, the narrator has managed to concentrate our attention on their existence as fictional objects, away from the strictures of reality and reference. I am not sure that the use of the present *bloom* has anything to do with it. I think the trick is in making us captive to a statement which evades both the simple denotation and the traditional authorial comment. We are left face to face with whatever we know the author has concocted. We are, in a sense, totally contemporary with the text: in the words of Gadamer, we are able to "experience from the occasion of its coming to presentation a continued determination of its significance" (1975: 130). It is as though the portrait of the women was in a category by itself: on the one hand, a simple type, consecrated by the comparison with other beauties (the roses, the women of Salem), and on the other hand, distinct individuals, each of whom represent the type, albeit none of them being singled out for a particular description. From their collective beauty then (the metaphor is followed by a synecdoche, as "their cheeks" is the part that stands for the whole model of these women) results a picture, which is not specifically determined (Who is each of these women?), *but increased in being*, as it were: not quite singular, nor quite typical. *Their power is, again, as in the case of Achilles' shield above, in their display*, only in the display, and the reader's reaction is to that display.

I should like to emphasize that this kind of (display) description has nothing to do with the traditional concept of description, where the reader is supposed to be impressed with the sheer bulk of informative or realistic detail. In fact, I even suspect that most of these traditional descriptions only interest us because we find in them something that indeed takes us away from the referential reality that they are supposed to educate and to inform us about. We are fooled into believing that it is the information displayed we are interested in, whereas what we really crave for is the display itself: the only thing with which we can feel contemporaneous, since most of what the narrator tells us is lodged in some remote past (or future). *What we want from fiction is not the truth, only the appearance of truth.* I am not using the word "appearance" in the sense that a new character, a new context suddenly "appears" to us as the plot thickens. The "appearances" of which I speak are not contingent upon the progress of the plot. In *Nana*, for instance, the *partie de campagne* is like a break from the ongoing Parisian story. What is important is that we be in tune with the display, with an indication that cannot be translated into anything of direct, pertinent significance. Because there is no definite goal to any description of this kind, because it is, so to speak, context-free, we too are free to wander away from the action and fantasize for a moment: which is what Melville invites us to do with him, when he lets himself be carried away to the Moluccas. In this sense, a display description superimposes a nonsignificant occurrence on a string of determined choices, with the paradoxical result that the fiction which was supposed to compete with reality through the patient weaving of description is now standing out on its own. And thus we are able to spend freely the portion of our desire not yet monopolized, that is, not yet signified in the all-out enterprise of the sign. We are able to revive what continues to lie dormant in the text as an excess of as yet unclassified, unsignified, and perhaps, unsignifiable meaning. Display-descriptions, whose function we have already seen in poetic texts (see Chapter 9), are thus the safety valves of the good prose writer: with them, he can, through the subtle manipulation of fictional meaning, altogether modify our conceptual modes. They are the regulative principle of fiction writing.

Before I close this part, just one word on the relationship of display-description to poetic genres, where the object is never truly individualized nor completely generalized, and stands out in an intemporal (*perennial*) present:

> There is a Yew-tree, pride of Lorton Vale,
> Which to this day stands single, in the midst
> Of its own darkness, as it stood of yore:
> . . . .
> Of vast circumference and gloom profound
> This solitary Tree! a living thing
> Produced too slowly ever to decay;
> Of form and aspect too magnificent
> To be destroyed . . .
> (Wordsworth, *Yew-trees* 1-13)[12]

I am suggesting that the versatility of display-descriptions, their adaptability to prose or to poetry, is a clear indication of their function in literary texts. In display-descriptions proper, *we are invited to poetize the object*, that is, to dwell on the possibility of such an experience, so that, in a sense, the experience is never completed. Such a display always tempts us each time, because it is like the beginning of a secondary story; it suggests that we go on and continue the narrative ourselves by fantasizing about the hero and his situation. Whether in prose or in poetry, however, such descriptions remain as the testimony to the possibility of considering fiction at a new distance, on the outer face of language, where we can be turned from readers and listeners into contemplators.

V. Before concluding this chapter, I would like to examine what happens to display-descriptions in texts where the display function seems to constitute the most important part of the narrative process. Let us take a passage from *Ulysses*:

His heart astir he pushed in the door of the Burton restaurant. Stink gripped his trembling breath: pungent meatjuice, slop of greens. See the animals feed.
   Men, men, men.
   Perched on high stools by the bar, hats shoved back, at the tables calling for more bread no charge, swilling, wolfing gobfuls of sloppy food, their eyes bulging, wiping wetted moustaches. A pallid suetfaced young man polished his tumbler knife fork and spoon with his napkin. New set of microbes. A man with an infant's saucestained napkin tucked round him shovelled gurgling soup down his gullet. A man spitting back on his plate: halfmasticated gristle: no teeth to chew chew chew it. Chump chop from the grill. Bolting to get it over. Sad booser's eyes. Bitten off more than he can chew. Am I like that? See ourselves as others see us. Hungry man is an angry man. Working tooth and jaw. Don't! O! A bone! That last pagan king of Ireland Cormac in the schoolpoem choked himself at Sletty southward of the Boyne. Wonder what he was eating. Something galoptious. Saint Patrick converted him to Christianity. Couldn't swallow it all however (Joyce 1961: 169).

Mr. Bloom, on his way to lunch, and full of expectation, his heart "astir" — he had just been daydreaming about "perfumed bodies, warm, full. All kissed, yielded" (1961: 168) — has just walked into the Burton restaurant ("Stink gripped his trembling breath: pungent meatjuice, slop of greens. See the animals feed. Men, men, men"). I chose this description, graphic to the point of being disgusting, as well as entertaining to the point of farce, to show the potential of display, and to demonstrate that the notion of precision discussed above can be conveniently explained by referring to the display function and its variations. For Joyce's text can be taken to the letter, as a very exact account of the way people eat in restaurants and the associations one can have by simply watching them; or it can also be taken in general, as a reflection upon the virtues of display itself.

   Let us, first, notice all that is typically Joycean in this text. The fast pace of the description follows Bloom's slowly panning view, as he surveys the dining-room to acquaint himself with the scene. As the narrator seems to want to intrude as little as possible, there are very few personal verbs ("polished . . . shovelled"), the syntax is generally disorganized with juxtapositions and breakups. This is very much in line with the quality of the viewing as well: seeing people, not as people, but as partial objects, set in various positions or modified by specific actions, without the whole object (or subject) ever being given due consideration ("swilling, wolfing"). As usual with Joyce, when there is no clear syntactic organization, the text weaves itself by association, the narrator substituting for the lack of organization a feeling of universal contiguity: first, a semantic contiguity, as in *swilling* and *wolfing*, and then a phonetic contiguity, as in "wiping wetted moustaches" or "chump chop". Because there is really no right or left, no real sense of a topography; rather a huge indistinct mass of food being absorbed or even rejected ("halfmasticated gristle") amidst utensils and gestures, the whole scene appears distorted, even farcical: from the "pallid suetfaced young man" to the man with an "infant's saucestained napkin tucked round him", with Joyce-Bloom making funny comments the while (*New set of microbes* . . . no teeth to chew chew chew it"), questioning whether the scene is real and whether his own manner of viewing is not in fact destroying the original relation between viewer and object ("See ourselves as others see us"), and finally ending the whole matter in a joke ("Couldn't swallow it"). Now, it is this uncertainty about the whole scene (What does it mean, from "sad booser's eyes," to "hungry man is an angry man"?), its possible *unreality* ("Am I like that?") which interests me here. I am not going to claim that it is typical of the disintegration of modern discourse in the modern novel, or that it is a symptom of the new aesthetics. I am simply suggesting that this is exactly what happens to a description, when the display function becomes so important that it takes over the narrative function. When Bloom entered Burton's, we could have expected Joyce to take over and, through the careful setting of spatial and temporal leads, the insertion of deictics, for example, *here*, there, and so on, to have presented us with a specific scene, for example, something could have happened in the restaurant: a fight or an accident, perhaps, pertaining to a specific place; for example, Bloom liked Burton's and lunched there often. Instead, nothing matters, as Bloom, disgusted by what he has seen, decides to leave and abstain from lunch altogether.

So what was the use of that description? Can we say that anything really happened there which could be of import to our understanding the rest of the work? But then, we would have to say that whatever happens to Bloom or Stephen at each stage of their progress through the day is equally important and significant. The truth is, most of *Ulysses* is actually made of this kind of display. Whether it be frying eggs in the morning or meeting prostitutes in the evening, the motivation for reporting such scenes is not in the quest for their meaning: all the actions in our lives are significant and deserve being reported; not in the point of view: there is none, there is no focusing on the object from a particular angle, no rationalization of an action appropriating it. One has the curious feeling that the narrator has simply taken leave of his common sense and that he is now discoursing about the world from the somewhat anti-Cartesian position, say, of someone seeing two faces of a cube, and still very much doubting whether he has a right to think and say there are a third and a fourth. The motivation is in the display:

filling one's eyes with partial features that are then taken for the whole objects themselves, organized and interpreted before they are referred to these objects we know-in-the-world. The point is rather in the pleasure afforded by representation itself, what Joyce, all ears, eyes and nose open, calls the *wealth of the world* and which he wants to impart to us. Let us ponder this a little. It is clear that there cannot be any wealth of the world without a representation of it, a representation which, because of the strictures of language, will automatically be limited to an interpretation derived from a great multiplicity of various representations (the multiplicity being in the semantic, phonetic, or any other content). This means that the idea of wealth, coincidentally one of the major connotations of the notion of display, will essentially be impoverished through its representation.

One way to obviate this is for the narrator to use description to *de*construct representation. By making a part of the representation of an object stand for the total representation of that object, he does not simply evidence a good command of synecdoche, a figure where the mouth of the voracious eater can be taken here to refer to the whole glutton. He suggests, rather, the possibility of a world where meaning is simply parceled out, disseminated and retrievable in more than one way at various stages along the associative line. This is perhaps why Joyce makes such generous use of the indefinite article: even the last pagan king of Ireland was possibly no more than "a man spitting back on his plate," much like the one that had "bitten off more than he can chew" and who "couldn't swallow" either, albeit both being angry for being too hungry, and all "men, men, men," anyway. The mode of retrieval is different according to everyone's experience, but the narrator intends to show, through an infinity of experiences coming on top of one another, and thus constantly expanding the field of possible reference, more the mode of retrieve than the object of retrieval itself. The wealth is in the extended possibility of retrieval: thus a cliché like "bitten off more than he can chew" applies both ways, literally (which is not its regular acceptation) and figuratively (which is). By moving from one display feature to another, the speaker and the narrator, have a chance to discover, side by side, the common pertinence of denotation and connotation, of finding more about their common role in the actualization (or should we say the *adumbration*?) of the object. Representation is then truly *displayed*. And, contrary to other types of description, where the narrator's criterium is exhaustiveness, here, exhaustiveness is replaced by a certain scarcity: we have to be satisfied by the exposure of a set of referents, without due consideration of an organizing narrative concept. Although it has already been argued that Joyce had every intention of having Bloom lunch at Burton's to begin with, because this stop was to represent but another in the long list of Bloom-Ulysses' stops throughout the city (the "swilling, wolfing" men would be the hypostases of Circe's pigs), it remains that the hero's progress is more *inside* the world than *through* it. He does not cross Dublin, as Odysseus crosses the Mediterranean, simply to go home (or to meet his "son"), but he is literally metamorphosized, as he lets himself *be visited* by the different spaces which he happens to be presented with. And in the end, he will only meet Stephen, so that the wealth of their individual experiences can be multiplied and exchanged for one another. That, indeed, is the main lesson of *Ulysses*: the display is not only made for him who watches, but *it is in the eye of the beholder, himself displaying his capacity for retrieving, for making meaning* (a lesson which was not to be lost on the French *Nouveau Roman*). In the last analysis, to experience the possibility of meaning in the world requires that one eventually abdicate the power of choice, where choice represents no more than the obligation to reduce the cosmos to hierarchical sets of antinomies, and that one open oneself, instead, to the chaos of display.

In the course of this chapter we reviewed some of the ways in which description tends to modify the system of the novel, by suggesting, alongside the logical options of its narrative, a world temporarily disconnected from the sequence of events, and where the reader is requested to involve himself purely in the pleasure of watching that which he knows is fiction *displayed as fiction*. Beyond the network of differences and opposites, there is, within the frame of any narrative, room for a naive contemplation of the world basking in the aura of its appearance, of its being shown, and vacillating on the brink of significance. No doubt these precious moments are quickly inventoried and intentionalized, that is, made fully significant: put to good use by an efficient narrator. They can, however, be retrieved in their originality, by patiently displacing the props of a narrative montage, the deictics, the figures of speech, the tone or register of the narrator's voice — all of which remain the reader's challenge, as they make it incumbent upon him to involve himself with constructing, putting together a fiction still enclosed in the pages of a book.

NOTES

1. For a theoretical background on this see Eichenbaum (1975).
2. For the concept of *deictic* and *shifter*, I am, of course, indebted to Roman Jakobson (1971: 130-147), who established the theoretical foundation for all phrases with a referent determined only by a relation to the speaker.

3. For blind people, it might, of course, be otherwise, although one would have to agree that no language is possible without some sort of conceptual image linked to the sound image or any other. Also, one would have to distinguish between the congenitally blind and the accidentally blind. Whereas the use of the Braille color wheel can be useful in the teaching of color differences, for instance, it is agreed that the acquisition of painting skills is extremely difficult for the congenitally blind (see von Senfen 1960).

4. I am adapting the Saussurean distinction to the context of *silent* interpersonal communication (writing/reading).

5. The problem of the difference between *designation* and *reference* already mentioned (see Chapter 7) is one of the most difficult and most neglected in the philosophy of language. Much work has been accomplished by Frege (1952: 56-78) and Quine (1960: ch. 5) in the area of logical determinations, where the distinction between *clear* and *opaque* contexts is of paramount importance. I am concerned primarily with avoiding a *semanticization* of the question, that is, explanation based on the distinction between the linguistic expression and the object that it denotes. I am not interested in that distinction, *but in that between the linguistic expression of reference and that of designation*. If one must distinguish between truths and falsehoods, however, I find that Strawson (1950) carries the best argument, as he distinguishes between *sentences*, which are mere series of words, and *utterances*, which are truths or falsehoods: I might say that I am concerned with the distinction between *sentence* and *utterance*, as it affects our reactions as readers and modifies our expectations of the narrative process.

6. I am referring here, not so much to the Kantian postulate inherent in the transcendental exposition of time and space, according to which "Time cannot be outwardly intuited, any more than space can be intuited as something in us" (Kant 1950: 68), because they are *a priori* intuitions, and as such, are *extensive* quantities, as to the anticipations of perception in the transcendental analytic, according to which, in all phenomena, "the *real* that is an object of sensation has *intensive* magnitude, that is, a degree" (Kant 1950: 201).

7. This process has been made abundantly clear by Lacan (1966: 89-97) in his analysis of the birth of the symbolic order (the *stage of the mirror*).

8. Jerphagnon's philosophical inquiry *De la banalité* (1965) is the best book I know on the subject of banality.

9. See Barthes (1968) who spells about the *checks and balances* of the narrative *vs.* description complex. Description relieves the boredom of straight narrative, and straight narrative balances out the flourish of description: it *watches out* for it.

10. Again, I am referring to Kant (1950: 151-175); this time, to the idea of *pure concepts of the understanding*, which are entirely heterogeneous, and can never be met with any intuition, except through the mediation of a *transcendental schema*. Thus the quintessential rose is a *transcendental schema*.

11. I am referring, in general, to the New Critics, and, as far as *Moby Dick* is concerned, to Horsford (1962).

12. For an interesting controversy on the interpretation of this poem, bearing on the theory of description, see Riffaterre (1973), and Hartman (1975).

Part Three: Desire

13

The Pleasures of the Text

I. It is now clear that there are in any text two levels of meaning which are distinct, albeit related. The first is the narrative level or level of *narration* where information is presented in the most economical manner, reality is brought down to the level of logical and semantic choices, and nothing else matters. The world is seen in differential terms of couples of actions: either the hero does *A* or he does *B*, or he does *A* and does not do *B*, and the meaning of the narrative arises precisely from the consciousness of those differences. In other words, the world can only exist in terms of which actions can be accomplished and which ones cannot. From this limited view of things which locates meaning in the selection process proper, one can build a system of probabilities which determines our ability to make choices against our social or cultural contexts; to decide which choices are possible in what context and which ones are not (see Chapter 6). The life of such a narrative depends essentially on how well one can balance our specific choices against others and how well the various choices add up to justify the necessary reversal or denouement inherent in any narrative.

There is also another level: the descriptive level or level of *description*, where not merely the selection (of one alternative against another), but rather the justification of that selection is more important. In a narration, possibility and probability are defined in terms of a relation of a past (the sequence of past actions), to a future (the sequence of actions yet to come): in any case, to a program already in operation. In a description, on the other hand, one tries to think not in terms of programs, of systems, but rather in terms of the time it takes the reader to actualize the choices made by the writer or his hero. This time is spent understanding, reconstructing the context of the choices through an associative process. One detail brings another and the writer, if he is, like Proust, an autobiographer, slowly becomes aware of his own place in relation to the narrative he is weaving, and also of his own self as reconstituted by the narrative. If he is a writer of fiction in the third person, he can slowly aggregate diverse features into one general picture: thus in Stendhal's *Le Rouge et le noir* (1964: 33-36) the description of the principal characters of the town of Verrières is what finally helps set off the personality of Julien Sorel — not simply as a special character different from anyone else in the novel, but as the only person to whom the establishment of this context finally matters.[1]

However, the problem of description can also be approached from another angle, for if one is willing to abstract oneself from a system of difference, one can get in touch with that which impels all of us to look for difference in the first place, which has its origin in a functional theory of symbolism. The problem can then be reformulated in the following terms: literature, through its narrative and, particularly, its descriptive passages, is a response to a desire to communicate which can never be completely satisfied, which constantly strives for, and delights in, the difference mentioned above: the difference between reality and fiction, and between one fictional world and another.

We have already seen how any narrative performs a constrictive function (Chapter 7). Because it uses those elements, and those elements only, which relate to a mere programming of the action, it can be said to limit not only our view of the world but our constant desire for representation *and imitation* (while it seems that it is precisely the function of description to obviate and relax those restrictions). One could go even further and state that the function of narration proper is the reverse of that of description. Unlike description, where reality is atomized and parceled out, where it is the details of form and style that define objects as well as people, narration synthesizes actions and events into sequences, whose practical end transgresses the end of each particular action and where what counts is not the action itself, but its relevance to the sequence and ultimately, to the whole set of sequences of which it represents only a small part. In the process, it limits our pleasure: the pleasure to be derived from the mere presentation of people and things. In description, on the other hand, one could say that, with pragmatic preoccupations no longer a factor, the narrator is at liberty to forget about the end, to be purposeless and to become a descriptor: to let himself be taken by the context and his reactions to it.

If we now investigate this discrepancy we shall soon find that it depends on the degree to which the narrative emphasizes or de-emphasizes a relation of appropriation with the object described — a relation where the object is or will be owned and possessed by the subject of the narrative and used by him for a certain purpose (for example A loves B and possesses him or her; or A uses B to get to C). In any description, this appropriation is deemphasized with the implication that the subject should indeed be defined through a symbiotic *association* with the object. Because the subject, the hero, is dependent on the world for the determination of his own identity, he cannot simply own or use objects for his own purposes; and because he must derive from them the meaning, the purpose of his own life, this relation often turns into a neurotic dependency (the hero both loves and hates his milieu), which can only be satisfied at the cost of any ongoing limited description. A long time ago, Norman O. Brown discussed the Freudian distinction between object-identification and object-choice and claimed that Freud had collapsed the distinction between the two. Brown seemed to imply that we ought to retrieve that original distinction, and cultivate the possibility of a true, nonneurotic association, in order to thwart the impatience to possess, manipulate and eventually annihilate, which accounts for the history of the death instinct in the world (Brown 1959: 40 ff). The comment could apply in part to the dialectic narration/description inherent in any narrative, where the object-identification of the description is at odds with the object-choice of narration.[2] In descriptions, the subject — and I mean by "subject" the consciousness formed in the triangulation writer-hero-reader by the establishment of a relation to a situational context — is associated with the objects described. Naturally, the model for this association is a psychoanalytic one. In this instance, even the linguist corroborates the psychoanalyst: when he (like Jakobson) defines description and the descriptive novel of the nineenth century through the process of metonymy, he simply means that the code of the message is essentially derived by association with a context. In other words, the descriptive subject associates with its context just as the Freudian child associates with his father or his mother.

To be sure, it may never be possible to define precisely the point at which a *description* ends and a *narration* begins in the overall narrative process, and descriptive phrases may never amount to more than bracketing devices (allowing us to stop and think by putting the narration between paren-theses). But my point is that the associative process has to do with annulling the process of difference inherent in narrative selection (the hero must act, and he does A or B). By helping annul this process, description returns the narrative subject to a state of rest, where the tension resulting from the maintenance of the selection process can be avoided. By avoiding this tension, it is as though the subject were offered the possibility of returning to the period preceding the beginning of narration: in some sense, to the time before the end. Hegel observed that to describe accurately is truly impossible, because objects are known to us mainly through the sum of their contextual or narrative differences, and that animals never have this problem, as they well know that objects are not mastered by naming them, but rather by eating them (Hegel 1970: A.1). Describing them is like pretending to eat the apple of knowledge without having to make the narrative and historical choice it entails — and Milton shows it well when in *Paradise Lost* he has the serpent shut up just before Eve eats, so that he can take the time to describe the surge of her desire and of her appetite (see Chapter 14). From this, it could be inferred that descriptions aim at integrating as fully as possible the stimulation and satisfaction inherent to the literary experience (the desire and appropriation of the literary phantasm); and because of the associative relation in which they implicate the subject, they are, to a large extent, self-indulgent and self-satisfying.

II. But to leave it at this and simply to abstract description from the rest of the narrative universe would be irresponsible. The truth is, by describing objects in a certain manner, the descriptor eventually elaborates a discourse whose ideology rests on the organization of these objects and people into a world of reference which by itself constitutes a narrative: thus the meticulous description of furniture in Balzacian households is always fraught with nascent, if not intense, narrative meaning. It could even be argued that the items of a description not only count as elements in a referential context (they contribute to our understanding of an action taking place or about to take place), they are already items of narration, just like the objects whose function is merely to help us perform daily tasks but which end up defining our existential context in one way or another. Not only can a description be made of them (their shape, their color, their weight), but they have their own story to tell (where they originated, who used them first), and this story, in turn, becomes our own (how we use them, how we live). We should thus be prepared to admit that descriptive-associative processes eventually contribute to the elaboration of narrative. On the model of how to get to the ultimate object (the mother) through the mediate object (the father), of how to get a sense of a character's capabilities through a comparison with his context, any description eventually eases into full-blown narrative, where the subject is fully operational. To be sure, the pleasure afforded by description is different from the pleasure afforded by narration. In a description, we are brought back to a stage of language practice and acquisition where we are supposed, much like children, to take stock in the expressive quality of language and to experiment with meaning, playfully, as it were, without forcibly having *to make sense*. It might even be that describing enables us to develop a language only for playing, with a release of (sexual) energy similar to that effected in the Freudian process of wit, where the adult indulges in punning, fully conscious that it will appear playful and nonsensical, and derives pleasure from an excitement interdicted by reason. Description in a narrative sequence would thus amount to an excursion into nonnarrative sense, and the pleasure afforded by this excursion would be that of excluding, or at least, of delaying, the organization of the nonnarrative sense — play-pleasure, the attractiveness of which, moreover, is that it can be taken under full narrative cover, while avoiding or delaying the object-choice and the sexual identification inherent in the narrative proper.

In the end, however, a description always turns into a narration of some kind. Using Freud in *Beyond the Pleasure Principle* (1955: 7-64), one could say that precisely because of description's dilatory tactics, the function of narration is to protect the enjoyment of primary processes which, otherwise exposed, might appear threatening: it must focus or fixate on that which allows it to avoid non(narrative)sense or the formative stage thereof. Let us take the example of the *Odyssey*, where Ulysses' narrative is essentially made of the tales of how he escaped from Calypso's island as well as from the Cyclops' den. In this context, it can be said that Homer's descriptions aim at isolating the element which will help the hero dominate his environment—in Ulysses' instance, the description of Circe's island leads to the discovery and display of Hermes' sacred blade (see Chapter 14), *moly*, with which he subdues the witch, and that of the Cyclops' cave, to the display of the pole with which he finally gouges out the Cyclops' eye. This element is usually a trick, whose performance allows the selection of the appropriate narrative device through which can be tested, with the repeated object-fixation, aggression and domination the test entails, the possibility of a return to the original state of bliss: say, the quasi-uterine condition of Ulysses at Calypso's, or, in the context of the return, the *nostos*, the final reunion of Ulysses and Penelope at the close of the *Odyssey*. The overall narrative thus fulfills two purposes. On the one hand, it compels the narrator and his hero to escape a situation which is intolerable, because it lacks objectification. On the other hand, the risk in each objectification is that it may subsequently return the subject to a state of nonobjectification, where he will barely subsist and remain passive, while others take care of him (Calypso, Circe, the Phaeacians). To obviate, or simply to delay this, it is then the responsibility of the narrator, each time, to reinstate a truly narrative perspective, by refreshing his hero's and our own awareness of the necessity of yet another objectification on the model of those already produced in the past. Such is the episode (*Odyssey* 8: 500 ff.), where the Phaeacian bard Demodokos

brings to Ulysses the realization of who he is and what he must do to be true
to his heroic model, and thus contributes to putting him back on the road, on
the boat, to Ithaca.

Within the overall narrative model, then, the place of description is
especially complex and ambivalent. While it represents a genuine desire to
return to or to remain in a nonnarrative state of association and nonobjectification, it also fosters a desire to prepare for that very objectification.
Returning to the model developed in *Beyond the Pleasure Principle*, one could
suggest that the particular pleasure of narration is eventually to transform a
mobile cathexis into a quiescent one by returning the psyche to a state of
nirvana and peace antedating all new activity; while, inside the total
narrative, the specific pleasure of description would be in the attempt to
thwart, or to delay the combination of Eros and Death in the certainty that
the pleasure is bound to be ended soon by an ongoing narrative process.
There, oblivious to the promise — or is it a threat? — of nirvana and death,
the Unconscious would thus give itself permission to enjoy without fear
(Death) something like the presence of Eros.

Let us pause a bit. To invoke Freud to account for distinctions in literary
criticism may seem farfetched, if not downright pretentious, particularly as
Freud himself always refused to become involved in discussions on the
nature of mimesis and fiction. On this point, however, not only did Freud
personally submit that it is one of the effects, one of the graces of poetry, to
achieve a masking effect, to take our attention off an expenditure of (sexual)
energy, but it seems that the use of the Freudian model of *objectification vs.
association* is particularly appropriate (Freud 1948: vol. 4, pp. 173-183).
Descriptions represent an attempt to preserve a flow of energy which is too
soon bound into the narrative process. In his study of "Jokes and their
relation to the Unconscious", Freud suggests that the pun can work only
through a *free* (that is, safe, because it is only fictitious) discharge of the
aggressive instinct inherent in any object choice (1960: 117-139). Translated
into our context, this would mean that, at the same time the descriptive
process contributes to generating a narrative process, it also creates an
expenditure of energy which transcends the narrative process and contributes to accrediting the reality of a pure fiction.

It is this pure fiction which I would now like to discuss. Description, it is a
known fact, creates an *illusion* of contextual reality (see Chapters 7 and 12).
And it is this illusion we crave. We think that by reading a description we
will better understand the subject, his motivations and his actions. *But in
fact, what we will understand is our own self*. Whether we find it attractive or
repulsive, the world appearing before us in a description is invested with
special interest: a particular segment of reality is magnified and dis-

played by the narrator in such a fashion as to appear an integral part of the characters' existence and to increase our share, or our stake, in it. The truth is, just as we need the world to reassure us of the concreteness of our existence, we need descriptions to protect the characters from disappearing into nothingness. And because we are fully aware that the pleasure we derive from descriptions is essentially temporary (every description must sooner or later turn into a narrative), we always look forward to them as a haven, a special place to get back in touch (properly: *to associate*) with our own uncommitted and unendangered self. Describing a character's context would thus not only fulfill our need for subsequent narrative determinations, but also protect our (the author's and our own) right to an unqualified and passive existence. Moreover, because the model narrative usually entails (the Bible; folktales) the recognition of an original loss and a subsequent attempt to recover the lost object (whether it be an entity distinctly separate from the subject or, more simply, a part of the subject himself), description is the place where, coemerging with the subject (the narrator and/or his hero) and awakening to the necessity of a program of action, we begin to identify in the world surrounding him those parts with which he wants to be associated and those with which he does not. Borrowing from Melanie Klein (1965: 87-116), we might say that description is the place where we see the subject project onto the world parts of himself he alternatively likes or dislikes, loves or hates (see also Jacobson 1964: 33-88). Finally, because descriptions are essentially meant to stimulate the reading of a narrative quest in a situation where the reader is, like the third party in the Freudian experience of jokes and puns by the joker, used as a facilitator whose function is to ensure that the expression of the aggressive instinct inherent in the subsequent narrative object-choice shall remain safe and innocuous, they are often construed as diversions from this very narrative and used by the narrator in excess to the point where they begin to extend indefinitely. They represent more than a mere delay or postponement of narrative determination; they establish the illusion that the idealizing of the self through the presentation of objects serving, like a sort of *ego*, to authenticate his existence-in-the-world is a temporary, albeit perfectly acceptable, substitute for the ensuing identification through object-choice inherent in any narrative sequence. Hence, again, in many novels (Balzac, Hardy, Zola), the sense that the entire work rests more on the combination of various descriptions than on some narrative determination and that the realization of a plot is due in large part to the simple juxtaposition of the descriptive loci.

Descriptions thus appear as the paradox of narrative fiction. Sublimating an unconscious ego-libido in an association with the objects surrounding the characters, they convince us of the truth, the reality of the narrative (its *realism*), while also remaining to some degree impervious, if not opposed, to the ongoing determination of the historical sequences they are supposed to introduce.

III. The proposition, however, has very serious implications. If we agree that all narratives do indeed *feature* this descriptive ambivalence, it is not only our view of the narrative process, that is, of the relation of descriptions to narrations, but our general attitude toward facts and data and their integration into a narrative set, in short, our whole view of the historical process, which is called in question and must be reexamined.

Overall, it is clear that the writing of history depends on a combination of narration and description. Even before he begins to write, every historian has before him two sets of narratives already constituted: the actions of men known as they have already been narrated (= narrations), and the series of other facts and information yet liable to enter into various kinds of new narratives (descriptions) — on this, see Chapter 15. He can decide to emphasize what should be termed the primary illusion — that something did happen, that it can be recreated as an event; or he may choose instead to emphasize the secondary illusion — that what happened is actually less important that what he thinks might have caused it to happen, and concentrate on it, so as to make it appear as a background to the action. In most cases, both methods are actually combined, with varying degrees of emphasis. The question, however, remains. How does *libido* manifest itself in the relationship of description to narration; and is our own relationship to the past as one of sympathetic reconstruction or one of overt rebellion? Must description be viewed as detracting from, or, on the contrary, contributing to, narration?[3] To try and understand these issues, I shall take the very convenient example of a narrative which combines fact and fiction, history and fantasy, *par excellence* and whose typological form, moreover, is that of an extended descriptive narrative, doubly compounded in this case (President Schreber's) by the original description of the patient and the added narrative commentary of the analyst (Freud). The narrative of the psychoanalytical cure, albeit of a cure never performed by the psychoanalyst himself (Freud had never treated Schreber) and its narrative commentary will, like the description which initiated it, forever remain within the pages of a book (Freud 1958: vol. 12; pp. 9-82).

In most psychoanalytical discourses (the patient's and his doctor's combined), the narration exists only in anticipation of a denouement — the implicit recognition of a dynamic lost in time, which, once it has been recreated and recognized, is understood and subsequently rejected as no longer pertinent to the present. The recreation and recognition of past situations indispensable to the identification process and the loss of narrative that ensues are essentially part of the process of achieving final mastery over the denied object — in the case of President Schreber, his father's love. But as the analytical scene is constantly turning up elements which bolster this repetition, psychoanalytical narration is essentially cumulative: it functions by derivations or displacement (metonymies), whose sum total represents the amount of discourse through which the subject must pull before he is made aware of what it is he is really talking about. It is by studying this process of derivation that one can hope to locate the libidinal energy invested in the narrative, and this is exactly what Freud did by superimposing his own narration to President Schreber's description of his own case.

In his account of *A Case of Paranoia*, Freud's main point is that a sexual delusion of persecution was transformed by the patient's mind into a religious delusion of grandeur. He explains how Schreber believed that he could save the world by being changed (and changing himself) into a woman, who, impregnated by the rays of God, could give birth to a new breed of men likely to be less hostile to him than his contemporaries. In order to make this condition appear not only necessary but inevitable, Schreber had also arranged his fiction to stipulate that, in the meantime, God, who should be caught up with his (Schreber's) body, could not properly play his part, that is, attract and incorporate into his own divine body the souls of the dead, because he (Schreber) was absorbing all or part of the divine rays. Schreber had thus put himself in the position of intercessor between the world and God, where he, and only he, could save the world from misery and destruction. At the same time and to perfect his fiction, he also claimed that his growing femaleness was indispensable to his experiencing the voluptuousness that comes from having intercourse with God: he was becoming God's wife.

To Freud, Schreber's fictional presentation and his insistence on being treated as God's wife can be read as the story of the president's homosexual love for his doctor, itself a displacement of the story of Schreber's love for his own father. In addition, he shows how Schreber's fantasy about being a woman represents a fictional transgression of the taboo, while also remaining perfectly consistent with the logic of his own narrative situation. It makes it possible for him to achieve what he could never achieve in real life, as he and his wife could not have children. Ultimately, as the transference of love from the father to the doctor (Flechsig) and from the doctor to God must be seen as part of a general process of paranoiac decomposition, through which a person endlessly divides and reports what he sees as of utmost importance to him, one understands that the aim of the psychoanalyst's (Freud's) deconstruction is to free from an egosocial repression, binding the unconscionable desires of the patient into acceptable figures of speech, the energy used in this repression to make it available for nonneurotic endeavor. What must be noticed, however, is that the repressive organization of the sociocultural ego, not being able to do away with those unconscionable desires (for example, Schreber's homosexual love for his father), not only lets them subsist, but justifies them as its libidinal components. Thus, in Schreber's system, whereby God is both enjoying him as a woman and trying to pull away from him as a man, the description of his elaborate precautions and successes, because it is read as a part of Freud's commentary (Schreber is seen as compensating for his homosexual frustrations as well as probable disappointments over *real* heterosexual relations), represents, through the narrativization of the descriptive construct, a *modification of libidinal pleasure*. In other words, Schreber's description, which was intended to derive pleasure from the masking of the original, albeit interdicted, historical sequence, is now reinserted into that historical sequence, and expected to produce, with the resolution of the neurotic dilemma a pleasure of another kind.

In more general terms, this means that, *for every lull, for every arrest in the ongoing narrative, the descriptive process also offers the possibility of an acceleration of the narrative and of the real history it purports to delineate, due to the binding of an otherwise free cathexis.* It means that in every narrative process where the narrative structure itself is essentially made of conflicts and their resolutions, the very sequence of conflicts and resolutions occasions a binding, a harnessing of libidinal energy conducive to accelerated problem-solving within the confines of this narrative. Now, the very concept of energy and of a binding of cathexis is very vague, primarily because the notion of energy has no value outside a physical context combining mass and movement. However, the analogy should be useful in helping us determine the quality and the function of each descriptive process. In the Schreber case, for instance, the way in which Schreber talks about himself is obviously integral to the overall fictionalization process and warrants, as such, Freud's narrative deconstruction and defictionalization. On the one hand, it is true that Schreber's account is meant to be one of purely pleasurable (delusive) experience. Thus in his discussion of his experience of being a woman, impregnated by God and going through the motions of birth, he does not attempt to justify himself on historical, autobiographical grounds, with a narrative tracing this femaleness back to his own childhood. What is important to him is to elaborate a very intimate, almost consubstantial *description,* where, by drawing, conjuring visual images: "durch zeichnen visuelle Vorstellen" (Freud 1964: 266), or rather, by describing how he is able to produce the drawing of feminine attributes in his mirror, using his own body as one would writing, he can enjoy the opportunity to experience himself as full of the energy and desire of a "woman luxuriating in voluptuous sensations" (Freud 1958: vol. 12, p. 34).

On the other hand, there is more to these constructs than mere descriptive fictionalization. Through Freud's commentary, Schreber's well-guarded fantasy becomes part of an overall narrative system. In Schreber's book the experiences described were almost context-free and time-free, in the sense that historical data were used only to certify the authenticity: it is as though Schreber had managed to rearrange his life and his mental universe to be able to take the time, to live and enjoy his fantasies:

"Sobald ich aber — wenn ich mich so ausdrücken darf — mit Gott allein bin, ist es eine Notwendigkeit für mich, mit allen erdenklichen Mitteln sowie mit dem vollen Aufgebote meiner Verstandeskräfe, insbesondere meiner Einbildungskraft, dahin zu wirken, dass die göttlichen Strahlen von mir möglichst fortwährend — oder da dies der Mensch einfach nich kann — wenigstens zu gewissen Tageszeiten den Eindruck eines in wollüstigen Empfindungen schwelgenden Weibes empfangen.

". . . ich glaube sogar nach den gewonnenen Eindrücken die Ansicht aussprechen zu dürfen, dass Gott niemals zu einer Rückzugsaktion vorschreiten würde, wodurch mein körperliches Wohlbefinden jedesmal zunächst erheblich verschlechtert wird, sondern ohne jedes Widerstreben und in dauernder Gleichmässigkeit der Anziehung folgen würde, wenn es mir möglich wäre, immer das in geschlechtlicher Umarmung mit mir selbst daliegende Weib zu spielen, meinen Blick immer auf weiblichen Wesen ruhen zu lassen, immer weibliche Bilder zu besehen usw" (Freud 1964: 267-288).

"No sooner, however, am I alone with God (if I may so express it), than it becomes a necessity for me to employ every imaginable device and to summon up the whole of my mental faculties, and especially my imagination, in order to bring it about that the divine rays may have the impression as continuously as possible (or, since this is beyond mortal power, at least at certain times of day) that I am a woman luxuriating in voluptuous sensations.

". . . I think I may even venture to advance the view, based upon impressions I have received, that God would never take any steps towards effecting a withdrawal— the first result of which is invariably to alter my physical condition markedly for the worse — but would quietly and permanently yield to my powers of attraction, if it were possible for me *always* to be playing the part of a woman lying in my own amorous embraces, *always* to be casting my looks upon female forms, *always* to be gazing at pictures of women, and so on" (Freud 1958: vol. 12, pp. 33–34).

However, these same data, set in logical order are used now by Freud to *support the narrative* account of the psychoanalyst reconstructing the paranoiac process and destroying the illusion:

Er kam dann zur sicheren Uberzeugung, dass Gott selbst zu seiner eigenen Befriedigung die Weiblichkeit von ihm verlange . . . Die beiden Hauptstücke des Schreberschen Wahnes, die Wandlung zum Weibe und die bevorzugte Beziehung zu Gott sind in seinem System durch die feminine Einstellung gegen Gott verknüpft. Es wird eine unabweisbare Aufgabe für uns, eine wesentliche genetische Beziehung zwischen diesen beiden Stücken nachzuweisen, sonst wären wir mit unseren Erläuterungen zu Schrebers Wahn in die lächerliche Rolle geraten, die Kant in dem berühmten Gleichnis der Kritik der reinen Vernunft als die des Mannes beschreibt, der das Sieb unterhält, während ein anderer den Bock melkt (1964: 267–268).

He then arrived at the firm conviction that IT WAS GOD HIMSELF who, for HIS own satisfaction, was demanding femaleness from him . . . In Schreber's system the two principal elements of his delusion (his transformation into a woman and his favoured relation to God) are united in his assumptions of a feminine attitude towards God. It will be an unavoidable part of our task to show that there is an essential *genetic* relation between these two elements. Otherwise our attempts at elucidating Schreber's delusions will leave us in the absurd position described in Kant's famous simile in the *Critique of Pure Reason*: — we shall be like a man holding a sieve under a he-goat while some one else milks it (1958: vol. 12, pp. 33-34).

The *free energy* available in Schreber's descriptive view of himself has been *bound* to prepare for true (Freud's) narrative resolutions, complete with beginning and end ("genetische Beziehung"). What has happened is that Schreber himself must continually defend his right to enjoy himself and Freud uses this as proof that the whole descriptive fantasy was merely an excuse to avoid the historical issue, which must now be spelled out and reset in its proper perspective. The same happens in literary descriptions, where the character is introduced by the narrator through a *separate* examination of the context (room, city, peers, etc.), and where the narrative process is delayed, as I pointed out earlier, by the experience of a forepleasure oblivious to the principle of natural return to quiescence underlying all narrative resolutions.[4] There (for example in Balzac and Flaubert), the narrator attempts to make us experience an arrest, a lull in the narrative, and the energy tapped by the descriptive process is still largely unused: free-floating and available — until it begins to appear that the description is only there to heighten the anticipation of the denouement in a straight narrative account setting all things right and having us take them for granted again. Extrapolating from this and attempting to reduce the ambiguity inherent in any description (autonomous from narrations while also contingent upon them as well as part and parcel of an overall narrative process), I suggest that we extend the above distinction between *free* and *bound* descriptions to the whole of narrative literature and propose a classification between free and bound *descriptions* according to whether they appear properly descriptive or more properly narrative. In the first sense, where description seems to create a lull, an arrest in the narrative process, one could say that energy is still free, that an attempt has been made at slowing down history. In the second, where description rather accelerates the resolution of conflicts, energy is bound and the historical process has been accelerated. Returning to our discussion of *associative vs. objective* processes, one could suggest that, in the first case, the experience of free energy is concurrent with an associative view of the context, where the subject, threatened by a historical situation, chooses to align himself with it and where the possibility of any action in opposition to, or in contradiction with, this context, is postponed, to allow a passive understanding of the world. In the second case, on the other hand, the binding of energy would be concurrent with an objective view of the world, where it is only through an obsessive construction leading to a fictional (Schreber's) or real (Freud's) resolution of conflicts that pleasure can be taken.

NOTES

1. I am using the terms *narration* and *description*, and not those of *story* and *discourse*, because I maintain that a semiological perspective on *description* cannot be limited to the examination of the various changes effected by a *discourse* on the thread of a *story*. What does interest me here in the problem of description is the definite appeal of the text to its narrator, to its reader, and the substance of the pleasure it affords — all things which seem to me to lie definitely beyond the limits of a structural or transformational examination of narrative. Moreover, and as long as I am taking my distance from structuralist studies, the articulation *story/discourse* (Benveniste 1966: ch. 5) appears to me to reduce descriptions to simple adjuncts to the *narrative* proper, forcing them into a narrative mold (see Hamon 1972b) where they lose all specificity. This obsession with narrativity, which might well pass for absurd in cultures where the distinction between story and discourse is irrelevant, or at best, unproductive (I am thinking of the sacred texts of India, for instance), literally blinds us to any other perspective. It also prevents us from asking questions relevant to the stylistic, phenomenological, and psychoanalytical specificity of the descriptive processes. The terms *narration* and *description* apply to diverse, albeit related *activities* (not actions) of the speaking subject (the hero, the narrator, or both) vis-à-vis his auditor or reader. These activities should not be viewed teleologically, in the perspective of a narrative using *story* and *discourse* as mere accessories to the definition of ends *a priori*. They should be considered an integral part of the production of fictional texts and the response to this production.
2. I am using the terms "object-choice," (*Objektwahl*) and "object-identification" (*Objekt-Identifikation*) again, although I am fully aware of Freud's own misgivings and hesitations and of Brown's impatient generalization. The fact is, *identification* — an operation where the subject establishes his own reality by association with another

subject or context — always remained, in Freud's thinking, the primary and necessary stage in the development of all narrative and historical representations of the subject in the world. In the standard edition of Freud's works (1957: 239-260) the editor, in an introduction to Freud's paper on "Mourning and Melancholia", remarks: "Freud seems to have been inclined at first to regard it [identification] as closely associated with, and perhaps, dependent on, the oral or cannibalistic phase of libidinal development. Thus in *Totem and Taboo* . . . he had written of the relation between the sons and the father of the primal horde that 'in the act of devouring him they accomplished their identification with him . . .' A few years later, in *Group Psychology* . . . where the subject of identification is taken up again . . . a change in the earlier view — or perhaps only a clarification of it — seems to emerge. Identification, we there learn, is something that *precedes* object-cathexis and is distinct from it, though we are still told that 'it behaves like a derivative of the first, oral phase'. This view of identification is consistently emphasized in many of Freud's later writings."

3. I am using the term *libido*, less in the context of a theory of the relation of the sexual instinct to the *making* of history (see Chapter 15) than in the context of the *distribution* of sexual impulses which determines the *representation* and the consciousness of historical reality (Freud 1957: 159-215). Now, as concerns this *distribution* between *description* and *narration* in the Freudian text, although it is obvious that President Schreber's account of his own neurosis constitutes in itself a narrative, *because it is also, as Freud shows, an attempt to avoid or delay a real solution to neurotic problems, it falls in the category of description* — while Freud's own commentary represents the narrative which effects this resolution.

4. Although Freud attempted to make a clear distinction between *Nirvana-principle* and *Pleasure-principle* by stating that the former strives to achieve a deathlike state of peace and repose while the latter underscores a desire to promote and maintain limitless enjoyment (Freud 1948: vol. 2, p. 257), insofar as they are both related to the operation of the *libido*, they must be considered together. This, however, can only confuse the issue of *descriptive* (limitless) *vs. narrative* (Nirvana) pleasures. A solution can be found in the conceptual pair *forepleasure–endpleasure*. *Forepleasure* represents an "incitement premium": "the increment of pleasure offered us in order to release yet greater pleasure" while *endpleasure* represents the final (genital) satisfaction indicating an imminent return to a state of quiescence (Freud 1948: vol. 4, p. 183). Applied here, the distinction between *forepleasure* and *endpleasure* could help clarify that between *free* and *bound* (energy) descriptions which I am advancing. Insofar as it is the *representation*, the fantasy of desire (as in the case of Schreber looking at himself *drawing* female buttocks in the mirror) which is emphasized, descriptive pleasure is really *forepleasure* or the pleasure of fantasy and it represents a release of energy. However, as soon as this representation is seen as a distortion of pragmatic reality, that is, as soon as the *forepleasure* turns into *endpleasure* (as in the case of Freud's narrative reconstructing Schreber's evasion of reality), the fantasy evidently points toward its own demise and this premonition, in turn, heralds, with the end of all evasion and delay, the coming of narrative: the victory of reality. Thus, in Freud's *A Case of Paranoia*, Schreber's descriptive fantasy is used (*bound*) to produce Freud's own narrative reality and the *forepleasure* in the original text (Schreber's) is transformed into the *endpleasure* of the corrective *narration* (Freud's). I am using the term *free* rather than *released* to avoid confusing, again, the separate determinations of the pleasure and death principles. By *free energy*, I mean an energy which is available for further *binding*: not properly released through the achievement of a particular motion or sequence of narration but identified and experienced as free and available through the mirror of description. One last word, to note that the concept of *forepleasure* may have influenced Herbert Marcuse in the writing of his chapter "Phantasy and Utopia" in *Eros and Civilization* (Marcuse 1966: 139-158).

14

Milton's Rhetoric of Desire

Considering all the historical, intentional, and thematic criticism lavished on Milton, one can only expect my precious title to suggest yet another symbolic interpretation of his work.[1] But there is more to the symbol than that which it symbolizes. Thus, working mostly on *Comus*, and later on the ninth book of *Paradise Lost*, my purpose here is to ask a few questions of import to the complex *mimesis* of the pastoral and the masque, and in the context of a semiology of *narration* and *description*, to try to clarify the relationship of poetic and dramatic texts to language and desire.[2] There the lines between *narration* and *description* are blurred, as rhetoric takes over the sequence, indeed, the production of the text.[3] *Comus* involves us in a very special way, which is somewhat beyond what is expected of a live audience. True, most of the trappings and mechanics of the Elizabethan and Jacobean masques are to be found in Milton's. First, the masque is essentially a compliment meant to contribute glory and beauty to a noble person, and in this sense, the story told in *Comus* only serves to enhance the presentation of the three young Egertons to their parents: the characters of Comus, on the one hand, and those of the Attendant Spirit and of Sabrina, on the other, are there to help deliver the proof of the Lady's virtue as she manages to ward off Comus' attacks. And since the masque is, again, the performance of the compliment, the parts of the characters are merely designed to give it a rhetorical structure. Such is the respect that Sidney's Lady of May pays to the Queen; such is the address of the Genius of the Wood praising the Countess of Derby in Milton's own *Arcades*, and such is the discourse of the Lady defending her chastity in *Comus*. Second, the use of magic and spells is also a favorite of masque writers. In Browne's *Masque of the Inner Temple*, Circe (more about her later) holds Ulysses' companions prisoner, until he can convince her to let them all go. And in Fletcher's *Faithful Shepherdess*, the nymph Sabrina sways the stream of the River Severn in a homage to her distinguished audience.[4] Finally, and this is in contradistinction with such delicate music and song as come from the Lady or Sabrina, there is even room in the masque for the antimasque: see, for instance, the *frolick* of Comus and his *crew*, and then the rejoicing of the country dancers appearing at the end of the performance to welcome the Attendant Spirit and his protégés to the castle (see Jayne 1968).

Yet, in another sense, the setting of *Comus* is like that of no other masque: the pastoral in it holds a very direct relationship to the unfolding drama. In most masques there is an element of pastoral; and in some, like Ben Jonson's *Pan's Anniversary*, performed in honor of King James I, the setting is a complete pastoral cliché. This connection between the pastoral and the masque is readily understandable, if one remembers that, after the Renaissance, pastoral literature is indeed on its way to becoming ornamental and academic, soon a repository of figures and stock phrases and situations. The masque being a compliment, the writer quite naturally turns to a genre that will provide him with easy formats: thus, in *Comus*, through the story of the preservation of the Lady's virginity deep in Comus' wood, it is naturally the new Lord President and the whole Egerton family who are complimented. In *Comus*, pastoral cliché has a much larger function.

I. Although the decor in *Comus* may appear *pro forma*, it has a function of its own.[5] We may know that the wood, where the yound Lady Egerton gets lost, was located near Ludlow Castle, that it actually refers to a real wood and a real event (the three Egertons having lost their way back to the castle that very year). But we also know that this wood of Comus, which is merely presented to us in the first scene as a generic piece of the whole setting ("The first scene discovers *a* wilde wood"), soon grows in importance, as the Attendant Spirit-narrator first warns us:

> Who [Comus], ripe and frolic of his full grown age,
> Roaving the Celtic, and Iberian fields,
> At last betakes him to *this* ominous wood
> (Milton *Comus* 59-61)[6]

and then, turned Thyrsis (one of the all-time good shepherds of classical pastoral), shares his fears with the two brothers:

> Within the navil of this hideous wood,
> Immured in cypress shades a Sorcerer dwels,
> Of Bacchus, and of Circe born, great *Comus*.
> (Comus 520-522)

But in the meantime, the wood's mystery also depends on our perception of a particular atmosphere: the night is pitch dark:

> Elder Brother: Unmuffle, ye faint stars, and thou fair moon,
> That wont'st to love the traveller's benison,
> Stoop thy pale visage through an amber cloud,
> And disinherit Chaos, that reigns here,
> (331-334)

and we can hear the wild row of the revellers inside:

> Attendant Spirit: The wonted roar was up amidst the woods
> And fill'd the Air with barbarous dissonance.
> (549-550)

What the whole *ekphrasis* then suggests is that the pastoral world is indeed a very dangerous place to visit. We remember that into those woods and vales of the Golden Age, tigers or bandits sometimes make devastating forays (*The Faerie Queene*, for instance), threatening the serenity of the romance; we also remember that if Thessaly was in antiquity the land of pastoral Tempe and of the sacred Peneus, it was equally the land of witches and wizards, as Ovid and Apuleius, Goethe and Nodier all well knew. Now one could, of course, argue that *Comus* is not a true pastoral, that it takes place in a wood at night, while most pastoral eclogues usually unwind in some pleasant clearing in the shade of the noonday, that there are no satyrs, no fauns, except in the nondescript *crew* of Comus and their *Measure*. Yet there are nymphs (Echo and Sabrina), there are suggestions of other pastoral divinities (including the river god Severn), and what is even more deceptively rustic, Comus himself as well as the Attendant Spirit choose to appear as shepherds:

> Second Brother: (*meeting the Spirit*): O brother, 'tis my father Shepherd sure
> Elder Brother: Thyrsis whose artful strains have oft delaid
> The huddling brook to hear his madrigal,
> And sweetned every musk-rose of the dale
> (493-496)

> Comus: . . . When once her eye
> Hath met the vertue of this magic dust
> I shall appear some harmles villager
> . . . .
> And hearken, if I may, her business hear.
> (464-469)

If in fact the world of Thyrsis and Meliboeus old is the world of *otium* and balance, it seems that it can also very easily become the domain of

Dionysos-Bacchus leading his wild bands through the woods. From Sophocles to the Alexandrines, to Catullus, to Virgil and Ovid, we have a dual tradition of peace and violence associated with the ἄλσος, the wood, grove or pleasance of the pastoral landscape: it is *sacred* (ἱερόν), off limits, figuratively *and* literally.[7] Milton may have used it for two reasons.[8] On the one hand, the world of the pastoralist symbolizes a shelter, which is so unmistakably suggestive of the quiet of a nonurban environment:

> *Lady*: My brothers when they saw me wearied out
> With this long way, resolving here to lodge
> Under the spreading favour of these pines,
> Stepped as they said to the next thicket-side
> To bring me berries, or such cooling fruit
> As the kind hospitable woods provide,
>   (182–187)

that is soon loses any positive identification by becoming another cliché (the perfect setting for expressing one's frustration with the agitation of "civilized" society). On the other hand, the wood also has a tradition of harboring restive satyrs and fauns, who forever and mercilessly pursue nymphs from the mornings of the *Anthology* to the *Après-midi* of Mallarmé. In *Comus*, it is the Enchanter, the god of the wood himself, who emanates and refracts this atmosphere of *sacrum* through his every move and resolution. In the old epic tradition, the Enchanter lives alone in an isolated place. Circe inhabits a secluded valley, the Sybil lives as a recluse, most witches from *Beowulf* to Goethe have always haunted inaccessible mountain caves or forests, and in the *Divine Comedy*, Dante meets Virgil in the wood. That Milton has selected a wood, that this wood is haunted by the son (masculine version) of Circe, brings to the fore what remains to us the most interesting aspect of the pastoral genre in its relation to the masque: its ambivalence.[9] The shelter may even be a "civilized" one:

> *Lady*: Shepherd I take thy word
> And trust thy honest offered courtesy,
> Which oft is sooner found in lowly sheds
> With smoaky rafters, then in tapstry halls
> And courts of princes, where it first was named.
>   (322–326)

It will, nonetheless, continue to be a receptacle for all the sacred things which our Western civilization cannot handle, except perhaps at a safe distance, and, as in magic, by remote control. If indeed the decorated and miniaturized world of classical and Renaissance pastoral appears to us today so pretty and empty, it might just be that we fail to understand how this excessive emphasis on expression could actually be allopathic and curative, by disseminating through language, and thereby controlling the "ugly" pulsions of sex, violence and death, which could otherwise not be dealt with in a nonpastoral society,[10] which may be why translators of pastorals, from Thornley on, have always chosen to be modest and sometimes used their Latin in the rendering of an immodest Greek.[11] Later, when the world of the eclogue becomes more and more devoid of content, when the rococo entertainments of the Modern Age in England and on the Continent look to us like futile rhetorical exercises, it is just as possible that the eighteenth-century intellectuals, many of them deeply rooted in their class and cultural prejudices, found themselves unable to cope with the reality of true down-to-earth nature, and had to see it either in purely biophysiological terms (the philosophers), or in those totally abstract and disincarnated visions of the pastoral (the poets) — see Chapter 11. This is why Fontenelle and Pope, and Turgot after them, all stressed in their discussion of the eclogue the concept of *artistic* nature over *true* nature: a shepherd should not smell of the herd, and, as for fishermen, they did indeed cut too rustic a figure in those scenes from *The Green Cabinet* (Rosenmeyer 1969).[12] There again, our feeling of missing something comes from not experiencing a release of "real" emotions, and having to remain impervious to the tremendous charge of violence, which such productions as *Comus*, on the other hand, manage to communicate to us through the process of the masque.

It is true that the masque, because of its profoundly mimetic nature, seems to emphasize the merely representational aspect of the pastoral. Up front, everything, Comus' charming overtures as well as the majestic moves of the Attendant Spirit, is described in magnificent terms and set in beautiful rhythms. Yet the mime is also pantomime, the charm also comes with a scaring gait, and behind the descriptive front, the exterior, there lies a terrible ambiguity, which is but superficially resolved at the level of language and rhetoric. The poet can in fact delve into the innermost sensitive, sacred and dangerous matter of the pastoral, while at the same time preserve the mystique of his allegory to the last word. Although the brothers are able to wrest the dangerous potion from Comus' hand, it is up to Sabrina, and not to the Attendant Spirit himself, to free the Lady and undo Comus' charm with her own reverse of it:

> Next this marble venomed seat
> Smeared with gumms of glutenous heat
> I touch with chaste palms moist and cold.
> Now the spell hath lost his hold.
> (916-919)

It is as if Milton wanted to ensure that the magic could only be broken by magic.[13] This means that Comus has not been subdued, but merely routed. It leaves both contestants intact— and potentially ready for another round. Should Comus threaten the Lady's virginity again, the Lady would, no doubt, be able to fight him back with her words. In this sense, the spectator and/or reader is reassured of the propriety of terms and values: an attack on virginity, such as occurs in *Comus*, can only occur in a world as fairy-like as that of the pastoral; and when it does occur, there is always enough magic around so that it can be handled within the context of the pastoral. Sabrina, who is the only one able to thaw Comus' frost, thus symbolizes the perfect closure of a world where salvation and safety are but a corollary of the immanence of the pastoral norm and tradition: she herself was saved from death by the same ritual she will now use on the Lady.

II. I would like to show that this ambivalence of the *mimesis* and the unseen is quite functional and that it works at two levels: (1) at the level of language and rhetoric; and (2) at the level of desire, beneath the mask of words.

First, the distinctive feature of the masque is that it compels us to reexamine all the classic demarcations that we usually expect in a dramatic system, such as the one between audience and performers, that between actors as actors and actors as people, and that between reality and allegory (see Tuve 1968). Whereas a traditional play will relate matter and treatment in such a way that, say, Othello's behavior on the stage can be interpreted as representative of the conflict of reason and faith, while at the same time showing the triumph of raw jealousy, in *Comus*, on the other hand, the masque does not provide for such a wide range of interpretation, because there the end is attained less in working through the plot than in complimenting the actors and their audience of relatives and friends on qualities which they possess outside the stage, or which are conferred upon them by the very fact of their performance:

> Noble Lord, and Lady bright,
> I have brought ye new delight,
> Here behold so goodly grown
> Three fair branches of your own,
> Heav'n hath timely tried their youth,
> Their faith, their patience, and their truth,
> And sent them here through hard assays
> With a crown of deathless praise,
>   To triumph in victorious dance
> O'er sensual folly, and intemperance.
>   (966-975)

The mimetic system keeps the structure of imagery completely closed at all times: the Egertons do have one daughter and two sons; they have one *factotum* (Lawes) turned shepherd (Thyrsis). Since these are noble persons, since they are to remain so by virtue of and within the nondramatic format of the masque, their representation can only be fairly static. One could expect that Comus, on the other hand, not being a referential person, would have more freedom: since, living alone in his wood, he appears excluded from society, the member of the Egerton entourage who plays him is not so much concerned with respect of conventions. However, because the delicate balance between reality and its double must not be altered, the masque cannot tolerate direct confrontation with alienation or violence. Thus, when the tension which keeps content and expression together has been increased to the point where the masque is evolving toward tragedy, the whole process then requires for its catharsis — actually, as we shall see, for the resolution of a semiotic conflict between form of expression (rhetoric) and form of content (desire) — the vacation of at least one of the protagonists, of the symbolic perpetrator of violence. Comus, who must be expelled from the process, leaves the stage, so that a (two-level) ritual of purification can be accomplished. Sabrina *physically* frees the body of the Lady, and the Attendant Spirit taps the sexual energy of Comus, by suggesting an appropriate allegory in the Garden of the Hesperides:

> All amidst the Gardens fair
> Of Hesperus, and his daughters three
> That sing about the golden tree:
> Along the crispèd shades and bowres
> Revels the spruce and jocund Spring,
> The Graces and the rosy-bosomed Howrs
> ·
> In slumber soft, and on the ground
> Sadly sits th'Assyrian queen;
> But far above, in spangled sheen
> Celestial Cupid her famed son advanced
> Holds his dear Psyche, sweet entranced.
> After her wandering labours long,
> Till free consent the gods among
> Make her his eternal bride,
> And from her fair unspotted side
> Two blissful twins are to be born,
> Youth and Joy; so Jove hath sworn.
> (981-1011)[14]

By the same token, that Comus chooses to be a gentle villager, thus in fact usurping the semblance of the good shepherd, that the Attendant Spirit decides to appear to the brothers as Thyrsis is symbolic (1) of the conditions imposed on Milton for a proper functioning of the masque; and (2) of the ambivalence of the pastoral, and specifically of the complete reversibility of the pastoral cliché.

Mythology will attest that Comus was born of Circe and Dionysos-Bacchus. This parentage, nowhere recorded, and Milton's own creation, has bemused the critics, who, as usual, elect to fall back on literary history or psychology. They point out that Milton could not have failed to see Ben Jonson's *Pleasure Reconciled to Virtue*, in which Comus leads a band of pleasure-seeking revelers. But this explanation is of little help. First, Ben Jonson's Comus, otherwise known as the *Cheer* or the *Belly*, is but a Plautinian and grotesque picture of mere gluttony; far from being threatening, he is farcical.[15] Second, a reference to *Pleasure* does not give us any clues as to the metamorphosis of the meek ogre into the cool sarcastic devil of Milton. A bit of research will actually tell us that for the first representation of a Comus, we are indebted to Philostratus,[16] who describes a painting of Dionysos-Comus (κωμάω: "to revel") inebriated; there the word *Comus* is still understood as a mere attribute of Dionysos (Philostratus 1931: 9). Later, in Virgil, Ovid and others, we do have allusions to a Faunus god born of Circe and Jupiter. Faunus, one of the oldest gods of Rome, and worshipped by peasants and shepherds as the legendary representative of Arcadia in Italy, was soon to be associated with Pan and Dionysos (see Chapter 8). Whether Milton was actually aware of these filiations, as he well might have been from his classical studies at Cambridge, matters little (see Parker 1968: 23-115). There is something more mysterious and fascinating here than the question of Milton's scholarship, and, considering the text as the prism which focuses and refracts a somewhat confused mythology, I intend to show how the process of the masque coalesces and compounds strong elements not only from a pastoral, but also from an orgiastic tradition ("Stygian rites of Hecate . . . Cotytto, goddess of nocturnal sport"). Dionysos is the transvestite god, who likes to disguise himself. Mythology has it that he was dressed as a girl by his nurse to escape the fury of Juno [*Lady*: "Were it a draught for Juno when she banquets" (701)] jealous of the love of Zeus and Semele — which, incidentally, throws an interesting light on Milton's attention to a male Comus instead of a female Circe. He is worshipped by bands of satyrs, such as those that had already appeared in *The Winter's Tale*, and often disguised themselves as women or Bacchae, wearing masks and performing fertility rites [*Comus*: "And strangled with her waste fertility" (729)]. At this point, a quick investigation into the history of the masque shows us that the first masques originated with the revels and mummeries usual at carnival time, the *sociétés joyeuses* in France, and the moriscos in England. Then, under pressure from the extraordinary development of the civic pageant, while at the same time confused by the glorious memories of an age of chivalry, it slowly came to lose its ritual pertinence, and finally evolved into the more aristocratic court and noble mummeries of the late Renaissance. Now, bringing all these loose threads together, we can see that Milton managed to accomplish several things at once. With his Comus, he retained the pastoral context traditionally attached to Circe's progeny, while also emphasizing an orgiastic and mimetic aspect of the Dionysiac tradition, which had always been, albeit subliminally, significant in the masque; and finally, through the personalization of a character separate from both Circe and Dionysos, he was eminently successful in organizing and synthesizing conflicting pulsions and meanings through the powerful process of his own rhetoric.[17]

My point here becomes theoretical. If the structure of the masque—called the *hinge* by Tuve (1968) and Barber (1968) — is indeed particularly appropriate to the subject of *Comus*, because it works as a metaphor, dividing our attention between a *tenor* (for example revelry *vs.* temperance, or sex *vs.* virginity) and a *vehicle* (Comus *vs.* the Lady), making us feel a tension between (1) the two arguments; (2) the two characters; and (3) the arguments and the characters, and sometimes increasing our excitement by attempting to confuse our references (as when Comus addresses the Lady disguised as a shepherd); if it also works as a transformer for conflicts which would otherwise destroy the world (see, for instance, what happens in Euripides' *Baccahe*); *is it not, conversely, the only mechanism through which the text can let us glimpse and feel how representation structures and represses the sweeps of desire within the confines of a plausible debate?* If this is true, the effectiveness of the text, its power to repress, would depend on its reliability as a didactic model; its rejection of sense experience would be in direct relation to the fineness of its engineering and the *airtightness* of its composition (Fletcher 1964: 279-303). What then would be the semiotic impact of these two factors on the production of the masque?

There is a great bareness and simplicity about *Comus*. It is actually reducible to an *agon*, a debate between two archetypal characters: Comus (κῶμος) and the Lady — one standing for revelry and debauchery, and the other for chastity and virginity, as we have just seen. Milton had not invented the form of the debate: again, it comes from the pastoral, where two shepherds try to maintain the equipoise of the noontime by jousting for their love, and then later, as the Theocritan idyll gives way to the Virgilian eclogue, the *pastor bonus*, to the *pastor felix*, and the Classics are expurgated and *moralized*, by arguing points of moral teaching and theological dogma.[18] But Milton, writing more in the tradition of Prudentius and Augustine, focused the debate on the specific issue of sex, physical love and the sensuous appetites. Yet, what is actually very new, and typically Miltonian, is the intimation that, partly because the sensuous and/or erotic experience offered by Comus engages mostly to silence:

> . . . Come, no more!
> This is mere moral babble, and direct
> Against the canon laws of our foundation;
> I must not suffer this, yet 'tis but the lees
> And settlings of a melancholy blood . . . ,
> (806-810)

the salvation of the Lady must rest in language. Thus, by forcing a debate, where he could show the power of words (of reason against the voice of unreason), while at the same time suggesting the attractiveness of Comus' philosophy, Milton was able to explore the perilous shelter of pastoral, while also remaining within the proper confines of the masque. Here, and in contradistinction to *Paradise Lost*, the Lady must resist and win. Yet, if it should appear that neither she nor Comus are really triumphant, because, as we have seen, magic can only be undone by magic, and that the debate therefore does not resolve anything, it may be that the true function of pastoral rhetoric has never been to move, but, on the contrary, to stablilize and delay (Rosenmeyer 1969: 65-97).

III. On both sides, the Lady's as well as Comus', there is the acknowledgment that their dogmatic opposition may only be a question of semantics, within two arguments whose setup is identical. The distribution of lexical items remains constant; only their value changes through pairs of opposites. Comus praises luxury, and the Lady, temperance, but the two arguments are teleologically oriented toward nature, conformed, each in its own way, with its own rhetoric, to nature's (God's) offering. Comus cares not to let nature fade away in time: he is the hedonist, and to the Lady, a swinish glutton; the Lady wants to preserve the same nature's riches through temperance: she is the true Epicurean, and to Comus, a Cynic and a Stoic. Both discussants are caught in a linguistic quibble. What they communicate to each other as intended differences are in fact mere equivalences, as the Lady well enough admits, when she claims that Comus is unworthy to know more:

> And thou art worthy that thou shouldst not know
> More happiness than this thy present lot.
> (788-789)

The sad truth is, she must learn, language in itself does not mean anything, and rhetoric, through its process of displacement, for example:

> What need a vermeil-tinctur'd lip for that
> Love-darting eyes, or tresses like the Morn?
> (753-754)

and condensation, for example:

> If you let slip time, like a neglected rose
> It withers on the stalk with languish't head,
> (743-744)

is nothing else than the staging of those differences and/or equivalences. Her only way out is to appeal to those higher mysteries she speaks of, and Comus', to the magic he brags about. One could sum the whole debate between the two by saying that Comus does *not* in fact succeed in keeping rhetoric out of a very physical situation. Indeed, the one passage, where he tries to wrest the Lady away from her own praise of virginity, by suggesting the plain truth of sexual encounter— cleverly enough, not in the context of forcible rape, but in that of "mutual . . . partaken bliss" — was actually deleted from the Ludlow performance

> List Lady be not coy, and be not cosened
> With that same vaunted name, Virginity,
> Beauty is Nature's coin, must not be hoarded,
> But must be current, and the good thereof
> Consists in mutual and partaken bliss,
> Unsavoury in th'enjoyment of itself.
> (737-742)

And because rhetoric is not kept out of the debate, but rather articulates it, both characters must deal with each other at a level which is not really *deliberative* (that is, in any case, *persuasive*, or *leading to action and narration*), but merely demonstrative: they each get involved with discussing the merits of their respective model, which is but a reflection of, a cover for, their desire.

Comus starts off with a *friendly* approach. He wants to share with the Lady his feeling for the strength and beauty of life anew:

> When the fresh blood grows lively and returns
> Brisk as the April buds in primrose-season.
> (670-671)

Nothing special in this, except the argumentation. The approach derives its *friendliness* from a natural proposition rather prevalent in Aristotelian philosophy — something in the order of "too much worrying is not only not pleasant, but also not good, because it increases the secretion of bile and fiery humors", or, using a Scholastic paradigm, where the biological inference has been lost and the tropic value alone remains, that "fire and gold are *friendly*".[19] There is Comus' first sophistication: adorned with an inviting *ekphrasis*: "And first behold this cordial [biology again] Julep here" (672), his address is meant to elicit a biological response:

> Is of such power to stir up joy as this
> To life so friendly, or so cool to thirst.
> (677-678)

Let us notice that the biological motif and its adornments, which symbolize the god's attempt at what rhetoricians would call simple *communication*, that is, the tentative, albeit implicit, inclusion of the opponent in support of one's own allegation:

> *Comus*: Why are you vext Lady? why do you frown?
> Here dwell no frowns, nor anger, from these gates
> Sorrow flies far,
> (666-668)

is translated into a metaphorical model of functioning nature: man-the-borrower from nature-the-lender. I am not going to discuss here the tradition and the propriety of this model. The relationship between the processes of nature and the exchange of money is surely something that the Middle Ages consciousness enjoyed and which the Renaissance writers knew how to use well (see, for example, the whole dicussion on nature, moneylenders, and debt in Rabelais' *Tiers livre in Pantagruel*. Let us merely consider how, through a slip from a biological or organic imagery to a financial and legalistic or nonorganic imagery, we are suddenly removed from the plane where our senses have as much to say as our mind, to that where our mind becomes the sole agent of our metalinguistic understanding:

> Why should you be so cruel to yourself,
> And those dainty limbs which nature lent
> For gentle usage, and soft delicacy?
> But you invert the covenants of her trust,
> And harshly deal, like an ill borrower
> With that which you received on other terms,
> Scorning the unexempt condition
> By which all mortal frailty must subsist,
> Refreshment after toil, ease after pain,

> That have been tired all day without repast,
> And timely rest have wanted. But, fair Virgin
> This will restore all soon . . .
>
> (679-690)

By shifting the discussion from a level where sensuality is a part of the
process of relating ("And first behold . . .") to a level where it is purposely
masked under that very process, and becomes a distant reference for it
("Why should you be so cruel to yourself"), Comus chooses to place the
debate on the firm footing of rhetoric, thereby putting the Lady in a position
where she can readily accuse him of rationalizing falsehoods and being a
traitor:

> 'Twill not false traitor,
> 'Twill not restore the truth and honesty
> That thou hast banished from thy tongue with lies.
>
> (690-692)

The vocabulary of "covenants", "trust", "lent", "unexempt condition",
because it is removed from the biological context, implies a misuse of
what is a natural function through an unnatural image, and far from
helping to reinvest those natural processes into the text and within the
frame of Comus' invitational remarks: ". . . But fair Virgin, This will
restore all soon", provokes the Lady's anger and her forceful rejoinder.

But this first attempt will also backfire in another sense. By rhetoricizing
his desire and metaphorizing reality, Comus may well induce the Lady,
once she has got past her initial reaction of outrage, to consider his plea in
rational terms. Yet, in doing so, he will have had to alter the semantic
context of his offer and may have lost the sense of spontaneous freedom
which had inspired the *wordless* dance of his *Measure* at the opening of the
masque:

> Com, knit hands, and beat the ground,
> In a light fantastic round.
>
> (143-144)

As expected, the Lady rejects the:

> . . . fair pretence of friendly ends,
> And well placed words of glozing courtesy
> Baited with reason not unplausible,
>
> (160-162)

but without really touching Comus's argument: her remark that

> . . . such as are good men can give good things
> And that which is not good, is not delicious
> To a well-governed and wise appetite,
>
> (703-705)

is not a response in kind, but in degree: governance, or the lack of it can in no way change the fact that there is natural pleasure in the satisfaction of our appetite. Encouraged, Comus pushes ahead. And after a couple of cracks at the Stoics and the Cynics, he soon resorts to the full-fledged rhetoric of an *adunaton* (see Chapter 6): the impossible picture of a world where pleasure is defined according to the terms of his metaphor. Using the Lady's own critique (her "well-governed appetite" has become "lean and sallow abstinence," and her call for restraint has been ridiculed as a "pet of temperance" in the face of nature's bounty), he cleverly manufactures a syllogism: if, where nature has entered into a contract with us and given us plenty, it is our responsibility to relieve her of her burden; the more so, if we are truly her *sons*, not her *bastards*, we must be diligent and execute our part of the contract. Finally assured of his point, he boldly emphasizes the sexual tone of his argument through a metonymy: the riches of the Lady are like the riches of nature; the *deixis* of the statement (Nature → Lady) has been modified thanks to a crude dichotomy, very suggestive of the sexual act (*bastards vs. sons*), and exemplified with the "partaken bliss" which grows out of the contractual enjoyment of the lovemakers. With this last shift, pleasure through lovemaking has become not only functional, but the overt reference of the discourse. All in all, Comus' danger lies not in the overtness of this appeal to sexual instincts, but rather in his rhetoric, which, *normalizing*[20] them, robs the sacred (social and religious) function of virginity: "the sage/And serious doctrine of virginity" (786-787), of its mystery. The demonization of sex is nothing else but its demystification.

To protect herself from this, and because, as we have seen, there is nothing wrong with Comus' basic argument, the Lady has no choice but to try and expose the fallacy of his *adunaton*, which she does by building her own, a picture of communal socialism very reminiscent of Gloucester's speech in *King Lear*. Her model is as normalized as Comus'; only, picking up his metaphor, and speaking about love and exchange, she stresses not the universal but the distributional aspect of it. In Comus' speech, the emphasis was on *bounty* of supply, and the necessity for a universal response:

> Wherefore did Nature powre her bounties forth,
> With such a full and unwithdrawing hand,
>
> (710-711)

to keep her from being "strangled with her waste fertility." But she points out that her defense of *virginity* has nothing to do with *waste*. *Virginity* symbolizes the protection of the individual through a system of measure, *temperance*:

> As if she [nature] would her children should be riotous
> With her abundance. She, good cateress,
> (763-764)

of which chastity is but a particular aspect (to be sparing of one's body, as one is of divine nature's):

> Natures full blessings would be well dispensed
> In unsuperfluous even proportion,
> . . . .
> . . . swinish gluttony
> Ne'er looks to Heaven amidst his gorgeous feast,
> But with besotted base ingratitude
> Crams, and blasphemes his feeder. Shall I go on?
> Or have I said enough? To him that dares
> Arm his profane tongue with contemptuous words
> Against the sun-clad power of chastity; . . .
> (772-782)

At this point, she becomes enthused with her demonstration, and gets carried away by her praise of virginity ("the sage/And serious doctrine . . ."), just as Comus had got carried away by his attack of it:

> Yet should I try, the uncontrollèd worth
> Of this pure cause would kindle my rapt spirits
> To such a flame of sacred vehemence,
> That dumb things would be moved to sympathize,
> And the brute Earth would lend her nerves, and shake,
> Till all thy magic structures reared so high,
> Were shattered into heaps o'er they false head.
> (793-799).

While being sarcastic about his rhetoric:

> Enjoy your dear wit, and gay rhetoric
> That hath so well been taught her dazling fence,
> (790-791)

she is caught with her own: the phrase "rapt spirits" suggests an Orphic trance (Fletcher 1971: 186-194), where "dumb things would be moved to sympathize," and she ends up threatening him in return:

> *Comus*:   Nay Lady sit; if I but wave this wand,
>   Your nerves are all chained up in alabaster
>   (659-660)

I

> *Lady*:   Till all they magic structures reared so high,
>   Were shattered into heaps o'er thy false head.
>   (798-799)

This is the end of all rhetoric: Comus tries to subdue her with his potion.

IV. Let us go back a bit. As stated above, Comus' ancestry is unclear. What is very clear, however, is that the introduction of a rhetorical element into a loose body of mythology helps control the diversity of pulsions and symbols which it contains, and can best dispose of the excesses of desire, particularly sexual desire. That is to say, rhetoric charging the text with descriptive features mandates an arrest in the narrative sequence. By giving the Lady the power to hold off Comus for a while — and Comus' line: "Her words set off by some superior power" (801) covertly Christian under the reference to *Jove's thunder*:

> . . . a cold shuddering dew
> Dips me all o'er, as when the wrath of Jove
> Speaks thunder,
>   (802-804)

does translate into Milton's Christian context the shift of power between the adversaries — the poet robs the god of his magic. Thus it is the Lady who, for a moment, has the power, through the magic of her words: like Jove, she "speaks thunder." Now let us look at the Circe-Odysseus episode, to which Milton at this point specifically refers. The two brothers, using *Haemony*, which is but another version of Homer's *moly* (*Odyssey* 10. 305), given to them by the Attendant Spirit (the Hermes of the *Odyssey*) and much like Ulysses himself (*Odyssey* 10. 294, 321) their swords drawn, will presently rout Comus and his crew. We can see that there is indeed a major difference between Homer's and Milton's treatment. In the *Odyssey*, mention of sexual relations is only made (1) with respect to *Ulysses* who can alone intimidate Circe with his sword; that none of his companions is involved simply means that it is he, Odysseus, who, *par excellence*, has the power to make love; (2) *after* Odysseus has indeed drunk Circe's potion. In *Comus*, however, by keeping the Lady chained, and shifting the physical violence to the brothers and Comus, *before* the Lady can drink the evil potion, Milton has made impossible the consummation of the sexual act, avoiding the sexual context of Circe's change of her men into pigs, *filling the time* between the capture of the Lady and her liberation by her brothers with a rhetorical debate, and then, at last, resorting to Sabrina, to effect a complete liberation.

Again, the question is: What induced Milton to promote a format where rhetoric would take precedence over action, and why did he not entrust the Lady's immediate liberation to her brothers?

The answer is twofold. First, a point of conventions: granted the conditions of the masque, Milton could not very well expose the young Lady Egerton to physical violence, or even to the mere violence of words, for instance something like Phaedra's attempt on Hippolytus in Racine. And, by making her liberation contingent on the magic of Sabrina, who, as Fletcher (1971: 219 ff.) has shown, liberates not only the Lady but also herself, Milton closes according to conventions and to the requisites of an *aesthetic distance*.

The second point has to do precisely with the importance of rhetoric and its relation to the expression of sexual desire. By insisting on Comus' temptation, by reversing the roles (Comus has taken the place of Circe), by investing the brothers and Sabrina with the task of liberation, Milton *delays* the whole process of desire. This "structural" delay, which we will also find in the ninth book of *Paradise Lost*, when Satan tempts Eve — let us note in passing that the motif of feminine temptation does not seem to inspire Milton: the woman does not tempt; she is tempted — represents a subversion of Comus' desire in the context that he himself set up ("well placed words of glozing courtesy"). *It is this delay* which allows Milton to verbalize the conflict between the Lady and Comus and which can help him demonstrate the arresting power of the *logos* in a situation of direct confrontation. But, most important, it also indicates that it is eventually language itself which has both a dilatory and *disseminating* function (Derrida 1972): speech acts as a transformer, and if Comus loses his crude strength, it is because he chooses to resort to a rhetoric which tones down his passion and normalizes it into organized discourse. It is surely no small paradox that Comus' ancestral frenzy gives way to a cool new logic adorned with sarcasms:

> O foolishness of men! that lend their ears
> To those budge Doctors of the Stoic Fur,
> And often their precepts from the Cynic tub,
> (706-708)

while the Lady's expected reserve by and by yields to a growing fantasy ornate with figures: "Yet should I try, the uncontrolled worth. . ." One cannot help feel that rhetoric soon becomes the outlet, and even perhaps the analogue of sexual gratification.[21] Semantically, the phrases "shake," "reared so high," "o'er they false head," and, metrically, the overflow "Were shattered" can leave little doubt as to the transparency of the symbolism. Comus is overwhelmed by the Lady's reply (note the alliteration):

> She fables not, I feel that I do fear
> Her words set off by come superior power.
> (800-801)

Yet, theologians, philosophers and transcendentalists notwithstanding, if we can for a moment leave Milton's alleged concerns and his critics' obsessions aside, if we can allow this reponse to be more than a mere reference to the power of the Almighty in the context of the poet's ambiguous Christianity, we shall find that it is actually at some level a very short, but very basic remnant, something like a trace, or more appropriately in this case, like an echo, of the pleasure principle implicitly negated and sublimated through the Lady's "holy dictate of spare temperance", the "sun-clad power of [her] chastity" and her "serious doctrine of virginity" (Lacan 1971: 151-191; also Kristeva 1974: 17-100). Indeed, as the unmediated *signifier* stands closest to the external object of desire, the alliterative pattern of the phonogical substance "She fables not, I feel that I do fear" would seem to indicate the presence of a reality not yet *signified*, that is, not translated (metaphorized or allegorized) through the sign processes of language. But Milton cannot allow this pleasure principle to be realized, and, quickly mastering the sublimal, he wilfully returns to an old *signified* of concepts and allegories ("words. . . superior power") through the distancing of clichés (metonymy, synecdoche, and so on):

> . . . as when the wrath of Jove
> Speaks thunder, and the chains of Erebus
> To some of Saturn's crew . . .
> (803-805; emphasis added)

Two objections: first, this interpretation is surely very debatable in itself; and, second, assuming that it is correct, why does Comus not act accordingly?

The answer to the first objection is, of course, that the text carries more than one meaning, and that it is only in the context of its own ambiguity that it proves more effective. This Milton himself suggests, when he has the Lady quip, on the one hand, "Thou art not fit to hear thyself convinced" (792) and fantasize, on the other, "Yet, should I try . . ." (793). The question here is not only whether the proof is admissible, but also, and mostly, *whether one accepts the principle of the constant possibility of semiotic deconstruction or transgression of the text by text* itself: an operation, where the subject attempts to posit himself as one in an apparently monodic *sym*bolic process, and where only through his dissociation from the *thou* or the *you*, is he able to reinforce the feeling of his own existence (Kristeva 1974: 57 ff; see also Chapter 5). Again, see the Lady's quip: "*Thou* art not fit to hear *thyself* convinced." Comus, on his part — and this is my answer to the second objection — however desirous he may be of the Lady, is only allowed to perceive, albeit not comprehend her, bound and statue-like that she is in her frozen *virginity*. The linguistic quibble I mentioned before in the context of a substitution of lexical values can be traced here in another context, where the ambivalence in the determination of the semantic field (the Lady's tirade boasts selective, distributional pleasure, in the face of Comus' orgiastic, undisciplined revelry) actually points to an irreconcilable difference between form-free message and restrictive code, *which cannot itself be comprehended except in the context of the struggle of the speaking subject with his own utterance*. Let us watch, for instance, the subtle shift from the generalities of *everyman*:

> If every just man that now pines with want
> Had but a moderate and beseeming share
> Of that which lewdly-pampered Luxury . . .,
> (768-770)

to the specific deitic *thou*: "Thou are not fit . . .," to the hyperbole of the *I*: "Yet, should I try . . ."

In the discourse of the Lady, the symbolical-allegorical void of non-referential denomination ("luxury," and previously in contradistinction with it, "temperance," which Comus had called "sallow abstinence" in the face of "bountiful Nature") is replaced ("every just man") with a *binary* referential opposition between the *thou* and the *I*. On a structural level, this shifting appears perfectly consistent with the tight dialogic framework of Milton's mask, and the closed debate between Comus and the Lady. Yet, if it were only for that, the Lady's allegory would not really be very *productive*. To provide relief from the interlocking of a *binary* opposition (*thou/I*) which oppresses her, and to instigate a feeling of resolution or, as in the context of her style, of *salvation*, through a *triple* instancing (*him/I/thou*) is precisely the regulatory function of her rhetoric:

> . . . To *him* that dares
> Arm his tongue with contemptuous words
> Against the sun-clad power of chastity;
> Fain would *I* something say; — yet to what end?
> *Thou* has nor ear, nor soul to apprehend . . .
> (780-784; emphasis added)

It means that the Lady can escape Comus now made ineffective ("To him . . . *fain* would I . . . thou has *nor* . . . thou art *not* fit . . ."), by giving herself the *temptation* of vicarious rapture ("Yet, should I try . . ."). She knows that Comus, dumbfounded, will not be able to *apprehend* how he stands excluded from the process, robbed of his power. He will have to "try her more strongly": note the corespondence between the two *try*'s. He has now realized that this rhetoric of his, whose process he started and which has now become another person's "mere . . . babble," has actually been subverted from inside: "direct/Against the canon laws of our foundation". Satan, in *Paradise Lost*, will know better, staying with the pulsion through the outside object, the apple. Here the potion is but a testimony to Comus' failure: it will not be allowed to work.

V. To be sure, the obvious difference between the two episodes, the one in *Comus*, and the other in *Paradise Lost*, is one of tradition and convention. Eve must be led into temptation and succumb; the Lady cannot and will not. Yet, assuming for a moment that this difference is but a free variation (Satan/Comus; Eve/the Lady) of a systemic model (*tempter vs. tempted*) within the context of a given style (*Biblical vs. non-Biblical*), the only major real difference remains, literally and phenomenologically, an objective one: whether the object of the debate is a real object or a sign, and if a sign, what kind of sign it is.

It can be argued that Comus' rhetoric is circular and that it misses its goal, because the object of the debate with the Lady (reveling or sexual debauchery) actually never materializes in any form or shape, except perhaps in the vial of julep, which she has been offered, but which she will not touch. In *Paradise Lost*, on the other hand, the focalization of the debate on the Tree of Knowledge makes it easier for Satan to persuade Eve to eat of the fruit:

> . . . or will God incense his ire
> For such a petty Trespass . . .
> (Milton *Paradise Lost* 9. 692-693)

The eloquence this time is *deliberative*; it may extrapolate around the object by discussing its metaphysical or moral context, but is is essentially geared toward making this object the object of a particular action in the context of Milton's epic narrative:

> Till on a day roving the field, I chanced
> A goodly tree far distant to behold

> Loaden with fruit of fairest colours mixed,
> Ruddy and gold: I nearer drew to gaze
> ·
> To satisfy the sharp desire I had
> Of tasting those fair apples, I resolved
> Not to defer: hunger and thirst at once,
> Powerful persuaders, quickened at the scent
> Of that alluring fruit, urged me so keen.
> (9: 575-588)

In other words, Comus' attempt to sway the Lady fails because he fails
to invest his rhetoric in the appropriative process.[22] The convention of
his ekphrasis:

> And first behold this cordial julep here
> That flames and dances in his crystal bounds
> With spirits of balm and fragrant syrups mixed
> Not that Nepenthes which the wife of Thome
> In Egypt gave to Jove-born Helena
> Is of such power to stir up joy as this . . .,
> (Comus 672-677)

the indeterminacy of metonymical space:

> Here dwell no frowns, nor anger, from these gates
> Sorrow flies far; See here be all the pleasures
> That fancy can beget on youthful thoughts . . .
> (*Comus* 667-669)

—are in striking contrast with the precision of Satan's argument:

> When from the boughs a savoury odour blown,
> Grateful to appetite, more pleased my sense
> Than smell of sweetest fennel, or the teats
> Of ewe or goat dropping with milk at even,
> Unsucked of lamb or kid, that tend their play . . .
> About the mossy trunk I wound me soon,
> For high from ground the branches would require
> Thy utmost reach or Adam's: round the Tree
> All other beasts that saw, with like desire
> Longing and envying stood, but could not reach.
> Amid the Tree now got . . .
> ·
> Sated at length, ere long I might perceive
> Strange alteration in me . . .
> (*Paradise Lost* 9. 579-599) [23]

It all appears quite simple at first. The differences between the vial of
julep and the fruit of the Tree of Knowledge is a difference between a

simple trope and an allegory. But what does it mean? While the vial of Comus is but a metonymy for the life of revel, to which the god and his *crew* are inviting the Lady, the Tree of Knowledge remains isolated from and standing above all other objects in the world. It has its own mystery, which cannot be explained, either literally or figuratively. Whereas the content of the julep is determinated by a mythological tradition, and, categorized as a magic device, cannot itself be the object of desire, but merely a sign for it, the Tree of Knowledge is out of context, quite properly set beyond reach. Its *significance* is contained in a presupposition for its existence (see Fillmore 1965),[24] which, if transgressed, offers the subject a place in narrative complete with agent, patient, ally, adversary, causal relations and time sequences:

> . . . *Now I feel* thy *Power*
> Within me clearer, not only *to discerne*
> *Things in their causes*, but *to trace the ways*
> Of highest *agents*, deemed however wise.
> Queen of this Universe! do not believe
> Those rigid *threats* of death: *ye shall not die*:
> How should ye? by the fruit? *it gives you Life*
> To Knowledge . . .
>   (*Paradise Lost* 9. 680–687; emphasis added)

The rhetoric of the Serpent has had the effect of questioning this presupposition. In fact, questioning it, he literally strips the object of its symbolic significance. The fruit of the Tree is shown to be *just a fruit*, available to desire, a free desire like his own: "Goddess humane reach then, and freely taste" (9. 732). At this point, the text itself underlines, through Milton's detached commentary, the delayed triumph of a silent descriptor and the victory of desire over the sign:

> He ended, and his words replete with guile
> Into her heart too easy entrance won:
> Fixed the fruit she gazed, which to behold
> Might tempt alone, and in her ears the sound
> Yet rung of his persuasive words, impregned
> With reason, to her seeming, and with truth;
> Meanwhile the hour of noon drew on, and wak'd
> An eager appetite, raised by the smell
> So savory of that fruit, which with Desire
> Inclinable now grown to touch or taste,
> Solicited her longing eye; yet first
> Pausing a while, thus to herself she mused
>   (9. 733–744)

The idea of *taste* (understood as *touch and eat*, as in *"freely taste"*) has grown to that of *tasting good*, and so has the *appetite*. The rest follows: "Forth-reaching to the fruit, she plucked, she ate" (9. 781).

The relationship of language, and specifically, of rhetoric, to desire is ambiguous at best. While seemingly structuring the expression of desire into highly formalized components, for example in *Comus*: (phonology and metrics) a decasyllabic blank verse, and in some cases, an octosyllabic lyrical recitative, both with frequent alliterative patterns; (syntax) compound adjectives ("low-thoughted care", "Sin-worn mould", etc.); or (semantics) clichés and allegories from the tradition of the pastoral and the masque, rhetoric does, at the same time, rationalize and repress the content of this desire through the concurrent elaboration of rigid hermeneutical models of metaphysics and morals. To put it another way, it is because of the explosiveness of desire that the speakers resort to rhetorical devices, which in turn help them form and regulate the expression of that which, like the Tree of Eden, defies expression in the first place:

> Thy praise he also who forbids thy use
> Conceals not from us, naming thee the Tree
> Of Knowledge, knowledge both of good and evil;
> Forbids us then to taste. But his forbidding
> Commends thee more, while it infers the good
> By thee communicated, and our want . . .
> (9. 750-755)

What has now become the contest of rhetoric and desire implies an internal dialectic of the text directly related to the opposition between narration and description. Seen *constructively*, poetic and dramatic text is the organizer, the programmer, of a loose, ineffable and generally inexpressible substratum into a set of linguistic hierarchies and semantic taxonomies. In which case, whether the performance is for an audience or by the reader, there is not much action: words merely delay the outcome, and rhetoric is nothing else than the process of that delay: the wording up and stabilization of two irreconcilable positions. On the other hand, *destructively*, the same text as a group of organized constructs is also, and at the same time, the agent of its own destruction, concealing the libidinal process involved in the establishment of abstract sign-relations. That this *semiotic* process threatens the unity and the reliability of the text is made exceedingly clear by the fact that the rhetoric is interrupted on stage by a substitute repressive action (*Comus*) preventing any possibility of real identification and wish fulfillment, and in the epic poem, by the silence which propitiates the emergence of desire (*Paradise Lost*), then by the narration of the fulfillment of the wish, and the punishment meted out for satisfying desire.

Of such a basic conflict there can be no resolution. On stage, the only cure may be amnesia: what was said must be unsaid:

> . . . without his rod reversed
> And backward mutters of dissevering power,
> We cannot free the Lady that sits here . . .
> (*Comus* 816-818)

and within the confines of the masque, the magic ritual of words in reverse is enough to erase, and thereby terminate the performance (*mimesis*) while in the epic narrative, the price for transgressing the limits of description is the wrath of God and the guilt of man. As in

> . . . the gardens fair
> Of *Hesperus*, and his daughters three
> That sing about the golden Tree
> (*Comus* 981-983)

we are for ever caught between the one and the other, as between the Garden and the Tree. [25]

NOTES

1. Take, for instance, the case of *Comus*. Is there anything left to say about *Comus*? Students of the old School of Ideas are still stuck with A. S. P. Woodhouse's overbearing exegeses (1941, 1950), while phenomenologists and structuralists alike wonder how to add to Angus Fletcher's theory (1971).

2. In this Chapter, the term *semiology* refers to a general theory of sign-systems — one of which is hopefully language, and another one, language-in-literature; the term *semiotic* (a noun or an adjective), used mostly in sections IV and V, refers to the nonsign, nonsymbolic process, which helps generate desire and fulfill the wish, as against a sign, symbolic (structural) process which represses it, while ordering it. My discussion will thus reflect the current Continental debate between *structuralism* and *poststructuralism*, from Saussure and Hjelmslev to Derrida and Kristeva.

3. *Production* means here: (1) in a Marxist context, the process of the text reflecting the exchange between Labour and Capital; (2) in a psychoanalytical context, the process of the text reflecting the working through of contradictions between language and desire at all levels; and (3) in the context of this chapter, the process of the text reflecting the exchange between language and desire at a very high symbolic level. For another context of *production* see Chapter 5.

4. Critics have often pointed out the influence of Fletcher's play on Milton. The reference is particularly interesting in view of Fletcher's defense of his own play as a new form of drama. For a comprehensive review of possible influences on Milton, see Fletcher (1971: 40-115).

5. Let us recall here the Hjelmslevian distinction (see Chapter 2, note 1) between *content-form* and *content-substance*. This distinction will help us differentiate between the stylistic datum of our text (the pastoral decor in *Comus*), perceived as substantially different from the aesthetic norm (pastoral decor in general) and the system (or form) of structural relations involved in making this specific illustration possible (Milton's use of rhetoric).

6. I am quoting from the Rinehart edition with introduction by Northrop Frye (New York, 1955).

7. As Fletcher reminds us, Thyrsis' presence in *Comus* is more than a mere cliché. Thyrsis appears in Theocritus' *Idylls* 1: "But the irony of his name is deepened by a pun, since the *thyrse* is the Bacchic wand, as in the Ancient Greek proverb: 'Many are the worshippers of Bacchus, but few are the true bearers of the Thyrse' . . . Comus . . . only pretends to possess the power of benign transformation. Thyrsis, however, has this power" (Fletcher 1971: 165). As for the reference to *Meliboeus old*: "Som other means I have which may be used/Which once of Meliboeus old I learnt/The soothest shepherd that e'er piped on plains" (*Comus* 821-823), it is generally agreed that Milton wanted to pay homage to Geoffrey of Monmouth, although we need not rule out other possibilities (Chaucer?). But, in Greek mythology, Meliboeus is the shepherd who discovers Oedipus tied on Mount Citheron. The two names, Thyrsis and Meliboeus, thus refer to a tradition much larger than the eclogue's.

8. See Sophucles *Oedipus Coloneus*; Theocritus *Idylls* 7; Virgil *Aeneid* 6, Ovid *Metamotphoses* 5. 391 (Pluto rapes Proserpina in a Sicilian meadow); Ovid *Fasti*: 4. 749 (shepherds must keep their sheep off the *lucus*, and so on). Even a linguist like Quintilian seems to substantiate the ambivalence of the wood, when he claims (*Institutio oratoria* 1. 6. 34) that the word *lucus* is derived *by antiphrase* from *lux, lucere*. Rosenmeyer (1969: 190) maintains a distinction inherited from Curtius (1953: 194-195) between the *grove* and the *pleasance*, and claims that only the pleasance, because it is never properly a precinct, belongs to the pastoral world. However, this distinction, which may apply to a thematic study of Theocritean literature, is much too theoretical (that is, structural only) when tested as a semiotic level, where it becomes largely academic.

9. For a theoretical background on this ambivalence, see Fletcher (1964: 147-180).

10. There is not much psychoanalytic literature on the pastoral proper: nothing in Freud, and aside from the obvious diagnosis of a castration complex and a regression to infancy (see Lerner 1972: 81-104), nothing in modern criticism, particularly on the relationship of the pastoral cliché to desire.

11. See Longus (1962), with "the English translation of George Thornley, revised and augmented by J. M. Edmonds." Thornley himself may well have been a fellow student of Milton at Christ's College.

12. For a more extensive discussion of this problem, see Chapter 11, note 10.

13. We must remember that the brothers do not heed the advice of the Attendant Spirit: they let Comus escape, without seizing his magic wand. On the use of Sabrina as a mode of existential (ritual) repetition, see Fletcher (1971: 222-223).

14. Most commentators have already pointed out the paradisiac feeling conveyed by these lines. But one could also notice the *symbolism* of numbers: *three* (daughters); *two* (Psyche and Cupid, Youth and Joy); *one* (the Assyrian Queen, that is, Venus, the goddess of both earthly and spiritual love) — and remember that there are three Egerton children, two contestants and one intercessor (the Attendant Spirit of Sabrina). The allegory of the Hesperides, by shifting the scene from the *three* to the *two* (+ two → four) seems to attempt some sort of *structural* resolution of the problem. Or is it only *structural*? And could it not be said that critics who try to take advantage of the *symbolism* do miss the point and confuse form and substance (for example the essentialist debate on the triarchy of *Temperance, Chastity* — or is it *Charity*? — and *Virginity*)?

15. "Room! Room! make room for the Bouncing Belly/First father of sauce, and deviser of

jelly . . ./Hail, hail, plump pauch! O! the founder of taste,/For fresh meats, or powdered, or pickle, or paste,/Devourer of broiled, baked, roasted, or sod . . ." (Jonson 1890: 222).

16. See Chapter 9 for an insight into Philostratus' work.

17. Which makes Milton's outward puritanical stance all the more striking in *Comus*. Barber (1968: 203) sees in *Comus* a reflection of changing social conditions: the urban class is seeking new pleasures (its revels) in a traditional agrarian context. On this see Chapter 15.

18. See Greg (1959: 79-103); and also Curtius (1953: 228-246).

19. For a historical account of the function of rhetoric in theological writings, see Fish (1967: 69-80).

20. A terminology introduced by Greimas (1966) to define the setting up of a metalinguistic framework, within which ideological contents can be actualized (see Chapter 1, note 3).

21. For a theoretical background on this, see Lyotard (1973: 135-156).

22. For narration as appropriative processes, see Chapter 13.

23. Note the striking mixture of pastoral clichés (". . . more pleased my sense/Than smell . . .") categorizing and regulating the object of desire and its mode of apprehension, and of "straight" admissions of desire (". . . with like desire"), which are really what the serpent acts on ("Stated at length . . .").

24. From a logical point of view, the *presupposition* or *entailment* means that, if it is not true, the statement of which it is a part, cannot be true or false. But this presupposition also has a pragmatic value; the selection of a particular statement with such or such entailment can introduce into a discourse the key-structure of repression; for instance: Of each Tree in the Garden we may eate,/But of the Fruit of this fair Tree amidst/ The Garden, God hath said, Ye shall not eate/Thereof, nor shall ye touch it, least ye die (*Paradise Lost* 9. 659-660).

25. Because the semiotic process, as we have defined it, takes place beyond the realm of language and rhetoric, it might be appropriate to move from the field of linguistics proper to that of the philosophy of language. Following Derrida (1973: chs. 2, 3), I shall say that the relation of language to the referential world must be defined by using two criteria: (1) *indexicality*: the fact that language is an *index*, a system of signs for something else; (2) *expressionality*: the fact that, spoken or written, it intuits, on the threshold of meaning itself, the notion of a self-conscious independent existence. Comus' rhetoric, because it constantly confuses the two, fails to convince the Lady, not only of what he talks about, but of what he merely suggests. Satan's argument, on the other hand, because it clearly concentrates on (indexes) one object, does succeed in making Eve forget the given value of her wish (*Wunsch*), thus leaving her desire (*Lust*) free to express itself — even if for only a moment — outside the realm of rhetoric, *through* her own words, and soon *through* the poet's own discursive commentary.

15

Masks of History in Nineteenth-Century Fiction

I. In this chaper, my objectives are twofold. First, returning to the discussion of the relation between narration and description in prose, I want to investigate the consequences of the delay or the acceleration which, we have seen, it involves for the overall narrative process (Chapter 13). I want to suggest that in the context of nineteenth-century fiction — and as an alternative to having the subject set up his own image against the world in which he lives (*Madame Bovary*) — description can cause him to *fictionalize* his own historical tradition, his desires and aspirations as well as those of his economic and social class. Second, I would like to show that this process of fictionalization usually covers the range of differences and contradictions between, on the one hand, a pastoral (positive) representation, where history still remains unborn or suppressed, and, on the other hand, a farcical, burlesque and grotesque (negative) representation, where history progessively looms larger and ominous. Eventually, I hope that this discussion will lead to a reevaluation of the overall relationship between history and fiction, money and desire, and more specifically, that it will help shed some light on little known aspects of the nineteenth-century novel.

Before we proceed any further, however, we must consider the following points on historical narrative.

First, historical narrative, like purely fictional narrative, is essentially involved with programmatic considerations: the *presentation, projection* and *actualization* of a performance, in relation to other performances. That is to say, the recognition of a fact (*factum*), either directly established, or patiently reconstrued from documentary evidence, must then be referred to a subject or a group of subjects, and to an object or group of objects in their specific context, in order to appear as an action (*gestum, res gesta*). At this point, the narrative process proper takes over and introduces this *gestum* in the foreground of a world which it both constitutes and by which it is constituted (*presentation*). Once this process is operative, the relation of, the discourse on, the *gestum* becomes essentially motivational: actions are endlessly confronted with the possibility of other actions (*projection*), and this introduces a multiplicity of points of view. Finally, from the organization of these points of view, for instance, Columbus' arrival in the Caribbean becomes the discovery of America, the sack of the Bastille means the end of tyranny and the beginning of the French Revolution, the *gestum* is constituted as complete, and shown to be significant (*actualization*). This actualized *gestum* then stands as a reference for others, in what we call *history*, if we simply mean by *history* the organization of the past, for example, the Fall of the Roman Empire, the invention of printing, the American Revolution, and so on.

Second, in the course of this programmatization, every historical narrative draws its energy from three processes: a process of objectification; a process of emplotment; and a process of fictionalization proper (Chapter 14).

The objectification process specifically includes the locating and the instancing of the narrating subject. When instead of remaining explicit, this instancing becomes merely implied, *then we move from the purely historical to the fictional narrative*. This is very important, as the relation of an idea or a concept to a place is typically the historian's privilege (Le Goff and Nora 1974: 3–41). His objectification of the world is determined by the clarity of his relation to a particular space and time. It is obvious, for instance, that Stendhal's description of the battle of Waterloo through the eyes of Fabrice is a highly successful piece of *fictional* narrative, emphasizing the inability of an individual under stress precisely to actualize the *res gestas* around him. But from a historical point of view, Stendhal's Waterloo could have taken place anywhere. There seems to be no order, no sequence in the organization of the facts, and because the narrator (the instance of the speaking subject) chooses to act only as an unconcerned (even mocking) mediator for his character, the account of every action lacks the dual reference to a context and a point of view, and the actualization of *facta* into *gesta* remains incomplete:

"Ah! m'y voilà donc enfin au feu! se dit-il. J'ai vu le feu! se répétait-il avec satisfaction. Me voici un vrai militaire." A ce moment, l'escorte allait ventre à terre, et notre héros

"Ah! So I am under fire at last!" he said to himself. "I have seen shots fired!" he repeated with a sense of satisfaction. "Now I am a real soldier." At that moment, the escort began to go hell

comprit que c'étaient des boulets qui faisaient voler la terre de toutes parts. Il avait beau regarder du côté d'où venaient les boulets, il voyait la fumée blanche de la batterie à une distance énorme, et, au milieu du ronflement égal et continu produit par les coups de canon, il lui semblait entendre des décharges beaucoup plus voisines; il n'y comprenait rien du tout (Stendhal 1973: 49).

for leather, and our hero realised that it was shot from the guns that was making the earth fly up all round him. He looked vainly in the direction from which the balls were coming, he saw the white smoke of the battery at an enormous distance, and, in the thick of the steady and continuous rumble produced by the artillery fire, he seemed to hear shots discharged much closer at hand: he could not understand in the least what was happening (Stendhal 1962: 54).

Now one could object to this analysis on the grounds that the real Battle of Waterloo must have been very much like Fabrice's experience indeed, and furthermore, that novelists always manage to express later what is too vast and too complex for contemporaries to understand. But this kind of objection is like a point of privilege; it simply begs the question of the respective value of emplotment in historical and fictional narrative, to which I must now turn. In the meantime, I will offer the preliminary statement that, although the narrative of Fabrice's experiences appears to convey what is likely to have happened at Waterloo, and thus to fulfill Aristotle's criteria for probability, it only appears so for being an imitation, and not a historical account.

The process of emplotment can take several forms or modes, which Hayden White (1973) has clearly defined in his book on *Metahistory* as the ethic, ideological, aesthetic or linguistic modes. Choosing for the moment to limit myself to a linguistic or semiotic point of view, I can say that the emplotment of historical narrative is mainly dependent on the activation of a single string of probable sequences in a dual system of alternate logical choices: it is because Napoleon chose to wait for Grouchy (who never materialized) that he lost at Waterloo. Any comprehensive account of the battle must emphasize the decisive choice made by Napoleon, as against the other possibility:

Nie waren Napoleons Dispositionen umsichtiger, seine militärischen Befehle klarer als an diesem Tage: er erwägt nicht nur den Angriff, sondern auch seine Gefahren, nämlich, daß die geschlagene, aber nicht vernichtete Armee Blüchers sich mit jener Wellingtons vereinigen könnte. Dies zu verhindern, spaltet er einen Teil seiner Armee ab, damit sie Schritt für

Never had Napoleon's dispositions been more circumspect, his military orders clearer than on this day: he considers not only the attack but also its dangers, i.e. that the defeated, but not annihilated army of Blucher might join forces with that of Wellington. In order to prevent this he splits off one part of his army so that it might pursue

Schritt die preußische Armee vor sich herjage und die Vereinigung mit den Engländern verhindere.

Den Befehl dieser Verfolgungsarmee übergibt er dem Marschall Grouchy: ein mittlerer Mann, brav, aufrecht, wacker, verläßlich, ein Reiterführer, oftmals bewährt, aber ein Reiterführer und nicht mehr . . .

Daß er in Grouchy keinen Heros hat und keinen Strategen . . . weiß Napoleon wohl. Aber die Hälfte seiner Marschälle liegt unter der Erde, die andern sind verdrossen auf ihren Gütern geblieben, müde des unablässigen Biwaks. So ist er genötigt, einem mittleren Mann entscheidende Tat zu vertrauen (Zweig 1950: 128).

closely the Prussian army and prevent its merging with the English.

He hands the command of this army of pursuit to Field Marshal Grouchy: an average man, honest, upright, decent, reliable, a cavalry leader who had proven himself frequently, but a cavalry leader and nothing more . . .

That Grouchy is not a hero or a strategist Napoleon knows very well. But half his marshals are dead, the others have remained on their country estates, sulking, tired of never-ending bivouacs. Thus he is forced to entrust a decisive action to an average man (translated by Manfred Kusch).

This process of emplotment implies that the tension we are used to build into the historical process (whether we choose to emphasize conflict, as in a Marxist perspective, or whether we follow Ranke or Croce and prefer to emphasize unity) is already built in the presentation of the historical narrative. It also means that the vision provided by the historical narrative is esentially one of difference and irreversibility. The choices regulating the emplotment process can be made to appear conscious as in the pure historical narrative, where the historican decides everything on the basis of his information, or, on the contrary, to be guided by fate or chance, as in the fictional narrative, where the narrator seems to abstain from interfering with the decisions of his hero, which only become clear and definite to us later, as against the choices that were not made at the time:

Ce qui détermina Fabrice à rester, c'est que les hussards ses nouveaux camarades lui faisaient bonne mine; il commençait à se croire l'ami intime de tous les soldats avec lesquels il galopait depuis quelques heures. Il voyait entre eux et lui cette noble amitié des héros du Tasse et de l'Arioste (Stendhal 1973: 53).

What made Fabrizio decide to stay where he was was that the hussars, his new comrades, seemed so friendly towards him; he began to imagine himself the intimate friend of all the troopers with whom he had been galloping for the last few hours. He saw arise between them and himself that noble friendship of the heroes of Tasso and Ariosto (Stendhal 1962: 58-59).

Another important consequence of this differential model of emplotment is that it contributes a particular kind of tension, a particular kind of energy to the narrative: a negative energy. Because a narrative is basically emplotted according to a differential pattern (*presentation*), insofar as it tries to communicate to us (*projection* and actualization) the probability of the past having taken place, its mode of *representation* is basically a figurative one. Not only does a narrative activate a particular plot, which keeps our attention focused on the differential pattern, but it also points out, and most of the time, subtly implies, the credibility of the fiction represented. The performance that we are witnessing is not only possible, it is *convincing*. In the passage from Stendhal quoted above, we know perfectly well that Fabrice is completely wrong about his relationship to his impromptu comrades-in-arms: the "il voyait entre eux . . . cette noble amitié . . ." — which seems, with the imperfect, to prolong such a nice romantic dream — is patently ironic: we know that Stendhal, like Flaubert later, can in so many ways imply judgment of his characters at the same time as appearing sympathetic with them; as a matter of fact, the emplotment process being what it is, this total unawareness of Fabrice will soon almost cost him an arm. Yet the major part of our interest in Fabrice is that he can actually be made fun of, and we can then feel compassion for him. We can perhaps become as romantic as he is, while we also know that he is perfectly foolish, just as we can be fascinated, albeit without feeling much compassion, by the dry painting of Félicité's empty domesticity in Flaubert's *Un Cœur simple*. In the end, the process of *narrativization* (implicit in the use of the imperfect), is superseded by a process of *fictionalization*, which represents more than the difference between two kinds of emplotment and triggers our reference to a world beyond mere conceptual denotation (see Katz and Fodor 1964: 491 ff).

We have now come to our third process. In view of the above, it can be granted that *fictionalization* is basic to any narrative, in the sense that it determines the nature and the extent of our involvment in the world of *mimesis*. It is the process through which a narrative choice, based on a simple linguistic opposition (for example, in the above passage, Fabrice's decision to stay with the army in the thick of battle as opposed to his returning home), suddenly opens a whole series of positive identifications which modify the substance, the quality of the mimesis. The comment: "c'est que les hussards . . . lui faisaient bonne mine . . ." soon leads to: "il commençait à se croire l'ami intime" (instead of the reverse implied by the restrictive "avec lesquels il galopait depuis quelques heures"). This substantial modification interests me here, not because it immediately suggests the familiar problematic of an author/ narrator-narratee relationship, but rather because it is totally pertinent to the relation of narrative to history in general, and specifically, *because it can help understand how the superimposition of a fictional process on a narrative process will in the end make possible and illustrate the actualization of an* histoire *(simply understood as the organization, the emplotment of the past) into* history *(understood as the spirit which transforms the confrontation of narrative differences into a dialectic interchange).* In this chapter, I intend to show a particular aspect of this operation, by concentrating on a particular range of substance modification, from pastoral to farcical, to burlesque, to grotesque fiction. In this way, we shall progress from a kind of mimesis where history is totally absent and where the narrative and the fictional processes being securely locked with one another, there simply is no evidence of cover-up, to another kind, where fictionalization soon becomes so intent and overly emphatic, that it must imply, through its own excesses, the kind of strategic difference, the crack through which history becomes rational and begins to make sense. Nineteenth-century fiction seems to offer a particularly convenient field for this experiment, as it appears, or rather, would like to appear, to have done away with both the pastoral and/or farcical tradition which the *Orlando* and the *Quixote* seemed to have installed in the catalog of European fiction (*The Faerie Queene, Astrée, Gil Blas, Tristram Shandy*). We shall see in a moment that this demise of conscious pastoral/farcical elements is but an apparent one, and that the general assumption that nineteenth-century fiction is less fictitious and more realistic than most needs to be reexamined.

II. There is, in nineteenth-century fiction, a large body of literature concerned with a very specific locus and a specific time in the history of post-Napoleonic Europe, when capitalism has joined ranks with nationalism in the overturning of the old hegemonies (see the combination of the adventurer Fabrice, the minister Mosca, and King Ranuce in *La Chartreuse de Parme*, for instance). And that time and locus are mostly those of the heroic (Fabrice) and the tragicomic (Fabrice, Ranuce). But, as the pressure of history weighs heavier, the hero (from Frédéric in *L'Éducation sentimentale* to Des Esseintes in *A Rebours*) is less and less heroic, while the urban monster of progress and industry devours everybody into anonymity (Gervaise dies crumpled and forgotten in some awful garret). There is also another body of fictional literature, which is best defined as that of pastoral Europe around and after 1830. Although

conceived by writers who reside in and are mostly familiar with the city (Balzac and Flaubert), it concerns itself with a story in the countryside: *Les Paysans, Madame Bovary, Middlemarch, Far from the Madding Crowd* — to which many other titles could be added: most of George Sand's novels, Zola's *La Terre*, and so on. The scene can be a castle, as in Balzac; it can be a small town, as in *Madame Bovary* or *Middlemarch*; or plain country as in Hardy.

In all these novels apparently dedicated to the glorification of an easy country living for the well-off and the praise of daily toil for those they employ, there is something indeed very powerful about the description of a community which is closed, self-supporting, and little, if at all, affected by outside events; a community, where, in addition to the implicit references to an oft-celebrated golden age, the praised qualities of a topical peace and repose, there is also apparent a desire to protect this daily serenity, to arrest the flow of time, and thus to cheat history, by secreting a history of one's own without any residue, one that can never escape the tight grip of a limited fiction. The end of *Middlemarch* is very interesting in this respect, because it suggests that the process of a stabil-ized fictionalization will go on forever, once the narrative, the actual story, has stopped. We learn that Tertius Lydgate, the rash young doctor, who, with his new ideals and methods, represents one of the intruders in the pastoral ring, will eventually go back to the metropolis and die there a successful but hard-working man's death. He will be survived by a Middlemarch of happy people, that of the Garths, of Sir James and Celia, and by another one, which, George Eliot tells us, we all carry in our heart:

for the growing good of the world is partly dependent on unhistoric acts; and that things are not so ill with you and me as they might have been is half owing to the number who lived faithfully a hidden life and rest in unvisited tombs (Eliot 1875: 621).

In this sense, the mimesis of the novel seems in perfect agreement with the ideals of pastoral literature, the capture of a world of *otium* and balance, which can represent a shelter from the bustle of urban environ-ment. In all the works mentioned above, there are indeed many (too many to be counted) passages which suggest just that: pure *tableaus* and timeless descriptions, whose obvious purpose it is to arrest the narrative and delight us with the picture of a world we seem to have forgotten; a world pure and virginal, but whose deemphasized, desexualized,

virginity makes it appear both natural and artistic:

J'ai enfin joui d'une campagne où l'Art se trouve mêlé à la Nature, sans que l'un soit gâté par l'autre, où l'Art semble naturel, où la Nature est artiste. J'ai rencontré l'oasis que nous avons si souvent rêvée d'après quelques romans: une nature luxuriante et parée, des accidents sans confusion, quelque chose de sauvage et d'ébouriffé, de secret, de pas commun (Balzac 1964: 11).

In a word, I have found much enjoyment in a region where art and nature are mingled without either being spoiled by the other, where art seems natural, where nature is artistic. I have discovered the oasis we have so often dreamed of as the result of reading certain novels: luxuriant, gayly-decked nature, irregularity without confusion, a touch of savagery and disorder, something unfamiliar and out of the common (Balzac 1899: 11).

In this world unartistic characters can be made to acquire the simplicity of Nature:

[Mrs. Cadwallader's] life was rurally simple, quite free from secrets either foul, dangerous, or otherwise important, and not consciously affected by the great affairs of the world (Elliot 1875: 41).

Soon, the narrator makes us feel that we belong in this pleasance, and he has us look for tracks, for *vestigia*, of our former existence in this Eden. Thus we have the *topoi* of the grots, the statues, the ruins, and the whole neoclassical environment, in which the Romantics do so much love to reminisce, to strike a pose, a dream:

L'Arcadie est en Bourgogne et non en Grèce, l'Arcadie aux Aigues, et non ailleurs. Une rivière, faite à coups de ruisseaux, traverse le parc dans sa partie basse par un mouvement serpentin et y imprime une tranquillité fraîche, un air de solitude qui rappelle d'autant mieux les Chartreuses que, dans une île factice, il se trouve une Chartreuse sérieusement ruinée et d'une élégance intérieure digne du voluptueux financier qui l'ordonna (Balzac 1964: 17-18).

Arcadia is in Bourgogne and not in Greece, Arcadia is at Aigues and nowhere else. A river, formed by diverse small streams, flows through the lower part of the park in a serpentine course, and imparts to it a cool tranquillity, an air of solitude which is the more reminiscent of the Chartreuse convents, in that there actually is, upon an artificial island, a summer-house — *chartreuse* — in the last stages of decay, whose interior splendor is worthy of the voluptuous financier who built it (Balzac 1899: 18-19).

All this as a testimony to some sort of unfinished business, of a history that is, perhaps, not quite real after all.

Finally, even in books where the intentions of the character already seem too straightforward, and the modern outlook already too close to ours to fit the pastoral image, for instance in Hardy, where the assumption of the Victorian era would seem to forbid recourse to the trinkets of Greece and Rome, the push toward the pastoral can unmistakably be recognized in these lulls, those pleasances of the mind that the novelist simply cherishes too much to abandon:

Bob Coggan was sent home for his ill manners, and tranquillity was restored by Jacob Smallbury, who volunteered a ballad as inclusive and interminable as that with which the worthy toper old Silenus amused on a similar occasion the swains Chromis and Mnasylus, and other jolly dogs of his day. It was still the beaming time of evening, though night was stealthily making itself visible low down upon the ground, the western lines of light raking the earth without alighting upon it to any extent, or illuminating the dead levels at all. The sun had crept round the tree as a last effort before death, and then began to sink, the shearers' lower parts becoming steeped in embrowning twilight, whilst their heads and shoulders were still enjoying day, touched with a yellow of self-sustained brilliancy that seemed inherent rather than acquired. The sun went down in an ochreous mist; but they sat, and talked and grew as merry as the gods in Homer's heaven. Bathsheba still remained enthroned inside the window, and occupied herself in knitting, from which she sometimes looked up to view the fading scene outside. The slow twilight expanded and enveloped them completely before the signs of moving were shown (Hardy 1918: 179).

However, fully pastoral as these indulgences may be, they remain mostly indulgences; and they cannot ensure the whole pastoral tenor of the novel. We have seen that the end of *Middlemarch* could be interpreted as the stabilization of fiction in an ahistorical process. But this is, surely, a one-sided interpretation. We soon remember a long tradition of threats to the pleasance (roving bandits and slave merchants in the Alexandrine romances, witches in the *Satyricon* and the *Golden Ass*, vicious tigers in *The Faerie Queene*, ill-advised shepherds in *Astrée* and devils in Milton), and we tell ourselves that this pastoral world of English provinces is just as threatened by the intrusion of foreign persons and foreign ideas. It is weighted down by the obscure and distant presence of London, "with its jealousies and social truckling"; threatened also by the involvement of some of its inhabitants with an unfinished past: thus Will comes back to haunt Cazaubon, and Raffles, Bulstrode — or with a reckless present: thus Fred Vincy risks the well-being of his family in order to pay his gambling debts. The same goes for *Far from the Madding Crowd*, where the triple incursion of Bathsheba, Troy, and Boldwood into the pastoral world of Gabriel Oak and the whole of Weatherbury village can only alter the peace modulated by the "dulcet piping of Gabriel's flute". With Balzac and Flaubert, the pastoral setting of the narrative is equally threatened by an ongoing process of instrusions: remember the arrival of the new nobility among the freeholders in *Les Paysans,* and the havoc wreaked by Emma's books and daydreams upon herself, her idiot husband, and the whole community in *Madame Bovary.* Yet it is not only threatened, but also defiled by a slow process of internal change, whereby the affects of the pastoral turn into those of the farce, and soon, as we said before, of the burlesque and the grotesque. The "heavenly" descriptions sent by Balzac's naive Parisian (the newspaper editor Blondet) to his hypothetical friend in the city, will eventually be replaced by the narrator's own cynical visions of a pastoral world crawling with horrid Satyrs and murderous Maenads. And as the narrative progresses from pastoral to farce, to burlesque and beyond, the myth of an ideal countryside will be blown to pieces: "Toute révolte, ouverte ou cachée, a son drapeau. Le drapeau des maraudeurs, des fainéants, des bavards, était donc la terrible perche du Grand-I-Vert. On s'y amusait!" (Balzac 1964: 65). ["Every rebellion, open or secret, has its standard. The standard of the marauders, the do-nothings, the wine-bibbers, was the awe-inspiring pole of the *Grand-I-Vert.* There was amusement to be had there" (Balzac 1899: 79)]. In an absolutely masterful way, the author of the *Comédie humaine* reminds us that, in the wake of the eighteenth century's discovery of the self, there also comes, with the memory of the French Revolution, the awareness of a course of history, which, though fully cyclical, is subverted by an erratic fictionalization process (for example, Stendhal's Waterloo).

Purposefully played down at first, this process eventually destroys all our illusions, and by exposing our own reification of fiction, our reverse dreams of nature into art, of beautiful monuments and lifelike paintings, by emphasizing the significant distance between masks and reality, it shows how the modification of political regimes and economic conditions leads to the major upsets of history (the revolutions of 1830 and 1848, both lived through by Balzac; the abolition of serfdom in Russia in 1863; the Commune of 1871, and so on). Thus the French Revolution, and the subsequent repurchase of church and noble property by the affluent boureoisie, the famous *Biens Nationaux* or *National Estate,* instead of expanding a class of freeholders, eventually served to endow much of the bourgeoisie with the land previously belonging to the privileged classes. With this modification in the forms of property, itself the consequence of a modification in the means of production, there also comes a modification in the age-old relationship the public may have had to familiar themes and *topoi* of fiction, through the commonplaces of pastoral rhetoric. The dangers that surrounded the *locus amoenus* and threatened its life had been sent from afar, a geographically distant Europe, as in *Paul et Virginie*, a culturally gross America, as in *The Last of the Mohicans*. Now, on the other hand, these dangers are right here, in the middle of pastoralia; they are the peasants, who, comical at first, then, like goblins and devils, more ugly and grotesque, keep General de Montcornet from sleeping and enjoying his freshly acquired domain. Looking like the illustrations in the books of cheap romance that will dull Emma to death in the midst of a flat and boring Normandy, the peasants of Balzac, strikingly made up of all the bad, the deformed, the sly and the beastly, all get together from behind the lovely woods and the rich underbrush, the extraordinary rivers and flower beds, to clown, thrill and scare, perhaps, but also and most definitely, to steal, rape and kill. One of the more obvious results of this modification is the reversal of the relationship of narrative to fiction and the demystification of our much-vaunted process of fictionalization. As Balzac says, entitling one of his chapters "L'Oaristys, XXVIIème églogue de Théocrite, peu goûtée en Cour d'Assise," and thus unmasking the rhetoric: "L'âge de fer et l'âge d'or se ressemblent plus qu'on ne le pense. Dans l'un, on ne prend garde à rien; dans l'autre, on prend garde à tout; pour la société, le résultat est peut-être le même (Balzac 1964: 61). ["The age of iron and the age of gold resemble each other more than you think. In one, you look out for nothing; in the other, you look out for everything; so far as society is concerned, the result is perhaps the same" (Balzac 1899: 75)].

III. In all the works briefly reviewed here, history becomes manifest through the crack between the narrative and its fiction — which is not to say *that history is the end of all fiction*; rather, that history can only appear under the mask of fiction; or, put another way, that it is only by being a myth of a fiction, that history can be made clear to us. Here, it might be useful to recall some of the clichés we all learned concerning the beginnings of history.

For instance, the fictions (the *histories*) of Herodotus, the father of history, duly represent the first production of history through a system of narrative fiction. Yet, avidly *recited* in their time, preserved, albeit consistently ridiculed as a bunch of old wives' tales or the scurried log of a particularly unscrupulous or gullible traveler, these stories also have a secret. In the process of presenting us with facts, most of which are largely fiction, they intimate, not so much that the pure historical truth is to be uncovered from the fiction, the mass (gossip, hearsay) of undigested material, but that the fictionalization of an original narrative, say, for instance, the report of Sataspes to Pharaoh Nekao on his circum-navigation of Africa, *is absolutely essential to the manifestation of history*. When Herodotus, acting in the name of a well-meaning objectivity, says he refuses to believe the *fiction* that, "when the Phoenicians sailed a westerly course round the Southern end of Lybia, they had the sun on their right" (Herodotus *History* 4. 43), we, on our part, do understand that fiction to represent nothing but the truth: the Phoenicians did actu-ally sail around Africa in the Lower Empire. Fictionalization and history, therefore, are indissolubly linked. More precisely, it seems that history (in the Hegelian sense, that which moves toward the realization of the spirit of the world) can only become actualized when produced as fic-tion. Something that Marx obviously knew, when he stated that history repeats itself, first as tragedy, and second, as farce, and he added that:

die Parodie des Imperialismus war notwendig, um die Masse der fran-zösischen Nation von der Wucht der Tradition zu befreien und den Gegen-satz der Staatsgewalt zur Gesellschaft rein herauszuarbeiten (Marx und Engels 1960: vol. 3, p. 203).	But the parody of the Empire was necessary to free the mass of the French nation from the weight of tradition and to work out in pure form the opposition between the state power and society (Marx 1963: 130-131).

The Marxist view, however, is essentially concerned with the exposition of historical processes, which, when pitted against the tragedy of the first *Eighteenth Brumaire*, appear farcical, simply because of the burlesque fig-ure of the "Prinz der Lumpen" himself and his bourgeois dupes. In other words, the contribution of a particular fiction (for instance tragedy *vs.* farce) to the production of history is not the major interest of the author of the *Eighteenth Brumaire*. To be sure, his study of events as fictions leads him, first, to reconstruct, to narrativize, contemporary events as yet unrecorded, undigested, and certainly misunderstood, and second, in order to prove his point that history is essentially a covert process, to rhetoricize and fictionalize this narrative process:

Changarnier teilte den Führer der Ordnunspartei die Todesanzeige mit, aber wer glaubt, daß der Biß von Wan-zen töte? Und das Parlament, so ge-schlagen, so aufgelöst, so sterbefaul es war, konnte sich nicht überwinden, in dem Duelle mit dem grotesken Chef der Gesellschaft von 10. Dezember etwas andres zu sehen als das Duell mit einer Wanze. Aber Bonaparte ant-	Changarnier informed the leaders of the party of Order of the obituary notice, but who belives that bedbug bites are fatal? And parliament, stric-ken, disintegrated and death-tainted as it was, could not prevail upon itself to see in its duel with the grotesque chief of the Society of December 10 any-thing but a duel with a bedbug. But Bonaparte answered the party of

wortete der Partei der Ordnung wie Agesilaos dem Könige Agis: "Ich scheine dir Ameise, aber ich werde einmal Löwe sein" (Marx and Engels 1960: vol. 3, p. 175).

Order as Agesilaus did King Agis: "I seem to thee an ant, but one day I shall be a lion" (Marx 1963: 94).

But in the end, Marx's enterprise marks the demise of fiction: farce is, of all the fictional processes, that which retains the least credibility. And the *Eighteenth Brumaire* symbolizes, with the learning and the practice of true historical content, the discard of an overrated model of reference:

So übersetzt der Anfänger, der eine neue Sprache erlernt hat, sie immer zurück in seine Muttersprache, aber den Geist der neuen Sprache hat er sich nur angeeignet, und frei in ihr zu produzieren vermag er nur, sobald er sich ohne Rückerinnerung in ihr bewegt und die ihm angestammte Sprache in ihr vergißt. . . . Dort ging die Phrase über den Inhalt, hier geht der Inhalt über die Phrase hinaus (Marx und Engels 1960: vol. 3, pp. 115-117).

In like manner a beginner who has learnt a new language always translates it back into his mother tongue, but he has assimilated the spirit of the new language and can freely express himself in it only when he finds his way in it without recalling the old and forgets his native tongue in the use of the new. . . . There the phrase went beyond the content; here the content goes beyond the phrase (Marx 1963: 14–18).

It is only by rejecting this now obsolete model that the nineteenth-century social revolution can "ihrem eigenen Inhalt anzukommen".

My own concern is partially the reverse of the Marxist enterprise: I want to show the constitution of texts of fiction as events, and to analyze their order of pertinence to the production of history. That is to say: tragedy and farce may just be two of the many possibilities of textual production of history. Indeed, an examination of the contribution of a seemingly ahistorical pastoral to the production of history through the growing processes of farce, burlesque and grotesque, might conveniently provide the sort of fictional field, the mimetic range, in which to understand the conditions of this production.

One final point, before coming to particulars. The term *production*, used here figuratively, is derived from a Marxist context, where it applies to the process of the text reflecting the exchange of *Labor* and *Capital*. We shall see, in another section, that this exchange between *Labor* and *Capital* can be derived again to mean in a psychoanalytical context, the process of the text reflecting the working through of contradictions between language and desire at all levels.

Pastoral, like Eden, lies on the threshold of history:

Iuppiter angusta vix totus stabat in aede,
Inque Jovis dextra fictile fulmen erat.
Frondibus ornabant, quae nunc Capitolia gemmis;
Pascebatque suas ipse senator oves;
Nec pudor in stipula placidam cepisse quietem,
Et faenum capiti supposuisse fuit.
Iura dabat populis posito modo praetor aratro,
Et levis argenti lamina crimen erat.

(Ovid *Fasti* 1. 201-208)

In those times scarcely could Jupiter stand at full length in his narrow temple, and in his right hand was a thunderbolt of clay. Then used they to adorn the capitol with boughs, which now they adorn with gems; and the senator himself used to tend his own sheep. Nor was it then reckoned a disgrace to have enjoyed undisturbed slumber on the bed of straw, and to have heaped the hay as a pillow under one's head. The consul used to give laws to the people, the plough being but just laid aside, and the possession of a small ingot of silver was deemed a crime.

(Ovid 1892: 16).

But this association is confusing because it fails to consider the close relation of pastoral to farce, and their common relevance to the production of history.

Without abandoning my argument, I would like to go back for a moment to the origins of historical narrative, and by using two examples from Greek drama, to establish a dual archetype pastoral/farce, which we will then be able to apply elsewhere. First, I shall assume that history cannot begin, unless there is a rational spirit which articulates contradictions in an understandable manner, so that the resolution of these contradictions, if not consciously effected by the interested parties, can at least be explained to an impartial observer (generally, the public). I shall then examine how this basic assumption is verified and developed as a theme in each of the works: the end of lawlessness and strife (of the talion) in Aeschylus' *Oresteia*, and the end of war in Aristophanes' *Peace*.

It could easily be shown that the end of *Eumenides*, where Apollo tames the Furies (the Erynies) into well-meaning deities, is essentially of a pastoral character, while the end of the *Peace*, where the happy peasants of Attica celebrate the mythical peace by helping the goddess (the Peace) out of the "deep pit where War has cast her", is not only of a pastoral, but also of a comic, even marked farcical character: the peasant Trygaeus goes to consult the gods on his dung-beetle, and has to deal with the buffoonery of Tumult and War, before he can free Peace. In *Eumenides*, Aeschylus, having his audience look back on the growth of mature Athens, is able to use the metamorphosized chorus of the Eumenides to forecast the beginning of a new era, and thus inscribe the beginnings of Greek history (say, the years of formation before the Persian Wars, the period of the institutionalization of law and order with Solon and Dracon) into the span of a *civilized* Golden Age:

> Let there blow no wind that wrecks the trees.
> I pronounce words of grace.
> Nor blaze of heat blind the blossoms of grown plants, nor
> cross the circles of its right
> place. Let no barren deadly sickness creep and kill.
> Flocks, fatten. Earth, be kind
> to them, with double fold of fruit
> in time appointed for its yielding. Secret child
> of earth, her hidden wealth, bestow
> blessing and surprise of gods.
>   (Aeschylus *Eumenides* 1960: 938–947)

There, of course, the dramatic performance will have to stop, because the plot begins to incorporate the past history of the spectators, now actualized in the rituals and festivals of classical Athens, and because Aeschylus does not intend to represent that which lies outside the realm of his tragedy proper and can best be narrativized in the accounts of a historian like Thucydides (where the order of history has become the order of a discursive reason in its many *logoi*). And because it stops there, the spectators must have been made to feel that this history, which seemed to separate them from those mythical beginnings of Athens, was indeed part of the original myth of the *transcendental locus* which Lukacs nostalgically praises in his *Theory of the Novel* (Lukacs 1971: 29–39). Pastoral then appears as the very consequence of this momentous decision: because conflicts will not be wasting the earth any more, the only history left will be that of the earth in its productions, and the Erynies, the awesome goddesses of the subterranean world, become the "above ground" benefactresses of the city. In other words, and to put this in the perspective of historical narrative, the *Eumenides* pastoral is no mere adornment to the dramatic text. Rather, one could say that it is the establishment of a strict procedure (in Orestes' case, the jury system) in the selection of narrative alternatives (murder upon murder, or acquittal and the growth of the city under the law) that will secure for the people the true promise of a pastoral world and deliver, so to speak, the reality of the fiction. In the *Peace*, on the other hand, although the incredible decisions of Trygaeus and the people of Attica seem to warrant a pastoral future of prosperity and tranquillity, and more specifically, although Peace has been freed and War and Tumult suppressed, no procedure is established for the prevention of new conflicts. The pastoral dream (and it is but a dream, as the Spartans will eventually conquer Athens) can only come across as a wishful fantasy, a farce, whose main device is a ritual of repetition: appealing to the gods for peace, when the gods are powerless; appealing for unity, when it is only the feasting and the reveling that interests the people, and so on. When the play is over, this ritual leaves the public with nothing to hold on to, except, as in all farces, the trick of an impromtu marriage, of the punishment of the thief, the humiliation of the conceited, and so on.

The conclusion could be this: as long as fictionalization is anchored in the narrative (*Eumenides*), history is reduced to the mere integration of both processes into one and thus very naturally appears homogenous as pastoral. However, when the fictionalization process has grown so autonomous as to warrant the whole narrative by itself, history begins to lack credibility. It can only appear as mere repetition and thus provides material for the closed–circuit game of the farce. Now, since farce cannot sustain itself, except in a play, within the limits of the stage, the narrative process must either unmask the farce (the historians will, for example, tell us that peace was but a dream, and that the Spartans took Athens) or require additional fictional differences, so as to try and make its well-worn picture still more different and more relevant. Yet, at the same time the farce expands, reality moves further and further away, and farce becomes burlesque, until the burlesque burns into the grotesque. When we do realize how far our illusions have taken us, the consequences are usually disastrous. What I have been saying here, is that Aristophanes' *Peace* does in fact represent the travesty of *Eumenides*: pastoral has deftly been turned into farce. We have smoothly moved from the lovely brush of Arcadia to the props of the stage: pastoral as representation has been exposed. The mere act of this exposure proves it to be a farce.

History as pastoral has now become history as farce, and farce promises but further slippage, because shepherds, occasional and real, are more apt to loot than wisdom — as beautifully exemplified in Hardy's picture of Gabriel and Bathsheba covering the ricks under the raging storm, while the beau of the ball, Sergeant Troy, now half soldier, half shepherd, lamentably sleeps off his brandy in the company of all the farm boys he has corrupted. Oak and Bathsheba represent the *good shepherds*, while Troy and his crew are now but a masquerade of themselves:

Here, under the table, and leaning against forms and chairs in every conceivable attitude except the perpendicular, were the wretched persons of all the work-folk,

the hair of their heads at such low levels being suggestive of mops and brooms;
. . . the united breathings of the horizontal assemblage forming a subdued roar
like London from a distance. Joseph Poorgrass was curled round in the fashion of
a hedge-hog, apparently in attempts to present the least portion of his surface to
the air; and behind him, was dimly visible an unimportant remnant of William
Smallbury. The glasses and cups still stood up on the table, a water-jug being
overturned, from which a small rill, after tracing its course with marvellous
precision down the centre of the long table, fell into the neck of the unconscious
Mark Clark in a steady monotonous drip, like the dripping of a stalactite in a cave
(Hardy 1918: 287-288).

Finally, that this dual picture of pastoral, on the one hand, and farce, on
the other, is rooted in the long tradition of *one* ambivalent symbolism,
can easily be demonstrated, by using mythological examples both in
literature and in painting, where the cliché world of pastoral is also
bathed in the farce of Arcadia (satyrs teased and cheated by nymphs,
shepherds ridiculed in contest, and Eros playing havoc with everyone's
heart); and by recalling well-known anthropological data, where the pastoral celebration of a bountiful uncultured nature usually implies a degree
of farce in the ritual (fertility rites, phallic dances and masquerades).
Goethe knew all this, when he painted the Upper Peneus as a place where
sphinxes, griffins, ants, pygmies and cranes take the place of the nymphs
and the Sirens of the Middle Course. Now that farce is established in its
own right in the midst of Arcadia, it will, given the time and the space,
quickly degenerate into the burlesque and the grotesque.

Farce remains a dramatic genre, where plot resolution, because it is
based on repetition, depends on the very artifice of the stage and its
theatrics. However, when used in prose narrative, where syntagmatic
repetition must be checked as against the diversity of people, time and
places, it often turns into burlesque, in order merely to continue to
sustain itself. It often happens that the narrator, apparently unconcerned
with the consequences of this transformation, seems to relish the feeling
of a growing pandemonium:

The longer Joseph Poorgrass remained, the less his spirit was troubled by the
duties which devolved upon him this afternoon [driving the hearse of Fanny
Robin to the cemetery for the appointed burial]. The minutes glided by
uncounted, until the evening shades were but sparkling points on the surface of
darkness. Coggan's watch struck six from his pocket in the usual still small tones
. . . "Nobody can hurt a dead woman" at length said Coggan with the precision
of the machine . . . "Drink, shepherd, and be friends, for tomorrow we may be
like her" (Hardy 1918: 336-337).

In a first stage, farce still permits some sort of identification through

the imagery:

Et après un port d'armes où le cliquetis des capucines se déroulant sonna comme un chadron de cuivre qui dégringole les escaliers, tous les fusils retombèrent.

Alors on vit descendre du carrosse un monsieur vêtu d'un habit court à broderie d'argent, chauve sur le front, portant toupet à l'occiput, ayant le teint blafard et l'apparence des plus bénignes. Ses deux yeux, fort gros et couverts de paupières épaisses, se fermaient à demi pour considérer la multitude, en même temps qu'il levait son nez pointu et faisait sourir sa bouche rentrée. Il reconnut le maire à son écharpe, et lui exposa que M. le préfet n'avait pu venir. Il était, lui, un conseiller de préfecture (Flaubert 1966: 170).

And after a present-arms during which the rattle of the metal bands as they slid down the stocks and barrels sounded like a copper cauldron rolling down a flight of stairs, all the rifles were lowered.

Then there emerged from the carriage a gentleman clad in a short, silver-embroidered coat, his forehead high and bald, the back of his head tufted, his complexion wan and his expression remarkably benign. His eyes, very large and heavy-lidded, half shut as he peered at the multitude; and at the same time he lifted his sharp nose and curved his sunken mouth into a smile. He recognized the mayor by his sash, and explained that the prefect had been unable to come. He himself was a prefectural councilor (Flaubert 1957: 158).

However, burlesque will soon revel in fiction for its own sake, by *rationalizing a farcical repetition*:

Tous ces gens-là se ressemblaient. Leurs molles figures blondes, un peu hâlées par le soleil, avaient la couleur du cidre doux, et leurs favoris bouffants s'échappaient de grands cols roides, que maintenaient des cravates blanches à rosette bien étalées. Tous les gilets étaient de velours, à châle; toutes les montres portaient au bout d'un long ruban quelque cachet ovale en cornaline; et l'on appuyait ses deux mains sur ses deux cuisses, en écartant avec soin la fourche du pantalon, dont le drap plus décati reluisait plus brillament que le cuir des fortes bottes (Flaubert 1966: 171).

All in this group looked alike. Their flabby, fair-skinned, slightly suntanned faces were the color of new cider, and their bushy side whiskers stuck out over high, stiff collars that were held in place by white cravats tied in wide bows. Every vest was of velvet, with a shawl collar; every watch had an oval carnelian seal at the end of a long ribbon; and every one of the gentlemen sat with his hands planted on his thighs, his legs carefully apart, the hard-finished broad-cloth of his trousers shining more brightly than the leather of his heavy shoes (Flaubert 1957: 159).

In the evolution of the novel, however, burlesque is a double-edged device, which cannot be used with too much caution. While farce, loosening pastoral from its mythical context, exposes history through the mere *possibility* of repetition (for example pastoral being attuned to the cycle of the seasons and the earth), burlesque, on the other hand, *by multiplying that possibility, actualizes history in the narrative*.[1] In the

Alexandrine romances, for instance, the succession of episodes reads much like a game, and the various stations occupied by the heroes (from slave to prostitute to soldier to governor) are no more than the stages where the incredible burden of history (the political instability of the Hellenistic world, the upsurge of the *knights* against the old aristocracy, the ruinous mercantilism of the middle classes, and so on — is relieved as fate, chance, or even magic (see *Daphnis and Chloe*). But the burlesque experience cannot be allowed to expand indefinitely, because it would eventually jeopardize the narrative structure it is supposed to reactivate. Thus, the narrative of a Heliodorus (see Chapter 9), of an Apollonius, an Apuleius, will only entertain us through a variety of somewhat identical adventures, up to the point where our reason begs relief, and everything is then straightened out by the appearance of an unsuspected witness (usually the narrator himself), who restores the original pastoral. In the nineteenth-century novel, a similar juxtaposition of burlesque vignettes is interrupted by a narrator careful to preserve the peace of his endangered pleasance. Thus, while Troy and his crew are sleeping from too much wine and food, which gave Hardy the opportunity to try his own hand at burlesque, Oak and Bathsheba must attend to the ricks, or see their harvest destroyed. In this sense, the narrative of their action, which takes on a pastoral flavor, is equivalent to the narrative of the unsuspected witness in the romances: Hardy tells us through which circumstances the ricks were saved from the storm. The implication of all this is that the peaceful resolution of conflicts is made possible only by preventing the fictionalization process *from ever becoming overwhelming*. The heroes of Greek romances are always rescued from potentially disastrous situations by the use of very believable stratagems, and Hardy's own heroes can still count on the benevolence of their mates or their servants. All is still well that ends well.

Yet, when the fictionalization process is allowed to grow unchecked, it may carry with it, not simply the weight of boredom through endless repetition, but through the burden of an increasing meaninglessness, chaos or death (Emma Bovary). Hence the transformation of laughter into rictus, and the growing importance of cynicism and sarcasm in the descriptive patterns. Wolfgang Kayser (1963: 21 ff.) defines the grotesque as the expression of an anxiety caused by the loss of belief in a rational order weakened or destroyed. But the belief in this natural order is first expressed in the pastoral, and the grotesque fascinates us because we know it originates in the pastoral and the farce. What could be more grotesque than the picture of a satyr or a faun? Yet it also frightens us, because it seems indeed so removed from the world of enjoyable fantasies, that we are afraid it could hurt us. It challenges our ability even to articulate basic elements of fiction, let alone to make up for the difference between fiction and reality, as was still possible with the burlesque.

In this review of farce and the burlesque as subgenres of the pastoral, we have only been talking about a form of writing designed to stimulate laughing and provide entertainment, without involving the spectator or the reader in a confrontation with himself. But there are instances where reason, when summoned, is important, where it seems that sense should be made out of things, and where it cannot. It all starts with a description, where the selection of patterns, quite challenging at first, appears more and more to cultivate the awry, the *uncanny*, by continually displacing and reintroducing into the discourse elements subliminally perceived as unworkable. In fictions of this type, the narrator (Walpole, Restif, Cazotte), facing incongruous realities, while also claiming to remain aloof and objective, will constantly hit upon this uncanny, isolate it, and isolating it, will symptomatize it in a system of rhetoric derivations and redundancies crystallizing the *Wunsch* and the *Gegenwunsch*. The practice of the uncanny, its conscious pursuit in the narrative, will, in most cases, lead to the pitting against the rational world of an irrational one, until or unless further identification produced by thorough analysis can dissolve this disturbing irrelation (Cixous 1976; Mehlman 1977). This, indeed, is the world of the grotesque, which we can recognize in the art forms of the late Romanesque and Gothic, in the elaborations of Bosch, and in the gothic side of literature.[2]

The complexity of the grotesque, its use of the trappings of the farce and the burlesque on the one hand, and on the other hand, its distinct, one-sided, noncathartic involvement with the singular, the odd, the bizarre, explains why, instead of inducing our laughing participation, as the farce and the burlesque do, it quickly sets us on edge. That such an involvement may have grown from the backdrop gargoyles and the witch tales of the Middle Ages to the metaphysical elaborations of *Faust* and has been interpreted as an attempt at overturning the forces of reason and at communing in evil, is perfectly understandable. The grotesque lurks in regions so distant from the waking mind, as to suggest the idea that it is indeed an irretrievable, cursed form of art. In this respect, it obviously threatens the stability of the pleasance: thus Marc's dwarf, perched on a high branch, spies on the secret reunions of Tristan and

Iseult; thus does smallpox strike Julie in her apotheosis as the Mistress of the Elysée. In the novels we are concerned with, the grotesque is the ultimate cover-up, which indicates, and at the same time dissimulates, an occurrence of extreme importance: Rigou's elaborate dinner, before he leaves on his Machiavellian mission (to rouse the countryside against the Aigues); Emma's encounter with the blind idiot on each of her adulterous expeditions to Rouen; Raffles' unexpected death at Bulstrode's; Fanny's drawn-out burial. All these episodes are grotesque, because they are odd in themselves: the narrator suspends judgment and avoids explanations. But we know that they are, in some obscure way, connected with the action: Fanny, for instance, was Troy's girlfriend, before he married Bathsheba, and her return to Weatherbury, which she hoped would be just in time for the baby's delivery, can only threaten the stability of Bathsheba's marriage. The grotesque is, as has been said, the *seemingly* unrelated, the uncanny. This apparent meaninglessness, however, is part of the signifying process, and the reader soon senses that in the odd, the bizarre, lies the sphinx, the riddle the narrative strives to resolve, which it can only resolve by letting things run their course. In other words, with the grotesque, the pastoral representation is coming full circle, mirrored as its very opposite: the Devil is already in the pastoral under the name of Pan. In this way, the grotesque is perhaps the ultimate form taken by history in the fictionalization process. With it, the character and the reader are suddenly confronted with their own distorted image, and the narrative bears the brunt of this introspection:

Weatherbury tower was a somewhat early instance of the use of an ornamental parapet in parish as distinct from cathedral churches, and the gargoyles, which are the necessary correlatives of a parapet, were exceptionally prominent . . . There was, so to speak, that symmetry in their distortion which is less the characteristic of British than Continental grotesque of the period . . . This horrible stone entity was fashioned as if covered with a wrinkled hide; it had short, erect ears, eyes starting from their sockets, and its fingers and hands were seizing the corners of its mouth, which they thus seemed to pull open to give free passage to the water it vomited . . . The water accumulated and washed deeper down, and the roar of the pool thus formed spread into the night as the head and chief among other noises of the kind created by deluging rain. The flowers so carefully planted by Fanny's repentant lover began to move and writhe in their bed. The winter-violets turned slowly upside down, and became a mere mat of mud . . . Troy's face was very expressive, and any observer who had seen him now would hardly have believed him to be a man who had laughed, and sung, and poured trifles into a woman's ears (Hardy 1918: 369-373).

The narrative thread, thus so eerily lost, will only be picked up to point out Troy's subsequent disappearance. In *Madame Bovary*, Emma's arsenic death, so ostentatiously disgusting, is like the crying antithesis of her lyrical dreams. In *Les Paysans*, Balzac, who seems to insist on a happy ending, speedily takes us away from the devilish countryside abandoned by his heroes. He does, however, bring us back, if only for a brief moment in the very last page, to have us notice that:

Le pays n'était plus reconnaissable. Les bois mystérieux, les avenues du parc, tout avait été défriché; la campagne ressemblait à la carte d'échantillon d'un tailleur . . . La mise en culture avait dégagé le pavillon du Rendez-vous, devenu la villa il *Buen Retiro* de dame Isaure Gaubertin; c'était le seul bâtiment resté debout, et qui dominait le paysage, ou, pour mieux dire, la petite culture remplaçant le paysage. Cette construction ressemblait à un château, tant étaient misérables les maisonnettes bâties tour autour, comme en bâtissent les paysans (Balzac 1964: 371).

The neighbourhood was unrecognizable. The mysterious woods, the avenues through the park, all had been levelled and cleared; the country resembled a tailor's card of samples . . . The turning over to agricultural uses of the lovely park, formerly so well-cared for and so charming, had isolated Michaud's gate-house, which had become the villa Il *Buen-Retiro* of Madame Isaure Gaubertin; it was the only building left standing, and dominated the whole landscape, or, to speak more accurately, the collection of small cultivated fields that had replaced the landscape. The structure resembled a château, the little cottages built all about it were such miserable affairs as peasants build (Balzac 1899: 508).

In the last analysis, the riddle of the grotesque is that fictional characters, like every one of us, are unable to get a sense of their own life until it finally comes back to them, reflected in some strange mirror. For a while, they keep wondering at the strangeness, the otherness, only to discover that it is a part of themselves, slowly aggregated through the fiction of successive narrative processes — just as Fanny's life and motherhood is a part of Troy's own life, now unrecognizable under the muddy flood caused by the gargoyle; just as "il *Buen Retiro*" is the old "pavillon du Rendez-vous" wished out of its former existence by *dame* Gaubertin. The time it takes the novelist to drift from pastoral to the grotesque is eventually the time it takes history to actualize itself; and the nineteenth-century novel is one of the select times of this actualization.

IV. In all I have said about history's masks so far, I have only concerned myself with a classification process of history. In order to complete this part of my study, I ought now to examine the masking process itself, not so much the how, but the why of its constitution.

I have suggested that the grotesque, being something like the inverted representation of the pastoral, could be the space where history's riddle is finally constituted, and where man-the-spectator is made aware of the basic masking process in that riddle. Taking this one step further, I now would like to suggest that, in the pastoral/antipastoral range set above, the complex of differences and affinities which structures the relation of pastoral to the grotesque is expressed in a variety of rhetorical *topoi*, whose vagueness and indefinition — I shall call it a *marginal space* — are basic to the masking process itself.[3]

Now, in order to track the concept of the undefined, the marginal, we must, for a moment, abandon purely formal considerations and examine, not so much differences as *signata, but the concept of difference itself.* This difference, which we seem to have so much trouble defining, is technically undefinable, because it is the original locus of our need to define and structure everything differentially; it is the locus of our desire. And, in this sense, the *locus amoenus* being the retrieve of a pastoral Eden lost to desire, the representation, and even perhaps, the actualization of history, are directly related to the *emergence of this desire*.

The borders of the pastoral world are ill-defined, because it is but a juxtaposition. Its charm is that, kept away from the bustle of civilization, but close enough to the real world to be threatened by it, it is maintained in a constant posture of vulnerability. It must be saved time and again, and it must also be threatened time and again, because the original quality of pastoral literature is in direct relation to the magnitude of the threat and the subsequent triumph of its purity, its virginity. Again let us note that the ritual of repetition is a key to the understanding of the mimesis, as the act of representation becomes more important than the representation itself, and the pastoral takes on the farce and other related masks. That the original pastoral world cannot be destroyed, but must live and remain as the perennial symbol of lost ideals, merely invites the manifestation of jealous and destructive forces on its borders. And that these forces have traditionally been made to originate from the outside (tigers, bandits, foreigners, and so on) in turn suggests a need to clarify obscure internal conflicts, by projecting and externalizing them on the outside. The concept of *margin*, which indicates this idea of outer projection, while at the same time pointing to the interior space which it is supposed to delineate, is thus particularly appropriate here (Derrida 1972).

With this I seem to be implying that we should resort to a psycho-analytical interpretation of literature. What interests me, however, is less the programming of a narrator's particular desire than the theoretical

articulation of the concept of desire in relation to that of representation (*mimesis*). Nor am I particularly concerned with the symbolism of
psychoanalytical interpretation, which has monopolized much of the
thematic and theoretical criticism today: in our case, one could easily
imagine a likely debate on the relation of pastoral to either the loss of the
mother or, more directly, to castration.

By *desire*, I mean, not the *libido*, which is a metacritical concept, but the
manifestation of *Lust* through the accomplishment of *Wunsch (Wunscher-
füllung)*. Now, we must understand that one of the paradoxical aspects of
this accomplishment is that desire (*Lust/Wunsch*) is both dependent on
and rejecting of, the symbolic, figurative, and one should say, phantas-
matic setup, that is related to it. As Lyotard says:

> There is an innate complicity between figure and desire. This is the hypothesis
> which leads Freud to the understanding of dream processes. It helps give a sound
> structure to the realm of desire and the realm of the figural by using the category
> of transgression: the *text* of the preconscious (waking reminders, recollections) is
> subjected to tremors which make it unrecognizable, illegible; by this very illegi-
> bility the deep matrix where desire is caught profits: it expresses itself through
> disjointed forms and hallucinatory images (Lyotard 1971: 271).

Lacan had shown that the programming of desire is intricately linked
with the very symbolic structure of language used by the unconscious. In
the *Écrits*, the *instance of the mirror*, where the infant for the first time
recognizes both an image, that is, a phantasm, and his own self, is identical to the famous *instance of the (purloined) letter*, which is both different
and the same at each stage of the purloining process: desire is caught in
the grip of a dual sign system operating both at the conscious and the
unconscious level. Lyotard goes one step further, by showing how, in the
narrative/descriptive order of discourse, the association of desire with
language, far from suggesting a structure, where linguistic analysis might
eventually reduce and functionalize the *libido*, represents a mere "conni-
vence du désir et du figural". This I interpret to mean that (1) the compli-
cation, the "reasoned illegibility" of discourse, which is what delights us
in the reading of literature, as well as what obsesses us in the course of
our lives, is part and parcel of the manifestation of this desire; (2) because
our representation of desire cannot be traced to a beginning without
implying an *arche*, an origin, for which we have no explanation nor
justification (how would this origin not be part of the process of desire
itself?), there is no possibility of ever establishing, within a space of a
specific text, the linguistic model which might account for the manifestation of desire as a manifestation of discourse; (3) far from attempting to

locate, to gather desire on the inside limits of a specific text, either at a purely phenomenological level, or at the level of a pyscho-physiological *Gestalt*, something like Lyotard's own *figure-matrice*, we must attempt to consider the reality of desire as the actualization, the enjoyment of differences between the forms of established conscious representation, as well as those, unconscious, of all potential representations. Desire then is nothing but a *locus* of added or surplus-values.

Eventually, it is in this locus that history will also materialize. The vague, the undefined, the outside and the inside, are in relation to the processes of masking and unmasking, and the masking and the unmasking themselves are the *locus* of a differential desire. Through the masks then, desire is history's main booster. On the one hand, history cannot be actualized directly, because it is fraught with the energy of a yet unfulfilled desire, which, if allowed to be fulfilled, would soon reduce the hope of a coherent narrative to shambles: hence the artifice of masking. On the other hand, this masking process, which is essentially protective, is also, in the reconditioning of the mimesis that it warrants, for example the weakening of the cultural context of the pastoral and the shifting from the reference of the mask to the mask itself, suggestively delaying desire, and, in turn, calling for more fictionalization and more masking.

In *Les Paysans*, for instance, the imminent rape of the countess' little *protégé*, the Péchina, by a beastly peasant, is prevented *in extremis* by the arrival of the countess herself and of her party, including the *curé* of the village. Appropriately enough, the countess declares: ' "C'est à faire fuir un paradis terrestre",' which is another way of implying the end of the pastoral dream. From now on, the whole countryside is pregnant with the war between the classes. The narrator, however, unconsciously led by the symbolism of the unconsummated rape, wants to find out the truth behind his own fiction, and summarily attempts to tear away at the masking process: ' "Vous êtes des monstres," cria le curé, "vous mériteriez d'être arrêtés et envoyés en cour d'assises . . ." ' (Balzac 1964: 211) [' "You are monsters!" cried the curé; "you deserve to be arrested and sent to the assizes." ' (Balzac 1899: 281)]. But ending the story and giving up the whole narrative would not be possible at this point. The reader already knows too much of other preparations made by the peasants toward a general confrontation with their enemies, and this last incident must serve only as a premonition in the entelechy of the story:

Ce fait minime en apparence, dans la situation irritante où se trouvaient les Aigues vis-à-vis des paysans, devait	This incident, apparently of trivial importance, was likely to have a decisive influence in the irritating condi-

avoir une influence décisive, comme dans les batailles où la victoire ou la défaite dépendent d'un ruisseau qu'un pâtre saute à pieds joints et où s'arrête l'artillerie (Balzac 1964: 216).

tion of affairs as between Aigues and the peasantry, just as, in a battle, the question of victory or defeat may be decided by a little stream which a shepherd leaps with his feet close together, but by which the artillery is held in check (Balzac 1899: 288).

I have emphasized the dual reference to history and pastoral, which must be combined with the reference to erotic desire discussed here. The countess, however, is terrified:

J'irai, s'il le faut, dit la comtesse, voir moi-même mon cousin de Castéran, notre préfet, mais d'ici là, je tremble . . . (1964: 214)

"If necessary," said the countess, "I will go myself to see my cousin De Castéran, our prefect; but I tremble to think of what may happen between now and then . . ." (1899: 284)

and Balzac summarizes the situation with one of her phrases: "nous verrons" — which means that we must expect yet more plotting and simulating. Indeed, the next chapter title brings just that: "Comme quoi le cabaret est la salle de conseil du peuple" (1964: ch. 12). History in the making, leading to the ousting of the bourgeois and the nobles from the country, has merely been *delayed*.

To return to the scene of the rape above: as the peasant assulting the young woman is about to confront the party whose sudden appearance prevented him from consummating his crime, he extracts from his victim the promise that she will publicly disculpate him, and testify that they were *merely playing*; to which the others will, of course, react incredulously: ' "Comment vous battez-vous donc, si c'est comme cela que vous jouez?" s'écria Blondet' (1964: 211) [" 'How do you fight, then, if that's the way you play?' cried Blondet" (1899: 281)]. But the characterization is interesting, if only because it emphasizes the playful instance of the atrocious mask. The peasant Nicolas tries to present his action as a farce (which is the way it had appeared to the young Péchina, when she was seduced into sharing the drinking and the ribald conversation by Nicolas' female companion and coplotter, his sister Catherine). The farce degenerates into burlesque and grotesque, with the true purpose of the seduction becoming clear:

Avec une rapidité foudroyante, Catherine Tonsard, en disant cette horrible phrase, saisit la Péchina par la taille, la renversa sur l'herbe, la priva

As she uttered those ominous words, Catherine Tonsard, with overwhelming rapidity, seized La Péchina by the waist, threw her down on the grass,

de toute sa force en la mettant à plat, et la maintint dans cette dangereuse position (1964: 210).

reduced her to helplessness by putting her arms out straight, and held her in that dangerous position (1899: 279).

The Péchina reacts violently:

En apercevant son odieux persécuteur, l'enfant se mit à crier à pleins poumons, et envoya Nicolas à cinq pas de là, d'un coup de pied donné dans le ventre; puis elle se renversa sur elle même comme un acrobate avec une dextérité qui trompa les calculs de Catherine et se releva pour fuir (1964: 210).

When she caught sight of her hateful persecutor, the child began to shriek at the top of her voice and kicked Nicolas in the stomach with a force that sent him reeling five yards away; then she threw herself over like an acrobat with a dexterity that upset Catherine's calculations, and sprang to her feet to fly (1899: 279).

Then the countess' party turns up, and all is stopped. However, and here one can admire Balzac's own awareness of the importance of the masking process, the playful or farcical element is thought so important by the narrator, as to be carried across psychological and social boundaries. To his interlocutors, who do not for a second believe that he was playing, Nicolas curtly responds:

"Ah! ça! que faites-vous dans vos salons, vous autres?" demanda Nicolas, en regardant la comtesse et Blondet qui frémirent. "Vous jouez, n'est-ce pas? Eh! bien . . . les champs sont à nous, on ne peut pas toujours travailler, nous jouions . . . Demandez à ma soeur et à la Péchina (1964: 211).

"Bah! what do you people do in your salons?" demanded Nicolas, looking at the countess and Blondet, who shuddered at his glance. "You play, don't you? Very good, the fields are ours, we can't work all the time, so we were playing! — Ask my sister and La Péchina" (1899: 281).

By his offensive comment, Nicolas implies that they who are most prompt to spot the evidence of the mask in the actions of others, particularly when those others are beneath them (the lowly, the peasants, the small-town dwellers), are indeed blind to their own masking process (' "Que faites-vous dans vos salons, vous autres?" '). Farce, understood as the masking process, is everywhere. Only those who initiated this masking process would rather delude themselves and call it *pastoral*, just as Marie-Antoinette would rather call bread *cake*. In the next section, when I tackle the relation of history, not only to the masque of desire, but to the processes of exchange of money and labor in a capitalist culture, I will show that, if history is indeed the same Reason for all, it is essentially visualized as a pastoral product by the upper class, and perhaps, as more of a farce by the lower classes. As long as there is a mask on either desire, they mirror and neutralize each other (the farce of the lower classes is the negative of the pastoral of the upper class), and no progress can be made. A few pages later, however, the exasperated peasants will kill the count's gamekeeper, thus setting the stage, not for the full-fledged battle the Count (General de Montcornet) hoped to wage, but for the retreat that he must make. Apprised of the gravity of the situation through the good offices of a drunken servant and a former soldier, he finally understands that masks are off, and that it is time to leave:

Huit jours après cette conversation singulière, tout l'arrondissement, tout le département et Paris étaient farcis d'énormes affiches annonçant la vente des Aigues par lots, en l'étude de Maître Corbineau, notaire à Soulanges (1964: 370).

A week after that curious conversation, the whole arrondissement, the whole department, and Paris itself were plastered over with huge posters announcing the sale of Aigues in lots, at the office of Maître Corbineau, notary, at Soulanges (1899: 506).

Similar examples could be taken from the other novels. In *Madame Bovary*, for instance, it is the vagueness of Emma's aspirations, and what Flaubert no doubt conceived as the cheapest form of Romanticism, which makes it easy for her to associate so easily — with lovers who love the same clichés (the pastoral):

et le livre d'un romancier ayant mis à la mode la manie des plantes grasses, Léon en achetait pour Madame, qu'il rapportait sur ses genoux dans l'Hirondelle, tout en se piquant les doigts à leurs poils durs.

Elle fit ajuster, contre sa croisée, une planchette à balustrade pour tenir ses potiches. Le clerc eut aussi son jardinet suspendu; ils s'apercevaient soignant leurs fleurs à la fenêtre (Flaubert 1966: 132).

When a new novel launched a craze for exotic plants, Léon bought some for Madame, holding them on his knees in the Hirondelle and pricking his fingers on their spikes.

Emma had a railed shelf installed in her window to hold her flowerpots. The clerk, too, had his hanging garden, and they could look out and see each other tending their blossoms (Flaubert 1957: 112-113).

— as well as with those who just want to take advantage of her emptiness (the farce):

La campagne était déserte, et Rodolphe n'entendait autour de lui que le battement régulier des herbes qui fouettaient sa chaussure, avec le cri des grillons tapis au loin sous les avoines; il revoyait Emma dans la salle, habillée

The countryside was deserted, and the only sounds were the regular swish of the tall grass against his gaiters and the chirping of crickets hidden in the distant oats. He thought of Emma in the parlor, dressed as he had seen her, and

comme il l'avait vue, et il la déshabillait. . . .

Il se rencontre un jour répéta Rodolphe, un jour, tout à coup, et quand on en désespérait. Alors des horizons s'entr'ouvrent, c'est comme une voix qui crie: "Le voilà!". Vous sentez le besoin de faire à cette personne la confidence de votre vie, de lui donner tout, de lui sacrifier tout. On ne s'explique pas, on se devine. On s'est entrevu dans ses rêves (et il la regardait). Enfin, il est là, ce trésor que l'on a tant cherché, là devant vous; il brille, il étincelle. Cependant on en doute encore, on n'ose y croire; on en reste ébloui, comme si l'on sortait des ténèbres à la lumière.

Et en achevant ces mots, Rodolphe ajouta la pantomime à sa phrase. Il se passa la main sur le visage, tel qu'un homme pris d'étourdissement; puis il la laissa retomber sur celle d'Emma (Flaubert 1966: 173-174).

he undressed her . . .

"Yes, it comes along one day," Rodolphe repeated. "All of a sudden, just when we've given up hope. Then new horizons open before us: it's like a voice crying, 'Look! It's here!' We feel the need to pour out our hearts to a given person, to surrender, to sacrifice everything. In such a meeting no words are necessary: each senses the other's thoughts. Each is the answer to the other's dreams." He kept staring at her. "There it is, the treasure so long sought for— there before us: it gleams, it sparkles. But still we doubt; we daren't believe; we stand there dazzled, as though we'd come from darkness into light."

As he ended, Rodolphe enhanced his words with pantomime. He passed his hand over his face, like someone dazed; then he let it fall on Emma's hand (Flaubert 1957: 161-162).

All in all, her amorous experiences only take her further down the path of degradation. This degradation is accompanied by the realization of the fatefully high cost of her dreams and the revelation of the implacable logic of monied exchanges (Léon cannot find money for her, and L'Heureux has her assigned to court). But it is also bitterly mixed in the grotesque, when, her wish to die ironically parodying the hunger of others, Emma, led by the idiot Justin to a cupboard next to the room where the *farcical* Homais are *stuffing* themselves, promptly seizes the bottle of arsenic and swallows it. In *Far from the Madding Crowd*, it is Bathsheba's original fickleness, her play with her own desires, which drives her away from her only true admirer, Gabriel Oak, a man incapable of dissimulating anything, and to associate with Sergeant Troy, who has hidden from her his attachment for Fanny Robin. Unfortunately, dead and about to be buried, Fanny comes back to haunt them both three times: a first (burlesque), when Poorgrass gets drunk and forgets all about his hearse and the funeral, a second (grotesque), when the casket is pried open by an inquisitive Bathsheba, and a third (perhaps the most grotesque yet), when Troy's bizarre and erratic behavior is displayed under the watchful eye of a spouting gargoyle. In *Middlemarch*, things are more subdued. But it might be argued that Dorothea's love for the grotesque Cazaubon is only the unwitting cover-up of her passion for Will, and of her desire actually to be liberated from her own rigid personage. Dorothea's story thus fulfills George Eliot's own notion that the seeds of history lie buried in everyone's own self; masked twice: under the weight of one's own rejection, and under the weight of universal oblivion:

Who that cares much to know the history of man, and how the mysterious mixture behaves under the varying experiments of Time, has not dwelt, at least briefly, on the life of Saint Theresa, has not smiled with some gentleness at the thought of the little girl walking forth one morning hand-in-hand with her still smaller brother, to go and seek martyrdom in the country of the Moors? . . . Theresa's passionate, ideal nature demanded an epic life: what were many-volumed romances of chivalry and the social conquests of a brilliant girl to her? . . . Here and there is born a Saint Theresa, foundress of nothing, whose loving heartbeats and sobs after an unattained goddess tremble off and are dispersed among hindrances, instead of centring in some long-recognizable deed (Eliot 1875: viii).

V. To stop here, however, would be to admit that nineteenth-century fiction, involved as it may have been with masks, energized as it may have been by desire, is not really a part of the underlying reality that it set about to imitate and mask. And the truth is, the novel, especially the nineteenth-century novel, is also the privileged locus of a particular exchange: that between desire and money, as reflected in the figures of the text.

Let us, first of all, take a look at the role of money in the books studied here. In all of them, the obvious problem is one of establishment: in *Les Paysans*, the count wants to settle down as a part of the restored king's new gentry; and in the end, excessive poaching, gleaning and wood gathering by the peasants on his domain and the financial loss which he incurs from all of those, will make his life impossible. In *Madame Bovary*, Emma is constantly looking for more money or more loans to cover her purchases of clothes and furniture. In the end, we see her and her husband die, and we know full well that Charles' purse could never have met the expense required by Emma's unbounded desire. In *Middlemarch*, most of the narrator's preoccupations have to do with money and its difficult relation to feelings and passions: Lydgate is constantly devoured by his anxiety about meeting bills, while Bulstrode, the town banker, the very seat of money in the novel, must squander it on silencing the importune Raffles; as for Dorothea, it is Cazaubon's legacy which, in the end, will enable her to live with (and support) Will. In *Far from the Madding Crowd*, it is, of course, Bathsheba who has the money, hires Oak, turns Bold-wood down, and regretfully lends her fortune away to her husband, so he can continue to bet at the races. In the end, her feelings will allow her to accept Oak, which is all to the good, since he also is the man best qualified to manage her estate. In the meantime, however, her anxieties are always expressed in terms of money:

"That I'm willing to pay the penalty of" said Bathsheba firmly. "You know, Gabriel, this is what I cannot get off my conscience — that I once seriously injured him in sheer idleness [she teased Boldwood by sending him a valentine card]. If I had never played a trick upon him, he would never have wanted to marry me. Oh! if I could only pay some heavy damages in money to him for the harm I did, and so get the sin off my soul in this way . . ." (Hardy 1918: 419).

That money is thus so clearly one of the main preoccupations, one of the main subjects of these novels, no doubt testifies to the fact that fiction, now the privileged entertainment of the bourgeoise, instead of remaining the playful erotic game for women of the nobility, responds to the preoccupations of this bourgeoisie, by depicting its ascent in the world of landed capitalism. Such an interpretation, however, only takes into account a surface manifestation of the text, that is, the generation of a code by the context (context → semantic values → stylistic values). Emma, born the daughter of a rich peasant, and married to a would-be prosperous country doctor, falls in love with her romantic dreams of castles, knights, clothes and equipage:

Emma se sentit, en entrant, enveloppée par un air chaud, mélange du parfum des fleurs et du beau linge, du fumet des viandes et de l'odeur des truffes (Flaubert 1966: 82).

Here the air was warm and fragrant; the scent of flowers and fine linen mingled with the odor of cooked meats and truffles (Flaubert 1957: 54).

And this, in the midst of rural Normandy, tends to give the narrative an inescapable pastoral flavor, ready to be spoiled by Flaubert's carefully appointed masquerade. What remains to be explained, is the relation of that surface manifestation to a content: (1) how the masking process is, at the beginning, through the pastoral, essentially a monied process; (2) how the exchange of masks is partially that of money; and finally (3) how the desires of the characters appear, through the masking process, to have been affected, corrupted by the use of money. In this triple perspective, nineteenth-century fiction, at least a large segment of it, represents the precise means of production of a narrative history through the covert exchange (that is, the dialectic) of desire and money.

Pastoral is for the rich, the endowed. I have already pointed out that the main characters in our novels are bourgeois, that they have money, or want more of it, and that one of the main preoccupations of the narrator is with the handling of this money, or of its substitutes (estates, expenses, and so on). What is more significant, however, is the fact that this privilege is also one of aesthetics. Balzac makes us aware of it, when he introduces us to the world of *Les Paysans* through the cliché subterfuge of a letter by the Parisian Blondet to one of his writer friends remaining in the capital. Note the subtlety of the *mimesis* already. The picture of the Burgundian countryside is mediatized through the book, itself mediatized through the letter of Blondet, itself addressed to a writer "qui procure[s] de délicieux rêves au public aves [tes] fantaisies," whose girlfriend is a famous and luscious actress (desire, the mask, money):

Tu mesureras la distance à laquelle nous sommes du temps où les Florine du dix-huitième siècle trouvaient à leur réveil un château comme les Aigues dans un contrat (Balzac 1964: 9).	You shall measure the distance that lies between us and the time when the Florines of the eighteenth century found, upon awaking, a château like this of Aigues in their contract (Balzac 1899: 9).

To perfect this mediating process, Blondet claims that he can make his friend Nathan dream, not with illusions, but with the truth. To be sure, this raises the question of the book itself as the mediator, and in a sense, perhaps, the very substitute for the money, which it fictionalizes, by using it to purchase aesthetic illusions and thus artfully play with desire. I shall come back to this. Right now, we simply know that this countryside, which is described to us as something devoid of the ugliness and pollution of the capital, as well as delightfully free-spirited:

De chaque côté des pavillons, serpente une haie vive d'où s'échappent des ronces semblables à des cheveux follets. Çà et là, une pousse d'arbre s'élève insolemment. Sur le talus du fossé, de belles fleurs baignent leurs pieds dans une eau dormante et verte (Balzac 1964: 10),	On each side of this double gatehouse winds a quickset hedge, from which bramble-bushes protrude like straggling hairs. Here and there a clump of trees insolently raises its head. On the sloping bank of the ditch, lovely flowers bathe their feet in a sluggish, slime-coated stream (Balzac 1899: 9-10),

is actually owned and exploited by the rich:

D'immenses forêts, posées sur une vaste colline côtoyée par une rivière, dominent cette riche vallée, encadrée au loin par les monts d'une petite	Vast forests, lying along the horizon on an extensive hillside skirted by a small river, overlook that fertile valley, framed by the distant peaks of a lesser

Suisse appelée le Morvan. Ces épaisses forêts appartiennent aux Aigues, au marquis de Ronquerolles et au comte de Soulanges, dont les châteaux et les parcs, dont les villages, vus de loin et de haut, donnent de la vraisemblance aux fantastiques paysages de Breughel-de-Velours (1964: 10).

Switzerland called the Morvan. Those dense forests belong to Aigues, to the Marquis de Ronquerolles and to the Comte de Soulanges, whose châteaux, parks, and villages, viewed from a distance and from an elevation, give an air of probability to the fantastic landscapes of Breughel de Velours (1899: 10-11).

And when we arrive at the Château des Aigues, we realize that, just as in Versailles, there is a park: "cette grille d'ailleurs encadrée par deux pavillons de concierge semblables à ceux du Palais de Versailles" (1964: 12) ["The gate stands between two porter's lodges like those at the palace of Versailles" (1899: 12)]; there are magnificent rooms with painted ceilings:

un plafond peint à fresque dans le goût italien, et où volent les plus folles arabesques . . . Toutes les embrasures sont en mosaïque. La salle est chauffée en-dessous (1964: 18-19).

a frescoed ceiling in the Italian style, in which the most fantastic arabesques are intertwined . . . All the window recesses are in marble mosaics. The room is heated from below (1899: 19-20).

The pastoral has indeed become a painting, a mimesis, whose price only few can afford:

Et l'on a coupé le cou, mon cher, à des fermiers-généraux en 1793! Mon Dieu! comment ne comprend-on pas que les merveilles de l'Art sont impossibles dans un pays sans grandes fortunes, sans grandes existences assurées? Si la Gauche veut absolument tuer les rois, qu'elle nous laisse quelques petits princes, grands comme rien du tout (1964: 19).

And yet, my dear fellow, they cut off farmer-generals' heads in 1793! *Mon Dieu!* how could people fail to understand that the marvels of art are impossible in a country without great fortunes, without great careers assured. If the Left is absolutely determined to kill off all kings, let it at least leave us a few little princes as big as nothing at all! (1899: 20-21).

This aestheticization is extremely important, because it indicates that the dialectic process begins exactly *at the point* where the masking process begins. Blondet is partially aware of it, when he states: "Voici l'*histoire* de mon Arcadie" (Balzac 1964: 21; emphasis added). To the poor, peasants and farmers, the land is nothing if not real. And Balzac knows it fully:

La Révolution de 1789 a été la revanche des vaincus. Les paysans ont mis le pied dans la possession du sol que la loi

The Revolution of 1789 was the vengeance of the vanquished. The peasants placed their feet in possession of the

féodale leur interdisait depuis douze cents ans. De là leur amour pour la terre qu'ils partagent entre eux jusqu'à couper un sillon en deux parts, ce qui souvent annule la perception de l'impôt, car la valeur de la propriété ne suffirait pas à couvrir les frais de poursuites pour le recouvrement (1964: 104).

soil, which the feudal laws had kept from them for twelve hundred years. Thence comes their affection for the land, which they divide among themselves to such a point as to cut a furrow in two, which often puts an end to the collection of taxes, for the value of the property would not suffice to cover the expense of proceedings to recover them" (1899: 133).

The rich, on the other hand, can only express their relationship with the land in terms of a relationship with nature, and that one is essentially fictitious, as fictitious as their own economic status, and the money they accumulated and spent to buy it. How did the bourgeoisie ever get to be rich, and a career soldier like Montcornet become the owner of the sumptuous castle of Les Aigues? Marx's answer would be that the nobility enriched itself through the original division of labor by appropriating or later taxing the fruits of this labor and by constantly attempting to extend this tax base through war (the only occupation a noble could engage in without losing caste). As for Montcornet, he would have seen him as a farmer's son only moved out of his class by helping Napoleon achieve his grand design of European domination. However, during the Revolution, the Empire and the Restoration, the land also passes from the hands of the nobility to those of the bourgeoisie, in a process which includes the accumulation of capital through the marketing and exchange of labor, the purchase of land formerly owned by the *émigrés* and, last but not least, the authentication of the purchase by the king, ensuring, with a peerage, an automatic share as *duc et pair* in the political process. This last form of land acquisition is particularly fictitious, since it involves, not only a division of labor (Montcornet's estate can only be his if some peasants slave for him and others are driven or kept away from it, and starve because of him), but also the profit-making which alone made it possible in the first place:

Les Aigues furent alors achetés par Montcornet, qui dans ses commandements en Espagne et en Poméranie, se trouvait avoir économisé la somme nécessaire à cette acquisition, quelque chose comme onze cent mille francs, y compris le mobilier (Balzac 1964: 24).

Aigues was thereupon purchased by Montcornet, who found that he saved, during his commands in Spain and Pomerania, the amount required for the purchase — something like eleven hundred thousand francs, the furniture being included (Balzac 1899: 25).

As for the family of his wife, it was a classical case of being poor, but:

ancienne et puissante, [elle] comptait un pair de France, le marquis de Trois-ville, chef du nom et des armes; deux députés ayant tous nombreuse lignée et occupés pour leur compte au budget, au ministère, à la cour, comme des poissons autour d'une croûte (1964: 137).

His family, an ancient and powerful one, included a peer of France, the Marquis de Troisville, chief of the name and arms; two deputies, both having a numerous family and intent upon their own interests in the budget, in the ministry, and at court, like fish around a crust (1899: 176).

For Montcornet, acquiring and owning the land represents an attempt at changing his capital from fictitious into real, that is, obtaining the status and security of a landowner, and thus achieving a respectable position in the social order, while also investing his money in what promises to be a profit-making venture. Unfortunately, profit based on profit is but a deceit. And the peasants will show him just that, but turning his pro-jected elevation into his demise: they will first keep him from developing his estate and thus from making profit; and then they will make the place so unsafe for him, that, finally totally insecure, he and his wife will have to leave.

The ultimate proof that Montcornet's relationship to the land is fictitious is that it matters little where he eventually invests his money:

"Une des plus belles propriétés qu'il y ait à vingt lieues à la ronde," dit le sous-préfet; "mais vous retrouverez mieux aux environs de Paris . . ." "On a," dit Blondet, "un château royal aujourd'hui pour cinq cent mille francs aux environs de Paris. On achète les folies des autres . . ." "Je croyais que vous teniez aux Aigues," dit le comte à sa femme. "Oui, mais je tiens encore plus à votre existence" (1964: 368).

"One of the finest properties within a radius of twenty leagues!" said the subprefect; "but you will find finer ones in the environs of Paris . . ." "You can obtain a royal chateau in the outskirts of Paris for four hundred thousand francs today," said Blondet. "People are buying other people's fol-lies." "I thought that you were fond of Aigues", the count said to his wife. "Do you not think that I care a thousand times more for your life?" (1899: 503-504).

It is not the land, but the reason for having it that keeps the general speculating. No wonder then, if the relationship to the land being so fictitious, the history of its acquisition is actualized as pastoral. Since it is only by being blind to the aspirations of the peasants and to his own system that Montcornet can keep his estate, he and his friends need to make the most of the fiction: as long as it lasts, the romance lasts. The presence of the writer (symbolized in Blondet) is here one of the requisites of the experiment; it will be his job to perfect, to cover and hide the ugly and the threatening. And Balzac accepts this role, at least for a while. The book, producing a literary fiction of the rich (the bourgeois and the nobles), thus becomes the perfect mediator of an economic fiction:

Quelques esprits, avides d'intérêt avant tout, accuseront ces explications de longueur. Mais il est utile de faire observer ici que, d'abord l'historien des mœurs obéit à des lois plus dures que celles qui régissent l'historien des faits; il doit rendre tout probable, même le vrai (1964: 182).

Some minds, greedy for interesting narrative above everything, will charge that these explanations are too long; but it is well to remark at this point that, in the first place, the historian of manners is bound by stricter laws than those which govern the historian of facts: he must make everything seem probable, even what is true (1899: 239).

However, and precisely because the narrative includes the meticulous account of this mediating process (the beauty of Les Aigues is only in contradistinction to the shabbiness, not of nature, but of the poor who inevitably live from it), Balzac soon must undo what he set out to do, deconstruct what he had constructed (and I have shown the purely literary aspects of this process in my analysis of the relation of pastoral to farce, to burlesque and grotesque):

Vous allez voir cet infatigable sapeur, ce rongeur qui morcelle et divise le sol, le partage, et coupe un arpent de terre en cent morceaux, convié toujours à ce festin par une petite bourgeoisie qui fait de lui à la fois son auxiliaire et sa proie. Cet élément insocial créé par la Révolution absorbera quelque jour la Bourgeoisie comme la Bourgeoisie a dévoré les Nobles (1964: 4).

You are about to see that indefatigable sapper, that rodent who subdivides and parcels out the land and cuts an acre into a hundred bits, always invited to the banquet by a petty bourgeoisie which makes of him its auxiliary and its prey at once. This anti-social element created by the Revolution will some day absorb the bourgeoisie, as the bourgeoisie has devoured the nobility (1899: 4).

Now, that all these monied processes are related to desire is obvious. Money is what keeps the phantasm of pastoral going. In the first pages of the novel, Balzac (Blondet) has hardly finished introducing his *locus amoenus*, and explained to us the economics and the politics around it, when he cannot resist mentioning how the big boorish general had simply been tamed by Eros, that is, his wife, most appropriately named Virginie (there are many other references to Bernardin de Saint-Pierre's exotic pastoral). Meanwhile, he has also told us that the former proprietress of Les Aigues was, like Nathan's girlfriend, an actress, who had bought the property with money accumulated from her various lovers. All this in the background of mythological scenes, of erotic paintings, and last, but not least, of burlesque basket-bearing character-columns and grotesque frescos of food:

Des femmes en stuc finissant en feuillages soutiennent de distance en distance des paniers de fruits sur lesquels portent les rinceaux du plafond. Dans les panneaux qui séparent chaque femme, d'admirables peintures, dues à quelque artiste méconnu, représentent les gloires de la table: les saumons, les têtes de sanglier, les coquillages, enfin tout le monde mangeable qui, par de fantastiques ressemblances, rappelle l'homme, les femmes, les enfants, et qui lutte avec les plus bizarres imaginations de la Chine. . . . Cette salle communique à une salle de bains d'un côté, de l'autre à un boudoir qui donne dans le salon. La salle de bain est revêtue en briques de Sèvres peintes en camaïeu, le sol est en mosaïque, la baignoire est en marbre. Une alcôve, cachée par un tableau peint sur cuivre, et qui s'enlève au moyen d'un contrepoids, contient un lit de repos en bois doré du style le plus Pompadour. Le plafond est en lapis-lazuli, étoilé d'or. Les camaïeux sont faits d'après les dessins de Boucher. Ainsi, le bain, la table et l'amour sont réunis (1964: 18-19).

At intervals, female figures in stucco, ending in foliage, hold up baskets of flowers, which join the branches in the ceiling. In the panels between the women are admirable paintings, the work of unknown artists, representing the glories of the table: salmon, boars' heads, shell-fish; in short, the whole world of eatables, which, by curious points of resemblance, remind one of men, women, and children, and which rival the most whimsical conceptions of China. . . . The dining-room adjoins a bath-room on one side; and on the other a boudoir which opens into a salon. The walls of the bath-room are of Sèvres brick, painted to represent cameos, the floor is inlaid, the bath-tub of marble. An alcove, hidden by a picture painted on copper, which is raised by means of a cord and weight, contains a gilded wooden bed of a most decidedly Pompadour style. The ceiling is of lapis-lazuli, starred with gold. The cameos are after Boucher's designs. Thus the bath, the table, and love are united (1899: 19-20).

I am throwing all this pell-mell, to show that, if the first pages of the novel are packed with this sort of pastoral/farcical information, it is because the relation of money to love, desire and the instincts is simply mediatized through the book, and because it will also, by the same token, neutralize the unrefined drinking and lovemaking that goes on in the taverns or in the woods:

Avez-vous bien saisi les mille détails de cette hutte assise à cinq cents pas de la jolie porte des Aigues? La voyez-vous accroupie là, comme un mendiant devant un palais? Eh bien, son toît chargé de mousses veloutées, ses poules caquetant, le cochon qui

Have you thoroughly grasped the thousand and one details of this hovel, situated some five hundred yards from the pretty gate of the Aigues estate? Do you see it crouching there like a beggar at the gate of a palace? Ah! well, its moss-covered, velvety roof, its cack-

vague, toutes ces poésies champêtres avaient un horrible sens. A la porte du palais, une grande perche élevait à une certaine hauteur un bouquet flétri, composé de trois branches de pin et d'un feuillage de chêne réunis part un chiffon. Au-dessus de la porte, un peintre forain avait, pour un déjeuner, peint dans un tableau de deux pieds carrés, sur un champ bleu, un *I* majuscule en vert, et pour ceux qui savent lire, ce calembour en douze lettres: Au Grand I-Vert [hiver]. A gauche de la porte, éclatent les vives couleurs de cette vulgaire affiche: *Bonne bière de mars*, où de chaque côté d'un cruchon qui lance un jet de mousse, se carrent une femme en robe excessivement décolletée et un hussard, tout deux grossièrement coloriés. Aussi, malgré les fleurs et l'air de la campagne, s'exhalait-il de cette chaumière la forte et nauséabonde odeur qui vous saisit à Paris en passant devant les gargotes des faubourgs (1964: 51).

ling hens, its wallowing sow, its lowing heifer, all this rustic poesy had a ghastly meaning. At the gate in the fence was a tall pole with a withered bouquet, composed of three pine branches and a cluster of oak-leaves, tied together with a rag, at the top. Over the gate a travelling painter had, for a breakfast, painted on a board two feet square a capital *I* in green on a white ground, and, for those who knew how to read, this pun, in twelve letters: *Au Grand-I-Vert*. At the left of the gate the eye was struck by the commonplace legend: *Good March Beer*, in bright colors, on a sign, whereon were the figures of a hussar and a woman in an excessively low-necked dress, flanking a jug running over with foam — both gaudily and roughly colored. And so, despite the flowers and the country air, the hovel exhaled the strong, sickening odor of wine and stale food that assails your nostrils as you pass the low eating-houses in the faubourgs of Paris (1899: 61).

In this relation of desire and money then, the fiction of the capital is compounded, that is, translated, into another, where desire functions at two levels. For the rich who, like Blondet, the general and his wife, merely seek to enjoy the status and the amenities that their income permits, the pastoral is the only way to translate their added value or profit into art, and thus to allow themselves to fantasize about that which is not a real, but merely symbolic object, indefinitely representable and expansible, always strange, and yet always the same and always theirs:

Mon cher, je suis dans cette admirable campagne depuis six jours, et je ne me lasse pas d'admirer les merveilles de ce parc, dominé par de sombres forêts, et où se trouvent de jolis sentiers le long des eaux. La Nature et son silence, les tranquilles jouissances, la vie facile à laquelle elle invite, tout m'a séduit. Oh! voilà la vraie littérature; il n'y a jamais de faute de style dans une prairie. Le bonheur serait de tout oublier ici, même les *Débats* (1964: 28).

"I have been in this lovely spot six days, my dear fellow, and I do not weary of admiring the marvels of the park, dominated by frowning forests, where pretty paths run along beside the streams. Nature and its silence, the tranquil enjoyment, the indolent life to which it invites one, all have combined to seduce me. Oh! this is the true literature, there are never any faults of style in a level field. It would be true happiness to forget everything, even the *Débats* (1899: 30).

As for the poor, the peasants, on the other hand, who had been led to believe that they would eventually have access to the confiscated land of the *émigrés* and the properties of the Church, they were prevented, most of them (except for some of the less poor: the *laboureurs*), from enjoying the opportunity by the lack of funds, the impossibility of borrowing, as well as the gross devaluation of the revolutionary currency. They can only wish for the destruction of the dream of the *nouveaux riches*.[4] The transformation of pastoral into farce and the grotesque represents the explosion of one fiction by another.

In this demonstration, I have limited myself to an examination of *Les Paysans*, because, of all the novels here, it offers the most complex and sophisticated example of a dual fictionalization process. But the scheme could be extended to the other novels. In *Madame Bovary*, the relationship of desire and money would be set in a somewhat reverse perspective. Emma wants the fiction that Charles' income cannot justify; and the vacuousness of her dreams is in direct proportion to the smallness of her means; here, creditors like L'Heureux play the part of the peasants in Balzac: the fiction unravels at the mere contact of money. In *Middlemarch*, in order simply to establish himself, Lydgate needs Bulstrode's support, and the banker, haunted by his past and his fortune dilapidated by Raffles, cannot and will not readily supply it. Desire is strictly regulated, and therefore, repressed.

Even if the end of the book brings happiness to Dorothea, she will have gone through her marriage with Cazaubon before she can enjoy Will's company. George Eliot's novel is, in this sense, the least fictional of all four studied here. With her, the exchange of desire and money is limited to a mere exclusion: either money *or* desire. Hence the extraordinary stability of a fiction consisting mostly in the integration of the characters' discourse, and aiming at some sort of suspension of history (Miller 1974). In *Far from the Madding Crowd*, the dialectic of desire and money throws Bathsheba between the dissipation of penniless Troy and the melancholy of rich Boldwood, both of whom are equally dangerous, and whose separate and conflicting story (Boldwood kills Troy at the end of the book) Hardy weaves to span the time between the original encounter of Bathsheba and Oak in the first pages of the book and their final reunion in the last pages. In all the novels, there is a happy ending (in *Les Paysans*, after the death of the count, Blondet marries the countess, and on their honeymoon, they come back to contemplate what had been their fiction). *Les Paysans*, however, is the only novel which really offers the perspective of a generalized class conflict. And this should, perhaps, be related to the design of the *Comédie humaine*. Whereas the other authors concentrate on character stories with heroes, Balzac is the only one to engage in the painting of mass passions and desires. His multiplicity of characters and actions enable him to give us the feeling of some sort of grandiose epic in one limited space. But, in the end, the peasants' victory, even if it seems that it was going to be borne out by history (a few years after the publication of Balzac's novel, Marx will remind us that Napoleon III was elected by the mass of those peasants), is but an empty one. Napoleon will use the peasantry simply to dupe the bourgeoisie, and in truth, the freeholders, the victors of the general, will eventually die, as Balzac had predicted, under the weight of an indiscriminate parcelling. Indeed, in the last page of the novel, the narrator cannot make up his mind which fiction to leave us with: Blondet's regret for the pastoral lost to the peasants, or the antipastoral, fought and won against the nobles and the bourgeois, and then soon to be lost by the peasants against themselves. In this sense Balzac's uncertainty is perhaps more significant than Eliot's or Hardy's smugness or Flaubert's cynicism; it is the uncertainty of a man for whom reality means to be caught between fictions, tortured by the opposition of ravenous desire and legitimate history.

VI. It is time to pull our threads together. The display of a close, albeit complicated relation of pastoral to farce and its derivative, as evidenced in the nineteenth-century novel, may appear as just another step toward the reduction of all literature to the mere manifestation of surface level differences. In this sense, fictionalization processes, indispensable to any narrative, would represent no more than the coded reference to a socioeconomic (money) or psychological (desire) context, subject to variation only as the context itself changes. But this is not the case. If it is true that fictionalization processes are in fact determined by structures of referential content: for example the pastoralization of the Burgundy countryside by Blondet would be determined by his association with the new breed of landowners operating on a fictitious capital, these fictionalization processes, on the other hand, regulate structures of content, to the degree that these structures are dependent for their expression, their actualization, on the opposition and/or substitution of stylistic features. Thus, in Hardy, a beastly and undecorous Troy is substituted for a gentle and proper Gabriel Oak, and the translation of pastoral into farce is capped by Troy's return to England in a traveling carnival. They also regulate structures of content to the extent that connotative and denotative elements being interactive, meaning is *both* overt (connotation) and covert (denotation). Thus the Boucher pastorals of Les Aigues are really beautiful, but also better than real, and therefore more fictitious than the reality they adorn. This copresence in the description of the truth and nontruth of imitation is the only thing which enables us to sense history in the making: or is it fiction in the making of history? Whatever the case, the problem is one of the place of representation (*mimesis*) in human discourse. As the argument between Nicolas and the countess and her party reminds us, the question is not *who is master of the language*, but what the relation of someone's *playing* is to someone else's own *play*, what is the relation between the painted splendor of Les Aigues and the smelly sleaziness of Le Grand-I-Vert complete with its cheap poster on a greasy wall. If it should prove the case that historical conflicts are first and foremost identifiable as conflicts of symbols, one should perhaps seek, not only the proper relation between the forms and the means of narrative but also and mostly, to consider the role played by the forms in the actualization of the means. It would then be possible to add to the order of successive conflicts another order of symbolic resolutions, according to a dialectic mask/unmask in each. *Doing history* would consist less in transcribing events or ideas into stories as it would in integrating two processes: one of covering up, the other of uncovering the text of fiction. In this sense, the history of the text as mask and unmask from Milton to Hardy remains to be written.

NOTES

1. Naturally, because it makes such short change of all rules and references, burlesque, even more than farce, is the world where the lowly and the poor get their revenge on the rich and the powerful. Hence, later, the social significance of the burlesque in the picaresque novel. In the nineteenth-century novel, however, society is tightly structured around the bourgeois establishment both in the cities and in the country; bandits, privateers and highwaymen have all but disappeared, and the only *picaros* left to roam the countryside are a bunch of migrant workers and an occasional furloughed soldier with mischief in mind.

2. In late Romanesque sculptures, where monsters and other dubious beings suddenly meet us at the turn of some capital or in the semidarkness of some porch, it is clear that man is part of an immense zoomorphy, that he is tied together with all other creatures, animal and vegetal, to the mass of his column, his church, his Christian ideal, and that he cannot be dissociated from them. Culturally, of course, the Romanesque taste for the bestiary can be explained as going back to the Bible, the Gospels, and especially to Saint John the Divine's Revelation, whose success, linked to a fear of the Millennium, of invasions, the plague and calamities of all sorts, makes it one of the best known discourses throughout the Middle Ages. During the Gothic period, human figures, following

the lead of Christ incarnate revealing himself over the front portal, slowly, but definitely, emerge from the architectural mass (Baltrusaitis 1960). Striving for more autonomy, they became more human, they detach themselves from the animals ones, and by and by, monsters disappear. Some critics have seen in the separation of the Gothic figure, not only the glorification of the Incarnation, but also the triumph of mind over matter, and with it, of religion over sin. However, resistance to this Enlightenment remains strong, throughout the Middle Ages, revived, time and again, by a pessimism based on social and economic realities, and fanned by an opposition to the religious estabishment (Bosch). In the world of Renaissance and post-Renaissance art, the grotesque is that which lies in a grotto, away from the light, and strikes one as odd and bizarre. But with the rediscovery of Rome and antiquity during and after the Renaissance, grotesque forms, like every other bit of the ancient patrimony, soon become a matter for artistic imitation. From now on, the grotesque is a style, tied to a period. In the seventeenth century, it is part of a growing awareness of the independence of the cosmos, of its physical separation from the Kingdom of God. It contains the first positive indication that this cosmos should be discovered and enjoyed, not in its stability and fixity, in its opposition to God and its relation to the Devil, but in its constant movement and expansion. The grotesque is part of the baroque liberation and fantasy, while remaining also a part of a symbolic and religious emblematic. Temporarily drowned under the weight of French classicism and the burden of rules for a clear presentation, it will soon reappear in the eighteenth-century reaction to neoclassical dogmas, when the grotesque portrayal of ideas and men becomes a prime weapon in the arsenal of great satirists (Hogarth). At the end of the eighteenth century and in the nineteenth century, the grotesque is used to question the cold postulates of a reason grown academic. Hugo, expanding on his *Réponse à un acte d'accusation*, where he sees himself as having placed a revolutionary *bonnet rouge* on the Dictionary, writes *Le Satyre*, where he uses the mythological model to break concepts, social and political, as well as geographical and historical. Others (Balzac, Nodier, Lewis) indulge in illumination and look at the grotesque merely as an occasion to test our negative capabilities.

3. Just a note here in passing, to stress that this marginal space is that of the pastoral, not of Utopia. Because Utopia is not *against* or *outside* anything (*outopos*: "no place; nowhere"), its realities are generally syntagmatic and successive in their representation: they exist only in direct relation to their inscription in the discourse. Maps can be drawn, graphs and schedules can be made, but only to convert textual contradictions into a game of spatial differences. Think, for instance, of More's description of *Utopia*, where the center of the circular island (of Utopia) is supposed to be by the sea. This contradiction can only be resolved by adopting a design, in which the island is of the form of a half moon bay, with the capital in its center (Marin 1973: 197). In the pastoral, on the other hand, such resolutions are impossible, *because difference is only a way to mask, not to resolve essential contradictions*: for example Milton's Comus attempts to seduce the young Lady Egerton by parading as a wise man (see Chapter 14).

4. For an earlier presentation of this problematics, see Chapter 11.

References

Aeschylus (1960), *Eumenides*. Trans by R. Lattimore. Chicago and London, University of Chicago Press.

Alexandrescu, Sorin (1974), *Logique du personnage (réflexion sur l'univers faulknérien)*. Paris, Mame.

Aristotle (1956), *De Arte Poetica Liber*. Ed. by Rudolfus Kassel. Oxford, Oxford University Press.

— (1968), *Poetics*. Introduction and appendices by D. W. Lucas. Oxford, Clarendon Press.

Auerbach, Erich (1953), *Mimesis: The Representation of Reality in Western Literature*. Trans. by W. R. Trask. Princeton, Princeton University Press.

Augustine (1961), *Confessions*. Trans. by R. S. Pine-Coffin. Baltimore, Penguin.

Bally, Charles (1951), *Traité de stylistique française*. Paris, Klinksieck.

Baltrusaitis, Jurgis (1960), *Réveils et prodiges: le gothique fantastique*. Paris, A. Colin.

Balzac, Honoré de (1899), *The Peasants*, vol. 3 of *Scenes of Country Life* in *The Novels of Honoré de Balzac*. Trans. by G. Burnham Ives. Philadelphia, George Barrie.

— (1964), *Les paysans*. Paris, Garnier Frères.

Baraz, Michaël (1968), *L'Etre et la connaissance selon Montaigne*. Paris, José Corti.

Barber, C. L. (1968), 'A mask presented at Ludlow Castle: the masque as a masque' in *A Maske at Ludlow*, ed. by John S. Diekhoff, 188–206. Cleveland, Press of Case Western Reserve University.

Barthes, Roland (1957), *Mythologies*. Paris, Seuil.

— (1964), *Eléments de sémiologie*. Paris, Seuil.

— (1966a), *Critique et vérité*. Paris, Seuil.

— (1966b), 'Introduction à l'analyse structurale des récits', *Communications* 8: 1–27.

— (1967), *Système de la mode*. Paris, Seuil.

— (1968), 'L'Effet de réel', *Communications* 11: 84–89.

— (1970), *S/Z*. Paris, Seuil.

— (1975), *S/Z*. Trans. by R. Miller. London, Jonathan Cape.

Baudelaire, Charles (1964), *Oeuvres complètes*. Paris, Bibliothèque de la Pléiade.

Baudrillard, Jean (1976), *L'Echange symbolique et la mort*. Paris, Gallimard.

Benveniste, Emile (1966), *Problèmes de linquistique générale*. Paris, Gallimard. (Originally published 1963).

Bernanos, Georges (1961), *Journal d'un curé de campagne*. Paris, Plon.

— (1962), *Diary of a Country Priest*. Trans. by P. Morris. New York, Macmillan.

Bertrand, Louis (1968), *La fin du classicisme et le retour à l'antique dans la seconde*

moitié du XVIIIème siècle et les premières années du XIXème en France.
Geneva Slatkine Reprints.
Blanchard, J.-M. (1973), 'Pierre Jean Jouve et l'intégration du poème', *Cahiers de l'Herne* 19: 274–299.
Blanchot, Maurice (1955), *L'Espace littéraire*. Paris, Gallimard.
Bloch, Marc (1955), *Les caractères originaux de l'histoire rurale en France*, vol. 1. Paris, Armand Colin.
Bobik, Joseph (1965), *Aquinas: On Being and Essence.* Notre Dame, Indiana, University of Notre Dame Press.
Boccaccio (1947), *Decameron.* Trans. by J. Payne. Cleveland, World Publishing.
— (1960), *Decameron*, vol. 2. Ed. by Vittore Branca. Florence: Felice Le Monnier.
Bonheim, Helmut (1975), 'A theory of narrative modes', *Semiotica* 14(4): 329–344.
Booth, Wayne (1961), *The Rhetoric of Fiction.* Chicago, University of Chicago Press.
Brecht, R. B. (1974), 'Deixis in embedded structures', *Foundations of Language* 11(4): 489–518.
Brémond, Claude (1964), 'Le message narratif', *Communications* 4: 4–32.
— (1966), 'La Logique des possibles narratifs', *Communications* 8: 60–76.
— (1973), *Logique du récit.* Paris, Seuil.
Brombert, Victor (1966), *The Novels of Flaubert.* Princeton, N.J., Princeton University Press.
Brown, Norman O. (1959), *Life Against Death.* Middleton, Conn., Wesleyan University Press.
Callistratus (1931), *Descriptions.* Trans. by A. Fairbanks. New York, G. P. Putnam's Sons; London, William Heinemann.
Catullus (1957), *Thetis and Peleus. The Poems of Catullus.* Trans. by J. Michie. New York, Random House.
Chalk, H. M. O. (1960), 'Eros and the Lesbian pastorals of Longus', *Journal of Hellenic Studies* 80: 32–51.
Charolles, Michel (1973), 'Le texte poétique et sa signification', *Europe* 51 (529–530): 97–114.
Chatman, Seymour (1971a), 'The semantics of style', in *Essays in Semiotics*, ed. by Julia Kristeva, Josette Rey-Debove, and Donna Jean Umiker, 399–422. The Hague, Mouton.
— (1972), *The Style of the Later Henry James.* Oxford, Blackwell.
— (1978), *Story and Discourse: Narrative Structure in Fiction and Film.* Ithaca, Cornell University Press.
Chatman, Seymour, editor (1971), *Literary Style: A Symposium.* London and New York, Oxford University Press.
Cixous, Hélène (1976), 'Fiction and its phantoms: a reading of Freud's Das Unheimliche [The "uncanny"]', *New Literary History* 7(3): 525–548.
Conrad, Joseph (1974), *The Nigger of the Narcissus and Typhoon and Other Stories.* London, J. M. Dent and Sons.
Coquet, Jean-Claude (1973), *Sémiotique littéraire; contribution à l'analyse sémantique du discours.* Paris, Mame.
Crane, Ronald S. (1957), 'The concept of plot and the plot of *Tom Jones*' in *Critics and Criticism*, ed. by Ronald S. Crane, 62–93. Chicago, University of Chicago Press.
Culler, Jonathan (1975), *Structuralist Poetics.* Ithaca, Cornell University Press.
Curtius, Ernst Robert (1953), *European Literature and the Latin Middle Ages.*

Trans. by W. R. Trask. New York, Pantheon Books.

Damisch, Hubert (1973), *Théorie du nuage*. Paris, Seuil.

Deleuze, Gilles and Felix Guattari (1972), *Anti-Oedipe*. Paris, Minuit.

Delille, J. M. (1833), *Oeuvres de Delille*, vol. 7. Paris, Furne.

Derrida, Jacques (1972), *La dissémination*. Paris, Minuit.

— (1973), *Speech and Phenomena*. Trans. by D. B. Allison. Evanston, Northwestern University Press.

— (1974), *Glas*. Paris, Galilée.

— (1976), *Of Grammatology*. Trans. by G. Spivak. Baltimore, Johns Hopkins University Press.

Diderot, Denis (1951), *Oeuvres*. Bibliothèque de la Pléiade. Paris, Gallimard.

— (1965), *Oeuvres esthétiques*. Paris, Garnier Frères.

Diekoff, John Siemon, comp. (1968), *A Maske at Ludlow: Essays on Milton's Comus*. Cleveland, Press of Case Western Reserve University.

Dijk, Teun A. van (1972), *Some Aspects of Text Grammars*. The Hague, Mouton.

Donato, Eugenio and Richard Macksey (1971), *The Structuralist Controversy*. Baltimore, Johns Hopkins University Press.

Eco, Umberto (1971), *Le forme del contenuto*. Milan, Bompiani.

— (1972), *La structure adsente*. Trans. by E. Esposito-Torrigiani. Paris, Mercure de France.

— (1975), *A Theory of Semiotics*. Bloomington, Indiana University Press.

Eickenbaum, E. (1965). 'La théorie de la "méthode formelle" ', in *Théorie de la littérature*, textes réunis, présentés et traduits par Tzvetan Todorov, 31–75. Paris, Seuil.

Eliot, George (1875), *Middlemarch*. London, William Blackwood.

Encyclopédie, ou Dictionnaire raisonné des sciences, des arts et des métiers. Mis en ordre et publié par M. Diderot et quant à la partie mathématique par M. d'Alembert (1775), vol. 5, 426. Paris, Briasson.

Encyclopédie of Diderot et d'Alembert (1954), *Selected Articles*. Ed. by J. Lough. Cambridge, Cambridge University Press.

Fillmore, Charles J. (1965), 'Entailment rules in a semantic theory', in *Project on Linguistic Analysis*. Report 10: 60–82. Columbus, Ohio, ERIC Document Reprint Service.

Fish, Stanley (1967), *Surprised by Sin: The Reader in Paradise Lost*. New York, Macmillan.

— (1973), 'What is stylistics and why are they saying such terrible things about it?', in *Selected Papers from the English Institute*, ed. by S. Chatman, 109–152. New York and London, Columbia University Press.

Fittschen, Klaus (1973), 'Der Schild des Achilleus', *Archaeologia Homerica* 2(N–1).

Flaubert, Gustave (1926), *Correspondance*, Deuxième série (1847–1852). Paris, Louis Conard.

— (1957), *Madame Bovary*. Trans. by F. Steegmuller. New York, Random House.

— (1966), *Madame Bovary*. Paris, Garnier-Flammarion.

Fletcher, Angus (1964), *Allegory, The Theory of a Symbolic Mode*. Ithaca, Cornell University Press.

— (1971), *The Transcendental Masque*. Ithaca, Cornell University Press.

Fontenelle, B. L. B. (1968), *Oeuvres complètes*, vol. 3. Ed. by G.-B. Depping. Geneva, Slatkine Reprints.

Frege, Gottlob (1952), *Translations from the Philosophical Writings of Gottlob Frege*. Ed. by Peter Geach and Max Black. Oxford, Basil Blackwell.

Freud, Sigmund (1948), *Collected Papers*, vols. 2, 4. London, Hogarth Press and the Institute for Psycho-Analysis.

— (1955), *The Standard Edition of the Complete Psychological Works of Sigmund Freud*, vol. 18. Trans. by J. Strachey. London, Hogarth Press.

— (1957), *The Standard Edition* . . ., vol. 14, Trans. by J. Strachey. London, Hogarth Press.

— (1958), *The Standard Edition* . . ., vol. 12 Trans. by J. Strachey, London, Hogarth Press.

— (1960), *The Standard Edition* . . ., vol. 8. Trans. by J. Strachey. London, Hogarth Press.

— (1961), *The Interpretation of Dreams*. Trans. by J. Strachey. New York, John Wiley.

— (1964), *Gesammelte Werke*, vol. 8. London, Imago.

Friedrich, Hugo (1968), *Montaigne*. Trans. by R. Rovini. Paris, Gallimard.

Gadamer, Hans Georg (1975), *Truth and Method*. Trans. by G. Barrett and J. Cumming. New York, The Seabury Press.

Genette, Gérard (1966), *Figures 1*. Paris, Seuil.

— (1969), *Figures 2*. Paris, Seuil.

— (1972), *Figures 3*. Paris, Seuil.

Gernet, Louis (1968), *Anthropologie de la Grèce ancienne*. Paris, Maspéro.

Gessner, Solomon (1771), *The Death of Abel*. London, T. Collyer.

— (1802), *The Works of Solomon Gessner*, vol. 2. London, T. Cadell Junr. and W. Davies.

— (1972), *Sämtliche Schriften*, vols. 1, 2. Zürich, Orell Füssli.

Gombrich, E. H. (1969), *Art and Illusion*. Princeton, Princeton University Press.

Goodman, Paul (1954), *The Structure of Literature*. Chicago, University of Chicago Press.

Gray, D. H. F. (1947), 'Homer's epithets for things', *Classical Quarterly* 41: 109–121.

Gray, Floyd (1958), *Le style de Montaigne*. Paris, Nizet.

Greg, Walter Wilson (1959), *Pastoral Poetry and Pastoral Drama*. New York, Russell and Russell.

Greimas, Algirdas Julien (1966), *Sémantique structurale*. Paris, Seuil.

Greimas, Algirdas Julien (1976), *Maupassant, la sémiotique du texte, exercices pratiques*. Paris, Mame.

Greimas, Algirdas Julien, editor (1970), *Du sens*. Paris, Seuil.

Gros, Léon-Gabriel (1959), 'Poésie-bien-disante, poètes maudits', *Cahier du sud* 48: 3–9.

Hamon, Philippe (1972a), 'Pour un statut sémiologique du personnage', *Littérature* 6 (mai): 86–110.

Hamon, Philippe (1972b), 'Qu'est-ce qu'une description?', *Poétique* 12: 465–485.

Hardy, Thomas (1918), *Far From the Madding Crowd*. New York, Harper.

Hartman, Geoffrey (1975), 'The use and abuse of structural analysis: Riffaterre's interpretation of Wordsworth's "Yew-trees"', *New Literary History* 7(1): 165–190.

Hegel, Georg Wilhelm Friedrich (1967), *The Phenomenology of Mind*. Trans. by J. B. Baillie. New York, Harper and Row.

— (1970), 'Phänomenologie des Geistes', vol. 3 in *Werke*. Frankfurt, Suhrkamp.

Heliodorus (1895), *An Aethiopian History*. Trans. by T. Underdowne. London, David Nutt.

Hemmings, F. W. J., editor (1974), *The Age of Realism*. Baltimore, Penguin.

Herodotus (1928), *The History of Herodotus*. Trans. by G. Rawlinson. New

York, L. MacVeagh, The Dial Press; Toronto, Longmans, Green and Company.

Hesiod (1959), *Opera et Dies. The Works and the Days; Theogony; The Shield of Herakles.* Trans. by R. Lattimore. Ann Arbor, The University of Michigan Press.

Hjelmslev, Louis (1961), *Prolegomena to a Theory of Language.* Trans. by F. J. Whitfield. Madison, University of Wisconsin Press.

Homer (1964), *Odyssey*, 2 vols. Ed. with commentary by W. B. Stanford. London, Macmillan; New York, St. Martin's Press.

— (1967a), *Odyssey.* Trans. by R. Lattimore. New York, Harper and Row.

— (1967b), *The Iliad.* Trans. by R. Lattimore. Chicago, University of Chicago Press.

Horsford, H. C. (1962), 'The design of the argument in *Moby Dick*', *Modern Fiction Studies* 8(3): 233–251.

Hugo, Victor (1931), *Les misérables.* Trans. by Charles E. Wilbour. New York, The Modern Library.

Husserl, Edmund (1952), *Ideas.* Trans. by W. R. Boyce. New York, Macmillan.

Ingarden, Roman (1965), *Das literarische Kunstwerk.* Tübingen, Niemeyer.

Jacobson, Edith (1964), *The Self and the Object World.* New York, International Universities Press.

Jakobson, Roman (1960), 'Closing statement', in *Style in Language*, ed. by Thomas Sebeok, Bloomington, Indiana University Press.

— (1971), *Selected Writings*, vol. 2. The Hague, Mouton.

— (1973), *Essais de linguistique générale*, vol. 2. Paris, Minuit.

Jakobson, Roman and Claude Lévi-Strauss (1962), ' "Les chats" de Baudelaire', *L'Homme* 2: 5–21.

Jameson, Fredric (1971), *The Prison-house of Language: A Critical Account of Structuralism and Russian Formalism.* Princeton, Princeton University Press.

Jayne, Sears (1968), 'The subject of Milton's Ludlow Mask', in *A Maske at Ludlow*, ed. by John S. Diekhoff, 165–187. Cleveland, Press of Case Western Reserve University.

Jerphagnon, Lucien (1965), *De la banalité.* Paris, Vrin.

Jonson, Ben (1890), *Masques and Entertainments.* Ed. by Henry Morley. London, George Routledge.

Joyce, James (1956), *Dubliners.* Harmondsworth, Penguin.

— (1958), *Finnegan's Wake.* New York, The Viking Press.

— (1961), *Ulysses.* New York, Vintage Books.

Kant, Immanuel (1950), *Critique of Pure Reason.* Trans. by N. K. Smith. London, Macmillan; New York, St. Martin's Press.

Katz, Jerrold J. and Jerry A. Fodor (1964), 'The structure of a semantic theory', in *The Structure of Language*, ed. by Jerry A. Fodor and Jerrold J. Katz, 479–518. Englewood Cliffs, N.J., Prentice-Hall.

Kayser, Wolfgang (1963), *The Grotesque in Art and Literature.* Trans. by U. Weisstein. Bloomington, Indiana University Press.

Klein, Melanie (1965), *Contributions to Psycho-Analysis 1921–1945.* London, Hogarth Press.

Kristeva, Julia (1968), 'La sémiologie en U.R.S.S.', *Tel Quel* 35.

— (1969), *Séméiotikè*. Paris, Seuil.

— (1974), *La révolution du langage poétique.* Paris, Seuil.

— (1977), *Polylogue.* Paris, Seuil.

Kristeva, Julia, Josette Rey-Debove and Donna Jean Umiker, editors (1971), *Essays in Semiotics.* The Hague, Mouton.

Lacan, Jacques (1966), *Ecrits*, vol. 1. Collection *Points*. Paris, Seuil.
— (1971), *Ecrits*, vol. 2. Collection *Points*. Paris, Seuil.
La Fontaine, Jean de (1884), *Oeuvres de la Fontaine*, vol. 2. Paris, Hachette.
Le Goff, Jacques and Pierre Nora, editors (1974), *Faire de l'histoire*, vol. 1. Paris, Gallimard.
Lejeune, Philippe (1975), *Le pacte autobiographique*. Paris, Gallimard.
Lerner, Laurence (1972), *The Uses of Nostalgia: Studies in Pastoral Poetry*. London, Chatto and Windus.
Levin, Samuel R. (1962), *Linguistic Structures in Poetics*. The Hague: Mouton.
Lévinas, Emmanuel (1967), *En découvrant l'existence avec Husserl et Heidegger; réimpression suivie d'essais nouveaux*. Paris, Librairie Philosophique J. Vrin.
Lévi-Strauss, Claude (1950), 'Introduction', in *Sociologie et anthropologie*, by Marcel Mauss, ix–lii. Paris, Presses Universitaires de France.
— (1966), *The Savage Mind*. Chicago, University of Chicago Press.
— (1969), *The Raw and the Cooked*. Trans. by J. and D. Weightman. New York, Harper and Row.
— (1973), *Tristes tropiques*. Trans. by J. and D. Weightman. London, Jonathan Cape.
Lewis, Philip (1966), 'Merleau-Ponty and the phenomenology of language', *Yale French Studies* 36/37: 19–40.
Longus (1962), *Daphnis and Chloe* with English translation by G. Thornley, revised and augmented by J. M. Edmonds. Cambridge, Mass., Harvard; London, William Heinemann.
Lord, Albert (1965), *The Singer of Tales*. New York, Atheneum.
Lubbock, Percy (1931), *The Craft of Fiction*. London, Jonathan Cape.
Lucretius (1942), *De Rerum Natura*. Ed. with introduction and commentary by William Ellery Leonard and Stanley Barney Smith. Madison, University of Wisconsin Press.
Lukács, György (1971), *The Theory of the Novel*. Trans. by Anna Bostock. Cambridge, Mass., M.I.T. Press.
Lyotard, Jean-François (1971), *Discours Figure*. Paris, Klinksieck.
— (1973), *Des Dispositifs pusionnels*. Paris, Dix/Dix-huit.
Malraux, André (1967), *Anti-mémoires*. Paris, Gallimard.
Malraux, André (1968), *Antimemoirs*. Trans. by T. Kilmartin. New York, Holt, Rinehart and Winston.
Marcuse, Herbert (1966), *Eros and Civilization*. Boston, Beacon Press.
Martin, Louis (1971), *Etudes sémiologiques*. Paris, Klinksieck.
— (1973), *Utopiques*. Paris, Minuit.
Martinet, André (1960), *Eléments de Linguistique générale*. Paris, A. Colin.
Marx, Karl (1963), *The Eighteenth Brumaire of Louis Bonaparte*. New York, International Publishers.
Marx, Karl und Friedrich Engels (1960), *Werke*. Berlin, Dietz.
May, Gita (1964), *De Jean-Jacques Rousseau à Madame Roland*. Geneva, Librairie Droz.
Mazon, Paul (1959), *Introduction à 'l'Iliade'*. Paris, Edition Les Belles Lettres.
Mehlman, Jeffrey (1977), *Revolution and Repetition*. Berkeley, University of California Press.
Melville, Herman (1962), *Moby Dick*. New York, Macmillan.
Mérimée, Prosper (1951), *Romans et nouvelles*. Texte établi et annoté par Henri Martineau. Paris, Bibliothèque de la Pléiade.
— (1966) *The Venus of Ille and Other Stories*. Trans. by J. Kimber. London, Oxford University Press.
Merleau-Ponty, Maurice (1948), *Sens et non sens*. Paris, Nagel.

— (1962), *Phenomenology of Perception*. Trans. by C. Smith. London, Routledge and Kegan Paul.

— (1964), *Signs*. Trans. by R. McCleary. Evanston, Ill., Northwestern University Press.

Meschonnic, Henri (1973), *Pour la poétique*, vol. 2. Paris, Gallimard.

Metz, Christian (1971), *Essais sur la signification au cinéma*. Paris, Klinksieck.

Miller, J. Hillis (1974), 'Narrative and history', *English Literary History* 41(3): 455–473.

Milton, John (1955), *Paradise Lost and Selected Poetry and Prose*. New York and Toronto, Rinehart.

Mittelstadt, Michael (1967), 'Longus: Daphnis and Chloe in roman narrative painting', *Latomus* 26(3) 752–761.

Monglond, André (1966), *Le préromantisme française*, 2 vols. Paris, J. Corti.

Montaigne, Michel de (1962), *Essais*, 2 vols. Ed. by Maurice Rat. Paris, Garnier.

— (1965), *Essays of Montaigne*. Trans. by D. Frame. Stanford, Stanford University Press.

Mornet, Daniel (1907), *Le sentiment de la nature en France*. New York, Burt Franklin.

Nagler, Michael (1975), *Spontaneity and Tradition, A Study in the Oral Art of Homer*. Berkeley, University of California Press.

Nietzsche, Friedrich (1910), *The Complete Works of Friedrich Nietzsche*, vol. 10. Ed. by Dr. Oscar Levy; trans. by T. Common. Edinburgh and London, T. N. Foulis.

— (1971), 'Rhétorique et langage', textes présentés et traduits par Jean-Luc Nancy et Philippe Lacoue-Labarthe, *Poétique* 5: 99–142.

Ovid (1892), *The Fasti, Tristia, Pontic Epistles, Ibis and Halieutica of Ovid*. Trans. by H. T. Riley. London, George Bell.

— (1896), *The Fasti of Ovid*. Ed. by G. H. Hallam. New York, Macmillan.

— (1955), *Metamorphoses*. Trans. by R. Humphries. Bloomington, Indiana University Press.

Parker, William R. (1968), *Milton: A Biography*, vol. 1. Oxford, Clarendon Press.

Parthenius (1962), *The Love Romances*. Trans. by S. Gaselee. Cambridge, Mass., Harvard University Press; London, William Heinemann.

Peirce, Charles Sanders (1931), *Principles of Philosophy*, vol. 1 of *Collected Papers*. Cambridge, Harvard University Press.

Philostratus (1931), *Imagines*. Trans. by A. Fairbanks. New York, G. P. Putnam's; London, William Heinemann.

Pike, Kenneth (1954), *Language in Relation to a Unified Theory of the Structure of Behavior*. Glendale, California.

Plato (1951), *Symposium*. Trans. by W. Hamilton. Harmondsworth, Penguin.

Plutarch (1975), *The Greek Questions of Plutarch*. Trans. by W. R. Halliday. Oxford, Clarendon Press.

Poétiques (1971), Rhétorique et philosophie. Paris, Seuil.

Poulet, Georges (1950), *Essais sur le temps humain*, vol. 1. Paris, Plon.

Prévost d'Exiles, Antoine François (1746–1749), *L'histoire générale des voyages*. Paris.

Propp, Vladimir (1958), *Morphology of the Folktale*. Ed. by Svatava Pirkova-Jacobson; trans. by L. Scott. Bloomington, Indiana University Press.

Quine, Willard (1960), *Word and Object*. Cambridge, Mass., M.I.T. Press.

Quintilianus, M. Fabius (1886), *Institutionis Oratoriae*, vol. 1. Ed. by Ferdinandus Meister. Pragae, Sumptus Fecit F. Tempsky.

Rabelais, François (1973), *Oeuvres complètes*. Texte établi par Guy Demerson. Paris, Seuil.

Rastier, François and Algirdas Julien Greimas (1970), 'Le jeu des contraintes sémiotiques', in *Du Sens*, ed. by A. J. Greimas, 135–155, Paris, Seuil.

Richard, Jean-Pierre (1955), *Poésie et profondeur*. Paris, Seuil.

Riffaterre, Michael (1968), 'Malraux's *antimemoirs* [*sic*]', *Columbia University Forum* 11 (4): 31–35.

— (1971), *Essais de stylistique structurale*. Paris, Flammarion.

— (1972), 'Système d'un genre descriptif', *Poétique* 9: 15–30.

— (1973), 'Interpretation and descriptive poetry: a reading of Wordsworth's "yew-trees"', *New Literary History* 4(2): 229–256.

Rimbaud, Arthur (1960), *Oeuvres*. Ed. by Suzanne Bernard. Paris, Garnier Frères.

— (1973), *A Season in Hell, The Illuminations*. Trans. by E. R. Peschel. New York and London, Oxford University Press.

Roscher, Wilhelm Heinrich (1965), *Ausführliches Lexicon der griechischen und römischen Mythologie*, vol. 3.1. Hildesheim, Georg Olms.

Rosenmeyer, Thomas G. (1969), *The Green Cabinet*. Berkeley, University of California Press.

Roudaut, Jean (1959), 'Les logiques poétiques au XVIII siècle', *Cahiers du sud* 48: 10–32.

— (1962), 'Les exercices poétiques au XVIII siècle', *Critique* 18: 533–547.

Rousseau, Jean-Jacques (1964), *Oeuvres complètes*, vol. 2. Paris, Bibliothèque de la Pléiade.

— (1973), *Les confessions*, 2 vols. Paris, Gallimard.

Said, Edward (1976), *Beginnings: Intention and Method*. New York, Basic Books.

Saint-Augustin (1961), *Les confessions*, 10. 33, vol. 2. Texte établi et traduit par P. Labriolle. Paris, Les Belles Lettres.

Saint-Lambert, Jean-François Marquis de (1769), *Les saisons*. Amsterdam.

Saussure, Ferdinand de (1971), *Cours de linguistique générale*. Paris, Payot.

Segre, Cesare (1973), *Semiotics and Literary Criticism*. The Hague, Mouton.

Senden, M. von (1960), *Space and Sight*. Trans. by P. Heath. London, Methuen.

Serres, Michel (1968), *La communication*. Paris, Minuit.

Spitzer, Leo (1948), *Linguistics and Literary History: Essays in Stylistics*. Princeton University Press.

Starobinski, Jean (1970a), *La relation critique*, vol. 2 of *L'Oeil vivant*. Paris, Gallimard.

— (1970b), 'Le style de l'autobiographie', *Poétique* 3: 257–265.

— (1971), *Jean-Jacques Rousseau. La transparence et l'obstacle*. Paris, Gallimard.

Stendhal (1962), *The Charterhouse of Parma*. Trans. by C. K. Moncrieff. London, Zodiac Press.

— (1964), *Le rouge et le noir*. Paris, Garnier-Flammarion.

— (1973), *La Chartreuse de Parmer*. Ed. by Antoine Adam. Paris, Garnier.

Stevens, Wallace (1954), *Collected Poems*. New York, Knopf.

Strawson, P. F. (1950), 'On referring', *Mind* 59(235): 320–344.

Tesnières, Lucien (1969), *Eléments de syntaxe structurale*. Paris, Klincksieck.

Theocritus (1963), *The Idylls of Theokritos*. Trans. by Baviss Milss. West Lafayette, Indiana, Purdue University Studies.

Tocqueville, Alexis de (1967), *l'Ancien régime et la révolution*. Paris, Gallimard.

Todorov, Tzvetan (1966), 'Les catégories du récit littértaire', *Communications* 8: 125–151.

— (1969), *Grammaire du Décaméron*. The Hague, Mouton.

Trahard, Pierre (1931–33), *Les maîtres de la sensibilité française au XVIIème siècle,* 4 vols. Paris, Boivin.

Turgot, A. R. J. (1919), *Oeuvres de Turgot*, vol. 3. Paris, Félix Alcan.

Tuve, Rosemond (1968), 'Image, form and theme in *A mask*', in *A Maske at Ludlow*, ed. by John S. Diekhoff, 126–164. Cleveland, Press of Case Western Reserve University.

Valley, G. (1926), *Über den Sprachegebrauch des Longos*. Uppsala.

Virgil (1906), *Aeneid*. Trans. by E. Fairfax Taylor; introduction and notes by E. M. Forster. London, Putman.

White, Hayden (1973), *Metahistory*. Baltimore, Johns Hopkins University Press.

Wilson, Edmund (1968), *The Fruits of the MLA*. New York, New York Review.

Woodhouse, A. S. P. (1941), 'The argument in Milton's *Comus*', *University of Toronto Quarterly* 11: 217–271.

— (1950), '*Comus* once more', *University of Toronto Quarterly* 19: 218–223.

Wordsworth, William (1932), *The Complete Poetical Works of William Wordsworth*. Boston, Houghton Mifflin Company.

Zola, Emile (1893), *The Experimental Novel*. Trans. by B. Sherman. New York, Cassell.

— (1927), *Nana*. Trans. by E. Boyd. New York, Random House.

— (1967), *Oeuvres*, vol. 4. Texte établi sous la direction de Henri Mitterand. Paris, Cercle du livre précieux.

— (1968), *Oeuvres*, vol. 10. Texte établi sous la direction de Henri Mitterand. Paris, Cercle du livre précieux.

Zweig, Stefan (1950), *Sternstunden der Menschheit*. Frankfurt, S. Fischer.